Indecent Exposure

THE MIDDLE AGES SERIES

Ruth Mazo Karras, Series Editor
Edward Peters, Founding Editor

A complete list of books in the series
is available from the publisher.

INDECENT EXPOSURE

Gender, Politics, and Obscene Comedy
in Middle English Literature

NICOLE NOLAN SIDHU

PENN

UNIVERSITY OF PENNSYLVANIA PRESS

PHILADELPHIA

Published by
University of Pennsylvania Press
Philadelphia, Pennsylvania 19104-4112
www.upenn.edu/pennpress

Printed in the United States of America on acid-free paper
1 3 5 7 9 10 8 6 4 2

Library of Congress Cataloging-in-Publication Data
ISBN 978-0-8122-4804-3

To my parents,
Phyllis Fitzsimmons and Bernard Nolan,
for the humanitarian values they taught me
and that I hope are reflected in this book
(subject matter notwithstanding).

CONTENTS

NOTE ON THE FABLIAUX

Unless otherwise noted, all quotations from the fabliaux are from the *Nouveau recueil complet des fabliaux*, ed. Willem Noomen and Nico van den Boogaard, 10 vols. (Assen: Van Gorcum, 1983–98), abbreviated hereafter as NRCF and cited parenthetically in the text by volume, fabliau, and line numbers.

Indecent Exposure

Introduction

Obscenity in Medieval Culture and Literature

> Blameth nat me if that ye chese amis.
> The Millere is a cherl; ye knowe wel this.
> So was the Reve eek and othere mo,
> And harlotrie they tolden bothe two.
> Avyseth yow and putte me out of blame;
> And eek men shal nat maken ernest of game.
> (*Miller's Prologue*, 3181–86)

In the final words of the *Miller's Prologue*, Chaucer-the-narrator issues an extended defense of the two tales that will follow. They are "harlotrie," he admits, a word that in Middle English denotes ribald talk, foul jesting, scurrility, or obscenity.[1] Readers should not blame Chaucer for the offensive content of a "cherles tale," however, for he only transcribes it out of a duty to truth (3169). These are the stories the miller and the reeve told, so the narrator must repeat them, "Or elles falsen som of my mateere" (3175).

The narrator's self-defense is as false as it is emphatic. It is, in fact, highly unlikely that anyone in Chaucer's original audience would have associated the tales of the miller and the reeve with the lower orders. Both entries derive from the Old French fabliau, a genre whose ruling-class affiliations in England are attested by the fact that all English fabliaux before Chaucer are written in Old French or Anglo-Norman.[2] Nor (of course) is the tales' appearance in the first fragment the result of anything other than the artistic choice of Chaucer the author.

If the narrator's self-defense does little to explain Chaucer's interest in these tales, it is effective in drawing our attention to the question itself. Why *does* Chaucer see fit to begin his master work with not one but two (three, if we count the fragmentary *Cook's Tale*) pieces of "harlotrie"? While the narrator discourages further inquiry with the demand that we "nat maken ernest of game" (3186), Chaucer the author invites the opposite. Just as surely as most audience members can be guaranteed not to follow the narrator's advice to "turne over the leef, and chese another tale" (3177) but to read on, their prurient interest stirred by the very warnings meant to discourage them, so will they be tempted to ask what exactly it is in these seemingly ridiculous and offensive "games" that Chaucer the author finds so compelling.

The purpose of this study is to answer that question, for Chaucer and for a number of other Middle English authors, all of whom invoke "harlotrie" in writing of serious purpose and intellectual ambition. As works that are humorous and include language and behavior that violate social prohibitions, the *Miller's Tale* and the *Reeve's Tale* partake of a popular and widespread medieval discourse that I call "obscene comedy." Set in domestic spaces and featuring primarily members of the lower and middle ranks, obscene comedy evokes laughter by portraying socially outré behavior (like adultery, theft, and disobedience), as well as body parts and activities (like genitalia, sexual intercourse, and farting) whose mention is socially taboo. In plots that are centrally concerned with heterosexual relationships and sexuality, obscene comedy inverts social hierarchies and invites its audience to laugh at the transgression of the decent, the good, and the seemly.

While a medieval tradition of scatological obscenity exists and has been the subject of a couple of recent studies, my focus in this study is primarily on sexual obscenity, a phenomenon that largely defines obscene comedy in the Middle Ages.[3] Certainly examples of obscene humor can be found that do not involve male-female relationships or sexuality, but these are the exceptions that prove the rule in a tradition that is intensely, some might even say obsessively, focused on the relations of men and women, particularly within the family.[4] In an illustrative study, Per Nykrog counts 150 narrative patterns (what he calls "themes") in the fabliau and notes that, of these, only a quarter are not sexual.[5]

In spite of its pervasive influence in medieval culture, obscene comedy has not been regarded—or even named—as such. Centuries of embarrassment over obscenity have meant that the study of it is still in a nascent stage. There have been few attempts to read it systematically. In Middle English studies, Chaucer's fabliaux—and other conspicuous instances of obscene comedy, such as the Noah pageants of the biblical drama—are popular subjects of study, but they tend to be read in isolation, not only from obscene comedy generally but even from other works in the same corpus. The profusion of critical writings on Chaucer's *Miller's Tale*, for instance, includes few attempts to explain why it appears with two other similar works, or indeed why Chaucer was so compelled by the fabliau that he returned to it over and over again, making it the most-used genre in the *Canterbury* collection. Similarly, critics have analyzed the Noah pageants extensively, sometimes brilliantly, but have not connected them to the unruly women and angry husbands that punctuate other biblical drama pageants.

The isolationism that we see in the critical treatment of Middle English texts reflects a tendency in medieval studies generally, wherein analyses of obscenity are almost always confined within generic boundaries. Studies of obscene manuscript marginalia, or the Old French fabliau, for instance, focus on their own particular genre or art form and do not consider it as part of a more widespread system of meaning. Only analyses of lexicon consider obscenity as a broader cultural phenomenon.

Neither the generic nor the lexical approach is able to encompass the full scope of obscene comedy. Studies of words cannot account for the fact that, while references to sex acts and sexual body parts are part of the tradition, they do not fully describe it.[6] Equally characteristic of obscene comedy is its household setting, its focus on the middle and lower ranks, its tendency to associate women and certain other social types with riotous behavior, and its celebration of a "world upside down."[7]

Generic analyses, meanwhile, take in the nonlexical elements of obscene comedy but cannot account for continuities between forms of obscene comedy in different genres and artistic mediums. Scholarship on the fabliau, in particular, has produced sophisticated analyses regarding the genre's gender politics, relation to medieval social hierarchies, and engagement with a variety of social issues.[8] The generic basis of these analyses, however, means that their insights have not been extended to other, similar works in the literary and visual arts.[9] The rigidity of generic classification is precisely the difficulty Peter Dronke encounters in his discussion of obscene comedy in medieval Latin literature. Lacking a term to express the similarities between works in medieval Latin and those in Old French, Dronke detaches the word "fabliaux" from its generic and national context, using it to mean "amusing stories of deception and outwitting, especially of a sexual kind."[10]

Nowhere are the troubles involved in the generic approach better exemplified than in the ongoing debate over how to classify the fabliau. The controversy is, as Keith Busby has remarked, "one of the most notorious problems of French literary scholarship."[11] Early anthologies of fabliaux printed in the late eighteenth and nineteenth centuries group them in with other fables and short tales. In their 1872 collection, Montaiglon and Raynaud omit all fables, including those of Marie de France, as well as tales from the *Disciplina Clericalis*.[12] In his 1893 study of the fabliau, Joseph Bédier provides a minimalist definition of the genre as "contes à rire en vers" and, on that basis, eliminates a number of works from Montaiglon and Raynaud's edition.[13] Per Nykrog advocates a further narrowing of Montaiglon and Raynaud's selections but argues against excluding the fables of Marie de France.[14] Scholars of Anglo-Norman literature, meanwhile, are critical of the French fabliau anthologies for excluding Ango-Norman texts.[15] One of the central reasons for the fabliau debate is that medieval authors themselves did not define their works according to any strict generic parameters. As Jean Rychner has remarked, it is a questionable practice "to constitute a genre retrospectively, despite a vacillating terminology and in the absence of testimonials concerning the unity of intention of the authors."[16]

Similar troubles have dogged the study of English comic tales. Attempts to classify these tales as fabliaux have been thwarted by differences that forbid an identical generic classification. Thomas Cooke notes of English comic tales that, while "the customary practice has been to refer to them as fabliaux," a number of the tales do not have clear connections or similarities to the Old French genre, making scholars reluctant to call them fabliaux, "either preferring more cautiously to refer to them as 'fabliaux-like,' more skeptically to call them 'quasi-fabliaux,' or more radically to ignore the term altogether."[17]

This study aims to arrive at a better understanding of the function of comic obscenity in Middle English literature and culture by considering it as a discourse rather than a genre or a lexicon. In spite of the fact that they were created in different periods and in different artistic media, there are profound continuities among an Old French fabliau about a couple fighting over the "pants" of the household, a fifteenth-century misericord of a woman beating her husband, and the fisticuffs that Noah and his wife exchange in the Towneley *Noah* pageant. These similarities are best understood according to Michel Foucault's concept of a "discursive formation," which can be said to exist whenever we can perceive a regularity or similarity "between objects, types of statement, concepts, or thematic choices."[18]

Thinking about obscene comedy as a group of utterances that repeat similar concepts in similar ways but that are not confined to particular genres or modes of expression allows us to encompass both the remarkable diversity of medieval obscene comedy and its equally remarkable unity. It allows us to see that, even as the examples I have cited above differ in context, artistic medium, and language, they nevertheless exist as part of a recognizably distinct system of thinking and speaking about women, men, and domestic power relations that would have been immediately recognizable to medieval audiences. In addition, Foucault's theory of discourse allows us to appreciate how any medieval work that includes elements from that discourse (the unruly woman, a pair of battling spouses, a henpecked husband) is in conversation with a long history of other, similar representations, not only within its own medium or linguistic community, but across a variety of different textual, aural, and visual expressions.

The Context: Obscene Comic Discourse in Europe

Although obscene comedy does not enter English-language literature until the late fourteenth century, it has a long career as a widely dispersed discourse in the visual arts, in Latin and in other European vernaculars dating from at least the eleventh century. The earliest examples of obscene comedy from the European Middle Ages appear in several songs of the *Carmina Cantabrigiensia* (Cambridge Songs), a collection of Latin poems dating from the middle of the eleventh century. Frequently referred to as *ridiculum* by their narrators, the songs tell fabliau-like stories relating to domestic contests, sexual betrayals, and trickery. One Cambridge song tells a tale that is very similar to the fabliau *L'enfant qui fu remis au soleil* (5.48) in which an adulterous wife claims that the son born in her husband's absence was conceived by means of a snowflake. The husband avenges himself by taking the child on a trip and selling him as a slave. When he returns he tells his wife that the boy melted in the sun.[19] The Latin elegiac comedies that appear in the middle of the twelfth century (sometimes referred to as Latin comic tales because of their tenuous relationship to theatrical performance) also focus on adultery, sexuality, and contests of power in the domestic sphere. The Latin comedy *Babio*, for instance, features an elderly husband being cuckolded by his servant.[20] While these are the earliest extant examples of obscene comedy in the Middle Ages, they cannot, as Dronke asserts, be taken as a definitive starting point for comic tales of this nature. Earlier literature—like the poetry of the troubadour William of Aquitaine—includes similar motifs of sexual comedy, and the comic plots of the Cambridge songs are executed with a level of mastery that suggests the possibility that an earlier, now lost, tradition existed in medieval Europe.[21]

The late twelfth century marks the first appearance of the Old French fabliau, the most influential form of obscene comedy for Middle English writers. Authored from the thirteenth through the early fourteenth century, the fabliau's popularity is attested by the existence of more than 150 tales in manuscript.[22] Similar comic narratives of sex, deception, and domestic power contests also appear in other continental languages during this period, including the Middle

High German tales by Der Stricker (dating from the early 1200s), the Middle High German *maeren* (composed between the mid-thirteenth and fifteenth centuries), the Italian *novelle* (late thirteenth century), and the Middle Dutch *boerden* (first half of the fourteenth century).[23]

Obscene comedy is also a feature of ecclesiastical writing. The narrating of humorous tales was an approved rhetorical technique for sermon authors. In his *Forma Praedicandi* (early fourteenth century), Robert of Basevorn advises his readers to use "opportune humor," noting the positive results "when we add something jocular which will give pleasure when the listeners are bored."[24] These include tales of domestic strife and sexuality. Among the sermon exempla listed by Frederic Tubach in his compendium, at least forty-nine feature fabliau-style plots of marital or sexual discord punctuated by a humorous turn or trick.[25] A case in point is the exemplum included in the *Sermones Vulgares* of the theologian and cardinal Jacques de Vitry (ca.1160–1240), which plays on the familiar obscene-comedy theme of an old man married to a young wife. When the old man's house is invaded by a robber, his wife turns to him out of fear, and he is able to have intercourse with her, something she had not allowed him to do since their marriage. When the wife asks why he did not interrupt the robber, the old man tells her that the robber stole his gold but gave him something much more valuable in return.[26] In another exemplum, Phyllis, the consort of Alexander the Great, repeats the tricks and stratagems of the unruly women of secular comic tales when she arranges for Aristotle to carry her on his back.[27] Other forms of ecclesiastical writing also make reference to the tropes and characters of obscene comedy. In his treatise *On Conversion*, Bernard of Clairvaux characterizes the fleshly will, opposed to reason and divine will, as a lascivious old woman: "Siquidem voluptuosa sum, curiosa sum, ambitiosa sum, et ab hoc triplici ulcere non est in me sanitas a planta pedis usque ad verticem. Itaque fauces, et quae obscena sunt corporis, assignata sunt voluptati" ["I am voluptuous, I am curious, I am ambitious. There is not part of me that is free from this threefold ulcer, from the soles of my feet to the top of my head. My gullet and the shameful parts of my body are given up to pleasure"].[28]

In the visual arts, both secular and ecclesiastical examples of obscenity abound. Manuscript marginalia depict naked, copulating couples and other obscenities, such as a lover defecating in a bowl and presenting it to his beloved.[29] In a Book of Hours owned by a wealthy Franco-Flemish lady in the second quarter of the fourteenth century, a naked man appears to embrace a naked woman while a bird pokes at his buttocks with its beak (see Figure 1).[30] In a manuscript of the *Roman de la Rose* produced by the husband and wife

FIGURE 1. A naked man embraces (?) a naked woman while a bird pokes
the man in the buttocks with its beak. Book of Hours, c. 1320–1329.
Morgan Library, MS M.0754, fol. 016v.

FIGURE 2. A nun picks penises from a penis tree. Mid-fourteenth century.
BnF MS Fr.25526, fol. 106v. Courtesy Bibliothèque Nationale de France.

team of Richart and Jeanne de Montbaston, marginalia depicts a nun and a
priest engaged in lecherous activities, as well as a nun picking penises from a
"penis tree" (see Figure 2). It is quite possible that these illustrations were, in
fact, produced by Madame de Montbaston, since another marginal depiction of
the couple at work on a manuscript shows the wife completing the illustrations
while her husband inscribes the text.[31] Churches built between the eleventh
and thirteen centuries along the European pilgrimage routes feature explicit
carvings that are both obscene and obscenely comic: peasants display their buttocks and anuses, women exhibit their vulvas in distinctive representations
known as "sheela na gigs," and acrobats pull open their mouths and adopt positions that expose their rear ends.[32]

Obscene comedy continues to be a popular discourse on the Continent
through the later fourteenth and fifteenth centuries. It appears in a variety of
works, including the Spanish author Juan Ruiz's *Libro de Buen Amor* (c. 1330);
the *Decameron* of Boccaccio (c. 1353); the *Facitiae*, the collection of Latin tales
written by the Italian Poggio Bracciolini (c. 1450); the German *Fastnachtspiele*

(Shrovetide plays) of the fifteenth and sixteenth centuries and Schwänke (prose "jest" tales) of the same period; and the farces authored by the Basochiens of fifteenth-century France.[33] In the visual arts, late fourteenth- and fifteenth-century misericords exhibit genitalia, sexual activities, and battling spouses, while archaeological digs in France and the Netherlands have unearthed obscene badges displaying ludicrous scenes of vulvas and penises riding on horseback, being carried on litters, and roasted on spits (see Figure 3).[34]

FIGURE 3. Badge depicting three phallus animals carrying a crowned vulva on a litter. Lead-tin. Bruges, 1375–1425. Van Beuningen Family Collection, Langbroek, The Netherlands.

Obscene Comedy in England

It is remarkable that, before the late fourteenth century, only a couple of examples of English-language obscene comedy exist. In Old English, a number of riddles derive humor from descriptions that equate household objects with sexual body parts, in one case inviting a solution that could be either "penis" or "onion" and in another describing an erect penis in terms that could also apply to a rising loaf of bread.[35] In Middle English, *Dame Sirith*, found in MS Bodley 1687 (Digby 86) and dated to around 1275, tells the story of an old bawd who procures the sexual favors of a married woman for a local clerk by making her believe that clerks turn the women who reject them into dogs. Finally, a dramatic piece, apparently derived from the same story and given the Latin title *Interludium de clerico et puella*, is preserved in an early fourteenth-century copy in British Library Additional MS 23986.[36]

The existence of *Dame Sirith* gave rise, at one time, to a theory that a tradition of fabliaux in English existed before the work of Chaucer and had been lost either through manuscript destruction or because the tales were primarily oral. This theory has, however, been largely discredited by scholars who assert that the absence of fabliaux in English is justified by the absence of an English-language tradition of refined romance to create an appetite for the fabliau's obscene transgressions.[37] Nevertheless, in spite of a paucity of works in English, it is clear that educated and elite English audiences before the mid-fourteenth century were familiar with obscene comedy in the visual arts, in Latin and in other vernacular languages. As their name suggests, the Latin "Cambridge Songs" of the eleventh century are found in an English manuscript, and a number of the elegiac Latin comedies are also likely to have had English origins.[38] The existence of some tradition of sexually obscene tale telling in thirteenth-century England is further suggested by an Oxford University Statute of 1292, warning students "non cantilenas sive fabulas de omasiis (*sic*) vel luxuriosis aut ad libidinem sonantibus narrantes, cantantes, aut libenter audientes" [not to tell, sing, or willingly listen to songs or tales of lovers or licentious persons or those who incite one to lust].[39] In addition, manuscript evidence attests to the popularity of the fabliau among Anglo-Norman speakers: seven fabliaux in Anglo-Norman exist in four different manuscripts of English provenance.[40] Another fabliau in Old French is found in a manuscript dating from the last quarter of the thirteenth century that was likely made for an Anglo-Norman audience, since it also includes material relating to the Norman coast of France.[41] In addition, four fables by Marie de France represent the wars between the sexes in a comical vein.[42]

Repeated strictures against the lecherous tales of minstrels in Langland's *Piers Plowman*—as well as complaints about the fondness of kings, knights, and clergymen for "vile harlotrye"—attest to elite English audiences' ongoing consumption of obscene works through the mid-fourteenth century.[43] Chaucer, too, seems to assume that his audience will have a close familiarity with the fabliau. In spite of his supposed concern over the rudeness of the *Miller's Tale* and the *Reeve's Tale*, Chaucer-the-narrator never remarks on their novelty, proceeding with the assumption that his readers will know exactly what kind of story the Miller will tell when he promises a tale of "a carpenter and of his wyf,/ How that a clerk hath set the wrightes cappe" (3142–3143).

In the ecclesiastical culture of England, the tradition of obscenely comic sermon exempla seems to have been as well accepted as it was on the Continent. The French-language *Contes Moralizés* (c. 1320) of Nicholas de Bozon, an English Franciscan, includes obscene comic exempla from the *Sermones Vulgares* of Jacques de Vitry, as well as from the *Disciplina Clericalis*.[44] In his late fourteenth-century *Festial*, John Mirk suggests that de Bozon was not the only English preacher with a fondness for sexually humorous exempla. Voicing his disapproval of priests who tell tales of "ribawdye," Mirk tells of the terrible fate of an Irish priest "that was lusty to speke of rybawdy and iapys that turned men to lechery."[45] That English clergy regarded tales of unruly wives as useful pedagogical tools is also witnessed in an allegory in the thirteenth-century Middle English treatise *Sawles Warde* (the Keeping of the Soul), in which a husband, Wit, must rule over his unruly and domineering wife, Will.[46] And although we cannot know how frequently such tales were recited in sermons, we do know that English clergy had access to obscene comic exempla in sermon collections like the *Disciplina Clericalis* (twelfth century), the *Alphabetum Narrationum* (early fourteenth century), and the *Gesta Romanorum* (compiled in England in the early fourteenth century).[47]

In the visual arts of medieval England, obscenity appears in ways that are quite similar to the obscenities of continental Europe. A late twelfth-century carving over a window arch in Whittlesford church near Cambridge, for instance, features a woman inserting her fingers into a slit-like vulva while a bearded ithyphallic male crawls toward her.[48] Misericords in English churches feature a variety of transgressive comic scenes. In Carlisle Cathedral, a misericord dating from the first quarter of the fifteenth century is one of many English misericords of the later Middle Ages that illustrate female shrewishness, featuring a woman who holds a man by his beard and beats him with a flax mallet (see Figure 4).[49] The English partake of the same manuscript culture we

FIGURE 4. A woman holds a man by the beard and beats him with a flax mallet.
Carlisle Cathedral misericord, c. 1400–1419. Photograph courtesy of Ken Fawcett.

see in continental Europe, wherein marginalia portraying sexual contest and lower-body humor are common, and badges unearthed from the banks of the Thames in London display obscenities similar to those found in French and Dutch excavations.[50]

Obscene Comedy in Middle English Writing: Literature and Political Expression

When obscene comedy does enter English-language writing in the mid-fourteenth century, it is remarkable not only for its late arrival but for the fact that it enters in works of self-conscious literary ambition. While the discourse certainly appears in literary works of other continental languages, these usually follow its appearance in more entertainment-oriented modes of writing, authored by low-profile, often anonymous, writers. In English, the discourse first makes its debut in works by two of the period's most admired and authoritative literary authors, appearing first in Langland's *Piers Plowman* (in the person of the unruly Dame Study and in numerous other references and tropes) and then, most famously, in the *Canterbury Tales* of Chaucer. The innovations of Langland and Chaucer leave an influential legacy to later writers. While the fifteenth century sees the appearance of entertainment-oriented versions of obscene comedy in English, in the form of a variety of English lyrics and tales, the discourse also retains its sophisticated imprimatur, appearing in works that present themselves as rigorous philosophical or religious explorations, including the *Book of Margery Kempe*, the biblical drama, and the writings of John Lydgate.

The uses to which obscene comedy is put in the works of Langland, Chaucer, and their fifteenth-century heirs are the focus of this study. Perhaps because it entered English-language writing relatively late, or perhaps because Langland's innovations, themselves so revolutionary, happened to have been taken up and developed with comparable sophistication by Chaucer, obscene comedy in English writing of the fourteenth and fifteenth centuries takes on a notably innovatory, philosophically complex character.

As might be expected of domestically oriented narratives, issues of gender, sexuality, and the family are at the forefront of Middle English obscene comedy. While they take up the fabliau focus on male-female contests in the household, a number of Middle English works, particularly those of the fifteenth century, move away from the fabliau obsession with genitalia and adultery to examine cultural norms of masculinity and femininity, as well as issues of equality and subordination within marriage. Diverging from the fabliau tendency to think about marriage solely in terms of masculine control and female resistance, Middle English writings participate in a re-evaluation of marriage and gender roles that reflects the new emphasis on conjugality and the development of companionate marriage that historians have seen emerging in Northern Europe in the later Middle Ages.[51]

Household politics are not, however, the only purview of the Middle English texts under consideration in this study. Although it has never been regarded as a significant political discourse, obscene comedy in Middle English writing is just that. First in Langland and Chaucer and then in later works, Middle English writers use the discourse to create a new political language capable of confronting the profound alterations in their society over the century and a half following the Black Death. Well known as a period in which longstanding social and economic relations were subjected to radical change, the later Middle Ages was also notably deficient in well-developed political and economic theories to account for these changes or think through their implications. A number of scholars have noted the innovative work of Middle English writers in attempting to fill the theoretical and philosophical gaps in their culture. Nicholas Watson has described the development of what he calls a "vernacular theology" in religious discussions by fourteenth-century English writers.[52] Elizabeth Fowler has observed that William Langland uses medieval marriage law to construct a theory of contract relations in an environment that lacked the philosophical grounding developed in later centuries by thinkers like Hobbes and Rousseau.[53] Similarly, English writers of the fourteenth and fifteenth centuries use obscene comedy to develop what might be called a "vernacular political theory" to account for and examine the power relations of their world.

The political valence of the unruly woman in the medieval and early modern period has been famously outlined by Natalie Zemon Davis, who asserts that the struggles between disobedient wives and their husbands function as a metaphor for a variety of subordinate-superior relationships in the medieval and early modern periods.[54] Davis's emphasis on metaphor, however, conceives of the relation between the political and the domestic as a rather distant one. By definition, metaphor divides the two areas into separate spheres and presumes their absolute alterity. While the works I address in this study certainly do use household struggles as a metaphor for other social interactions, they also imagine a much more interdependent relationship between the two spheres. As the work of Mary Hartman and Martha Howell have demonstrated, family politics are not separate from the economic and political conditions of the worlds they inhabit but are closely tied to them in relations of mutual interdependence and influence.[55] In particular, Howell asserts that the development of companionate marriage among middle-rank people in the late medieval period is closely related to changing economic circumstances wherein increasing numbers of the well-to-do were no longer tied to the land but gained their assets from more mobile and fluid forms of wealth, a situation that required family relations to be stabilized through bonds of affection rather than a common dependence on a shared piece of property.[56] While Howell does not credit the middle ranks with a conscious sense of their own familial differences from the past and from other sectors of medieval society, a number of the works in this study show them exhibiting precisely this awareness, associating the unruly woman with a nascent middle-rank identity and either condemning or celebrating her on those grounds.

Finally, for Middle English writers, the ludicrous spirit of obscene comedy not only provides a rich dialectical atmosphere that facilitates scrutiny of social power relations, it also allows them to issue critiques of established powers that would have been too dangerous to air in other, less abject, discourses. As such, obscenity represents an important chapter in the history of English political thought and literary culture, encouraging innovative responses to the challenges of the post-Black Death period and facilitating the emergence of secular, middle-rank voices into the culture's literary and political spheres.

The Status of Obscenity in Medieval Culture

We can understand the function of obscene comedy in Middle English writing only if we understand the unique status of the obscene in medieval culture. Medieval "bawdiness" is legendary in the modern popular imagination, second only to the period's reputation for elaborate and gruesome forms of torture. And yet the precise status of the obscene in medieval culture has not been subject to close scholarly investigation. An influential school of thought in medieval studies has interpreted the seemingly unselfconscious displays of sexual acts and body parts in medieval arts and letters as evidence that medieval culture lacks a sense of the obscene.[57] A number of sexual theorists, Foucault among them, have followed suit in positioning the Middle Ages and modernity on either side of a divide marking a radical alteration in attitudes to sexuality and gender.[58] Neither of these analyses, however, can account for the many instances in which medieval thinkers, artists, and writers reveal a sense of taboo relating to sexual activity and lower body parts that is remarkably similar to that of the modern West; nor do they acknowledge that modern laws relating to sex, gender, and the family are rooted in medieval jurisprudence in ways that suggest a strong continuity between modern and medieval sexual values.[59]

Determining the exact nature of medieval obscenity and its relationship to modern norms requires careful thought. Emerging from complex and often unspoken cultural norms and values, the obscene is a notoriously difficult concept to pin down. In its classical definition, obscenity is that which is hidden from representation. The word itself means, literally, "offstage" (*obscaena*) in Latin. More generally, obscenity can be described as "the expression, representation or display . . . in certain contexts or situations, of something that is culturally regarded as shocking or repugnant."[60] What these shocking or repugnant representations might be, however, is more difficult to determine. As the anthropologist Weston La Barre observes, there is no particular set of images or ideas that all cultures regard as obscene:

> All we can postulate of the social animal, man (*sic*), is that
> he has the *capacity* for repression through socialization or
> enculturation, and hence can have very intense *reactions* to
> the prohibited or the obscene as defined by his society—
> but so far as any "universality" of descriptive *content* of

these categories is concerned, this is wholly the prescription, cultural or legal, of his own social group or subgroup.[61]

The difficulties involved in defining obscenity according to strict parameters is witnessed in the famous remark by U.S. Supreme Court justice Potter Stewart in a 1964 decision on whether the state of Ohio could ban the showing of the French film *The Lovers*, which officials had deemed "hard core" pornography. Stewart declined to list all the different types of material that might be embraced under the term "hard-core pornography," musing that it was unlikely he could ever do so intelligibly, even if he tried. He nevertheless reserved his right of judgment, affirming that even if he could not provide a precise definition, "I know it when I see it."[62]

Justice Stewart's reservations notwithstanding, a serviceable definition of obscenity in the modern West associates it with references to, and images of, human nudity, genitalia, scatology, or sexual activity, made outside scientific or medical contexts and in a language "that is itself subject to the same inhibitions as the thing it describes."[63] The 1973 U.S. Supreme Court decision in *Miller v. California* defines the obscene as "a work that depicts or describes, in a patently offensive way, sexual conduct or excretory functions."[64] In the United Kingdom, the Williams Committee report on obscenity in 1979 similarly describes obscenity as material that is "offensive to reasonable people" by reason of "the manner in which it portrays, deals with, or relates to violence, cruelty or horror, or sexual, fecal or urinary functions or genital organs."[65]

At first glance, we might agree that medieval culture lacks a sense of the obscene since it diverges markedly from modernity in the level of publicity and respectability it accords to certain displays of sexuality and body parts. Modernity separates out the exhibition of sexual activities and body parts from other forms of discourse and restricts it to private forms of media: to books, magazines and Internet films. Audiences for explicit sexual content tend to consume it alone and secretly. This is hardly the case in medieval visual culture which, as we have seen, displays obscene images in venues both public and respectable. Literary culture exhibits the same lack of separation between public and private, decent and obscene. The use of obscene exempla in sermons and the appearance of Old French fabliaux in manuscripts alongside saints' lives, fables, courtly poems, and moral tales attests to obscenity's status as an acceptable public discourse.[66] Indeed, the manuscripts containing Anglo-Norman fabliaux are a case in point. Oxford Bodleian Library MS Digby 86, containing one Anglo-Norman fabliau, is a late thirteenth-century "commonplace book" that also includes romances, devotional texts, and didactic writings. In the early fourteenth century, MS Harley 2253 (which contains four of the seven extant Anglo-Norman fabliaux), the fabliau *Les trois dames qui trouverent un vit* [The three women who found a penis] (8.96) is just one page away from an English translation of the "Sayings of St. Bernard." The fourteenth quire of Harley 2253, meanwhile, includes both *Le chevalier qui fist parler les cons* [The knight who could make cunts speak] (3.15), and the English religious verse piece *The Way of Christ's Love*, as well as the French *Enseignements de saint Louis à son fils* (Advice from St. Louis to his son).[67]

Nor is there a developed culture of censorship relating to the obscene in the Middle Ages. While the regulation of obscenity has obsessed modern jurisprudence for some time, medieval authorities appear to have had little interest in regulating what obscene representations could contain or who could see them. In medieval canon law, the only reference to the obscene is concerned with the problems sexually suggestive activities present for clerics.[68] Surveys of English secular court records from the Middle Ages show that there were no prosecutions for sex language except where it was defamatory against individuals.[69] Writers of religious treatises also display little interest in dirty talk. One list of sins of the mouth in English has nothing to say about suggestive or ribald language.[70] The sole exception to this general lack of concern (an exception whose significance I discuss in more detail below) lies in ecclesiastical dictates against nontextual phenomena, like popular performances and games, that occasionally deride them as "obscaenas."

In spite of these seemingly unselfconscious displays, medieval culture exhibits a sense of taboo relating to sexuality, defecation, and the lower body that is remarkably similar to the one that predominates in the modern West. These similarities should not be surprising given that, as James Brundage has demonstrated, the modern West derives much of its sexual theory and practice from the Middle Ages.[71] While obscenity is not "offstage" (*obscaena*) in the Middle Ages the way it is in modern culture, it is nevertheless "hidden in plain sight," consigned exclusively to particular marginalized spaces or artistic forms. In medieval literature, obscenity is reserved exclusively to debased genres like the Old French fabliau, with its proclivity for lower-rank characters and its focus on trifling conflicts over food, money, and sex. Obscenity is largely absent from the more exalted medieval genres like love lyric, romance, or epic, whose central characters are aristocratic and whose subject matter concerns war or *fin amor*.[72] In medieval visual arts, obscene representations are consigned to the margins of manuscripts; obscene carvings appear on the peripheries of church architecture, on window lintels, corbels, and misericords. This "hidden in plain sight" quality of medieval obscenity is also evident in the Anglo-Saxon riddles, which derive their humor from issuing descriptions of sexual intercourse, vaginas, and (most frequently) the penis in terms that might also denote banal household objects (a penis could be an onion, an erection is a rising loaf of bread).[73]

The literature of medieval France, well known for its influence on Middle English writers, reveals a sense of taboo relating to sexual body parts and acts that remains fairly consistent over at least two centuries. Fabliau authors often refer to their works' violation of social taboos, prefacing their tales with apologias for ribaldry (a convention that Chaucer himself evokes in the *Miller's Prologue*).[74] The words and behavior of fabliaux characters also bear witness to a sense of taboo associated with sexuality or bodily functions. The young maiden of *La damoiselle qui ne pooit öir parler de foutre* [The young lady who could not stand to hear talk of fucking] (4.26) cannot bear to hear dirty talk, and the wife in *Le fevre de Creil* (5.42) is offended when her husband begins to describe the size of his assistant's penis in detail, telling him,

> Quar parlez a moi d'autre chose
> . . .
> Quar, par la foi que je vos doi,
> Se plus en parlez devant moi,
> Je ne vous ameroie mie!
> Tel honte ne tel vilonie
> Ne devroit nus preudom retrere. (70, 73–77)
>
> [Talk to me about something else! . . . For by the faith I owe
> you, if you speak any more about it in front of me, I won't
> love you any more: a decent man should never discuss such
> a shameful, dirty business.][75]

A similar indication of the taboo nature of sexual language occurs in the thirteenth-century *Roman de la Rose*. During poem's infamous "testicles" debate, the Lover chastises Lady Reason for her indecorous use of language:

> Si ne vous tieng mie à cortoise,
> Quant ci m'avés coilles nomées,

Qui ne sunt pas bien renomées
En bouch à cortoise pucele.
Vous qui tant estes saige et bele,
Ne sai comment nomer l'osastes,
Au mains quant le mot ne glosastes
Par quelque cortoise parole,
Si cum prode fame parole.

[I do not consider you courteous, when just now you named
the testicles to me; they are not well thought of in the
mouth of a courteous girl. I do not know how you, so wise
and beautiful, dared to name them, at least when you did
not gloss the word with some courteous utterance, as an
honest woman does in speaking of them.][76]

Scholars have debated the extent to which the *Roman*'s original audience
would have been sympathetic to the Lover's objection. For my purposes, the
outcome of these debates is less significant than the fact that a medieval author
could conceive of a character who would object to such language on the basis of
its social impropriety. Such objections attest to a notion of taboo violation
inherent in sexual language, even if that violation is not equally offensive to all.
Indeed, while Reason defends her language usage as proper and right, she nevertheless acknowledges the existence of a differing viewpoint on the matter
when she notes that

Se fames nes noment en France,
Ce n'est fors desacoustumance:
Car le propre non lor pléust,
Qui acoustumé lor éust.

[If women in France do not name these things, it is only that
they are not accustomed to, for the right names would have
been pleasing to those who were accustomed to them.][77]

A similar distaste for frank sexual language is found in the late fourteenth-
century advice book written by the Ménagier de Paris to his young wife. There, the
elderly husband advises his wife against "vulgar" speech denoting sexual body parts:

Et certes, femmes ne doivent parler de nulle laidure, non
mye seulement de con, de cul ne de autres secretz membres
de nature, car c'est deshonneste chose a femme d'en parler.
Je oy une foiz raconter d'une jeune preudefemme qui estoit
assise en une presse de ses autres amis et amyes. Et par
adventure elle dist par esbatement aux autres: "Vous me
pressés si fort que bien la moictié de mon con me ride."
Et jasoit ce qu'elle l'eust dit par jeu et entre ses amis, cuidant
faire la galoise, toutesvoyes les autres sages preudefemmes
ses parentes l'en blasmerent a part.[78]

[And certainly women shouldn't speak of anything vulgar,
certainly not about cunt, ass or other private parts, for it is
unseemly for women to talk of these things. I once heard of
a virtuous young lady who was seated in a crowd of male
and female friends. And by chance she said teasingly to the
others: "You are crowding me so much that at least half of
my cunt is wrinkled." And although she said it in fun and
among her friends, thinking she was gallant, nevertheless in
private the other young ladies blamed her parents.][79]

The Ménagier's advice is part of a complex web of meaning, tied up with his
own status as an upwardly mobile merchant, subordinate in terms of the
courtly culture represented by the "gallant" young lady of his anecdote. What
is most relevant for my purposes, however, is the fact that his strictures reveal a
taboo relating to sexual body parts and that this sensibility is quite similar to
the one expressed by the Lover in the *Roman de la Rose* more than a century
earlier.

The *Querelle de la Rose*—a debate on the merits of the *Roman de la Rose*
carried out between Christine de Pisan and a number of French clerics and
writers in the early years of the fifteenth century—also testifies to taboos associated with genitalia, sexuality, and nudity. In a letter to Jean de Montreuil (c.
1401) disputing the work's claim to literary greatness, Christine cites the testicles discussion as evidence of the poem's corrupt sensibilities. Responding to de
Montreuil's argument that, since there is no ugliness in the things God made,
there should be no need to avoid naming them, Christine asserts that such a
position is only viable in the absence of original sin and that Adam and Eve's
error requires a code of silence around the "secret members":

> Et que honte doye estre deboutee en parlant des choses dont
> nature meisme se hontoye, en publique, je dis que, sauve la
> reverance de l'aucteur de l'avostre, grant tort commettés
> contre la noble vertu de honte, qui de sa nature restraint
> les gouliardises et deshonnestetés en dis et fais; et que ce
> soit grant vice et ors ordre de pollicie honneste et de bonnes
> meurs appert en mains lieux en l'Escripture sainte . . . Et si
> comme naturelmant le mucierent nos premiers parens,
> devons faire en fait et en parolle.[80]

> Thus should modesty be respected when speaking publicly
> of things about which Nature herself is ashamed. Saving
> your reverence and the author's, I say that you commit a
> great wrong against the noble virtue of modesty, which by
> its nature bridles indecency and dishonorable conduct in
> words and deeds. Holy Scripture makes clear in many places
> that this is a great wrong, outside the range of decent con-
> duct and good morals. . . . Just as our first parents hid their
> private parts instinctively, so ought we to do in deed and
> word.[81]

Christine's ally in the *querelle*, Jean Gerson, chancellor of the University of Paris, agrees with her views on the shameful nature of sexual body parts and the language used to describe them. Speaking through the figure of Theological Eloquence in an allegorical trial of the *Roman de la Rose*'s Lover, Gerson asks, "n'est ce pas raige dire que on doye parler nuement et baudement et sans vergoingne, tant soient deshonnestes les parolles au jugement de toutes gens, nes de ceulx qui seroient sans loy ou sans vergoingne?[82] ["is it not madness to say that one should speak fully and openly and without shame, no matter how dishonorable the words are in the judgment of all men, even of those who were without law or without modesty?"][83] By such logic, Theological Eloquence continues, "on doit aler nus et fere nus tout et par tout sans avoir honte . . . Or voise, qui ainssy le maintient, parmy les rues pour esprouver comment Raison le defendra d'estre huyés et abayé et ordoyé!"[84] ["people should go about naked and do as they please anywhere openly and shamelessly. . . . Anyone who believes this should go naked through the streets, and then he would find out whether Reason would prevent him from being scorned, booed, and reviled"].[85]

Media Control and the Regulation of the Obscene

We can reconcile the seemingly contradictory valences of medieval culture—which make it appear at once censorious and unselfconsciously obscene—if we make a distinction between what a culture regards as obscene and what it regulates. Theories that say the Middle Ages lack a notion of obscenity proceed from the flawed assumption that the *regulation* of a given representation is an exact reflection of its taboo status or lack thereof. In fact, European history reveals that, while authorities frequently cast their objections to the obscene in moral terms, their efforts at censoring it align more closely with their own control over its production and dissemination than with its offenses against decency. Official attempts at controlling obscenity in Europe only begin to appear after the invention of the printing press, which allowed a wider variety of people greater access to media, as producers and consumers, than they had ever had before. Before this time, as the authors of the 1986 Meese Commission on pornography note, "almost all written, drawn or printed material was restricted largely to a small segment of the population that undoubtedly constituted the social elite."[86]

As Joan de Jean demonstrates, the development of a discourse locating obscenity as a social problem in seventeenth-century France is not the result of a sudden growth in obscene content (sexually explicit content had been a feature of French arts and culture for centuries). Rather, French authorities begin to be concerned when a print culture arises that extends obscene material beyond the elites to a more general readership.[87] The same chronological sequence is evident in the history of obscenity regulation in Italy. In the early part of the Italian Renaissance, when the circulation of erotic imagery is limited to privileged groups, there is very little censorship. It is only with the arrival of the printing press that Italian authorities begin to express concern about its indecent influence.[88] The sixteenth-century scandal over *I Modi* (the Postures) is a case in point. In 1524, the engraver Marcantonio Raimondi made a set of engravings based on drawings by the painter Giulio Romano of a couple engaged in coitus in a variety of positions. The publication prompted outrage on the part of Pope Clement VII, who had Marcantonio put in prison. The artist himself, meanwhile, went unpunished, revealing that, for Italian authorities, the crime was not the creation of the images themselves but their public distribution.[89] Offense at the erotic writings of Pietro Aretino, the poet who later, famously, wrote sonnets to accompany a series of woodcuts based on the

I Modi engravings, arose from the fact that he, like Raimondi, "exposed the vices of the upper classes to an indiscriminate readership."[90]

More important, perhaps, than mere access to obscenity is the fact that print culture allows marginalized groups the opportunity to use obscenity's power to critique and degrade social and political authority.[91] Aretino prompts outrage not only because he distributes sexually explicit images widely but because he uses pornography "as a vehicle to attack everything from the humanist educational program to clerical piety to the vicissitudes of court life."[92] The passage, in 1791, by the National Assembly in France of a law against "the exposition and sale of obscene images" reveals a similar attempt to control obscenity's use as a political weapon. Although the law was ostensibly created in response to obscenity's corruption of young people and its "insult against the modesty of women," its real impetus was the publication of pamphlets like *Les Enfans de Sodome à l'Assemblée Nationale*, which characterized aristocratic and clerical delegates to the National Assembly as sodomites.[93]

The seemingly carefree medieval attitude toward obscenity can be credited less to a lack of taboo relating to nudity and sexuality than to the fact that the conditions of textual and artistic production in the Middle Ages give medieval authorities precisely the kind of control over the political valence and distribution of obscenity that authorities in later periods were obliged to seek through legal regulation.[94] Medieval manuscript culture and the low rates of literacy in medieval society give the majority of the medieval population very little access to texts or images. Indeed, such is the paucity of images in the Middle Ages that, when sinful "looking" is discussed in pastoral writings, it means looking at a living person rather than a picture, since that practice would have been unavailable to most people.[95] During their heyday, fabliaux are consumed primarily by audiences with funds to afford a professional jongleur or to commission manuscript copies of the tales. Obscene manuscript marginalia is visible only to those wealthy enough to own books. Misericords are located in the choir stalls of medieval churches, and thus only accessible to the clergy who stood there. While sexually explicit carvings on church architecture are available to a broader public, their creation is controlled by the church. The same goes for sermons invoking obscene comedy, which might be heard by many but are authored exclusively by priests.

Tellingly, the single example of a broadly accessible art form in medieval culture, the performing arts, also provides us with the only instance wherein medieval authorities are known to have become upset by "obscene" displays and the damage they inflict on public morals. Disapproval of theatrical activities begins with the church fathers and continues through medieval church thinkers, who condemn them specifically on the basis of their obscenity. The most influential of these is Isidore of Seville, who, in his *Etymologies*, decries the theaters as places of prostitution.[96] Bernard of Clairvaux laments the degradations of tumblers and jugglers who go about with their heads down and their feet up and condemns the theater, "which excites lust with feminine and lascivious wrigglings and represents wanton acts."[97] Attempts by church officials to eradicate theatrical activities also condemn them specifically in terms of their obscenity. In 1207, Innocent III forbids the "ludi theatrales" held by minor clergy in churches on feast days after Christmas, which he describes as "ludibria, insania, debacctiationes obscoenas."[98]

In England during the century before Chaucer's birth, the English episcopacy makes a concerted effort to enforce Innocent III's restrictions on clergy and extend them to lay activities. In a series of letters dating from 1236 to 1244, Bishop Robert Grosseteste of Worcester excoriates the ludi of the clerici as conducive to lechery and condemns customs in his diocese including miracle plays, "scotales," drinking bouts, ram raisings, and "festum stultorum."[99] In 1333, Bishop John de Grandisson of Exeter complains that vicars put on masks and engage in activities he calls "debacchationes obscoenas."[100] The *Summa Predicantium* of the Dominican friar John Bromyard (d. c. 1352) condemns the use of parish cemeteries as fairgrounds for dancing and other lewd and lascivious activities.[101]

Information is scarce on the exact nature of the offending performances since we have no written records from their creators. What information we do have, however, suggests that they included send-ups of religious authority. One sermon describes a "somergame" as a parodic game in which some people dress up as devils to taunt Christ and are rewarded as best taunter.[102] In 1348, de Grandisson describes an episode in which a group of men calling themselves the "order of Brothelyngham" roam the streets of Exeter in monkish habit, blowing horns, capturing laymen and clergy for ransom, then choosing a "lunatic" as an abbot, clothing him as a monk and setting him up "in theatro" for adoration as an idol.[103]

Medieval Categories of the Obscene

Although the most significant difference between medieval and modern obscenity lies in regulation rather than in what the two cultures categorize as obscene, there are a couple of notable differences between medieval and modern notions of the obscene. These represent differences of degree rather than a complete alterity between the two cultures but are nevertheless worth noting. The first difference lies in a marked distinction in medieval culture between two levels of taboo. While sexual body parts and normative heterosexual sex are, as I have described above, more publicly acceptable in the Middle Ages than in the modern West, other forms of sexuality are subjected to a censorship so profound they are rarely, if ever, visible. Cunnilingus, fellatio, homosexuality, bestiality, masturbation, and heterosexual sex acts that violate the gender conventions of male superiority and female inferiority are never (or very rarely) depicted in medieval texts and art.[104]

The second difference between medieval and modern notions of the obscene, and the one most significant for the purposes of this study, lies in a group of additional, nonsexual behaviors that medieval culture also places in the category of the obscene. While modernity defines obscenity primarily in terms of sexuality, scatology, or anatomy, the strictly hierarchical culture of the Middle Ages also invests disobedience and resistance to the established order with a level of obscenity equal to the display of lower body functions, body parts, or sexual acts. This is a phenomenon recently observed by Alastair Minnis in a study of the Wife of Bath, wherein he notes that, in spite of a general lack of obscene word usage in her prologue, the Wife nevertheless renders herself obscene "by blatantly and unashamedly engaging in behavior which is itself *dura, turpis,* and *immunda*—in a word, *obscenus.*"[105] The equivalence medieval culture makes between sexual obscenity and resistance to authority is witnessed in the way that obscene comedy often depicts the two qualities together: the unruly woman is almost always shown to transgress both sexually and in terms of her lack of deference to male authority. Indeed, obscene comic discourse tends to regard a resistance to male authority as a strong predictor of sexual transgression. As we shall see in subsequent chapters, some Middle English texts, like the Noah pageants and the mumming of John Lydgate, even drop the element of female *sexual* obscenity altogether (focusing solely on female disobedience) yet retain their claim to obscenity in the sense that they are still seen to portray behavior that is socially taboo.

The Politics of Medieval Obscenity

Appreciating the unparalleled levels of control that medieval authorities have over the creation and dispersal of most forms of obscenity is crucial to our understanding of its status in medieval culture, particularly in terms of the political valence that medieval audiences were likely to associate with the obscene. The fact that medieval authorities do not, for the most part, need to censor obscenity in order to limit its use by insurgent elements in the society means that they are free to exploit obscenity's power to their own ends. Thus, medieval obscenity (both comic and serious) is often used to uphold established powers, to dehumanize and degrade marginalized groups (like women, peasants, or religious minorities), and to illustrate the superiority of dominant ideologies relating to social hierarchies, morality, and sexual mores.

The tendency of medieval obscenity to uphold the established order has been elucidated in a number of different disciplines. In a study of obscene church carvings, Anthony Weir and James Jermain argue that the works originate as part of a campaign by twelfth-century celibate monks and clergy to uphold their own superiority by calling attention to the degradation inherent in human sexuality, particularly female sexuality.[106] The French poet Rutebeuf, in Leslie Dunton-Downer's analysis, directs his obscenity against social change in works that are moralistic and reactionary.[107] Susan Signe Morrison finds the same political valence in much scatological obscenity. Excremental discourse, she argues, is often directed against Jews, the poor, peasants, and women.[108] Examining the anti-Semitic Czech play *The Ointment Seller*, Alfred Thomas argues that medieval writers use obscenity to make a distinction between an unmocked majority and a ridiculed minority of outsiders.[109] In his analysis of the obscene art on the margins of medieval manuscripts, Michael Camille notes how frequently it chastises weaker groups in the social order.[110] Similarly, studies of the Old French fabliau have remarked both on its misogyny and on its tendency to favor the secular powers of medieval society over the lower orders and low-ranking clergy.[111]

Obscenity's prominent role in upholding the status quo means it would have had a different political valence for medieval audiences than it does for modern ones. In the modern West, obscenity is seen to exist in one of two categories: it is either pornographic, in which case it is credited with being largely apolitical, dedicated only to sexual stimulation, or it is artistic, in which case its politics are generally insurgent and attack the status quo.[112] Feminists and gay rights activists have rightly interrogated the notion of pornography's apolitical status. Antiporn feminists, for instance, have noted that mainstream pornography upholds gender hierarchies in ways that reflect women's second-class social status.[113] Angela Carter and Laura Kipnis, meanwhile, have noted that pornography associated with an oppositional politics tends to attract a disproportionate amount of censorship.[114] Nevertheless, the fact remains that the majority of those in the modern West *perceive* pornography and other forms of sexual obscenity as a sexual, rather than political, mode of expression and only read politics in obscenity when it is used in avant garde art.

In the Middle Ages, the political valences of the obscene are much more obvious, precisely because it is so completely controlled by elites. The control medieval power holders exercise over the obscene is far more blatant, and far easier to recognize, than the media controls in the modern West. In a culture wherein explicit representations of sexual body parts are engraved on church architecture, obscenity's capacity to enforce the established order is not a hidden element of its expression, to be discerned only by the most perspicacious reader or viewer, but an established and well-accepted fact. Thus, obscenity's capacity to uphold the status quo would have been far more perceptible to medieval audiences than it is to modern ones.

Recognizing obscenity's conventional status in medieval culture is of signal importance to our understanding of Middle English texts because it reveals that writers interested in using obscenity to interrogate the status quo would have been obliged to alter its traditional narratives and modes of characterization. Germane to Foucault's notion of discourse is his emphasis on the relationship between discourse and the "wider social processes of legitimation and power."[115] By determining what can be said and how it is said, discourse is crucial to the construction of certain "truths" that maintain social power relations. Thus, not only would traditional modes of depicting men, women, and marriage in obscene discourse have worked to affirm existing hierarchies, they would also have been *perceived* as affirming those hierarchies by medieval audiences. Conversely, alterations to the discourse would have appeared to medieval writers and their audiences as possible challenges to the established order. This is a recognition that is still largely missing from studies of Middle English literature. The critical history of Chaucer's *Miller's Tale* provides an illustrative example. While feminists like Karma Lochrie and Elaine Hansen have noted that the *Miller's Tale* upholds the gender status quo established by the Knight, other readings equate it unproblematically with resistance to the established order.[116] Lee Patterson, for instance, reads the insertion of the *Miller's Tale* after the *Knight's Tale* as indicative of peasant resistance to established authority without accounting for the fabliau's aristocratic provenance.[117]

The Semiotic Instability of Obscene Comedy

To say that obscenity has a socially normative valence in medieval culture is not to say that it is devoid of countercultural elements. As a violation of propriety, obscenity is, by definition, invested with an insurgent energy even in its most conventional iterations. The fact that many medieval expressions of obscenity are able to direct that countercultural energy toward the enforcement of the status quo means only that its insurgency is contained, not eliminated. Indeed, the semiotic instability of obscene comedy is the key to its success, even as an enforcer of the status quo, for it gives to that enforcement a thrill of the forbidden that makes it all the more compelling.

The difficulties that scholars have had in coming to terms with the semiotic instability of obscene comedy is best witnessed in the debates over Mikhail Bakhtin's theory of medieval "carnival." Associating the festivals that accompanied medieval feast days with an expression of what he calls "folk carnival humor," Bakhtin describes a culture of laughter that is opposed to official ecclesiastical and feudal culture.[118] Emphasizing parody, a celebration of the lower body functions, and a delight in featuring a "world upside down," these festivities were, according to Bakhtin, insurgent forces that "celebrated temporary liberation from the prevailing truth and from the established order," suspending "all hierarchical rank privileges, norms, and prohibitions."[119] Bakhtin's characterization of carnival as an insurgent and antiauthoritarian ritual has been critiqued by Umberto Eco and Terry Eagleton, among others, as an idealization of behavior that actually affirms the established order by providing a safety valve through which pent-up aggression in the general populace can be vented without risk to those in power. Carnival is, in Eagleton's words, "a *licensed* affair in every sense, a permissible rupture of hegemony, a contained popular blow-off."[120] Others have noted that carnival often works to promote official authority by encouraging the majority to relieve their frustrations by abusing weaker groups, like women and minorities. As James Grantham Turner notes in a critique of Bakhtin, "This sympathetic but misty-eyed interpretation underestimates the edge of real violence in carnival, sometimes directed against authorities but often unleashed on their behalf."[121]

While these are legitimate critiques of Bakhtin's work, the most accurate reading of carnival is one that recognizes the impossibility of pinning it down to one consistent meaning. As Stallybrass and White note of the debates over carnival's political status, "it makes little sense to fight out the issue of whether or not carnival is intrinsically radical or conservative, for to do so automatically involves the false essentializing of carnivalesque transgression."[122] Because carnival has the capacity to embody a variety of political valences, "the politics of carnival cannot be resolved outside of a close historical examination of a particular conjunction: there is no a priori revolutionary vector to carnival and transgression."[123] In her discussion of the unruly woman, Natalie Zemon Davis makes a similar point, noting that the unruly woman is a multivalent figure who could both reinforce and undermine the existing social structure, depending on the particular circumstances in which she was being invoked.[124]

In this respect, both carnival and medieval obscenity partake of the changeability and instability that Foucault identifies as a constituent element of all discourse. While Foucault emphasizes the connection between discourse and the preservation of the established order, he also asserts that no discourse has the totalizing capacity to uphold power relations absolutely:

> We must make allowances for the complex and unstable
> process whereby discourse can be both an instrument and
> an effect of power, but also a hindrance, a stumbling block,
> a point of resistance and a starting point for an opposing
> strategy. Discourse transmits and produces power; it rein-
> forces it, but it also undermines and exposes it, renders it
> fragile and makes it possible to thwart it.[125]

The dual nature of discourse that Foucault describes in this passage is key to our understanding of Middle English obscene comedy. While discourse often upholds the established order, it also has the capacity to undermine that order. Of particular note are the qualities of inventive freedom and experimentation that Bakhtin associates with carnival (and, by extension, with a number of medieval literary works, like the fabliau and the biblical drama, that he identifies with the carnival spirit).[126] In Bakhtin's analysis, carnival's celebration of disorder and its inversion of social hierarchies provide "a temporary liberation from the prevailing truth and from the established order," offering audiences "the chance to have a new outlook on the world, to realize the relative nature of all that exists, and to enter a completely new order of things."[127]

Since the publication of Bakhtin's work, thinkers in the fields of anthropology and sociology have expanded on his insight, exploring how celebrations of license and inversion offer groups and individuals the opportunity to rethink their society and its hierarchies. Victor Turner associates rituals of inversion with "liminality," a state in which a society sets itself apart from its everyday existence in order to mark key transitions (from season to season or war to peace, for instance). In liminal spaces, "profane social relations are discontinued, former rights and obligations suspended, the social order turned upside down" and "factors or elements of culture may be recombined in grotesque ways."[128] While Turner associates the liminal primarily with tribal societies, he deems ritual celebrations of disorder like the medieval carnival and its literary representations as "liminoid," the manifestation of the liminal in what he calls "contractual societies" (a rubric under which he includes medieval feudalism).[129]

In Turner's analysis, the suspension of normal social hierarchies liberates "human cognition and creativity from the normative constraints incumbent on occupying a sequence of social statuses."[130] While the potential for innovation resulting from liminal states is minimal in tribal societies, it is a primary function of the liminoid, which is able to extend the experimental space resulting from a suspension of social hierarchies for a longer period than is possible in tribal societies. In contractual societies, the liminoid is a space of self-evaluation, in which members of a given society can evaluate how their society measures up to its own ideals and can experiment with new ideas. In Turner's view, rituals like carnival can never be regarded as a safety valve or a mere letting off of steam; rather, they are places where society measures itself and can propose, "in however extravagant a form, new paradigms and models which invert or subvert the old."[131]

The concept of play is foundational to both the liminal and the liminoid. Drawing on the work of the sociologist Brian Sutton-Smith, Turner theorizes that the play and disorder in liminoid phenomena such as charivaris, fiestas, Halloween, and mummings are key sites of learning and innovation in a culture: "we may be disorderly in games either because we have an overdose of order and want to let off steam or because we have something to *learn* from being disorderly."[132]

Understanding obscene comedy's status as a discourse with an unparalleled capacity both to enforce the status quo and to interrogate it allows us to explain Middle English writers' perennial attraction to it. Each of the authors in this study does something different with the discourse, but they all exploit its paradoxical mixture of the conventional and the insurgent. Their interest in gender, sexuality, and the household, meanwhile, can take very different forms, but they are unified in their preoccupation with the connection between the political and the domestic.

The first section of the book examines obscene comedy's fourteenth-century pioneers, Langland and Chaucer. Chapter 1 points out the crucial role that obscene comic discourse plays in Langland's criticisms of secular and ecclesiastical authority. In passages that exploit the discourse's characters, voices, and tropes, Langland appropriates obscene comedy to interrogate social and political authority with a level of directness unmatched in any other parts of the poem. The discourse is useful to Langland for a number of interrelated reasons, providing him with a language to analyze the failures of social authority, with an aggressively critical voice in the speech of the unruly woman, and with a blind for some of his most radical critiques, its conventional nature and degraded status masking criticisms of secular authority in *Piers Plowman* that are often dangerously severe.

Chaucer follows Langland in using obscene comedy to criticize medieval power holders, in this case by exploring the operation of coercion and by underlining the devastating effects of chivalry's culture of violence. Unlike Langland, Chaucer does not break the discourse down into its constituent characters and tropes, choosing instead to create works in the image of the fabliau. As a result, Chaucer must struggle more than Langland to overcome the discourse's tendency to affirm the status quo and to unleash its capacity to pose questions of aristocratic ideology. Chapter 2 examines Chaucer's experimentations in the *Reeve's Tale* and the *Legend of Good Women*, showing how they reveal his discovery that the fabliau's capacity to critique aristocratic authority is only enabled by a revision of its misogyny. Although Chaucer's obscene comedy appears, on the surface, to be more generically identifiable than Langland's, Chaucer also breaks down the discourse from within, fusing fabliau and classical legend in the *Reeve's Tale* to undercut the genre's strongly misogynist valences and to grasp hold of its insurgent energy.

The second section of the book, comprising Chapters 3, 4, and 5, examines how fifteenth-century writers take up Langland and Chaucer's legacy. While the fifteenth century sees the emergence in England of entertainment-oriented obscene comedy in the form of tales and popular lyrics, a number of writers continue Langland and Chaucer's practice of using the discourse in works of thematic seriousness and intellectual rigor. These writers take obscenity in a number of different directions.

Chapter 3 turns to John Lydgate, a writer committed both to misogyny and to the claims of fifteenth-century elites. Unlike Langland and Chaucer, Lydgate does not favor obscene comedy, eschewing it in the majority of his writings. As an establishment writer who avoids a discourse that, in other periods and national contexts, is a beloved language of the powerful, Lydgate bears witness to the influence of Langland and Chaucer's innovations. Nevertheless, in particular circumstances, Lydgate does resort to obscenity, and these are well worth examining. Although Lydgate differs from Chaucer and Langland in his support for established authority, he, too, occasionally has need of obscenity's semiotic instability and spirit of playful experimentation. In the *Mumming at Hertford*, Lydgate brings warring lower-rank spouses before the king in an attempt to revise royal authority to better suit the changed social and economic conditions of the fifteenth century. Elsewhere, Lydgate appeals to the discourse's wittily negative portrayals of women in order to upend the popularity, in the early years of the fifteenth century, of Christine de Pisan's anti-misogynist critiques.

The fourth chapter examines a work whose obscene-comedy heritage has been largely unrecognized. While the capacity of the *Book of Margery Kempe* to evoke laughter has always been treated as accidental, my analysis proposes that it is actually a purposeful technique that enables far-reaching criticisms of the fifteenth-century English church. Of particular importance is the way the *Book* deploys obscene comedy to carry out a sustained critique of the Church's anti-Lollard campaign, highlighting the way an obsession with heresy has led the church to violate its most sacred commandments relating to compassion and the sanctity of divine revelation. Putting gender at the forefront of its exploration of power, the *Book* positions gender-based discrimination against a female visionary as the ground on which it explores the flaws in the church's anti-Lollard campaign. As in Langland's *Piers Plowman*, obscenity in the *Book of Margery Kempe* functions as a blind for some of the author's most trenchant critiques, concealing the *Book*'s most radical interrogations of secular authority in passages that appear, on the surface, to be conventionally misogynist depictions of an unruly woman.

The final chapter examines how the fifteenth-century biblical drama uses obscene comedy as a discourse of political expression. Most notable is the way the pageants evince a revised vision of the unruly woman, challenging the discourse's tendency to villainize her by characterizing her as figure whose self-command and assertiveness are useful, as well as disruptive. A fascinating element of this revision lies in the pageants' use of the unruly woman as a voice in which to interrogate ecclesiastical and secular powers, having her oppose a punitive religious ideology in the Noah pageants and attack, quite literally, aristocratic authorities in the "Massacre of the Innocents" plays. In doing so, these pageants highlight the interrelation between class and gender, celebrating the unruly woman as part of a middle-rank identity whose rights and perspectives they assert against the dominant order.

PART I

Fourteenth-Century Pioneers

CHAPTER I

Comedy and Critique

Obscenity and Langland's Reproof
of Established Powers in *Piers Plowman*

The final passus of *Piers Plowman* is generally known as the apocalyptic and pessimistic conclusion of Will's journey, chronicling the disintegration of the Christian community in the face of corrupt political leadership, a cynical commons, and a Church that fails to protect Christian values. It is rather surprising to find, in the midst of this grim scenario, a comical passage on a wife's disappointment in her elderly husband's impotence. Angered by Will's objection to the path he has shorn through the dreamer's hair, Elde subjects Will to yet more indignities of old age, rendering him deaf and dumb with cuffs to the mouth and ears and shackling him with gout. Will's wife, meanwhile,

> ... wisshed wel witterly that I were in hevene.
> For the lyme that she loved me fore, and leef was to feele—
> On nyghtes, namely, whan we naked weere—
> I ne myghte in no manere maken it at hir wille
> So Elde and heo it hadden forbeten. (B.XX.194–98)[1]

The passage's description of the sexual act, its domestic setting, its critical wife, and its elderly husband recall fabliau-style scenarios of marital strife. And yet William Langland is not typically identified as an obscene writer. Indeed, one might say just the opposite, given the impassioned condemnations of "harlotrie" that appear at regular intervals throughout *Piers Plowman*. Nevertheless, the impotence episode is far from being an anomaly in Langland's poem, which frequently makes use of the characters, tropes, scenarios, style, and language of obscene comedy.

Langland's debts to the discourse are less immediately recognizable than Chaucer's because he does not include complete, generically identifiable units in the manner of Chaucer's fabliaux.[2] Langland tends to be more diffuse in his evocations, importing different elements of obscene comedy at various points in *Piers Plowman* with differing degrees of intensity. The poem sometimes makes glancing references to certain tropes and characters, as when the Samaritan cites the allegory of the shrewish wife as the wicked flesh that will not be chastised (B.XVII.317–34) or when Wit makes reference to the bacon of Dunmowe (the prize for couples who go a year without quarreling) and advises men to marry "Whiles thow art yong, and thi wepene kene" (B.IX.170, 182). More extended uses of obscenity occur in Lechery's C-text confession, which features oversize sexual appetites, old bawds, clever tricks, and the fabliau's comically euphemistic terms for the sexual act.[3] Most significantly, the discourse plays a major role in the Meed episode and in the argumentative exchanges between Will, Study, Clergy, Scripture, Reason, and Ymaginatif in the dreamer's third vision, as well as in the impotence passage I have cited above.

In spite of Langland's persistent interest in the funny domestic tales that were omnipresent in his fourteenth-century milieu, his relationship to obscene comedy has not often been a topic of discussion in studies of *Piers Plowman*.[4] Recent years have seen some analyses of gender in the poem and a few studies on the influence of secular genres like romance.[5] But while critics often note that particular passages are "comical" or derived from "satire," thorough investigations into Langland's use of particular comic or satirical traditions are rare.[6]

My purpose in this chapter is not only to point out the existence of obscene comedy in *Piers Plowman* but to argue for its constitutive role in some of the poem's most famous and intellectually demanding segments. The Meed episode, the third vision, and the impotence vignette all draw extensively upon obscene comedy: on its manner of examining power; on its voices of resistance to authority; on its playful capacity to open up new ways of looking at social hierarchies, and even on its ridiculous and abject status. Stylistically, Langland's use of obscene comedy varies tremendously. Sometimes it emerges as a voice, sometimes it informs interpersonal dynamics between characters, and sometimes it provides only a particular language or situation. Thematically, however, Langland's evocation of the discourse always aligns with those moments when his interrogation of authority, particularly secular authority, is most aggressive. The three episodes under consideration in this chapter are also the episodes that constitute Langland's most severe condemnations of both secular powers and the Church. In each case, Langland draws on obscene comedy to provide him with a language and a paradigm for political analysis that is unavailable in any other medieval discourse.

We must pay particular attention to Langland's obscene comedy, for, in many respects, it sets the stage for Middle English writers' unusually politicized and sophisticated use of the discourse. Although Chaucer is almost universally identified as the writer who brings the fabliau into English, it is actually Langland who is the true pioneer in this respect. It is Langland who first expresses ideas of philosophical complexity using the characters, tropes, and language of the funny stories that entertained English elites, who provides an exemplar of how obscene comedy can be reconfigured to push the discourse beyond its own limits, and who shows how it can pose questions of those in power. Langland's importance in the history of obscene comedy in England is due not only to his influence on Chaucer (although that is profound) but to the wide dissemination of *Piers Plowman* in late medieval England.[7] As John Bowers has argued, it is likely that Langland's power in this respect was greater than Chaucer's, since Langland's work was more widely known and copied in later medieval England.[8]

One might ask how a case can be made for Langland's interest in obscene comedy, given that lecherous tales and their tellers are often condemned in *Piers Plowman*. A classic bit of Langlandian censure can be found in Dame Study's complaint regarding the goods that "harlotes...And japeris and jogelours and jangleris of gestes" win from the rich, who eagerly consume their "vile harlotrye" while ignoring those who speak of Christian doctrine (B.X.30–31, 45).[9] Langland's distaste for obscene comedy in its conventional form is certainly made clear in this passage, but we ought to distinguish between this and a complete disavowal of obscene comedy as a literary discourse. Study's condemnation might explain why Langland only deploys fragments of obscene comedy, rather than reproducing it in complete tales, but it should not be taken as a wholesale rejection of the obscene. Indeed, Dame Study herself is a case in point, as a figure whose own unruly personality bears witness to her creator's desire to recoup elements of very tales she condemns.

Crucial to an understanding of obscene comedy's function in *Piers Plowman* is an appreciation of Langland's commitment to rebuke the established powers of fourteenth-century English society (both ecclesiastical *and* secular) for their failure to embody Christian doctrine regarding just rulership and care of the poor. I am aware that this view of Langland goes against the predominant reading of him as a politically quietist poet whose primary interest is in religious thought.[10] As Larry Scanlon points out, however, Langland is regarded as a political and religious dissident for most of English history. It is only in the mid-twentieth century that scholars begin to characterize him as political moderate so disturbed by the 1381 rising that he altered his poem to eliminate rebel misreadings of its politics.[11] This view, as Scanlon notes, is not motivated by a careful reading of *Piers Plowman*, but by the desire to uphold a theory of single authorship across the three versions of the poem by accounting for the C-text's movement away from some of the more radical statements of B.[12]

To describe Langland as a religious thinker with little interest in politics is to overlook his commitment to embody Christian values in the human world. For this reason, the political and the religious are intertwined for Langland. Many passages in *Piers Plowman* testify to the Christian's duty to speak truth to and about the powerful when they commit injustices. This is not to say that Langland was a democrat *avant la lettre*. Much in his writing reflects his commitment to the traditional political hierarches of medieval society. However, as Scanlon notes, the categories of "radical" and "conservative"—wherein an interest in social reform is aligned with a desire to break from the past—are ill suited to fourteenth-century political discourse.[13] Langland is better characterized as an author who is both traditional and radical, who, in Susan Crane's words, "attributes oppression to wrongful distortions of fundamentally valid institutions."[14]

To understand Langland's obscene comedy, we must also appreciate his awareness regarding the dangers of speaking truth to power. One does not need to look far into later medieval history to find evidence of the risks involved in criticizing authorities. As the narrator of *Mum and the Sothsegger* avers,

> And yf a burne bolde hym to bable the sothe
> And mynde hym of mischief that missereule asketh,
> He may lose his life and laugh here no more,
> Or yputte into prisone or ypyned to deeth
> Or yblent or yshent or sum sorowe have,
> That fro scorne other scathe scape shal he nevre. (165–70)[15]

Even before the violence of the 1381 rebellion and Henry IV's overthrow of Richard II, English history provides evidence that lower-rank resistance to secular powers was met with severe punishment. In 1377, for instance, some anonymous Londoners publicly criticized John of Gaunt by reversing his arms (the sign of a traitor) and posting lampoons around the city that declared the duke to be the son of a Flemish butcher. In retribution, Gaunt summoned community leaders before the king at Sheen, where they "professed their innocence and begged on their knees for pardon." To placate the duke, the Londoners acceded to his demands that they depose their mayor and set up a marble pillar in Cheap, adorned with Gaunt's coat of arms. The anonymous authors of the lampoons were never found, but, if they were, the duke vowed they would be sentenced to death.[16]

In the aftermath of the 1381 rebellion, such views became even more dangerous to hold. In 1388, the Cambridge parliament passed a statute that "gave legal sanction to the suppression of adverse criticism of the aristocracy," dictating that anyone who was "so bold as to fabricate any further defamations or any such false things concerning the prelates, dukes, counts, barons, etc." would be punished.[17] As Scanlon notes, the political retreat of the *Piers Plowman* C-text can still be reconciled with the notion of a single author if we consider the possibility that the C rewrite was undertaken out of fear of external sanctions in the aftermath of the 1381 rebellion, rather than Langland's own, internally motivated repudiation of the 1381 rebels.[18]

Given this context, James Scott's theory of "the hidden transcript" provides a useful guide for reading the politics of *Piers Plowman*. Refuting the notion that the paucity of resistance so often seen among subordinates in coercive societies is due to their ideological complicity in their own oppression, Scott asserts that subordinates' approval of the status quo is often an illusion. In "a society of total clientage and dependency, where any open, identified resistance to the ruling power may result in instant retaliation, loss of home, employment, or tenancy," or even death, subordinates must mask their true feelings in front of superiors, producing a "public transcript" of compliance.[19] Concealed beneath this apparent approval lies the "hidden transcript," wherein subordinates resist established powers privately, among themselves. Public and unambiguous articulations of "the hidden transcript" only appear in the historical record when the established order breaks down completely, providing subordinates with the opportunity to resist without fear of immediate retaliation (as in the 1381 rebellion). Some expressions of resistance may still emerge into the public transcript at times when authorities' grip on power is firm, but, when they do, they appear in a manner sufficiently indirect and garbled that they are capable of two readings, one of which is innocuous and provides an "avenue of retreat" in the case of a direct challenge or interrogation on the part of authorities.[20]

Much of Langland's political expression occurs in the manner Scott describes: it is often garbled, or articulated in ways that provide an "avenue of retreat" in the form of an alternate, innocuous meaning. For twentieth- and twenty-first-century readers, Langland's disguises have perhaps been too successful, since modern scholars have overlooked or underestimated much of his most stringent commentary. The invisibility of Langland's politics presents a unique challenge to my project in this chapter. My primary aim is to discuss Langland's use of obscene comedy to criticize the leaders of his society, but because the very existence of that criticism in the passages I examine has been overlooked, I must preface my discussion of obscenity with a description of the criticism itself.

One might ask how Langland's commentary can be relevant if it is so obscure. To this I would answer that modern readers' inability to detect garbled or hidden political meaning may well be a disability more common to the citizens of Western democracies than to those who inhabit the nondemocratic and coercive regimes of the medieval and early modern period.[21] Langland's garbled meanings are perfectly obvious to the Protestant polemicist Robert Crowley (himself an inhabitant of a coercive society). In the introduction to his 1561 edition of *Piers Plowman*, Crowley acknowledges both Langland's criticism of secular authority and his practice of burying his most severe reproofs, noting that the poem describes the great wickedness of bishops and "some what of the powre and office of kinges and princes, and than secretly in latine verses, it rebuketh their cruelnes and tyranny."[22]

One of Langland's favorite garbling techniques is to pursue an analysis of secular power in the midst of a passage that advertises itself as being about something else entirely. The practice is facilitated by allegory, since the allegorical names of various characters explicitly announce the pursuit of a certain theme, thereby masking the other, more politically risky meanings the passage might contain. This is the case both in the Meed episode and in the third vision. In the Meed episode, the ostensible subject, trumpeted by Meed's own name, is financial reward, but in actuality the episode engages in an extended evaluation of royal governance. The third vision purports to be an allegory concerned with modes of learning (announced by figures named Study, Clergy, and Scripture), yet a close reading of the Latin biblical passages to which it refers shows Langland persistently identifying the failings of the ruling classes and pointing to biblical warnings of divine retribution against corrupt rulers. This is not to say that either episode is not also concerned with its ostensible subject, only that they engage at the same time in a separate inquiry that proceeds according to its own logic.

A suitable metaphor for the way that Langland pursues multiple meanings in his poem can be found in the relation between text and margin that we see in illuminated manuscripts. While the textual content of a manuscript page advertises itself as the document's primary meaning, the marginal illustrations offer alternate meanings. Marginalia may refer to the content of the text, or it may proceed according to a separate agenda all its own. Moreover, marginalia can proceed in a continuity of meaning over several pages, even as the subject of the main text alters. The Luttrell Psalter (c. 1325–35) provides a good example of this phenomenon. The pages of the psalter featuring Psalms 93 through 96 include a series of illustrations depicting the agricultural seasons, from plowing to sowing to harrowing and harvesting.[23] These scenes might have been somewhat inspired by the Psalms (Psalm 95 contains a line referring to agricultural labors), yet much of what they depict has little to do with the text they surround. Similarly, the nun at the penis tree in BnF MS Fr.25526 is one of a series of interconnected images depicting the lecherous activities of nuns and monks that is carried out over several pages of the manuscript. This pictoral narrative has little direct relation to the content of the *Roman de la Rose*, the poem whose text it abuts. Rather, the illustrations proceed according to a logic of their own. In the same way that a manuscript ostensibly presents the centrally positioned text as the main event while also including other content, so Langland's writing advertises the importance of one meaning, identified in the names and identities of the allegorical figures, while simultaneously pursuing others.

In medieval manuscripts, the marginal is a zone of experimentation, transformation, and innovation. The margins of the Luttrell Psalter not only include depictions of agricultural life, they also feature bizarre, hybrid creatures that defy what is known and accepted in the natural world. The top of one page of the Luttrell Psalter features a creature part man, part bird, part plant (see Figure 5). Lower on the page, another figure appears to combine the tippet-covered head of a man with the legs and abdomen of a wolf or lion. These images gesture to the way that the margins, in medieval culture, had permission to experiment with violations of convention and outlandish imaginings not permitted in other zones. Precisely because they are marginal (that is, not central, not authoritative), the margins can innovate and can ask questions of established truths in ways that the central text does not and cannot.

Obscenity and obscene comedy are part of this marginal world of innovation, play, and experimentation. It is only in the margins of medieval manuscripts that we see the copulating couples or the nuns picking penises from the

FIGURE 5. A man-bird-plant hybrid decorates the top of a page in the Luttrell Psalter.
Add MS 42130, fol. 60r. © The British Library Board.

penis tree (see Figures 1 and 2). The marginal obscene includes, too, insubordination and violations of established hierarchies. The same page of the Luttrell
Psalter that features the hybrid creatures also features a depiction of a man on
his knees, apparently begging for mercy while a tall woman towers over him,
about to beat him with her distaff (see Figure 6).[24]

The outrageousness of the margins provides a good place to engage in
political thought, their abject status providing a freedom to explore power relations in ways impossible in other, more culturally authoritative discourses. The
unruly woman is a case in point in this respect: because she is ludicrous and
funny, she is permitted an antiauthoritarian voice whose aggression is
unmatched by the voices available in any other medieval discourse, including
those accorded to men. Moreover, the permission to reimagine and recombine
accepted truths embodied in the hybrid man-plant, man-animal figures of the
margins illustrates how the marginal invites an interrogation of the established
order of things that is well suited to developing the kinds of nontraditional
responses that were necessary in the changed and changing world of the later
fourteenth century.

It is worth noting in this context that when Ymaginatif criticizes Will's
writing of poetry in Passus XII, saying that his writing is a waste when there are
books enough that describe Dowel, Debet, and Dobest and preachers to explain
it, Will defends himself by citing poetry's value as play (B.XII.16–17). Quoting
Cato's advice to his son, Will asserts the value of poetry as a relief from more
serious studies, noting that even though the son was a clerk, Cato counseled
him to "solacen hym som tyme—as I do when I make; / *Interpone tuis inter-
dum gaudia curis*" [give a place sometimes to pleasures amid your pressing
cares] (B.XII.21–23). Although we may think that play is simply about enjoyment, Will's subsequent remarks to Ymaginatif indicate that "pley" for Langland is an ethical practice and a heuristic device. Elaborating on his defense of

FIGURE 6. A woman threatens a kneeling man with a distaff.
Luttrell Psalter, Add MS 42130, fol. 60r. © The British Library Board.

poetry, Will tells Ymaginatif about the "holy men" of whom he has heard "how thei outherwhile / Pleyden, the parfiter to ben, in [places manye]" (B.XII.23–24). Will further justifies his "pley" by asserting that he would not have a need for poetry "if ther were any wight that wolde me tell / What were Dowel and Dobet and Dobest at the laste" (B.X. 25–26). Thus, Will characterizes the play of poetry as a way of learning, when neither books nor clergy can provide a satisfactory answer.

In creating a central meaning for various passages through the naming of allegorical figures (like Meed or Study) and at the same time "decorating" his text with thematic "marginalia," Langland gives himself the same kind of freedom that medieval manuscript producers gave to themselves in their juxtaposition of orthodox text and subversive marginalia. In the thematic "margins" of his poem, Langland can experiment more freely, knowing that his text is grounded in the less controversial and more orthodox meanings of its allegory. In the same way that the obscene is a definitive part of the margins' playful and experimental world, so in Langland, the obscene is often the avenue to the text's alternate meanings. If we follow Dame Study, if we follow the ludicrousness of the king and his unruly Meed, if we follow the rude and insubordinate Will, we will arrive at Langland's hidden thematic concerns.

And yet, one might argue that the margins are not truly insurrectionary, their violations contained within the larger, orthodox meaning of the text they abut. Indeed, this is true, and the margins' ultimate containment—the way that their insurrections and experimentations remain subject to the orthodox, central text—is crucial to a radical traditionalist like Langland, who wishes to criticize the failures of authorities but not disavow them entirely. This, too, is a quality of obscene comedy. Although works like the fabliaux might revel in the critique and examination of authority figures and hierarchical structures, they rarely advocate their demise. The fabliau makes fun of authority figures, particularly husbands, and often features subordinates undermining them, but it never depicts revolution. Husbands retain their titles and their claim to rule the domestic space, even as they are unofficially subverted from below. Other writers, like Chaucer and the authors of the biblical drama, attempt to remove these safeguards from obscene comedy and make it pose questions of authorities' right to govern. This is not the case in *Piers Plowman*, which retains obscene comedy's traditional deference to social and political authority even as it issues severe criticisms of that authority.

As well as providing Langland with a dynamic paradigm for political thought, obscenity is also, itself, another of his garbling techniques. Study's references to secular power are not only buried in Latin psalms, in an allegory ostensibly devoted to the intellectual faculties, they are also articulated in the voice of a figure rendered ludicrous through her relation to the unruly woman of obscene comedy. In this way, obscene comedy offers Langland an additional avenue of retreat: even as his characters' rebukes are issued, they can be dismissed as the ludicrous ranting of degraded individuals with no claim to authoritative speech.

Meed and the Unruly Woman

Meed's expensive clothing and her status as an aristocratic bride have blinded modern readers to her obscene comedy heritage. In a multiplicity of ways, Meed resembles the unruly, adulterous women of the fabliaux, the exempla, and the Latin elegiac comedies that were part of Langland's cultural landscape in the mid-fourteenth century. The friar's declaration that he will shrive Meed in spite of the fact that she has slept with both learned and unlearned men and Conscience's description of Meed as a woman who is "As commune as the cartwey to [knaves and to alle] / To monkes, to mystrales, to meseles in hegges" (B.III.132–33) make her a close cousin to those many obscene comedy women who pursue illicit sexual adventures with the help of degenerate clerics. The garrulous and adulterous fabliau woman is also a touchstone in Conscience's complaint that Meed "is frele of hir feith and fikel of hire speche" (B.III.122) and "tikel of hire tail, talewis of tonge" (B.III.131).[25] Conscience's assertion that Meed leads wives and widows to unchastity and teaches them lechery (B.III.125) recalls elderly go-betweens like the English Dame Sirith and Auberée of the eponymous fabliau (1.4), who trick innocent young women into sexual misbehavior.[26]

The king of the Meed episode is also characterized in obscene comedy terms, appearing in ways that resemble the frustrated and thwarted husbands of fabliau and elegiac comedy. While the king's involvement in Meed's marriage has a historical basis in the sense that kings did interest themselves in the unions of aristocratic wards, Langland's king is cast in a much more intimate and domestic relation to Meed than is dictated by the tradition of royal matchmaking, which was typically carried out at a distance, through agents.[27] The king's struggle to control the unruly maiden and the unceremonial, rather domestic nature of his conversations with Meed, Conscience, and Reason render him more similar to the hapless obscene comedy male, struggling to rein in his disobedient wife and household servants, than to a king.

While most scholarly treatments of Passus II to IV focus on its meditations regarding the corrupting effects of Meed, we should note that the episode
is equally interested in how the king *deals* with the problem of Meed. Langland's use of obscene comedy tropes and characters in the Meed episode is
rooted in his desire to examine the problems in the king's attitude toward
money. The intimate nature of obscene comedy struggles, wherein a man's
greatest enemy is not an outsider but his own wife, functions for Langland as
an apt metaphor for the insidious problem of financial reward, which is like the
adulterous wife in being both unruly and indispensable. A misbehaving outsider can be driven away, but a wife or daughter cannot. By the same token,
financial reward might be an irredeemably corrupting force, but it cannot be
eliminated from the court. Like the women in his household, financial reward
is indispensable to the king, and this very necessity makes it more difficult to
control than outside threats.[28]

The fidelity to patriarchal authority that is typically a feature of obscene
comedy, wherein even foolish or corrupt husbands are accorded the right to
command their households, is also well suited to Langland's meditations on
kingship in the Meed episode, which seek to criticize royalty yet also to honor
it as a political entity. Even as it delights in showing incompetent husbands,
obscene comedy tends still to honor their right to rule. The Anglo-Norman
fabliau *Les quatre souhais saint Martin* (4.31) is a case in point. Here, a husband
becomes a laughingstock for foolishly giving his wife the first of four wishes he
receives from St. Martin as a reward for his fidelity. Unhappy with his sexual
performance, the wife wishes him covered in penises. He repays her by wishing
her covered in "cunts." After expending the third and fourth wishes to first
eliminate the excess genitalia, then restore their originals, the couple is left no
better off than when they started.[29] While the fabliau excoriates the husband
for being stupid enough to give his wife a wish, it still supports his traditional
rights in its concluding moral, which declares that "cil ne fet mie savoir / qui
mieus croit sa fame que lui" (a man does not do right, who believes his wife
more than himself) (4.31.188–89).[30] Thus, the husband of *Les quatre souhais*
(4.31) is a laughingstock not because husbands ought not to have authority but
because he does not know how to assert that authority effectively. By invoking
obscene comedy in the Meed episode, Langland exploits audience familiarity
with the discourse to create a space in which he is able to criticize the king for
being weak and foolish without appearing to attack his authority.

As is characteristic of male authority figures in obscene comedy, Langland's king is inept at controlling underlings, particularly women with a ten-

dency toward sexual misbehavior. The king's initial evaluation of Meed as an innocent yet misguided maiden makes him similar to the obscene comedy husband, who often becomes a laughingstock by presuming the innocence of a wife who is actually corrupt. Although Meed is not the king's wife (a decision that reflects Langland's desire to configure a more attenuated relationship between royal authority and reward), her sexuality nevertheless troubles him in similar ways.[31]

We can observe the similarities between the king and the obscene comedy male if we consider the Latin elegiac comedy *Lidia* (c. 1175), an influential work in medieval Europe that is a possible source of Chaucer's *Merchant's Tale*.[32] The comedy narrates the machinations of Lidia, a high-ranking woman who (with the aid of her servant Lusca) tricks her husband in order to commit adultery with one of his knights, Pearus. Lydia's husband, Duke Decius, remains ignorant of his wife's adultery, blinded by his belief in her virtue: "Dux amat hanc, non illa ducem; male ducitur ille / Quo uult, quo non uult, Lidia ducit eum" (The duke loves her, but she doesn't love him; / he's badly mislead, for Lidia leads him / wherever *she* wants, not where *he* wants").[33] The tale culminates in a scene familiar to readers of the *Merchant's Tale*: Lidia and Pearus deceive Decius into witnessing their infidelity when Pearus claims that anyone climbing a certain pear tree will think the people below him are having intercourse. Decius tests the claim by climbing the tree himself, thus enabling Lidia and Pearus to cuckold him before his very eyes.

The story of the patriarch who mistakes a slut for a virtuous woman and who remains ignorant of her corrupting machinations in his household is an apt metaphor for royalty's problems in controlling money and its flow. By making his king into a Decius-like figure, Langland is able to reveal how an inadequate understanding of economics undermines political leadership. In Passus I, Holy Church emphasizes the importance of the second estate's capacity to use force when she advises kings and knights that they should keep truth by hunting down "transgressores and tyen hym faste / Til treuthe hadde ytermyned hire trespas to the ende" (B.1.96–97). The Meed episode illustrates that force is not enough; one must have information as well. The king cannot maintain control over his court because he does not understand how financial reward operates and underestimates the powerful influence this unruly entity has on his subordinates. Military might can quickly scatter Meed's entourage, but controlling the lady herself requires a more subtle, one might say more domestic, knowledge that can map out an intricate web of human desire and the cause and effect of its motivations.

The obscene comedy trope of a patriarch who exhibits an inadequate understanding of his wife and underlings also underlines the importance of information and knowledge in rulership, a key concept in the Meed episode. Gabrielle Lyons has observed that fabliau power struggles often play out a contest between *avoir* and *savoir*—between those who "have" by virtue of being accorded a superior position in a fixed hierarchy and those whose main resource is their wits.[34] Obscene comedy often faults male authority figures for lacking the knowledge or the wits to deal with underlings. Decius is deceived because he does not understand the true nature of woman, whom the narrator describes as a being who "steals away fidelity with deceit and / gravity with guile. By art, deceit, study, / she steals, she seduces, she ensnares" (33–35). Decius's wife controls him by controlling his cognition: that is, his analysis of information. In addition, Decius lacks correct information on the subordinates in his household, retaining a servant like Lusca who helps his wife in her adulterous liaisons. The same can be said for the husband of *Les quatre souhais saint Martin* (4.31), who mistakenly gives his wife a wish because he lacks full knowledge of her capacity for perfidy.

Also crucial to Langland is obscene comedy's interest in the function of desire. In the Meed episode, desire is closely linked to the matter of reward. While the episode's focus is ostensibly on financial corruption, the root of the problem for Langland is not actually reward itself, but the fact that individuals who have antisocial desires mobilize reward in ways that undermine the moral and religious principles of the society. The fulfillment of antisocial desire is the end to which the fiscal corruption of the Meed episode is inevitably directed: lecherous lords and ladies pay for windows in churches in order to be allowed to pursue their illicit sexual desires; merchants bribe the mayor in order to increase their profits (B.III.52–55; 87–90). The chain of causality that Langland emphasizes in the Meed episode is the stock in trade of obscene comedy, which delights in representing how various individuals lie and manipulate out of lust or greed. The close relationship that Langland perceives between fiscal corruption and antisocial desires is witnessed in the way that Meed's figurative status as "reward" and her literal status as a beautiful, sexually available woman merge in the scenes at court. When Meed disrupts the court by becoming an object of illicit desire to its officers, she is both an allegory for the corrupting effect of reward and, as a beautiful young woman who sparks sexual desire in the men around her, a literal illustration of the problem.

The connection between desire and fiscal corruption is also attested by the "properties" Meed and False receive at their enfeoffment. If the passage were to be consistent with the allegory of "reward being united with false principles," then we would expect the enfeoffment to focus on crimes such as bribery, simony, and the like. But, in fact, the enfeoffment is far more broad than this, including a whole range of behaviors whose common element is an unChristian pursuit of pleasure and power. Therefore, Meed and False's conveyance includes their right "To bakbite and to bosten and bere fals witnesse, / To scorne and to scolde and sclaundre to make" (B.II.81–82) and also accords to the couple envy and anger and domestic crimes like quarreling and "chaterynge out of reson" (B.II.85).

While Langland appropriates certain elements of obscene comedy in the Meed segment, he also alters its misogynist rhetoric to account for the ambivalent status of reward. On the figurative level, these revisions have to do with Langland's views regarding the appropriate management of reward. We should not, however, let the figurative meaning of the passages obscure the fact that they also have meaning on the literal level, as reflections on the problems inherent in received notions of gender. As Stephanie Trigg has argued, many readers have been too quick to assume that Langland presents Meed according to medieval stereotypes of gender, thereby failing to allow for the possibility that Langland may be interrogating those notions.[35]

Certainly there is a strong case to be made for Langland's interrogation of medieval gender stereotypes in the final passages of the Meed episode. When Conscience refuses marriage with Meed, he speaks in the voice of misogynist obscene comedy narrators who belittle husbands for being too credulous of their wives. Meed is fickle, he tells the king, leading men to "mysdo" many times and corrupting wives and maidens (B.III.123; 125–26). If this were a fabliau, Conscience's estimation of Meed might well be the moral of the story. Langland, however, suggests that Conscience's misogynistic condemnation of Meed is as flawed as the king's naïve trust in her. In fact, Conscience's view of Meed as an active corruptor who leads others into malfeasance is not an accurate reflection of Meed's behavior, for Meed is a passive character, not an active force in the way of a fabliau wife (who often initiates sexual misbehavior). Indeed, Meed's greatest flaw is her adherence to the most highly vaunted feminine qualities in medieval culture: her passivity and malleability. Unlike the adulterous obscene comedy wife, Meed's disruptions are based not in her own desires but in the desire of others *for* her. Meed is capable of bad behavior, certainly, but only when invited to do so. As Elizabeth Fowler observes, because Meed is wholly at anyone's "heste," she cannot be moral, but she cannot be immoral, either.[36]

Langland casts further doubt on Conscience's perspective by giving Meed
a compelling self-defense. If Langland had wanted to dismiss Meed in a definitive manner, it would have been easy for him to give Meed a self-defense that
did nothing but affirm all the worst suspicions about her character in the style
of la Vielle's confession in the *Roman de la Rose* or the Wife's revelations
regarding her manipulation of her first three husbands in Chaucer's *Wife of
Bath's Prologue*.[37] But Langland does not do so. Meed's assertion that everyone
wants or needs reward has a basis in Aristotle's *Ethics*, which was "a touchstone
for all later medieval commentary on the need for goods and services to be
equated by a process of exchange."[38] When she argues for the cohesive function
of reward in political relationships by noting that "It bicometh to a kyng that
kepeth a reaume / To yeve [men mede] that mekely hym serveth" (B.III.209–
10), she refers to a practice of gift and service that has too long a history in the
political tradition to be dismissed as mere foolish claptrap.[39] As Stephanie
Trigg notes, Langland offers Meed a moment of seeming triumph here, and
even though Conscience immediately collapses her back into an object of
exchange when he distinguishes between two different kinds of Meed, it is
notable that Langland "has allowed this moment of potential transgression of
gender roles."[40] While Meed's quotation from proverbs that "He that makes
presents shall purchase victory and honor" (Prov. 22:9) may be incomplete,
Conscience's rebuttal does not address the fact that the quotation is, in itself,
contradictory.[41]

Conscience's misogyny and the king's foolish gallantry reflect the two diametrically opposed notions of women—as dangerous sluts or passive innocents—that predominated in medieval culture. It is notable that Langland
characterizes both forms of extreme thinking as inaccurate and flawed. The
point applies equally to the concepts of reward and those of gender. It suggests
that a more moderated way of thinking is necessary in both cases: neither
women nor reward can be effectively integrated into the social order when both
are regarded according to such inaccurately extreme notions.

Also notable is the fact that Meed shows the greatest capacity for integration into the polity when she is permitted to break free from the gender constraints that render maidens silent and docile, and to speak for herself. If this
were obscene comedy, such impudent self-assertion would itself be evidence of
Meed's corruption, but, in Langland's passage, these qualities represent progress. By speaking, Meed reveals her own logic and motivations, allowing for a
better understanding of her that might ultimately lead to her productive integration. As Elizabeth Robertson has argued, the Meed passage suggests that

things will only be set right if Meed (and all women) can become figures of both agency and subjectivity whose consent is validated within the social order.[42]

The most profound illustration of the problems inherent in Conscience's misogyny is the fact that, in the conclusion, after the trial of Wrong, when the king accepts the arguments of Concience and Reason that Meed is a "sherewe" (B.IV.160), Meed is left as a dangerous loose end. Meed is a maiden, not a wife; thus, the king can dismiss her in a way that the husband of the unruly wife cannot. Whether he ought to, however, is another matter, for dismissing her does nothing to diminish her power. On the literal level, Meed retains her attractions for all sorts of men (an assizer and a summoner both pursue her after she has been condemned as a whore). On the figurative level, too, she maintains her power, since the very basis of the king's dismissal of her, that she costs him revisions, attests to the ongoing influence of money.

The Meed episode is not a simple allegory since Langland often merges Meed's literal and figurative levels. This assimilation of different allegorical levels suggests that, for Langland, the family and the realm are not just metaphors for one another, they are interdependent. The fact that Meed the woman is sometimes indistinguishable from the allegorical Meed indicates that Langland wishes his analysis of power to apply both to the political and the domestic realms: in whatever context it operates, whether that be in the court or in the household, authority is most effective when it can understand its subordinates and respond to them dynamically, rather than engaging in knee-jerk reactions based on simplistic beliefs that equate resistance with villainy.

The close interaction between the political and the domestic in Langland's obscene comedy helps shed new light on the gender politics of a poet whose attitudes to women have proven difficult to evaluate. Coming to terms with the women of *Piers Plowman* has been challenging for feminist critics, some of whom have even gone as far as to deny the importance of gender in the poem.[43] And yet, as Helen Cooper notes, Langland is remarkable for his avoidance of "the misogyny and hatred of sex that stalks so many medieval homiletic works."[44] While it is true that Langland does not exhibit an interest in women's experience of subordination in the way of other authors in this study (like Chaucer or Margery Kempe), reading Langland against the tradition of obscene comedy highlights his refusal to indulge in the discourse's characteristic misogyny. As the Meed episode reveals, furthermore, Langland's attitudes toward gender are closely aligned with his views on power relations in the wider community. This same alignment, as we shall see, is also important in the third vision.

Obscene Comedy in the Third Vision

Structurally, the third vision of *Piers Plowman* is modeled on Latin dialogues of counsel, featuring conversations between Will and a series of allegorical figures who seem to represent either the cognitive faculties or the educational disciplines. Even as they appear to reproduce Latin dialogues of instruction, however, the conversations of the third vision diverge considerably from that genre in both content and tone. As Anne Middleton has remarked, when Langland invokes the Latin dialogues of counsel, he tends to avoid the nurturing friendships or familial relations that traditionally define the genre, opting instead for relationships of conflict characterized by a "combative animus."[45] The third vision is particularly rife with hostile encounters: Study scolds Wit for teaching an idiot such as Will; Will interrupts Scripture and then denigrates her answers to his queries; Scripture scorns Will, causing him to weep; Will rebukes Reason for his poor care of human sexuality; and Reason and Ymaginatif scold Will for his rudeness.

While the aggressive tone of the third vision's dialogues has been noted, it has not been located in any literary source. A number of critics have linked the vision's arguments to university traditions of scholastic debate, a reading seemingly supported by Langland's use of academic terms like "contra" at various points in the vision.[46] The conflict of scholastic debate, however, proceeds according to a formalized model of statement and counterstatement that is very different from the free-flowing, back-and-forth arguments of vision three.[47] Nor does Langland identify any of his interlocutors with the scholastic tradition. In another attempt to identify Langland's source, Anne Middleton observes that he casts his expositors in "human social roles that conventionally permit such contention," like the "garrulous husband and scolding, censorious wife."[48]

Middleton is right to identify contentious marriage as a model for Langland's dialogues in the third vision. Its source, however, is literary rather than social. Indeed, it is in their literary nature that the primary value of these quarreling figures lies for Langland. In its characterizations, its tone, and its manner of representing social conflict, the third vision draws extensively from obscene comedy. As is the case in Langland's other evocations of the discourse, the third vision draws on bits and pieces of obscene comedy, rather than reproducing it in a generically identifiable whole. Nevertheless, obscene comedy is crucial to Langland in creating the vision's exceptionally stringent judgment of secular lordship and in the connections it makes between secular failings and doctrinal confusion within the Church. As a discourse that provides a unique way of thinking about power, obscene comedy allows Langland to examine social and political authority in the third vision in a way that is unavailable in any other discourse. At the same time, the discourse's degraded and comical status provides Langland with an "avenue of retreat," away from the dangerous ideas he expresses, offering up an alternate reading whereby the criticisms he offers are simply the ravings of ludicrous and abject figures.

In identifying a persistent critique of secular authority in the third vision, I am attending to a facet of it that has not been widely recognized. Critical discussions of the vision have focused primarily on the areas of inquiry invited by the allegorical figures. As a result, the vision has been characterized as a "turning inward" away from the political and communal concerns of the previous two visions.[49] In what follows, I wish to interrogate this approach to the third vision. While the vision's allegorical figures are a significant element in its meaning, they do not wholly define it. Indeed, some elements of the vision can only be perceived by putting them aside. Among these is a persistent insistence, through a variety of different conversations and figures, on the failure of secular authorities to embody Christian principles in their governance and an interest in linking those failures to theological confusion and to the failure of Church authorities to communicate Christian doctrine effectively to the laity. If the vision advertises a turning inward in a narrative that seems to concern the dreamer's own intellectual and spiritual development, I would argue that this inward orientation in the narrative actually enables a more probing exploration of politics than we see in the more explicitly political segments of the poem.

In the discussion below, I wish to follow a way of reading the poem pioneered by Anne Middleton, wherein we derive meaning from *Piers Plowman* by "reading past" the poem's figural elements.[50] In an insightful article, Middleton demonstrates how looking *through* the poem's allegorical representations (that is, setting them aside in order to examine how the poem functions as a narrative) enables us to see Langland's persistent interest in the argumentative encounter. Although Middleton's interest is in form and my own lies more in content, I wish to perform a similar "looking through" allegorical representation in the third vision to highlight an ongoing political evaluation that continues through Will's conversations with a variety of allegorical figures. Like Middleton, I do not wish to present my analysis as a refutation of figural interpretation, but rather as an exploration of the elements of the poem that have been overlooked in analyses that define the third vision's meaning exclusively in terms of its allegory.

Study

We can begin our consideration of obscene comedy in Passus X by appreciating
the exceptional nature of the shrewish Dame Study in the context of Langland's poetics. As Helen Cooper and Masha Raskolnikov have observed, Langland does not prefer female allegorical figures, often taking allegorical roles
traditionally accorded to females and making them male instead.[51] Study is
also more explicitly related to obscene comedy than any other figure in the
poem. Her status as a wife, her disrespectful attitude toward her husband, Wit,
and her aggressive speech link her to the shrewish wives of the fabliau and
other obscene tales.[52] She appears at the outset of Passus X lean of face and
body and severe in her criticisms of her husband Wit:

> She was wonderly wroth that Wit me thus taughte,
> And al starynge Dame Studie sterneliche seide.
> "Wel artow wis," quod she to Wit, "any wisdoms to telle
> To flatereres or to fooles that frenetike ben of wittes!"
> And blamed hym and banned hym and bad hym be stille
>   (B.10.3–7)

We can appreciate Study's close similarity to fabliau wives if we compare her
words and tone to those of the wife in Les quatre souhais saint Martin (4.31),
whom the narrator describes as the one who "chauce les braies" (wears the
pants) in the relationship and who castigates her husband in the following
manner when he returns home:

> . . . Vilains, mal jor aies!
> As tu ja si tost laisié ovre—
> Por lo tens qui un po se covre?
> . . .
> Onques n'anmastes laborage;
> Vous fetes mout volantiers feste:
> A mal eür aiez vous beste
> Quant vos n'en fetes vostre esploit! (36–38; 42–43.2)

> [What evil chance / brings you home now, oaf? Did you
> quit / work 'cause it's clouded up a bit? . . . You've never
> taken to the plow, / no—life for you is one big lark! / We

may as well sell off the stock, / since you won't work them
anyway!][53]

Langland's characterization of Study is also unusual in the context of his
attitude toward marriage. The shrewish wife is part of obscene comedy's misogamist mentality, in which marriage is figured as a burden on men that they
could better do without. Langland's attitude toward marriage is very different.
As a number of feminist readers have noted (and as I myself shall be discussing
in more detail in this chapter's concluding section), Langland tends to take a
favorable view of marriage, regarding it as a worthwhile Christian institution.[54]
Thus, his taste for the misogamist figure of the shrew is limited, and, indeed, we
do not find them outside the third vision.

Finally, Langland's appropriation of obscene comedy in the Study passage emphasizes the discourse's humor more consistently and explicitly than
any other segment of *Piers Plowman*. Like the unruly wives of the fabliau,
Study's shameless violation of social norms regarding women's deference
to male authority produces a shock that results in laughter. Study's funniness
is something that Langland is at pains to maintain throughout the episode.
Not only does she enter scolding her husband, but, after Study's speech,
Langland returns us again to the comic marital relationship of henpecked
husband and domineering wife, when he figures Wit struck dumb by his
wife's speech, able only to grimace and gesture to Will that he should submit
to Study's instruction.

Why does Langland evoke this figure, who in so many ways runs counter
to his tendencies as an author and social commentator? Why does he make her
so *funny*? My contention is that the shrewish wife and the humor associated
with her is, for a variety of reasons, crucial to Langland's critique of secular
authority in Passus X, an attack that is more direct and aggressive than we see
anywhere else in the poem, barring the conclusion.

The strength and persistence of Study's warnings regarding the bad behavior of secular authority are an underrecognized feature of Passus X. Most analyses of Study's speech focus on what she represents, identifying her either as a
representation of the liberal arts located below the higher forms of learning
symbolized by Clergy or as the representative of a more broadly based notion
of intellectual cogitation.[55] A close reading of Dame Study's monologue, however, reveals that her interest in teaching is fitful and episodic. The primary
focus of her concern, in many passages, is the failure of secular authorities to
live up to their responsibilities and to embody Christian doctrine, particularly

the Christian ethic of care for the poor. These are sometimes linked to failures of instruction, but not always.

The critique of lordship in Passus X is persistent but rarely explicit. To discern it, one must often follow a referential trail or complete a train of logic toward which Study gestures but that she does not make explicit. Study's speech occurs after a series of discussions in which first the friars, then Wit, attempt to answer Will's question as to what is do-well, do-bet, and do-best. When Study enters, however, she does not claim to have an answer to these questions, and Will never poses them to her, until her speech is over, at which point she refers him to Clergy and Scripture. What, then, is Study's speech about? She never says. Instead, it must be discerned (or, we might say, *studied*) from her words. Study is an aggressive speaker, but the exact target of her aggression is often concealed, subject to number of feints and dodges. While certain parties may appear to be the object of Study's wrath on the surface, following the logical implications of her argument often reveals a quite different object.

Study enters angry at her husband, Wit, for casting pearls before swine by speaking wise words to "sottes" (B.X.8). The object of Study's aggression here appears to be Wit but is, in fact, his audience. Study does not say her husband is wrong. Rather, she is angry that he has wasted his words on a worthless listener. Since Wit's audience is Will, Study's criticism would seem to be relatively innocuous in political terms, restricted to the dreamer himself. Following the logical inferences of Study's argument, however, turns the target away from Will and toward other objects. After condemning Wit for casting pearls before swine, Study generalizes her argument away from the particular Wit-Will situation, to condemn those that "were levere lond and lordship on erthe, / Or richesse or rentes and reste at hir wille" (B.X.14–15). Although Study never says so outright, it can be reasonably inferred that the objects of her criticism here are the aristocracy and gentry, not only because the ambition of the unnamed individuals is for lordship and rents but because lords are the ones most likely to be paying for the wisdom that Study says is considered worthless unless it is "carded with coveitise" (B.X.18).

Study's target seems to move back toward entertainers or advisers a couple of lines later, when she condemns those who consult at manor courts and "lede lords with lesynges and bilieth truthe" (B.X.22). But one must note that those who can "contreve deceites and conspire wronges" are "to counsel cleped" (B.X.19, 21). The passive voice avoids an outright declaration of who calls these liars to counsel, but certainly the most likely inference would be that it is the lords themselves. In subsequent lines, Study's condemnation pertains directly to lords, although, in a feint that is typical of Passus X, Langland turns to biblical quotation to do the work for him. Here, Study paraphrases a passage from Job associating rulers with lawlessness ["And that thei ben lords of ech a lond, that out of lawe libbeth" (B.X.25)], then cites Psalm 72. The line she quotes is relatively mild, concerning "peccatores" [sinners] who "in seculo obtinuerunt divicias" [in the world obtain riches] (B.X.26a). The rest of the psalm (which Langland does not quote) goes on to say that the prosperity of the wicked is a problem upon which the speaker in the psalm has cogitated, indeed *studied*: "Existimabam ut cognoscerem hoc; labor est ante me [I have studied that I might know this thing; it is a labor in my sight]" (72.16).[56]

The psalm's reference to cogitating on the prosperity of the wicked is fascinating both in light of Study's allegorical status and of her monologue's ultimate subject. Nicolette Zeeman has insightfully questioned previous critical assumptions that Study must represent scholarly activity, the institutions of medieval education or the intellectual disciplines. She points out that in medieval culture, Study is a more capacious term, "an ambitious and complex development of an Augustinian tradition of thought about the intense effort, labor, difficulty, even reverie, involved in the pursuit of understanding and spirituality."[57] While Zeeman usefully revises the definition of Study, she still reads the passus as a discussion of method, rather than an illustration of a method *directed toward* a particular end. While the unquoted portion of Psalm 72 turns us to precisely the notion of study that Zeeman describes, it also suggests that this meditation is focused on a particular object. Study as method is being discussed here, but Psalm 72 suggests that it is a method specifically directed at considering the problem of unjust authority.

The result of that "study" in Psalm 72 provides a radical correction of the notion, fundamental to most interpretations of medieval-estates theory, that those in power are put there by God. It asserts that not all of those in authority are there by God-given right but that some are an embodiment of wickedness and injustice that God will ultimately correct. Everyone is familiar with Clergy's famous prediction, later in Passus X, that a king will arrive to correct the sins of corrupt ecclesiastics (B.X.316–29). Less recognized is the fact that Study issues a similar threat against wicked secular authorities through a thread of inference that leads to Psalm 72. In this case, the avenging instrument is not a king but God himself:

Verumtamen propter dolos posuisti eis; dejecisti eos dum
allevarentur. Quomodo facti sunt in desolationem? subito
defecerunt; perierunt propter iniquitatem suam. Velut
somnium surgentium, Domine, in civitate tua imaginem
ipsorum ad nihilum rediges. . . . Quia ecce qui elongant
se a te peribunt; perdidisti omnes qui fornicantur abs te.
(72.18–20, 27)

[But indeed for deceits thou hast put it to them: when they
were lifted up thou hast cast them down. How are they
brought to desolation? They have suddenly ceased to be:
they have perished by reason of their iniquity. As the dream
of them that awake, O Lord; so in thy city thou shalt bring
their image to nothing. . . . For behold they that go far from
thee shall perish: thou hast destroyed all them that are dis-
loyal to thee.]

Immediately after citing Psalm 72, Study, or perhaps the poet himself (the
speaker is not entirely clear) quotes "holy lettrure" (holy scripture), who
exclaims, "Lo!...whiche lordes beth thise sherewes" (B.X.27). The sentence's
construction is an interesting one, perhaps referring to the biblical "sherewes"
of the Psalms but also conceivably referring to the contemporary lords mentioned previously. The following line is again rather vague in its object, describing those to whom God "moost good giveth" (B.X.28), but then skates very
close to lordship in the fourteenth-century English context, when it uses a
contemporary political term in complaining that those with the greatest wealth
are "mooste unkynde to the commune" (B.10.29).[58]

This is followed by a citation from Psalm 10. Once again, Langland cites a
relatively mild line from a psalm whose content is ultimately quite threatening
and punitive toward unjust rulers. The citation's fragmentary nature invites
readers to further investigation: "Que perfectisti destruxerunt; iustus autem"
[Who have destroyed the things which thou hast made; the just man however]
(B.X.29). Readers who peruse or call to memory Psalm 10 in its entirety will
arrive at a passage that promises, quite literally, to rain fire and brimstone on
the iniquitous: "Dominus interrogat justum et impium; qui autem diligit iniquitatem, odit animam suam. Pluet super peccatores laqueos; ignis et sulphur, et
spiritus procellarum, pars calicis eorum" [The Lord trieth the just and the
wicked: but he that loveth iniquity hateth his own soul. He shall rain snares

upon sinners: fire and brimstone and storms of winds shall be the portion of their cup] (Ps. 10, 6–7). Attenuated and vague though it may be, to those willing to follow the trail of literary breadcrumbs it scatters, the first part of Study's speech offers up a reading wherein contemporary English lords are condemned for their bad behavior and wherein obliteration and punishment is are predicted against them for these failings.

After citing Psalm 10, Study moves back, ostensibly, to focus on "japeris and jogelours and jangleris of gestes" (B.X.31), but again there is slippage between the minstrels and their lords. Study is angry that jesters are better appreciated than those who speak of holy writ. On the surface, our attention seems to be directed toward the entertainers, but, in reality, those to blame are the lords who pay the fees, as is made explicit several lines later when Study avers that, if there were no such thing as "vile harlotrye," then "sholde nevere kyng ne knyght ne canon of Seint Poules" give minstrels a single grote for their New Year's gift (B.X.45–47).

Study then moves on to the tale of the laymen who tell blasphemous jokes after dinner. As well as blasphemy, the sin of these individuals is that they eat elaborate meals while poor people beg at their gate. The referent is vague here. Who are these laymen? Wealthy merchants or lords? And the object of analysis moves again back to those who serve lords, rather than the lords themselves. (All of this happens, Study says, because the friars go about preaching intellectual paradoxes to the people). A few lines later, however, the focus is back on lordship and this time, Langland is uncharacteristically direct in identifying the objects of Study's criticisms, for now she speaks about "lordes," (B.X.92), who should love to hear advice on how to spend generously and provide for their households, rather than going like friars to other men's houses, a practice that harms the poor:

> Elenge is the halle, ech day in the wike,
> Ther the lord ne the lady liketh noght to sitte.
> Now hath ech riche a rule—to eten by hymselve
> In a pryvee parlour for povre mennes sake (B.X.96–99)

Here, once again, we see a move from the ostensible subject of the monologue, teaching and learning, to a political point about the ways that lords are failing in their duties. Aside from issuing a stringent criticism of contemporary lords, this passage also represents further evidence of what Larry Scanlon has described as Langland's interest in reconceptualizing the estates from the

perspective of the lower orders and his view of authority as "the social con-
cretization of communal will." As Scanlon has pointed out, this view is evident in the Prologue's description of the king's might deriving from "the
communes" (B.Prologue.113), a passage that he says represents a "radically
communal notion of political sovereignty."[59]

Study's appraisal of secular authority is quite remarkable in the context of
the poem as a whole. Direct criticism of the gentry or aristocracy is rare in
Piers Plowman. The Prologue is explicit about corrupt priests, but the failings
of secular authority inspire a move into one of the poem's few episodes of figural allegory, with the tale of the rats belling the cat. In spite of the relative
mildness of this evaluation—the allegory concludes with the rodents admit-
ting that they would run wild without the cat—it seems to require further
disavowals in the form of Will's invitation to others to divine the dream's
meaning since he dares not (B.Prologue.209–10). Other criticisms are so mild
that they could actually be construed as compliments, as when the knight fails
to discipline the lazy workers during Piers's plowing of the half-acre because
he is too gentlemanly.

We might assume that Langland's reluctance to issue direct criticism of
lords and gentry is due to his support for secular authority and to a view that
secular authority is less corrupt than the clergy. This, certainly, is the way that
he was interpreted by Protestant readers who supported Henry VIII's disend-
owment of the Church.[60] In fact, Langland's reluctance to issue explicit judgments of the aristocracy or gentry likely had more to do with a reasonable fear
of retribution than with a higher regard for secular powers.

That Langland regarded Study's references to rulers as politically risky is
strongly suggested by the revisions to this passage in the C-text, written in the
aftermath of the 1381 rebellion and generally regarded as a regression from the
more radical politics of the B-version. In the C-version, Study's specific reference to lords being misled by corrupt counselors is removed and replaced with
a reference to those who deceive "the rightfole" (C.XI.16). C also eliminates
both the accusatory paraphrase from Job and the line referring to "the commune," as well as the specific titles and the description of harlotry that we see in
the B-passage. In C, the B-version's remark that neither "kyng ne knyght ne
canon of Seint Poules" would give a grote to a minstrel if they were not being
regaled with harlotry (B.X.46) is replaced with a milder passage regarding how
little preachers are loved "among lords at festes" (C.XI.32). Finally, and most
significantly, the C-version eliminates B's diatribe against lords and ladies who
sequester themselves in private chambers and refuse to eat in the hall.

In spite of the risks involved, the duty that Langland felt as a Christian to speak truth to power is implied by the ongoing debate on public condemnation that we see throughout the third vision. This debate concerns the question of whether it is ethical for an individual who is himself not free from sin to blame others publicly. As well as documenting Langland's ethical qualms about whether a sinner ought to accuse other sinners, the debate includes an emphasis at various points on the duty of Christians to speak out about un-Christian behavior. It is notable that Clergy says Dobest is "to be boold to blame the gilty" (B.X.258), even if he qualifies this by saying it can only be done by one who is himself clean in soul. A few lines later, Clergy returns to the merits of public condemnation when he cites a passage from Mark 13.9 in which Christ tells his followers that they should not be afraid to stand before kings because God will "yyve yow wit at wille [with] konnyng to conclude hem" (B.X.446). The importance of public condemnation emerges again in the inner dream, when Will argues that he ought not to blame the guilty and Lewtee encourages him to testify to their wrongs by citing a passage from Leviathan that commands, "Non oderis fratres secrete in corde tuo set publice argue illos" [Thou shalt not hate thy brothers secretly in thy heart, but rebuke them publicly] (B.XI.88), asking Will what purpose the law possesses if no one reproves falseness and fraudulence (B.XI.92) and stating that "It is *licitum* for lewed men to segge the sothe" (B.XI.96).

Just as the various feints and dodges that characterize Study's speech align with Scott's description of garbling, so Study's unruliness functions as an avenue of retreat for Langland. This is particularly germane to Langland's use of the dialogue of counsel in the third vision. While the dialogue of counsel works well as a vehicle for intellectual investigation, it is, in its conventional form, a rather dangerous mode in which to reprove powerful individuals. Since the tutelary allegorical figure typically occupies a position of authority in the dialogue of counsel, any words that the character speaks are identified with the author's intent, making the author responsible for the words of the tutelary figure. By making Study a shrew, Langland robs her of the authoritative status usually accorded to allegorical figures in dialogues of counsel. Her status as a wife and her violations of appropriate wifely behavior to Wit mean that she does not possess the tutelary figure's unimpeachable authority. Instead, she becomes somewhat laughable and degraded. This degraded status enables Langland to issue his most severe and explicit judgments of secular authority in Study's voice, since her words can always be divorced from authorial sanction and dismissed as the ranting of a ridiculous woman in a way that they could not if they came from a respectable figure like Philosophia in Boethius's *The Consolation of Philosophy.*

And yet, even as the unruly woman is degraded, her voice retains a certain legitimacy, and her interrogation of authority makes certain claims on audience sympathy. While she is often characterized as a corrupt and disruptive force, the shrewish wife's resistance to authority is also celebrated in obscene comedy: the audience is invited to laugh *with* her as she bests various authority figures. In *Les quatre souhais de St. Martin* (4.31), for instance, the wife is outrageous, yet the tale makes the audience complicit by inviting them to laugh as she registers her dismay at her husband's sexual performance by wishing him covered in penises.[61] Study's manner may be shrewish, but there is still space in obscene discourse for the audience to absorb her judgments, particularly when that space is bolstered by her status as an allegorical teacher.

The dual status of the unruly woman also suits Langland's own ambivalence regarding the ethics of public rebukes. On the one hand, the assertive nature of the unruly woman's voice embodies what Langland sees as the legitimate outrage of the Christian observing the corruption of his world. On the other hand, her unruly status embodies the notion of public reproof as an unChristian form of behavior.

Scripture, Reason, and Ymaginatif: Will as Unruly Woman

Although Study departs midway through Passus X, neither the unruly woman nor Langland's persistent concern with the failings of secular authority dissipates in the remainder of the third vision. Rather, they undergo "a sea change," fading somewhat in intensity but remaining very much present. In a fascinating shift, Study's combative tone and her disregard for authority are transferred onto Will himself. Will argues with Clergy's wife, Scripture, in the same castigating tone that marks Study's scolding of Wit. Responding to Scripture's emphasis on Christian behavior in securing salvation, Will castigates her: "This is a long lesson . . . and litel am I the wiser! / Where Dowel is or Dobet derkliche ye shewen" (B.X.371–72). Will's role as a subordinate resisting the authority figures who attempt to discipline and control him throughout the rest of the vision also closely approximates the position of the disobedient wife of obscene comedy, and the reproof Will later receives from Reason to "rule thi tonge bettre" (B.XI.385) identifies him with the wagging tongues of shrewish women.

Will's parade in "unruly woman" drag through the third vision may seem unlikely, but in fact it aligns with longstanding tropes relating to the allegorical figure of "the will." As a number of readers have noted, Will's identity as an allegorical representation of the psychological faculty of "the will" is particularly acute in the third vision, which puts him in conversation with other psychological faculties like Thought, Wit, and Ymaginatif.[62] Both Middle English and Latin spiritual writings include a tradition of characterizing "the will" as an unruly woman. Bernard of Clairvaux characterizes the fleshly will, opposed to reason and divine will, as a lascivious old woman: "I am voluptuous, I am curious, I am ambitious. There is not part of me that is free from this threefold ulcer, from the soles of my feet to the top of my head. My gullet and the shameful parts of my body are given up to pleasure."[63] In the thirteenth-century English *Sawles Ward*, similarly, Reason is the master of a house ruled over by the unruly Will who, "if the household follows her lead, reduces it to chaos, unless Reason as master disciplines her better."[64]

While much of Passus XI and XII is taken up with discussions of salvation and how it is achieved, it would be wrong to say that Langland's concern with lordship falls away. Indeed, a discussion of lordship is the initial impetus for the salvation debate of the third vision, which begins in Passus X, when Will asks Scripture whether Dowel and Dobet are "*dominus* and knyghthode." Scripture says "no," and Will refutes her by saying that only baptism can save (B.X.330–45).

Early modern Protestants made famous Clergy's Passus X vow that a king will come to punish corrupt clergy, casting it as a prescient vision of Henry VIII's coming justice.[65] To this day, Passus X is associated with a condemnation of the Church that favors secular authority. In fact, the passage is as focused on secular corruption as it is on the Church. Clergy's own speech concludes with a citation from Isaiah that concerns God's punishment of *rulers*, not clerics. Taken from Isaiah 14, which predicts the overthrow of the king of Babylon during the Babylonian occupation of Jerusalem, Langland's citation reads: "Quomodo cessavit exactor, quievit tributum? Contrivit Dominus baculum impiorum et virgam dominancium cedencium plaga insanabili [How is the oppressor come to nothing, the tribute hath ceased? The Lord hath broken the staff of the wicked, the rod of the rulers . . . that struck . . . with an incurable wound] (B.X.327a). In the Latin Vulgate, verse six in its entirety reads: "Caedentem populos in indignatione plaga insanabili, subjicientem in furore gentes, persequentem crudeliter" (Is. 14.6). Thus, the full meaning of verses five and six is as follows: "The Lord hath broken the staff of the wicked, the rod of the rulers, / That struck the people in wrath with an incurable wound, that brought nations under in fury, that persecuted in a cruel manner." Following as this does upon Clergy's condemnation of Church corruption, we might assume that Langland is only inviting us to draw parallels between the prophecies of Isaiah and the fourteenth-century English clergy. Certainly this is one, less politically dangerous, reading of the passage. However, Langland does not dismiss alternative readings and indeed even encourages them in subtle ways. We should note that the Latin noun for rulers that appears in the passage Langland quotes referring to their cruel beatings ("virgam dominancium") is repeated in its nominative declension just three lines later by Will in a sentence that refers explicitly to medieval lords ("Thane is Dowel and Dobet . . . *dominus* and knyghthode?" [B.X.330]). For her part, Scripture (tellingly characterized as a domineering woman) does not hesitate to deny any connection between ethical Christian living and lordship in her answer to Will's query regarding Dowel and Dobet:

> Kynghod ne knyghthod, by noght I kan awayte,
> Helpeth noght to heveneward oone heeris ende,
> Ne richesse right noghte, ne reautee of lordes. (B.X. 332–34)

Moreover, Scripture's assertion regarding the connection of faith and works is made in terms that warn elites against abusing their privilege in this world, lest they meet the wrath of God in the next. It behooves those who wish to be saved to love, she avers, and unless we do this in deed before the day of judgment,

> It shal bisitten us ful soure, the silver that we kepen,
> And oure bakkes that mothe-eten be, and seen beggeris go
>   naked,
> Or delit in wyn and wildefowel, and wite any in defaute.
>   (B.X.359–61)

Scripture's declaration makes a connection between salvation doctrine and the behavior of secular elites. Implicit in her statement (and in the psalms cited in the Study section) is the conviction that the principle of salvation through works is crucial to ensuring good Christian behavior in the powerful. The connection between good lordship and salvation is made repeatedly through the latter portion of the vision. Ostensibly, the Roman emperor Trajan is introduced in the "dream-within-a-dream" segment of Passus XI to show that a non-Christian can be saved based on his virtue. It is notable, however, that St.

Gregory's famous prayer for Trajan's salvation is prompted, according to the *Legenda Aurea*, by Trajan's exemplary behavior *as a ruler*.[66] After Trajan's speech, Langland emphasizes Trajan's political status and links him to the themes of divine retribution expressed by Scripture in the preceding lines when he has an unidentified speaker opine, "Wel oughte ye lordes that lawes kepe this lesson to have in mynde, / And on Toianus truthe to thenke, and do truthe to the peple" (B.XI.157–58). Threats of divine retribution for elite malfeasance are issued again in Passus XII when Ymaginatif condemns "riche renkes" who hoard money and predicts that those who "se so manye nedy folkes" and do not love them as God bid will "lesen hir soules" (B.XII.53–54). This theme is also touched upon in the last portion of Ymaginatif's speech, when he speaks of the peacock and peahen who represent "proude rich men" (B.XII.239). Just as the peacock is easily caught because of his trailing tail feathers, so will the rich man be caught, "if he is richesse kepeth / And deleth it noght til his deeth day" (B.XII.244–45). Even if he repents and starts to rue ever having gathered such a great amount of money and cries "to Crist thanne with kene wille, " says Ymaginatif, his cry will be like the chattering of a magpie in our Lord's ear (B.XII.251–52).

Langland's references to "the rich" in Ymagintif's speech are vague. It is not clear whether he means the wealthy bourgeoisie, the aristocracy, the gentry, or all three. Nevertheless, while Langland does not explicitly connect Ymaginatif's words to rulers, it remains *possible* to interpret his strictures in this way. Certainly Langland is anxious to keep the matter of lordship in readers' minds, making yet another reference to Trajan in Passus XII, this time in Ymaginatif's voice. Responding to Will's statement on the impossibility of salvation without Christianity, Ymaginatif cites Trajan as a figure who "was a trewe knyght and took nevere Cristendom" (B.XII.280).

There has been considerable discussion of Langland's salvation theology, including his views on works, grace, baptism, and universal salvation.[67] These are complex issues that are taken up in a dialectical process through almost the entirety of the poem; it is not my purpose to comment definitively on them here. For the purposes of my argument, I wish only to remark on the extent to which Langland's consideration of salvation theology is tied up with his desire to reform secular elites. This is something that has often been overlooked in discussions of Langland's theology, which tend to consider it only in terms of texts and theories.[68]

For Langland, the political ramifications of salvation theology are as important as the intellectual coherence of the theology itself; indeed, they are

intimately bound up with it. When Langland considers the role of grace, predestination, and works in salvation, one of his primary concerns is political.
Repeatedly, these passages return to the fact that a theology that does not
include works as an element of salvation threatens to remove the one certain
method of control that Christianity has over secular powers: its ability to
threaten those who do not live up to their obligations with divine retribution.
This is the promise made in the biblical passage Langland often cites in *Piers
Plowman*: "Michi vindictam et ego retribuam" (Vengeance is mine, and I shall
repay).[69] Even at the point where Nicholas Watson sees the poem advocating
universal salvation (in Christ's speech before the Harrowing of Hell in Passus
XVIII, wherein the Savior seems to imply that all baptized shall be saved),[70] the
matter of punishing the guilty is still on Langland's mind. Even as Christ
asserts his right to have mercy on all, he makes note of the fact that "Holy Writ
wole that I be wroke of hem that diden ille" (B.XVIII.391). Christ promises
that all will be cleansed and cured of their sins. How that will be achieved,
however, is a matter of secrecy that Langland refuses to articulate in the poem,
citing instead Paul's words from 2 Corinthians on his vision of heaven: "Audivi
[*sic*] archana verba que non licet homini loqui" (I heard secret words which it
is not lawful for a man to utter).[71]

As it does elsewhere in *Piers Plowman*, obscene comedy has a protective
function in the salvation debate of vision three, providing an avenue of
retreat wherein any potentially offensive statement can be dismissed as the
rant of a degraded or misinformed character. It is worth noting, too, that the
risks Langland takes in this portion of the poem involve not only his continuing criticisms of secular elites but also involve reproofs of the Church
that are more penetrating and far reaching than we have thus far seen. As
number of readers have noted, the third vision enacts "a series of aggressive
anti-institutional critiques and conflicts over the monopoly of knowledge
and authority" and examines the limitations of "authoritative institutional
discourses."[72] Since most of these discourses are controlled by the Church,
the debates of the third vision represent a particularly keen attack on this
institution. Dismay over the lower clergy is rampant in *Piers Plowman*, but
these criticisms are limited. Focusing primarily on the failure of the clergy to
live up to the Church's declared values, they do not interrogate the Church's
theology or its methods of teaching. The salvation debate is more radical
because it connects secular corruption to the Church's failure to resolve theological questions regarding salvation and to teach its own doctrine effectively
to the laity.

Church debates over the relation between faith and works were well known in the fourteenth century. The question was a subject of controversy in Oxford in the 1340s and 1350s and was the focus of a well-known treatise, *On the Cause of God Against Pelagius*, by Thomas Bradwardine.[73] While the allegorical identity of Scripture and Ymaginatif has been debated, it is undeniable that, whatever else they might represent, both figures are identified with the Church and are cast as teachers. Scripture is, of course, married to Clergy and has been identified as representing either the Bible or teaching of the Bible. While many have associated Ymaginatif with the capacity to think through images, he is also, as Fiona Somerset observes, "the poem's most committed spokesperson for 'clergie' in the conventional, status bound sense."[74]

Theologically speaking, Langland the author has little quarrel with Scripture, Reason, and Ymaginatif. All three express views regarding works, predestination, and the salvation of exceptional pagans that are affirmed in other portions of *Piers Plowman*. In their ideas, these three express the best of Church learning. Their manner of expressing and communicating that authority, however, is maladroit and expresses Langland's dismay over how Church doctrine is debated and taught. As in the Meed episode, obscene comedy in the Scripture, Reason, and Ymaginatif passages provides Langland with a paradigm whereby he can issue criticisms regarding the *practice* of authority while still maintaining those authorities' ultimate rectitude. By placing Scripture and Ymaginatif in the role of obscene comedy authorities, Langland criticizes the Church's theological confusions and its dismissive attitude toward the queries of laypeople while still upholding its ultimate authority.

By casting Will as the unruly woman, meanwhile, Langland is able to exploit the semiotic instability of obscene comedy to honor Will's interrogation of authorities, even as he dismisses his theology. In obscene comedy, there is rarely any doubt that the unruly woman is morally in the wrong. She is often adulterous, and even when she is not adulterous she tends to exhibit other blameworthy qualities such as greed and dishonesty. At the same time, the fact that audiences are invited to laugh at the unruly woman means that her resistance to authority and her dissatisfaction with its operation is accorded a certain legitimacy. Even as we are invited to condemn the unruly woman for her bad behavior, we are invited to laugh along with her as she interrogates an authority that we acknowledge as maladroit and inadequate. Will often expresses views, like salvation by baptism alone, that Langland dislikes. Thus, he is wrong in the same way that the wife of *Les quatre souhais St. Martin* (4.31) is wrong in making outrageous wishes. Like her, however, his resistance to insufficient authority figures exposes their failings in spite of his own compromised position.

When Will interrogates Scripture, Reason, and Ymaginatif, the tutelary figures do not rise above his unruliness but rather descend to his level. Instead of providing the clarifying lessons of Boethius's Philosophia, Scripture, Reason, and Ymaginatif respond to Will's rebellion with a sequence of accusations, stonewalling, and blank assertions of power whose rudeness matches that of their unruly interlocutor. Scripture provides a theologically questionable distinction between Christian and pagan routes to salvation, then responds to Will's speech questioning the value of learning not with further exposition but with scorn: "And lakked me in Latyn and light by me she sette" (B.XI.2). Reason, similarly, responds to Will's question regarding the rationality of animal sexuality by telling him it is none of his business what Reason does or does not permit (B.XI.376–77), and Ymaginatif follows up with further condemnations of Will's "entremetynge" and "rude speche" (B.XI.414; 418), which he says has led to the withdrawal of Reason's instruction. Ymaginatif's own lessons assert an orthodox doctrine of salvation and the importance of learned clergy but never explain how one might reconcile those views with his commitment to pagan salvation.[75]

In this respect, the tutelary figures behave much like the husband of the fabliau *Sire hain et dame anieuse* (2.5). Beset by a shrewish wife who will not obey him, the husband first responds in kind to his wife's scolding, then engages with her in a ridiculous fight for the "pants" of the family, wherein he literally battles her for the garment. As in many fabliaux, the humor of *Sire hain* (2.5) lies in the husband's inability to administer authority effectively in the household, a mismanagement that is most humorously witnessed in the way he descends to a level of equality with his wife by responding to her in kind, an act that robs him of masculine authority and renders him a laughingstock.

Like the fabliau husband, the tutelary figures fail because they do not respond dynamically to a challenge to their authority. As a result, they lose their claim to precedence and become comically ridiculous. In this way, Langland invites his audience to see that neither the doctrinal nor the sociopolitical problems that he points out in the third vision will be resolved without an alteration in conventional power relations and ways of conceptualizing information. Henri Bergson's theory of comedy asserts that we are inspired to laughter when we see others behaving mechanistically in situations that demand a dynamic and sensitive response. A man running along the street who stumbles and falls is funny because his behavior exhibits a "lack of elasticity, through absentmindedness and a kind of physical obstinacy, *as a result, in fact, of rigidity or of momentum.*"[76] He should have altered his pace to avoid the obstacle but did not. A correlative of Bergson's theory can be found in obscene comedy authority figures who often inspire laughter through their lack of discernment and their inability to respond appropriately to the challenges presented to them. Scripture, Reason, and Ymaginatif enter this comic mode and become laughable when they respond to Will's unruliness with anger, which constitutes a mechanistic response to his questions. They are comical because, like the man whose rigidity prevents him from avoiding the stone in the street, they fail to create new ways of relating to the dreamer that might accommodate for his questions and incorporate his resistance into productive intellectual change. Like the husband of *Sire hain* (2.5), they degrade themselves by descending to their subordinate's level, rather than effectively asserting their authority.

The close interdependence between the political inquiries of this segment and its obscene comedy are revealed in the C-version edits of the poem. The C-version eliminates both the aggressive, obscene comedy exchanges between Will and the tutelary figures and many of the poem's concerns over Church knowledge and teaching. C does not include Scripture's statement on the efficacy of poverty in achieving salvation, Will's rude "Contra!" interruption, or his complaint about her long lesson. Will's remarks regarding predestination, the salvation of heathens, and the role of learning in salvation are, meanwhile, transferred to Recklessness. As Pearsall notes, the transfer of these ideas away from the dreamer "withdraws a further degree of authorial sanction from them."[77] Rather than being characterized in the morally ambivalent obscene comedy mode, the C-version exchanges on salvation humorlessly characterize Recklessness as a rude individual who attacks the good arguments of the tutelary figures. The narrator remarks disapprovingly that Recklessness "in a rage aresenede Clergie / And Scripture scornede that many skilles [good arguments] shewede" (C.XIII.129–30).

In the B-version, Langland not only invests Will with the unruly woman's comic appeal, but he also alters the moral trajectory associated with her. In obscene comedy, in spite of her charm, the unruly woman often justifies authorities' punitive and distrustful attitudes toward her through her own intransigence and lack of regret. Unruly wives will never be anything but resistant to authority. Therefore, the only solution to the problem she presents is a blank assertion of power, either by physically overcoming her, as the husband of *Sir hain et dame anieuse* (2.5) does, or by ignoring her input, as the narrator of *Les quatre souhais saint Martin* (4.31) advises.[78] Langland's Will is different. Even as he resembles the unruly woman in his surliness and rude speech, he diverges from her by showing a capacity for shame and a willingness to obey. Throughout the episode, Will's divergence from submission to unruliness is prompted not by his own character but by the inadequacies he perceives in the authorities' answers: Will initially greets Clergy and Scripture "and worshiped hem bothe" (B.X.224) and only becomes rude when he perceives Scripture's answer to be inadequate; his response to Reason's reproof is to feel ashamed and woeful and subsequently to submit to Ymaginatif, an obedience that is only fractured by Ymaginatif's accusations regarding Will's poetic endeavors.

The fact that the tutelary authorities cannot effect a rapprochement with Will in these moments means that, even though they are right and he is wrong, he is not integrated into their way of seeing the world, remaining an alienated outsider and a perpetual loose end, much like Meed in the first vision. The conclusions of both of these episodes are worth remarking on in the context of Langland's famed political conservatism. They suggest that, while Langland may support hierarchical relationships on principle, he is aware that they must be moderated by a respect for the needs and perspectives of subordinates.

Obscene Redemption in Passus XX

The impotence vignette of Passus XX appears in the midst of a bleak scenario, in which the vision of a simplified apostolic Church appears to have been obliterated, with no real hope being offered for institutional renewal in the future.[79] Secular leadership, meanwhile, falls victim to greed and corruption more profoundly than anywhere else in the poem, when a lord and king at the conclusion of Passus XIX defend their right to take from their subjects. The impotence vignette is obviously meaningful for Langland, not only because it appears in the final passus but because it is the very last time we see Will in the poem. Although Will suffers other indignities of old age after Elde's attack, his impotence and his wife's response to it are Langland's main focus in the episode, taking up six lines of description, as much as all the other afflictions together.[80]

The vignette occurs in the midst of the assault on Unity by Antichrist, Pride, and their minions. In the aftermath of disease and death brought on by Kind and Death in defense of Unity, Life emerges as a carefree and high-living character who enjoys his good fortune without care for holiness or any other sacred value. Having been called out by Conscience to deal with Life's careless ways, Elde frightens off Life's child, Wanhope, then heads off in pursuit of Life. At this point, Will, who has been a spectator since the beginning of the battle episode, appears once again, complaining that, in pursuing Life, Elde has cut a swath over his own head, rendering it bald. This, Will objects, is bad behavior and scolds, "Sire yvele ytaughte Elde....Haddestow be hende . . . thow woldest have asked leave!" (B.X.186–88). Elde responds by cuffing him about the ears and mouth, rendering Will deaf and toothless. Will's wife, meanwhile, in the passage I have quoted at the outset of this chapter, laments the absence of the "lyme" she loved him for and used to like to feel at night when they were in bed naked.

The passage has attracted little attention in spite of its significant placement. Among those who have analyzed it, there is not much consensus. Teresa Tavormina regards it as a bit of gentle comic nostalgia.[81] Michael Calabrese links it to an ongoing conversation about Will's penis in the poem, which also includes Wit's advice to Will to get married "Whiles thow art yong, and thi wepene kene" (B.IX.182) and Will's misuse of his "wepene" at the advice of Concupiscentia Carnis in Passus XI. For Calabrese, the failure of Will's body partakes of the more general social and spiritual degeneration of the passus: "Society's failure, its sickliness and impotence in defeating Pride, are enacted in Will's body, which thus becomes the locus of the degeneration and frailty that bring the poem to an end."[82] James Paxson reads the episode as evincing a "queer" dynamic because, in describing Elde (as well as his wife) as having "forbeten" his penis, Will represents what fourteenth-century culture would have labeled an "unnatural sexual exchange" between two men.[83] While all of these analyses touch on salient elements of the passage, I wish to characterize it as both more optimistic and more substantive than previous critics have allowed. In particular, I wish to focus on how the impotence vignette represents marriage as an institution that fosters many of the values Langland holds most dear, particularly in terms of its capacity to encourage effective and compassionate responses both to external difficulties and to challenges from within.

The vignette is remarkable for the way that the couple's exchange bypasses the animus-driven character of Will's previous social relationships and instead embodies the qualities of humility and modesty that have been persistent themes in Langland's explorations of "do-well" throughout *Piers Plowman*. As I have already noted, Will's relationships in the poem are generally characterized by a pattern of accusation and defensive response, followed by counteraccusation or shame. A proximate example of this kind of exchange in Passus XX can be found in Will's angry objection to Elde and Elde's dismissive and violent response. As a supplement to Paxson's observation regarding the nature of Will's relationship with Elde, I would add that its queerness extends beyond the imagined physical contact to the social relationship between the two men. Once again, here, we see Will casting himself in the role of the unruly woman, bickering with his masculine superior, Elde.

The complaint of Will's wife regarding his impotence offers up the potential for a similar exchange, this time with Will in the superior role. It would be perfectly reasonable within the tradition of obscene comedy to expect that Will might respond to his wife's complaint with misogynist accusations either about women's faithlessness or their overblown sexual appetites. This is certainly the narrative arc of *Le pescheor de pont seur Saine* (4.28), a fabliau that has some notable parallels with Langland's impotence scenario. In this tale, a fisherman suspects that his wife would not love him without his penis. She denies it vehemently, so he crafts a plot to convince the wife he has lost his penis. At this, the wife immediately announces she is leaving him, leading the narrator to the misogynist moralization that "Que por la coille et por le vit / Tient la fame l'ome plus chier" [That for the balls and for the cock, / The woman holds the man most dear] (4.28.198–99).[84] And even if the woman has the most handsome count for a husband, if he is castrated, she will leave him for the lowest serving boy, if she finds he fucks her well and often, the fabliau narrator concludes (4.28.204–9).

The exchange between Will and his wife contains shadows of obscene comedy animus. The wife wishes Will were dead, and Will is not above apportioning some of the blame for his malfunctioning organ on his wife's excessive sexual desire. His penis fails, he says, because "Elde and *heo* it hadden forbeten" (B.XX.198; italics mine). But the exchange also shows the operation of some higher principles, indicating a successful social bond between two human beings that, in other respects, embodies Langland's favored qualities of humility, self-control, self-abnegation, and charity.[85] This is not a perfect marriage, to be sure, but it is also not the strife-ridden, jealous, or greedy marriage that we see in Wit's list of bad marriages.[86] Nor is there any suggestion of adultery. Will's wife may complain, but there is no indication that she will seek satisfaction elsewhere.

Masha Raskolnikov has argued that *Piers Plowman* documents an anxiety about interdependence, particularly with women, and notes that the poem gradually pares away its female interlocutors, leaving Will, in the end, bound most profoundly to Liberum Arbitrum, a "Latin-named Will" who functions as a kind of second self to the dreamer.[87] In general, I am in agreement with Raskolnikov, but I think the impotence segment represents an alternative that, while it is not fully developed, gives us some insight into Langland's persistent interest in marriage throughout *Piers Plowman*.

Elizabeth Robertson has pointed out the centrality of marriage in the poem as "a concept and practice that for Langland most fully binds together the theological and the social."[88] The impotence vignette gives us our most profound illustration of this disposition. Throughout the poem, Langland has been concerned with the social consequences of Christians' inability to forgo the satisfaction of temporary and worldly desires in favor of Christian truth and the common good. In the married couple of the impotence vignette, we see a pair who maintains their social bond through the application of Christian values. Langland's wife has desire, is disappointed at the frustration of that desire, and yet does not act upon her frustration. In addition, she is not without charitable sentiments. She does, after all, have "ruthe" (pity) on Will for the sufferings brought on by old age.[89] Will, meanwhile, does not express the kind of animus to his wife's sexual desire that the misogynist tradition would dictate. Indeed, there is self-abnegation and humility in his sympathy with her disappointment and in his own nostalgic memories of late-night activities in bed.[90]

The imperfection of the marriage is precisely what gives the moment its poignancy. Repeatedly, *Piers Plowman* has given voice to frustration over the distance between religious dictates and what actually occurs in the historical world. A saintly, idealized couple would only be a continuation of that dichotomy, the couple's perfection serving to emphasize the distance between theory and practice. The fact that this couple is flawed—that they are disappointed and angry with one another and yet persist—makes them some of the few characters in *Piers Plowman* who are able to unify dictum and lived experience.

As a number of other readers have noted, marriage takes a remarkably prominent place in *Piers Plowman*'s vision of the Christian life.[91] It is the primary locus of "do-well" in Wit's speech and is characterized as representative of the Trinity in Abraham's speech. Moreover, the poem's two central male characters, Will and Piers, are both depicted in the context of families. Unlike Hoccleve, Langland never figures Will bemoaning marriage or depicting his wife as a shrew. Indeed, Will's invitation to his wife and daughter to share in the joy of the resurrection in Passus XVIII is his first truly social or altruistic action in the poem.[92]

However, Langland never explicitly justifies his positive attitude to marriage. The impotence passage suggests that he admires the elasticity of marriage as an institution, specifically, its ability to withstand challenges to its own internal hierarchies and its capacity to alter its own relations of power. In this respect, we can see the impotence vignette as an extension of the observations Elizabeth Fowler has made regarding the importance of marriage as an exemplar of contractual relations during a period that provided few other models.[93] Fowler is primarily concerned with how marriage provides Langland with a model of agency relations, particularly as a model for exchange and conditions of consent, which she notes were much more highly developed in the marriage doctrine in common law and the church courts than they were in economic analysis and regulation.[94] The impotence vignette suggests that marriage is also important to Langland as a model of how a traditional institution can adapt itself to changing social circumstances.

As I have argued earlier in this chapter, one of the major issues isolated in both the Meed episode and the third vision is the rigidity of both secular and ecclesiastical hierarchies. In many cases, Langland characterizes these hierarchies as being unable to integrate challenges from within or to alter themselves to adapt to new circumstances. As silly and obscene as it might seem, the impotence passage actually represents a serious challenge to Will's dominance within his own marriage, since medieval marriage theory regarded the husband's sexual capacity as a key element in his command over his wife.[95] Moreover, the wife's unhappiness parallels Will's own declarations of discontent with the failings of authority figures in the third vision. Unlike the king and his counselors in the Meed episode, however, Will does not banish his wife as irredeemably antisocial nor does he dismiss and denigrate his subordinate in the manner of the tutelary figures in Vision Three. Rather, he keeps her within the marriage, accepting the reasons for her unhappiness. Will's ability to adapt to the changing circumstances of his marriage allows him to avoid the stasis and fragmentation that we see at the conclusion of the first and third visions, wherein authority figures fail to rethink or reorganize themselves in response to challenges from subordinates.

In the following chapter, I examine the way that Chaucer uses obscene comedy to pose questions of the aristocratic ethos and to associate its intense competitiveness and idealization of violence with the forces of social disruption. While Chaucer's use of obscene comedy is certainly more generically identifiable in the sense that the narratives of his fabliaux often follow their Old French antecedents more closely than Langland ever does, Chaucer, too, must break down the discourse to achieve his ends. Like Langland, Chaucer merges obscene comedy with other discourses, creating a symbiotic relationship in which each discourse undercuts elements of the other. Also like Langland, Chaucer uses obscene comedy to talk about larger political relations in ways that reveal the close interdependency between political theory and conceptions of power relations within the household. On the surface more accessible and entertaining than Langland's obscene comedy passages, Chaucer's fabliaux are ultimately closer to Langland than they are to their purported French sources. Undoing the origins of the fabliau even as he presents it as a harmless "game," Chaucer follows Langland in using obscenity to examine what is and imagine what might be.

CHAPTER 2

Chaucer's Poetics of the Obscene

Classical Narrative and Fabliau Politics
in Fragment One of the *Canterbury Tales*
and the *Legend of Good Women*

In the pivotal episode of Chaucer's *Reeve's Tale*, a visiting clerk has intercourse with the daughter of Symkyn the miller to gain "esement" for the grain Symkyn has stolen. Chaucer's description of the clerk's approach in the middle of the night is suggestive of rape:

> And up he rist, and by the wenche he crepte.
> This wenche lay uprighte and faste slepte
> Til he so ny was, er she myghte espie,
> That it had been to late for to crie,
> And shortly for to seyn, they were aton. (4193–97)

The couple's exchange at dawn, however, is all sweetness and light. The clerk Aleyn takes his leave in a manner that evokes the courtly aube, calling the daughter "sweete wight" and vowing to be "thyn awen clerk" (4236, 4239). Malyne, the daughter, responds in kind, addressing Aleyn as "deere lemman" (4240) and revealing to him the location of the cake baked from the purloined flour. Her revelation clinches her father's defeat: the two clerks scoop up the cake before escaping from the mill, leaving Symkyn beaten, cuckolded, and humiliated.

Although the *Reeve's Tale* has always been called a fabliau, many elements of its plot and characterization are uncommon in the Old French genre and do not exist in tale's seven known analogues. Aleyne's assault on Malyne may seem to manifest the fabliau's comical treatment of violence, but in fact sexual coercion is rare in the fabliau, which favors the exploits of willfully lusty women. The few fabliaux that portray rape avoid any suggestion of coercive violence, instead representing rape as a funny trick, carried out without pain on women who end up enjoying it.[1] A daughter's betrayal of her father is also highly unusual in the fabliau, whose primary focus is on erotic relationships rather than intergenerational ones. None of the extant Old French or Anglo-Norman fabliaux feature a daughter who betrays her father in the manner of Chaucer's Malyne. Nor are the anxieties over social status that obsess the men of the *Reeve's Tale* commonly seen in fabliau characters, who are motivated primarily by the needs of the body, like hunger and lust. The women of the *Reeve's Tale* are also unusual. With the exception of Malyne's act of rebellion in the final lines of the tale, they are passive, displaying little of the agency and subversive verve for which fabliau women are famous.

As many readers have noted, the *Reeve's Tale* is not much fun. Refusing its audience the fabliau pleasure of watching ludicrous characters engage in carefree transgression, the *Reeve's Tale* portrays instead a complex, anxiety-ridden world where men battle one another for social status and women are pawns manipulated and damaged in the men's violent contests. The tale's bleakness has earned it a reputation as a maladroit and not-terribly-valuable entry in the *Canterbury* collection, a vengeful narrative told by a bitter old man that signifies decline, either of morality, community, political resistance, or a combination of the three. The tale is, by far, the outlier in Fragment One, attracting considerably less attention than the tales of the Knight or the Miller.[2] In a statement that typifies the dominant critical evaluation of the tale, V. A. Kolve concludes that the Reeve "exhibits a fierce insight into human behavior, but it is a perception without purpose or future; it is not on the side of life."[3] In a more politicized vein, Lee Patterson says that the *Reeve's Tale* represents a retreat from the direct political commentary of the *Miller's Tale*: "by revealing its teller's culpable ignorance of his own moral failures and his small-minded vindictiveness, the *Reeve's Tale* comes ultimately to have the most relevance to the Reeve himself, to *quite* its own teller."[4]

An evaluation that dismisses the *Reeve's Tale* as inadequate or unimportant, however, cannot explain why Chaucer was at pains over the tale (almost everyone agrees on its technical brilliance), or why he gives it pride of place as the third entry in the *Canterbury* collection. This chapter argues that the *Reeve's Tale* plays a crucial role in Fragment One, working out a number of concepts that are adumbrated, but not fully realized, in the preceding two tales.

If its importance has gone unrecognized in Chaucer studies, it is because modern critics have failed to understand the poet's complex and ambivalent relationship with the discourse of obscene comedy, particularly with the legacy of the Old French fabliau.

Perhaps the most obvious candidate for a study of obscene discourse in Chaucer would be the Wife of Bath. While the Wife is certainly a notable example of Chaucerian obscenity, she is not the best choice for those seeking to understand the poetics that structure her representation. It is, rather, in the romance-fabliau-fabliau ordering of Fragment One that we see Chaucer working out his poetics of obscenity most clearly and profoundly.

My discussion of *Piers Plowman* in the first chapter of this study described how Langland exploits obscene comedy for its ability to analyze and critique social power relationships in ways unavailable in other medieval discourses. At the same time, I also noted a distaste for obscene comedy in its conventional forms that leads Langland to break down the discourse, using only bits and pieces of it. Although Chaucer reproduces (or seems to reproduce) the fabliau with a fidelity lacking in Langland's poem, he shares Langland's dissatisfaction with obscene discourse. Rather than breaking down obscene comedy as Langland does, however, Chaucer adopts the fabliau framework and deconstructs it from within.

While Chaucer shares Langland's interest in using obscene comedy to critique the power holders of his society, he differs from Langland in the sense that he wishes to question not only authorities' use of their power, but the ideologies that govern and justify their authority in the first place. As I have noted in Chapter 1, Langland does not interrogate—and indeed often depends on—the limits obscene comic discourse places on its political critique, in particular, the way it upholds the legitimacy of established power holders, even as it pillories them for way they use their power. Chaucer does not accept these limitations, working instead to push obscene discourse beyond its self-imposed boundaries toward a portrayal of elites that characterizes them and their governing principles as so corrupt and dysfunctional as to interrogate their right to hold power at all. Aware that the master's tools will never, as Audre Lorde has remarked, "dismantle the master's house," Chaucer takes apart the fabliau from the inside, making crucial alterations to certain elements of plot and characterization in order to unleash its potential to ask penetrating questions of official truths.[5]

The process through which Chaucer explored obscene comedy's supposed resistance to authority and found it wanting is manifested in the romance-fabliau-fabliau sequence of Fragment One. In the *Knight's Tale*, as many readers have noted, we have an attempt to justify aristocratic ideology that often seems to fall short of its teller's aspirations. Making visible "the suppressions and elisions that enabled chivalry to function both as an ideology and a form of practice," the *Knight's Tale* suggests that its teller's convictions regarding the rectitude and moral superiority of the aristocracy are mistaken.[6] The Miller vows to "quite" the Knight; his displacement of the monk and insistence on speaking seem to promise that his quitting will be political in nature. In political terms, however, the *Miller's Tale* is a disappointment, doing little to extend the critique of chivalric ideology Chaucer adumbrates when he draws our attention to the Knight's rhetorical weaknesses. Instead, we learn that beneath the Miller's self-conscious opposition lies a worldview that is very similar to the Knight's: like the Knight, the Miller invites us to identify women and their sexuality as the primary disruptive factor in any given society; he asks us to believe that established male authority is morally legitimate (even if sometimes insufficient in its execution), and to share the Knight's conviction that social order cannot be preserved when women and male subordinates escape the control of a senior male authority.[7]

The features of plot and characterization that disable the countercultural potential of the *Miller's Tale* are not unique to it alone but are characteristic of the fabliau generally. By violating fabliau convention in the *Reeve's Tale*, Chaucer not only ruins fabliau pleasures, he corrects for the fabliau's political failings, enabling a far more penetrating critique of chivalric ideology than the Miller can ever hope to achieve. Most remarkably, the *Reeve's Tale* invites its audience to see how destruction and chaos are the necessary outcomes of a militaristic ethos that asserts men can only achieve honor and power through the violent domination of other men. In doing so, the *Reeve's Tale* does not chart out new territory so much as return us to themes expressed in the classical source of the *Knight's Tale*, the *Thebaid* of Publius Statius, whose unstinting critique of aristocratic violence is suppressed in the Knight's retelling.

Also integral to Chaucer's attempt at undercutting aristocratic ideology is the Reeve's evocation of yet another classical narrative closely related to the *Knight's Tale*, the legend of Ariadne, which subverts the knight's lionization of Theseus by recalling the hero's history as a liar and a rapist. In its narrative outlines, so at odds with fabliau convention, the *Reeve's Tale* repeats the *Ariadne*. The Reeve's story of a power struggle between a patriarch and a male interloper, the interloper's erotic relationship with the patriarch's daughter, his fight to escape, and the help he receives from a daughter who betrays her father are all reminiscent of Theseus' imprisonment by Minos in Crete, his battle with the Minotaur, and his escape courtesy of Minos's daughters.

Chaucer's use of classical legend is so extensive in the *Reeve's Tale* that the work is more accurately described as a fusion of classical legend and fabliau than as a faithful rendition of the Old French genre. This fusion is crucial to Chaucer for many reasons. In terms of fabliau gender politics, Chaucer's use of a classical legend plot highlights contradictions in medieval culture's gender ideology that the fabliau typically obfuscates. While in some respects medieval culture exhibits an investment in masculine authority that is similar to the principle of *patria potestas* that predominates in the classical world, its conviction regarding the absolute nature of this authority is disrupted by Christian doctrines advocating women's right of consent in matters of sex and marriage.[8] By having his fabliau narrate classical-legend style plots like rape and a daughter's betrayal, Chaucer draws the attention of his late medieval audience to elements in their own culture that value women's exercise of free will and limit masculine authority.

Although gender is Chaucer's primary vehicle of political expression in Fragment One, his experiments with the *Ariadne* in the *Legend of Good Women*—as well as conversations between various male characters in the prologues of the *Legend* and the *Canterbury Tales*—indicate that what is at stake in Fragment One goes beyond gender to other power relations in medieval society. In particular, the *Legend of Good Women* and the *Canterbury Tales* prologues invite us to draw parallels between the status of women and that of male subordinates. These passages, as well as some oddities in Chaucer's portrayal of Malyne, suggest that Chaucer's interest in gender is prompted less by a concern for women than by its relevance as a metaphor for the difficulties encountered by men like himself within a violent and coercive political system.[9]

As a reflection on the two entries that precede it, the *Reeve's Tale* works on two levels, one literary and the other thematic. On a literary level, it comments on the *Miller's Tale* by exposing the limitations that result from that tale's adherence to fabliau conventions. On a thematic level, the Reeve's primary focus is the chivalric ethos of the *Knight's Tale*. The tale's dual purpose in speaking to both previous entries is embodied in its profound connection to each. While the *Reeve's Tale* is linked to the *Miller's Tale* by virtue of a common generic heritage, it has structural parallels to the *Knight's Tale* that are, as Elaine Hansen remarks, more exact than those of the Miller's entry: Symkyn's position as a patriarch in charge of a wife and a young, unmarried woman echoes the Theseus-Hippolyta-Emelye triad more accurately than the Miller's husband, wife, and lover triangle;

and the two clerks' entry as outsiders into Symkyn's rural kingdom reminds us of Palamon and Arcite's relationship to Theseus more than Nicholas and Absolon, who are resident in the patriarch's territory.[10]

To understand Fragment One, we must appreciate the interdependence of Chaucer's literary and political projects. It is only by violating fabliau convention that Chaucer is able to get at the suppressed classical content of the *Knight's Tale* and arrive a fuller and more complete critique of the aristocratic ethos that governs it. By foregrounding his own artistic process of revision in the romance, fabliau, fabliau sequence of Fragment One, Chaucer bears witness both to obscene comedy's subversive potential and to the powerful limitations placed on that potential by the fabliau as a genre.

As well as helping us understand Chaucer's political explorations in Fragment One, appreciating his awareness of the fabliau's limitations also accounts for an oft-remarked but unexplained difference between the *Miller's Tale* and the *Reeve's Tale*. As many readers have noted over the years, the *Miller's Tale* and the *Reeve's Tale* seem to be diametrically opposed in the sense that, while the tale of the Miller has no known sources or close analogues, the *Reeve's Tale* is sourced from "one of the most popular fabliaux in medieval Europe."[11] The tale has seven extant analogues in French, German, Italian, and Flemish, including a tale from Boccaccio's *Decameron* and three Old French fabliaux, *Gombert et les deus clers* (4.35) and *Le meunier et les deus clers* (7.80), which exists in two versions, B and C.[12] Why would Chaucer have paired an obscure, or very possibly original, tale with a widespread and popular one? We can make sense of this decision if we think about the fabliau-fabliau sequence of Fragment One as the conventional iteration of a popular genre, followed by a revision that corrects for the genre's failings. As Chaucer's rendering of a genre in its classic form, the literary brilliance of the *Miller's Tale* lies in its originality. As a reflection on the genre, the *Reeve's Tale* benefits from its derivative nature, for how better to announce one's dissatisfaction with a genre to the discerning members of one's audience than to disembowel one of its most famous works?

What the Knight Suppresses:
Violence and Masculine Competition in Statius's *Thebaid*

Although the *Knight's Tale* is known as a rewriting of Bocaccio's *Teseida*, the ultimate source of the tale lies in the account of Theseus's war on Creon in the twelfth book of Statius's *Thebaid*. As one of the most popular classical poems of the Middle Ages, widely imitated in both Latin and vernacular poetry, the *Thebaid* was well known to Chaucer and his audience.[13] Chaucer cites the *Thebaid* directly in the *House of Fame* and gives a full summary of its plot in *Troilus and Criseyde* (5.1485–1510).

The *Thebaid* differs from both the *Teseida* and the *Knight's Tale* in its frank portrayal of ruthless and power-hungry aristocrats whose fierce battles for pathetic rewards result in needless destruction. In the *Thebaid*, social and political dissolution is the direct result of an ethos wherein men gain honor through violent acts of domination. Narrating the fratricidal contest over Thebes between Oedipus' two sons, Eteocles and Polynices, the *Thebaid* is, in the words of one scholar, "a powerful poetic depiction of the horrific consequences of the negative exercise of power by rulers both human and supernatural."[14] In Book I of the *Thebaid*, the narrator condemns the Theban brothers for engaging in a vicious struggle for control that sacrifices social good for pathetically small rewards:

> . . . sed nuda potestas
> armavit fratres, pugna est de paupere regno.
> dumque uter angustae squalentia iugera Dirces
> verteret aut Tyrii solio non altus ovaret
> exsulis ambigitur, periit ius fasque bonumque
> et vitae mortisque pudor. quo tenditis iras,
> a, miseri?
>
> [. . . Naked power
> The brothers aimed for, battle joined to win
> A pauper realm. And while the pair dispute
> Which shall plough narrow Dirce's squalid fields,
> Which boast in exile on Tyre's lowly throne,
> Heaven's laws and men's have perished; righteousness,
> Honour in life and death have died. Alas,
> Poor wretches! How far will your anger reach?][15]

Earlier in Book I, the narrator outlines the ignoble motivations behind the brothers' struggle for power:

> protinus adtoniti fratrum sub pectore motus,
> gentilesque animos subiit furor aegraque laetis

invidia atque parens odii metus, inde regendi
saevus amor, ruptaeque vices iurisque secundi
ambitus impatiens, et summo dulcius unum
stare loco, sociisque comes discordia regnis.

[. . . At once wild passions stirred
The brothers' hearts, the madness of their race
Inspired them, envy grudging others' joy
And fear that fathers hate; then lust for power,
Alternate rule rejected, second place
Spurned by ambition, sole supremacy
The sweeter satisfaction, rivalry
That waits on kingdoms where the reign is shared.][16]

Medieval chivalric culture closely resembles the culture Statius portrays in the *Thebaid* in the high value it puts on a man's ability to dominate other men through violence. As Ruth Karras notes, violence in chivalric culture "was the fundamental measure of a man because it was a way of exerting dominance over other men of one's own social stratum, as well as over women and other social inferiors."[17] As a supporter of the chivalric ethos, the Knight must suppress Statius' commentary on the stupidity and brutality of this ethic.[18] Following Boccaccio's "romancing" of Statius, the Knight replaces the rivalry for a city with a rivalry for the love of a woman.[19] In doing so, the Knight converts a battle for political power into an erotic contest, thereby obscuring the way that male rivalries for power are a cause of social disorder and shifting the blame to female sexuality instead. In the place of Statius' exploration of the pointless violence sparked by powerful male rivals, the Knight attempts to make his tale a celebration of martial power exercised by the correct person. As Winthrop Wetherbee notes, "The role the knight assigns to Theseus is intended to express the highest ambitions of medieval culture in its secular aspect, transforming classical heroism into an enlightened chivalry capable of harmonizing valor in war with political responsibility and courtly grace."[20]

In the *Knight's Tale*, militarism is represented as an instrument of justice. Theseus' military force returns the Argive dead to their grieving widows and stems the disruptive potential of Palamon and Arcite's impassioned rivalry. As a number of critics have noted, there are parts of the *Knight's Tale* that reveal an "awareness of other, darker aspects of life which are inherent in its classical subject matter,"[21] but these are not made explicit or put forward as a central matter of thematic concern the way they are in the *Thebaid*.

While Statius shows a keen awareness of the harm to women that ensues from violent masculine conflict, the Knight does not. One of the unresolved contradictions of the *Knight's Tale* is that it attempts to make a benevolent patriarch out of a man famous, even in the Middle Ages, for his mistreatment of women. Theseus' war against Thebes in the *Thebaid* may have been prompted by *ira iusta*, but the hero was also notorious for his betrayal and rape of women.[22] Statius accentuates Theseus' paradoxical status when he invokes the image of Ariadne in the *Thebaid* as "a counterpart in Theseus' own story to the many suffering women whose lives have been blighted by the heroic enterprise of the Theban war."[23]

The Knight's own chivalric order presents similar threats to women. As Roberta Krueger notes, chivalry's combination of violence and its assertion of masculine control over women "makes women dependent upon, and victims of, the chivalric system: the threat of rape, or more generally of male violence against women, makes women need the protection of knights, and that protection makes them vulnerable to male aggression."[24] The Knight, however, characterizes martial authority according to the dictates of chivalric ideology, as a source of care and protection for women.[25] And although Theseus' own past behavior to Ariadne and Phaedra implicates him in "the drama of desire and exploitation of women that he seeks to control at the end of the *Knight's Tale*," the Knight, following Boccaccio's *Teseida*, avoids narrating his hero's past.[26] Nevertheless, Chaucer seems interested in reminding his audience of Theseus' Cretan adventure, even as the Knight seeks to ignore it. Diverging from Boccaccio's avoidance of the Cretan episode, Chaucer includes a reminder when he describes Theseus riding off to conquer Thebes under the banner of "The Mynotaur, which that he wan in Crete" (980).

The *Miller's Tale* and the Limitations of the Fabliau

Impressed with the Miller's violation of courtly decorum and his claim to "quite" the Knight, many readers have assumed that his tale is the primary locus for Chaucer's interrogation of the Knight.[27] As the extensive critical literature on the *Miller's Tale* indicates, the tale, one of Chaucer's most brilliant creations, undoubtedly responds to the Knight's romance on many levels.[28] Its interrogation of the Knight's chivalric ideology is, however, quite limited in a way that probably would not have surprised Chaucer's fourteenth-century audience. Since the publication of Per Nykrog's landmark 1957 study, scholars of the fabliau have acknowledged that the tales did not originate in the middle or lower ranks but were, in fact, upper-rank entertainments.[29] While scholars of Old French continue to debate the exact parameters and chronology of the fabliau's dispersal in French society, the linguistic history of the fabliau in England attests to its aristocratic provenance.[30] While only one fabliau-like tale (*Dame Sirith*) exists in English prior to Chaucer's *Canterbury Tales*, there are eighteen fabliaux in British Isles manuscripts that are written in Anglo-Norman.[31] Approaching the *Miller's Tale* with an awareness of the fabliau's aristocratic provenance, Chaucer's original audience would have been likely to read ironically Chaucer's description of the Miller's entry as a "cherles tale" (3169) and to expect a tale whose opposition to the Knight's romance would be more playful and literary than politically threatening.[32] Far from being a new or shocking occurrence, response to romance is a conventional element of the fabliau, which frequently invoke romance language, situations and characters for humorous effect.[33]

As I have outlined in my discussion of *Piers Plowman*, obscene comedy's delight in portraying subversive characters who upend the established order, and its tendency to characterize established powers as foolish and incompetent, would seem to offer medieval writers a fertile language in which to pose questions of social and political authority. The fabliau tradition as Chaucer knew it in the late fourteenth century, however, includes elements that short-circuit obscene comedy's subversive potential. First among these is the fabliau's use of the erotic to obscure the political. Like the Knight, the fabliau identifies women and their sexuality—rather than male ambition, war, or corruption—as the primary cause of social chaos. This fabliau tendency was likely to have been well known to Chaucer's original audience, given the fidelity that the extant Anglo-Norman fabliaux display to the principle of female sexuality as prime disruptive force. These include: *Le chevalier a la corbeille* (9.113) found in London BL Harley MS 2253, which centers on a lady's attempt to sleep with her paramour when her husband is away; *Un chevalier, sa dame et un clerk* (10.123) found in Cambridge Corpus Christi College MS 50, a tale preoccupied with a wife's clever ruse to sleep with her clerkly lover in spite of her husband's suspicions; *Le cuvier* (5.44) found in London BL Harley MS 527, wherein a wife hides her lover under a tub to conceal him from her husband, as well as *Les quatre souhais de Saint Martin* (4.31) found in Digby MS 86, wherein a wife frustrates her husband's attempt to make good use of the four wishes he receives from St. Martin by wishing him covered in penises.

Foucault's description of discourse's political function sheds light on how obscene comedy's obsession with women and heterosexual relations is central to its capacity to uphold the established order even as it seems to celebrate subversion. Of particular importance to Foucault is the phenomenon of exclusion, that is, the way that discourses exert power by excluding certain forms of knowledge, and certain ways of thinking about and seeing the world. Discourse, according to Foucault, is characterized by "a delimitation of a field of objects, the definition of a legitimate perspective for the agent of knowledge, and the fixing of norms for the elaboration of concepts or theories."[34] A Foucauldian analysis of the fabliau reveals that the genre's exclusive focus on the domestic sphere is an exclusion that contains the subversive potential of obscenity by shutting out the political order as a legitimate subject of consideration.

While the domestic focus of the fabliau obfuscates the political, fabliau misogyny works simultaneously to support the view that patriarchal authorities deserve their power. Even as the husband of the fabliau may be characterized as stupid, lazy, greedy, or otherwise insufficient, he maintains a moral superiority to his subordinates in his commitment to upholding the sanctity of marriage. As the Anglo-Norman fabliaux I have cited above attest, fabliau women are almost always figured as immoral beings, wholly focused on the needs of the body, who will do anything to satisfy their lust. So pervasive is the genre's misogyny that it is recognized even among those who credit the fabliau with more subversive tendencies. Although E. Jane Burns explores the expression of female desire in the fabliau, she also notes that the genre often defines female nature as "irrational, pleasure-seeking, and wholly corporeal in opposition to the rationally endowed thinking male." Similarly, Simon Gaunt remarks that the fabliaux "evoke and use a deeply misogynistic discourse, often to condemn . . . women's sexual desire."[35]

In addition, the fabliau shares the Knight's conviction that violence on the part of male authorities is an effective and necessary tool for enforcing the social order. Fabliau men who fail to use violence are pilloried as foolish weaklings, while those who do use violence are characterized as successful and wise. This view is embodied in the narrator's reproof of *Gombert* the miller in the *Reeve's Tale*'s fabliau analogue, *De Gombert et les deus clers*: "Or a Gombert bone mesnie, / Mout le mainent de male pile" (118–19) [Gombert had a good household, / but he ran it with a weak stick"].[36]

In spite of the Miller's showy boast to "quite" the Knight, his tale's adherence to fabliau convention means that its potential as a source of political interrogation is limited. By featuring a male character, Nicholas, who is motivated only by his lust for Allison, rather than any other form of power seeking, the *Miller's Tale* shares the displacement of the political onto the erotic that is part of both the fabliau and the Knight's "romancing" of Statius. In addition, as a number of feminist critics have noted, the *Miller's Tale* does nothing to interrogate the Knight's assumption that husbands and other male authorities have an unquestionable right to control women.[37] The two tales might seem to present us with diametrically opposed models of womanhood: the Knight's remarkably ductile Emelye, whose total capitulation to masculine desire and masculine prerogative is remarkable even in the context of medieval romance, contrasts with the Miller's rebellious Alison, who subverts her husband in order to follow her own erotic desires. The Miller's Alison, however, does little to interrogate the Knight's celebration of patriarchal authority. Alison violates the marriage vow. Thus, her husband's attempts to frustrate her desires are legitimate. John may be foolish and he may be defeated at the end of the tale, but his moral prerogative to direct his female charges remains as unblemished as that of the Knight's Theseus. In the matter of violence, too, the *Miller's Tale* does little to interrogate the Knight's view that Theseus's military might preserves the social order. Indeed, in positioning John's uxoriousness and naïve trust in Nicholas as a prime cause of his downfall, the tale seems implicitly to recommend a stern, suspicious, and authoritarian form of patriarchal rule.

This is not to say that the *Miller's Tale* fails to gesture at other possibilities. Alison is more passive than the average fabliau woman, seeming simply to go along with Nicholas' plot rather than initiating it herself, thus inviting questions about her culpability. And while Nicholas exhibits a pure, fabliau-esque lust, Absolon's imitation of aristocratic dress and his interest in courtly behavior suggest a social ambition whose sources are political, rather than erotic. Meanwhile, John's mistaken marriage to a young woman and his obsession with holding Alison "narwe in cage" weakens his moral authority. There is, moreover, a suggestion of sexual violence in Nicholas' grabbing of Alison "by the queynte" (3276). And Absolon's rapid change from besotted admiration of Alison to a plot of gruesome revenge suggests that courtly attitudes to women are not as noble or beneficent as the *Knight's Tale* proposes. But these touches are not fully developed in the *Miller's Tale*, which avoids the problem of rape by making Alison complicit in the adultery and bypasses the problem of male violence against women by having Nicholas take the brunt of Absolon's revenge.

The Reeve's Tale and Chaucer's Attempt to Unleash the Potential of the Fabliau

While the fabliaux impose strict limitations on the political valence of their obscenity, they are nevertheless works that, as Gaunt notes, "revel in the dismantling of the discourses, structures, and hierarchies through which the culture in which they lived made sense of its world and sought to justify its inequalities with morally ordered, divinely ordained schemes of human life and death."[38] As Foucault notes, every discourse contains the seeds of its own undoing:

> We must make allowances for the complex and unstable
> process whereby discourse can be both an instrument and
> an effect of power, but also a hindrance, a stumbling block,
> a point of resistance and a starting point for an opposing
> strategy. Discourse transmits and produces power; it rein-
> forces it, but it also undermines it, and exposes it, renders it
> fragile and makes it possible to thwart it.[39]

As I have noted in the introduction to this study, the shock of taboo violation that is integral to the obscene is often used in the Middle Ages to uphold the established order. Nevertheless, precisely because it is invested in this shock, the medieval obscene opens itself to subversive meanings. In its delight in overturning hierarchies and exhibiting taboo behavior, the fabliau cannot help but offer a potential for political critique. By removing those elements of the fabliau that limit its subversive valences, Chaucer unleashes its potential to interrogate the governing order in unprecedented ways.

Although the political failings of "harlotrye" have rarely been recognized by modern critics, they are front and center in the discussions carried out in the prologues to the Miller's and Reeve's tales. When, in the *Miller's Prologue*, the Miller announces his intention to tell a tale of a carpenter and his wife, the Reeve objects on the basis of such tales' negative characterizations:

> . . . 'Stynt thy clappe!
> Lat be thy lewed dronken harlotrye.
> It is a synne and eek a greet folye

To apeyren any man, or hym defame,
And eek to bryngen wyves in swich fame. (3144–48)

The Reeve's remark has customarily been taken as a personal objection, based on
the Reeve's own identity as a carpenter, but in light of what both Chaucer and his
audience knew about the fabliau, it is also a trenchant commentary on the class
politics of the genre. Although he does not state it explicitly, the Reeve's anger
over the Miller's defaming of other men in his tale of a carpenter gestures at the
contradictions inherent in the Miller's attempt to "quite" the Knight by telling
the sort of tale that often denigrates the lower orders. The carpenter Reeve's
objection begs the question: if the Miller is really delivering a riposte to the aristocratic values of the Knight, why does he do so in a narrative that can so easily
be read as disparaging to the third estate? Also notable is the connection the
Reeve makes between men's standing and those of "wyves." Unlike the Miller,
the Reeve does not appear to see himself opposed to women, but rather groups
himself, as a man of the third estate, in the same category as the "wyves" whose
defamation he abhors. The Reeve's objection foreshadows the way his tale will
undercut fabliau misogyny, suggesting that he regards such women as respectable
citizens, rather than as the unruly and sex-hungry creatures of the fabliau.

Chaucer continues to elucidate the Reeve's antipathy to obscene comedy in
the *Reeve's Prologue*. When the Miller has finished, the Reeve begins his addition
to the tale-telling game by declaring that he does not wish to "speke of ribaudye"
(*RvP* 3866). Instead, he begins a disquisition on the miseries of old men like
himself, focusing particularly on the lamentable persistence of sexual desire in
old men who lack the capacity to fulfill it. Critics have mined this monologue
for evidence of the Reeve's distasteful personality. What has gone unremarked is
the fact that the evidence comes from the Reeve himself, in a speech that is more
self-critical than that of any other man on the Canterbury pilgrimage. The subject matter of the Reeve's speech—drawn from a longstanding medieval tradition of elegies on old age—is an apt riposte to precisely what the Reeve has
found most offensive in the *Miller's Tale*, replacing the fabliau tendency to categorize failings according to social grouping by speaking to a universal condition,
and countering fabliau misogyny with a turn to the foibles of men.

The Men of the *Reeve's Tale*

Chaucer's greatest divergence from the European analogues of the *Reeve's Tale*
lies in his rendering of the tale's male characters. As clerks and a miller, the

men of the *Reeve's Tale* embody fabliau types. Their motivations, however, are markedly different from those of fabliau men. Here, for the first time in Fragment One, we see Chaucer turning away from an erotically focused model of male motivation to one in which men are driven by a search for power and a desire to advance themselves on the social ladder. In doing so, Chaucer returns us to a territory much closer to the *Thebaid* than we have thus far seen in Fragment One.

Evidence from the tale's Continental analogues suggests that this is a purposeful change on Chaucer's part. In the analogues, as in the vast majority of erotic fabliaux, the young male interlopers are motivated solely by sexual desire.[40] The only ambition of the patriarch in all but two of the analogues, meanwhile, is to maintain the status quo by protecting his wife and daughter from the interlopers. This characterization of the men, combined with the women's lasciviousness, means that the central conflict in the analogues is the conventional fabliau struggle between uncontrolled sexual desires (on the part of women and other male subordinates) and the status quo (enforced by patriarchal authority).

The picture Chaucer provides us in the *Reeve's Tale* is different. The tale is remarkable among fabliaux for the extensive time and trouble Chaucer takes explaining the motivations of his male characters. From these passages, we learn that all three men are motivated by an anxiety over their social status and a desire to move up the social hierarchy. As we learn from the long description of Symkyn at the outset of the tale, the miller is anxious to raise his status by aping aristocratic behavior. This is evident not only in Symkyn's ambition to marry Malyne "into som worthy blood of auncetrye" (3982) but also in his predilection for clothes of the aristocratically identified color red, his pride in his wife's "noble" descent from the town parson, his determination that he would not marry a woman "but she were wel ynorissed and a mayde" (3948) and his outcry over the disparagement of his daughter's "lynage" (4272) when he learns that she has had intercourse with one of the clerks.

Social ambition is also the impetus behind Symkyn's attempt to best the clerks. Chaucer is at pains to emphasize Symkyn's resentment of the fact that the clerks' intellectual skills give them a higher social standing. The desire to prove the superiority of his own shrewdness over the clerks' university education amounts to an obsession with Symkyn: when the clerks arrive at the mill, he vows to "blere hir ye / For al the sleighte in hir philosophye" (4049) and smugly notes the proverb that "The gretteste clerkes been noght wisest men" (4054); he returns to the subject again after the triumph of his plot, when he gloats, "Yet kan a millere make a clerkes berd, / For al his art" (4096–97). When the clerks ask him for shelter, he taunts them with uselessness of their abstract knowledge in the face of physical reality:

> Myn hous is streit, but ye han lerned art;
> Ye konne by argumentes make a place
> A myle brood of twenty foot of space. (4122–24)

Symkyn's insecurity sets him apart from the patriarchs of the analogues. In five of the seven analogues, the fathers are credited only with the desire to protect the honor of their wives and daughters. The two analogues that give the father a motivation beyond preservation of the status quo, the two versions of *Le meunier et les deus clers* (7.80), restrict the father's desire to simple greed in his plan to steal the clerks' wheat without any suggestion of Symkyn's complex social ambition or resentment of intellectual accomplishment.

The clerks are also motivated by social ambition. They are junior members of their community, low on the totem pole at Cambridge's Soler Hall. As Northerners, they are foreign to the powerful regions of London and Cambridge.[41] Their eagerness to set Symkyn straight (they must beg the college warden to let them try their luck at the mill) suggests that the journey is an attempt to solidify their status at the college by handily solving one of its annoyances.

While the clerks begin boldly, the horse's escape exposes the brash young rakes as jittery underlings, terrified of Soler Hall's reaction to the loss of a valuable animal. "Oure hors is lorn, Alayn, for Goddes banes / Step on they feet! Come of, man, al atanes!" cries John when the beast's disappearance is discovered, "Allas, our wardeyn has his palfrey lorn" (4073–74). The gaze of Soler Hall continues to haunt John as he considers the consequences of Symkyn's successful theft. Recognizing that Symkyn has stolen the flour, John worries over how their defeat will play out at college:

> "Allas," quod John, "the day that I was born!
> Now are we dryve til hethyng and til scorn
> Oure corne is stoln; men wil us fooles calle,
> Bathe the wardeyn and oure felawes alle,
> And namely the millere, weylaway!" (4109–13)

Like Symkyn's ambition, the clerks' concern with their standing in the broader society is absent from the tale's Continental analogues. In five of the seven analogues, the clerks are motivated solely by their sexual desire for the wife and daughter. In the only analogues to include a somewhat more complex characterization (the two versions of *Le meunier et les deus clers*, 7.8) the clerks are poor students who seek to relieve themselves from poverty by becoming bakers, their sole ambition being to grind their grain in order to make bread from it.

As John's laments reveal, the men of the *Reeve's Tale* are keenly aware that displays of dominance over other men raise one's social status. The contest in which they engage with one another is not just a contest between the three parties, but is a battle *performed* for an audience of other men with the aim of increasing the combatants' social status. As Pierre Bourdieu observes, this is often central to assertions of manliness: "manliness must be validated by other men, in its reality as actual or potential violence, and certified by recognition of membership of the group of 'real men'."[42]

In spite of their low social status and the tale's rural medieval setting, Symkyn and the clerks are in many respects more similar to Statius' corrupt princes than they are to the men of fabliau or romance. While Chaucer certainly suggests in the *Knight's Tale* that the Knight's optimistic vision of chivalry cannot contain the forces of violent disruption it unleashes, it is only in the *Reeve's Tale* that we see Chaucer explicitly portraying a world where masculine contest is stripped of noble pretensions and revealed as a raw struggle for power that inevitably leads to social breakdown. In Symkyn and the clerks' pathetic contest over a half bushel of flour, we see a return to Statius' "Pugna est de paupere regno" (1.151) and in their desperate and violent battle for social status, a return to the maddened and brutal rivalry of the Theban brothers.

Fabliau Wives and Classical Daughters: Rape and the Reeve's Return to Statius

The *Reeve's Tale* characterizes women not as the perpetrators of social disruption but as the victims of a destructive culture of male competition and aggression. This is not something that we see portrayed explicitly in either the *Knight's* or the *Miller's Tale*, although it is adumbrated in both. The Knight wishes to characterize Theseus's care of Emelye as loving and responsible; he protects her and places her with an appropriate husband. The tale itself sometimes undermines that view, both when it characterizes Emelye as resistant to marriage in her prayer at the Temple of Diana and in its intimations of rape at various points in the narrative.[43] These same issues are touched upon somewhat more explicitly in the *Miller's Tale*, both in the fact that Alison, unlike fabliau wives, is rather passive in her adultery with Nicholas, and in the fact that, as the original intended recipient of the hot kolter, she is almost subjected to an act of violence that is shocking even by fabliau standards.[44]

In the *Reeve's Tale*, Chaucer makes women's victimization more explicit than it is in either of the preceding two entries. Under the influence of feminist criticism, recent years have seen a growing consensus that Aleyne's "seduction" of Malyne is, in fact, a rape. Historically, however, an alarming number of critics have failed even to recognize sexual coercion in the scene and even fewer have considered why Chaucer might have added this detail, which appears to be original to his tale alone.[45] Those who do acknowledge the scene's brutality have, at the same time, dismissed the notion that Chaucer intends it to be read seriously, pointing to Malyne's apparent consent after the fact (symbolized by her loving words to Aleyn at dawn) as evidence that the scene is simply a reflection of the misogynist fabliau principle that women always desire sex, even when it is forced on them.[46]

In fact, the scene's suggestion of brutality is not at all typical of the fabliau. As I have already noted, rape of any kind is rare in the genre. The few fabliaux that do represent unwanted sex characterize it as a comical matter, devoid of sorrow and pain. A case in point is the Anglo-Norman fabliau *Cele qui fu foutue et desfoutue* (4.30) [She who was fucked and defucked]. In this tale, a silly young woman is tricked into coitus by a young man who tells her he will sell her his crane for "a fuck." Ignorant of the word's meaning, she admits to being without a "fuck," whereupon the young man "finds" it under her dress, an operation that is carried out painlessly.[47] It is notable that in all the *Reeve's Tale's* analogues, the maiden is willing. In the three fabliaux, the clerk seduces the daughter with a series of courtly love declarations and offers her a magical piece of jewelry, which he claims will maintain the wearer's virginity no matter how many times she has intercourse. The young lady accepts the ring and the two spend a night of mutual enjoyment.

In the *Reeve's Tale*, Chaucer violates fabliau practice by drawing our attention to the possibility of violence at the very moment when the fabliau elides it. There is a strong suggestion of brutality in the Reeve's remark that Aleyn approaches so stealthily that "he so ny was, er she myghte espie, / That it had been to late for to crie" (4195–96). The passage's reference to crying out is particularly noteworthy, given that a woman's outcry is one of the tests used by canon law to identify a sex act as rape.[48] This is not to say that *Reeve's Tale* is explicit about the rape (Malyne does not cry out, and perhaps she never would have) but Chaucer deliberately keeps the suggestion of violence alive by having the Reeve assert that it was *too late* to cry out, thereby preventing us from assuming that Malyne's lack of outcry signifies consent. Further suggestions of Malyne's lack of consent can be found in the passive image called up by Reeve's description of Malyne, lying flat—"uprighte" (4194)—and by Aleyn's later boast of having "swyved" the miller's daughter "bolt uprighte" (4266).

In its representation of sexual violence, the *Reeve's Tale* is much more similar to classical legend than it is to fabliau. The rape of Malyne is reminiscent of a number of scenarios in classical and pseudo-classical literature, several of which would have been well-known to Chaucer's audience from the Latin texts that formed the core of the medieval schoolboy's curriculum. These include Achilles' rape of Deidamia in Statius' *Achilleid*, a number of passages in Ovid's *Ars Amatoria*, and *Pamphilus de Amore*, the pseudo-classical Latin Elegiac comedy of the twelfth century.[49] All the poems include episodes that are frankly rendered as violent rapes. Their similarities to the Malyne-Aleyn coitus are notable. In the *Achilleid*, Achilles, disguised as a maiden, shares a bedroom with the beautiful Deidamia, the daughter of his host, King Lycodemes. Achilles, overcome with lust, eventually rapes Deidamia. In spite of this, Deidamia falls in love with the hero and weeps at his departure. The passage narrating Achilles' rape of Deidamia leaves us in no doubt as to its brutality:

> . . . et densa noctis gavisus in umbra
> tempestiva suis torpere silentia furtis
> vi potitur votis et toto pectore veros
> admovet amplexus; vidit chorus ominis ab alto
> astrorum et tenerae rubuerunt cornua Lunae.
> illa quidem clamore nemus montemque replevit. (1.640–45)

> [And happy that in the night's thick darkness timely silence
> lies inert upon his dalliance, he gains his desire by force,
> launching veritable embraces, with all his heart. All the
> choir of stars saw it from on high and the young Moon's
> horns blushed red. The girl filled wood and mountain with
> her cries.][50]

In a passage in the *Ars Amatoria* advocating rape as a seduction gambit, Ovid describes the rape of Deidamia in similar terms:

Forte erat in thalamo virgo regalis eodem;
Haec illum stupro comperit esse virum.
Viribus illa quidem victa est, ita credere oportet:
Sed voluit vinci viribus illa tamen.
Saepe 'mane!' dixit, cum iam properaret Achilles;
Fortia nam posito sumpserat arma colo.

[It chanced that in the same chamber was the royal maid;
by her rape she found him to be a man. By force indeed was
she vanquished, so one must believe; yet by force did she
wish to be vanquished all the same. Often cried she, "Stay,"
when already Achilles was hasting from her; for, the distaff
put away, he had taken valiant arms.][51]

Although a common feature of classical literature, depictions of rape that emphasize female suffering in this way are rare in writing native to the Middle Ages. As Corinne Saunders has noted, two of the period's most popular genres—chivalric romance and saints' lives—repeatedly invoke the specter of rape only to defer it: "Abductions occur, rape and enforced marriage are threatened, but the woman's honor is almost invariably upheld."[52] While we can find some instances of unapologetic rape in the classically inspired Latin Elegiac comedy, and in the Old French pastourelle, it rarely appears elsewhere in medieval literature.[53]

As Diane Wolfthal has demonstrated in her study of rape imagery in medieval and Renaissance art, views of rape in the Middle Ages are unstable and contradictory, varying dramatically between a variety of different discourses.[54] Censure of rape is common in Christian discourse, due to the canon law's emphasis on the importance of individual will. In spite of its narrow and idiosyncratic definition of the crime, canon law recognizes rape as an act of violence against women and classifies it as an *enormis delicta*. Gratian distinguishes rape as a crime more serious than any other kind of illicit coitus.[55] The English theologian and canonist Thomas of Cobham describes rape as "a detestable crime, according to both divine and secular law."[56] Condemnations of rape are also prevalent in Christian texts and imagery. Wolfthal's survey of picture Bibles produced through the twelfth to fifteenth centuries reveals that they often show rape as a terrible act of violence that causes pain and sorrow to women.[57] Both canon and secular statutes rendered the crime punishable by death.

Questions relating to female volition also carry over onto Chaucer's representation of Malyne's mother. As in the Malyne episode, Chaucer diverges from the tale's analogues by implying a violation in the second clerk's assault on the mother. While the analogues characterize the mother as innately devious and lascivious (*Gombert* refers to the mother throughout as "Dame Guile"), the mother of the *Reeve's Tale* is quite anxious to avoid the clerks. As she stumbles upon what she believes to be the clerks' bed, the mother quickly corrects herself, exclaiming "Ey benedicte! Thanne hadde I foul yspede!" (4220). The Reeve later seems to suggest that the mother enjoys the coitus ("So myrie a fit ne hadde she nat ful yoore" [4230]), but his description of John simultaneously implies that she undergoes a violent physical assault ("He priketh harde and depe as he were mad" [4231]).

The canon law's requirement that the victim be a virgin means that the assault on Malyne's mother would not be classified as rape in medieval law. And yet, classical discourse *does* classify the sexual assault of married women as rape. Most well known to Chaucer and his audience would have been the rape of Lucretia, which Chaucer narrates in the *Legend of Good Women*. Indeed, John's remark that "Unhardy is unseely" (4210), before he assaults Malyne's mother is very similar to Tarquinus's proverbial observation in the *Legend of Good Women* as he vows to assault Lucretia that "Hap helpeth hardy man alday" (1773).

By suggesting violence and lack of volition in the assaults on Malyne and her mother, Chaucer disrupts the fabliau obfuscation of rape as a fun and funny occurrence. In doing so, he accentuates the contradictions in medieval gender ideology, which at once dictates that women ought to be subject to male authority and yet values women's free will and autonomy. By characterizing the women as the victims, rather than the perpetrators, of the disruption that occurs in the miller's household, Chaucer implies that it is male rivalry, rather than female immorality and lust, that is a prime cause of social disorder.

The fact that these points are made in a tale that so closely parallels the *Knight's Tale* challenges the Knight's positive vision both of male violence and of chivalry's nurturing and protective approach to women. The Knight frequently mobilizes gender to justify and dignify Theseus' use of force. Theseus' conquest of Femenye instills civilization by defeating a barbarian female disorder and restoring women to their conventional passive supporting roles. Theseus' conquest of Thebes for the sake of the grieving Argive widows justifies women's subjection to male power by showing how male violence protects women. Finally, the Knight characterizes Theseus's command over Emelye as a benevolent exercise of power that protects Emelye and provides her with a good husband.[58]

The *Reeve's Tale* inverts that proposition, showing how women's subjection to an aggressive masculine authority does not protect them, but places them in the path of male violence. It is Symkyn's aggression and drive to dominate that sparks the clerks' violence; it is Malyne and her mother's status as Symkyn's property that makes them likely candidates for Aleyn and John's retribution. In the clerks' exchange in the darkened bedroom, Chaucer is at pains to show us that Aleyn and John are inspired to assault the women not by lust but by their shame at having been beaten by Symkyn and their desire to restore honor by exacting revenge. Aleyn lays out his motivations in the speech he makes to John directly before approaching Malyne's bedside:

> For, John," seyde he, "als evere moot I thryve,
> If that I may, yon wenche wil I swyve.
> Som esement has lawe yshapen us,
>
> . . .
>
> Oure corn is stoln, sothly, it is na nay,
> And we han had an il fit al this day;
> And syn I sal have neen amendement
> Agayn my los, I will have esement. (4177–79; 4183–86)

By his own report, Aleyn assaults Malyne because he regards her as Symkyn's property, and thus feels entitled to use her in compensation for the stolen flour. But this is only part of what the passage reveals. The esement justification is specious, even by Aleyn's own measure, since the flour for which he seeks compensation belongs not to him but to the college. Aleyn's reference to the "il fit" he and his companion have had that day indicates that his actual desire is not for compensation, but for revenge. He assaults Malyne because he has been shamed by Symkyn, and now seeks vengeance in a sexual assault that will at once assuage his damaged manhood by attesting to his ability to dominate others, and shame Symkyn by violating his daughter.

Aleyne's choice of Malyne as the instrument of his revenge, then, is based on her status as her father's property, both as a being who should, theoretically, be entirely under her father's control and as a vehicle for his social ascent. As Holly Crocker notes, later medieval English society regarded a man's regulation of the women and children in his household as the public account of his masculinity.[59] By raping Symkyn's daughter, Aleyn simultaneously illustrates

Symkyn's lack of power over his household and stymies his attempt to use his daughter as a vehicle of social advancement by compromising her value on the marriage market.

John's monologue in the passage following Aleyn's assault on Malyne emphasizes how rape can help a man avoid the shame of defeat. As John considers the consequences of Aleyn's action and meditates on his own situation, he indicates that Aleyn's violence will win praises from Soler Hall, while his own lack of action will earn him scorn as a fool (daf) and a weakling (cokenay):

> He has the milleris doghter in his arm.
> He auntred hym, and has his nedes sped,
> And I lye as a draf-sak in my bed;
> And when this jape is tald another day,
> I sal been halde a daf, a cokenay! (4204–8)

Fear of this shame finally motivates John's own assault. Immediately after considering the Soler Hall reaction, John rises from his own bed with the intent of tricking Symkyn's wife.

Chaucer connects the male conflicts of the *Knight's Tale* to those of the *Reeve's Tale* by his persistent use of chivalric language in the *Reeve's Tale*. Symkyn has obvious aristocratic pretensions, witnessed in the trouble he makes over his daughter's marriage and his fondness for the aristocratic color red. The clerks also mimic the nobility. They exit Soler Hall in knightly fashion, armed for battle, "With good swerd and with bokeler by hir syde" (4019). That pretension is comically dismantled when the clerks' horse is lost and they must put down their swords to pursue the errant beast. The desire to reverse this symbolic declassing through the rape is indicated by the clerks' return to chivalric language during the assaults on the women. When John cogitates on Aleyn's plan to "swyve" Malyne, he says Aleyn has "auntred him" (has taken a chance or a venture) and John, too, decides he will "auntre it,"—vocabulary that is often used in the context of chivalric bravery.[60]

The clerks' belief in rape as a means of restoring masculinity is in perfect keeping with what classical legend frankly acknowledges, but which romance and fabliau persistently obfuscate. As Marjorie Curry Woods has argued, the classical texts used by generations of medieval schoolboys closely associate rape with the development and assertion of masculinity. In the *Achilleid*, the rape of Deidamia marks the beginning of Achilles' transformation from a boy under the control of his mother to a hero of the Trojan war. Ovid also reflects this view in the *Ars Amatoria*, when he prefaces the rape of Deidamia with a lament about Achilles' feminine disguise:

> Quid facis, Aeacide? non sunt tua munera lanae;
> Tu titulos alia Palladis arte petas.
> Quid tibi cum calathis? clipea manus apta ferend est:

> [What does thou, Aeacides? wools are not your business; /
> By another art of Pallas thou seekest fame. / What hast
> thou to do with baskets? Thy arm is fitted to bear a shield].[61]

In the pseudo-classical *Pamphilus*, the old woman go-between encourages Pamphilus to rape by telling him to "be a man" when he is alone with Galathea and force the young girl into sex if she refuses it. In these texts, "boys learn about sexual violence as a method of defining their manhood and controlling their own lives."[62]

If defining manhood through rape was acceptable in classical culture, it was much less so in the medieval context wherein, as I have shown, Church authorities condemn rape as a terrible crime. By featuring men who engage in sexual violence in order to dominate other men, Chaucer underlines the fundamental contradiction in chivalric culture, which at once promises to protect women and makes them, through their subjection to men, pawns in male contests. This, too, represents a return to Statius, who shares Chaucer's interest in showing the damage that violent masculine conflict does to women.[63]

Malyne's Obscurity and Chaucer's Meaning

While the brutality of the rape scene is undeniable, Malyne's behavior the next morning seems to suggest that Chaucer agrees with the fabliau (and Ovid) regarding women's enjoyment of sexual violence. Malyne's adoration of the clerk and her willingness to help him is worth noting for reasons I will describe in more detail below, but I do not think we can ascribe it to Chaucer's desire to forward the belief that women love rape. Rather, the scene reveals Chaucer's dedication to making the women of the *Reeve's Tale* as passive and obscure as possible.[64]

When we consider Malyne, it is important to recognize how very little Chaucer tells us of her motivations and how much this is at odds not only with

the fabliau but also with classical legend treatments of female rape victims. If
Chaucer had wished to illustrate the misogynist principle that women love
rape, he could have told us that Malyne enjoyed the assault. This would have
been a simple matter, requiring the addition of no more than a single line of
poetry, and yet Chaucer includes no such information. After the narration of
Aleyne's assault, we hear nothing of Malyne or her perspective until John
addresses her in courtly terms and she responds in kind. Her eight-line aube, in
which she refers to Aleyne as "deere lemmen" (4240) and tells him the location
of the hidden cake, is her only speech in the entire 400-line tale. We are given
no additional information to justify her response to the coitus with Aleyne or
her motivation in betraying her father. The absence of explanation is remarkable not only in light of the attention Chaucer lavishes on the thoughts of the
tale's male characters, but also in the context of other fabliau rape narratives.
Although Malyne's quick and unexplained jump from girl being "swyved bolt
uprighte" (4266) to saccharine courtly lover appears to be in line with fabliau
misogyny, it is not, for the other extant fabliau rape tales are always careful to
dwell on the women's delight in their rapes.

Alternately, if Chaucer had wished us to read Malyne as a stupid and gull-
ible country girl, he could have followed the analogues in having the clerk
seduce Malyne with courtly language and the presentation of a "magic" ring
before the coitus. In the analogues, the young woman's motivations make psychological sense, her pretentions to gentillesse rendering her more than willing
to believe both in the ring's magic and in the clerk's love for her. Indeed, the
girl's active cooperation in the clerk's seduction is key to the tale's comedy and
to its burlesque use of romance tropes, for her undeserved pretentions to gentillesse are precisely what bring about her downfall.

Even in terms of the rape tales of classical legend, Chaucer's refusal to
provide us with an explanation for Malyne's behavior is unique. Like the
fabliau, classical legend portrayals of rape victims tend to make the reasons for
their reactions clear. Ovid is careful to tell us that Deidamia *wished* (*voluit*) to
be vanquished (700); Statius informs us that Deidamia keeps the rape a secret
because she fears her father will punish Achilles with death (665–67); and
Pamphilus de Amore is famous for Galathea's long speeches accentuating the
pain of rape.

Chaucer's refusal to explain Malyne's cooperative and loving attitude the
following morning renders her indulgence in courtly love language perplexing,
rather than amusing. As in so many other places in the *Reeve's Tale*, the faux-
courtly Aleyne-Malyne dialogue gestures at fabliau pleasures (in this case the

fun that could be made of an ignorant country girl) but then refuses to give the audience full access to them. Instead of laughing at the stupidity of an unrefined young woman, we are forced to puzzle over her motivations.

A Daughter's Desire: Malyne and Ariadne

At first glance, the *Reeve's Tale* seems to adhere to the fabliau trope of the male authority figure thwarted by unruly women. Like many fabliau husbands, Symkyn is cuckolded and suffers a humiliating defeat at the hands of a female relative. But in the nature of the betrayal, the *Reeve's Tale* and the fabliau diverge. Symkyn's most profound defeat occurs at the hands of his daughter, not his wife, a plot twist absent not only from the tale's analogues but from the fabliau generally. Like the rape, Symkyn's defeat at Malyne's hands introduces an un-fabliau-esque complexity into the narrative, once again putting pressure on the contradictions of medieval gender ideology by calling audience attention to a point where medieval discourses of gender conflict with one another.

Obsessed with the power dynamics of the marital relationship, the fabliau is rarely interested in intergenerational conflict. None of the approximately 150 extant fabliaux feature a daughter who betrays her father in the manner of Chaucer's Malyne.[65] The *Reeve's Tale's* three fabliau analogues are already somewhat unusual for their interest in a father-daughter relationship. None of them, however, include a daughter who causes her father to lose a contest with other men. Indeed, in *Le meunier* (7.80) (the sole analogue that includes Chaucer's grain-stealing miller), it is the wife, not the daughter, who tells the clerks of her husband's theft. Nor do the analogues, or any other fabliaux, characterize the daughter's sexual escapades as a violation of her father's social ambitions in the way that Chaucer does when he invests Symkyn with aristocratic pretensions and a hope that Malyne will marry up the social ladder "into som worthy blood of auncetrye" (3982).[66]

If the daughter who brings about her father's defeat in a contest with other men is absent from the fabliau, she is a familiar figure in classical legend, appearing in a variety of tales, many of which seem to have held a particular interest for Chaucer. Four of the nine classical narratives in the *Legend of Good Women*—those of Thisbe, Medea, Hypermnestra, and Ariadne—focus on daughters who betray their fathers.[67] In particular, the betrayal of Chaucer's Malyne gives the *Reeve's Tale* a rather uncanny resemblance to the Ariadne legend. Like Minos, who takes Athens, Chaucer's Symkyn has been victorious in depriving other men of property. Like Theseus, the clerks arrive in the victor's domain as representatives of those he has thwarted. And, also like Theseus, the clerks win back their lost property through an erotic engagement with the victor's daughter that prompts her to betray her father. The tale's final, climactic scenes (the frenzied battle in the darkened bedroom, the unexpected aid the clerks receive from the women, and their escape into the dawn) all echo Theseus' alliance with Ariadne and Phaedra, his battle with the Minotaur and subsequent flight from Crete.

As a betraying woman who is a daughter rather than a spouse, Malyne opens up an indeterminate middle ground between dutiful maiden and unruly wife that has been overlooked in the preceding two tales. While both the adulterous Alison and the compliant Emelye affirm men's right to control the desires of female family members, Malyne's erotic rebellion occurs at a moment of unusual conflict between medieval secular and ecclesiastical convictions regarding the limits of masculine authority over women. Secular culture tends to advocate the father's right to direct a daughter's erotic desires by choosing her husband. But ecclesiastical jurists and Church leaders advocate the doctrine that both men and women should exercise free will in their choice of marriage partner. Gratian's declaration in the *Decretals*, "ubi non est consensus utriusque, non est coniugium" (where they each do not consent, there is no marriage) sets Church policy.[68] From the twelfth century onward, Church courts dissolve marriages found to be arranged through fear or force and forbid families from forcing marriage partners on children or wards. According to canon law, even marriages already consummated could be dissolved if there were found to be serious defects in consent.[69] In England, as elsewhere, ecclesiastical courts consistently uphold the principle of free consent in marriages.[70] Throughout the thirteenth and fourteenth centuries, Church courts in England dissolve marriages if the complainant can prove that the alliance was conducted out of force and fear.[71]

Although the conflict between secular and ecclesiastical notions of marital consent is a perennial one throughout the high and later Middle Ages, the problem of rebellious daughters has particular pertinence in Chaucer's late fourteenth-century England. During the thirteenth and fourteenth centuries, English jurists introduce a number of statutes concerning rape and abduction that are aimed at giving families greater control over the romantic choices of their wards and daughters. Westminster II (1285) includes legislation aimed at closing a legal loophole that allowed young women to marry men of whom their families did not approve. Older statutes descended from Germanic law permitted a victim to marry her ravisher if she wished. The frequency with which such a measure was employed as a remedy in rape cases in post-conquest England strongly suggests that some young women were exploiting these laws by colluding in their own "abductions" as a way of publicly announcing a sexual relationship and thereby coercing reluctant families into accepting an unpopular marriage choice.[72] Westminster II closes this loophole by allowing juries to charge the ravisher, even if the woman herself consents to the ravishment after the fact. Thus, the family of the ravished woman does not have to depend on her to seek the indictment but can seek it themselves, a particularly useful right in cases where victim and ravisher are in collusion.[73]

A century later, the Statute of Rapes (1382) gives even greater privileges to families by allowing them to charge the ravisher with rape directly and to disinherit women from their dowers if they consent to rape after the fact, asserting that women who "post huiusmodi raptum huiusmodi raptoribus consenservint, quod tam Raptores sive Rapientes quam rapte et eorum quilibet decetero inhabilitentur et inhabiles sint ipso facto ad omnem hereditatem, dotem, sive conjunctum feoffamentum" (after such rape do consent to such ravishers, that as well as the ravishers, as they that be ravished, and every of them be from thenceforth disabled, and by the same Deed be unable to have or challenge all Inheritance, Dower, or Joint Feoffment after the death of their husbands and ancestors).[74]

The cumulative effect of these new statutes is to remove a woman's power to make her own choices—whether that means punishing her rapist or marrying a man of her own choosing—and to hand this power over to her male relatives or guardians. The importance of Sir Thomas West in the creation of the 1382 Statute of Rapes confirms that these laws were sought by the heads of upper-class families as a way to punish wards and daughters for making disadvantageous marriages and to limit the loss of land and assets should such a marriage take place. West lobbied for the 1382 statute after his only daughter was abducted by, and subsequently married to, one Nicholas Clifton, who was of lower social standing than the family.[75]

While the Symkyn family's peasant status would seem to set them apart from the concerns of English elites, Chaucer's use of an aristocratic vocabulary of marriage, inheritance and alliance in the tale invites us to read it in precisely this context. The parson, for instance, gives a generous dowry with his daughter so that Symkyn "sholde in his blood allye" (3946). Symkyn—proud that his wife is "ycomen of noble kyn" (3942)—is fiercely protective of Malyne's "lynage" (4272). Of particular interest is Symkyn's use of the term "disparage"

(4271) after learning of Aleyn's night with Malyne ["Who dorste be so boold to disparage / My doghtre, that is come of swich lynage?" (4271–72)]. Although Symkyn is responding to Aleyn's "swyving" of his daughter, the term is noteworthy because it is often used in Middle English to denote the social degradation of marrying below one's rank, a top concern for the authors of the 1382 statute.[76]

To a late fourteenth-century audience familiar with the conflicts between ecclesiastical and secular valuations of women's free will, Malyne's betrayal of her father calls attention to the fact that men's right to control women's desires is not as unassailable as the tales of the Knight and the Miller assume. Malyne may appear in the guise of an unruly fabliau wench but she is much less easy to condemn than the adulterous Alison because her betrayal of masculine authority occurs at a life stage when the Church advocates giving women's desire free play. Thus, Malyne's rebellion emphasizes that masculine command over women is not a natural, preordained condition but is a culturally determined concept subject to debate.

Why Gender? The *Reeve's Tale* and the *Legend of Good Women*

The notion that Chaucer's interrogation of fabliau gender politics in the *Reeve's Tale* is motivated by a desire to better women's status or examine their reaction to social oppression is disputed by his dismissive treatment of Malyne. While Chaucer's portrayal of Malyne reveals his desire to explore matters of free will and coercion, it also reveals that he had little interest in exploring women's perspectives. What Malyne thinks or how she reflects on her experience is simply left out, without explanation or justification. We are left to conclude that her perspective is simply unimportant.

Reading the *Reeve's Tale* in the context of the *Legend of Good Women* gives us insight into Chaucer's motivations for undercutting fabliau gender politics. In the *Legend of Good Women*, Chaucer also experiments with using fabliau discourse to enable a critique of aristocratic culture. Less successful than the sequence of Fragment One, Chaucer's failures in the *Legend of Good Women* reveal how the disruption of fabliau misogyny is essential to unleashing its capacity to critique the chivalric ethos. Similarities between the *Prologue* of the *Legend of Good Women* and the exchanges between men of the Miller's and Reeve's prologues, meanwhile, reveal that Chaucer sees gender as a useful heuristic device to explore relationships of socially legitimated coercion that were of concern to subordinate men like himself.

In the *Legend of Good Women*, Chaucer also combines the discourses of romance, classical legend, and obscene comedy as a way of exploring the contradictions and insincerities of chivalric culture. As in Fragment One of the *Canterbury Tales*, these experimentations center on Theseus and his history. In the *Legend of Good Women*, the Ariadne legend once again plays a central role in Chaucer's attempts to undercut chivalric ideology, only this time, its presence is literal rather than metaphoric. As he does in the *Reeve's Tale*, Chaucer brings together obscene-comic discourse and classical legend in the *Legend of Good Women*'s Ariadne. In the Ariadne, however, Chaucer does not make obscene comedy a separate object of critique the way he does in the first fragment of the *Canterbury Tales*. Instead, he focuses on a romance rendering of classical legend and attempts to use a traditional version of obscene comedy to undercut the courtly love discourse of the legend.

The results are very different from what we see in the *Reeve's Tale*. Rather than exposing the brutality and destructiveness of male struggles for power, the *Legend*'s Ariadne becomes a misogynistic send-up of aristocratic women, replacing courtly idealizations of noble ladies with the rapacious, sexually-hungry, and dishonest creatures of the fabliau. The failure of this particular fusion to interrogate forcefully or deeply the governing principles of the medieval aristocratic world is instructive, for it shows us why Chaucer chose to make the fabliau itself an object of interrogation, and how he came to be interested in defusing its misogyny.

Although it is difficult to place the *Legend of Good Women* chronologically, it has clear textual affinities with the *Knight's Tale* which indicate, as Lee Patterson remarks, "that Chaucer thought of them together."[77] Queen Alceste's reference in the *Legend*'s prologue to Chaucer's poem about "al the love of Palamon and Arcite / Of Thebes" (F, 420–21) indicates that some version of the *Knight's Tale* antedates the *Legend of Good Women*. Moreover, Chaucer's version of the Ariadne legend in the *Legend of Good Women* features several events that have no parallels with any other classical or medieval version of the Ariadne story, but that do parallel events in either the *Teseida* or the *Knight's Tale*.[78] In Boccaccio's *Teseida*, Palamon and Arcite are "in prigione / Allato allato al giardino amoroso."[79] In the *Knight's Tale*, the cousins' prison tower "evene joynant to the gardyn wal / Ther as this Emelye hadde hir pleyynge" (1060–61), while in the *Ariadne*, Theseus' prison is "joynynge in the wal to a foreyne" (1962) belonging to Ariadne and Phaedra. Although a toilet might not seem to have much to do with a garden, both garden and "foreyne" translate Boccaccio's "giardino."[80] In the *Teseida*, the proximity of the prison to Emilia's garden means that she overhears Arcite's complaints, in the same way that Ariadne and Phaedra hear Theseus' plaints as they stand out on the wall of their chambers in the moonlight (1970–72). In both the *Knight's Tale* and the *Teseida*, Arcite becomes the servant of Theseus. In the *Legend of Ariadne*, Theseus promises to serve in Minos's court as a page. The term of service Theseus promises in the Ariadne story is seven years, the length of Palamon's imprisonment in the *Knight's Tale*. Finally, the notion of the *Teseida* and the *Knight's Tale* as sources for parts of the *Ariadne* accounts for the strange slip wherein Ariadne and Phaedra's Cretan chamber is said to face "the maysterstrete / Of Athenes" (1965–66), the city in which both the *Knight's Tale* and the *Teseida* are set.[81]

As a number of critics have already pointed out, the *Legend of Good Women Ariadne* replaces the Knight's portrayal of an honorable leader with a sardonic critique of aristocratic pretensions to "gentillesse" that exposes, in the words of Florence Percival, the "lack of principle and naked expediency which are masked by the aristocratic ethos to which the *Legend*'s heroes conform and which was valorized in the *Knight's Tale*."[82] In the legends, as Patterson remarks, "*gentillesse* designates not nobility of spirit but social advantage, a superiority of place that unprincipled men use to victimize grasping women."[83]

The Ariadne legend is a natural choice for anyone wishing to interrogate Theseus' authority, since it exposes a rapacious and exploitative chapter in his career, of which medieval audiences thoroughly disapproved.[84] In the *Teseida*, Boccaccio suppresses Theseus's Cretan past by altering the classical chronology of his career and placing his encounter with the Minotaur *after* his defeat of the Amazons and dealings with Arcite and Palamon.[85] In the *Knight's Tale*, Chaucer also makes little mention of Theseus' past, but diverges from Boccaccio in cleaving to the original chronology, drawing his audience's attention to Theseus' shady past when he features the hero riding out to Thebes under a banner displaying "The Mynotaur, which that he wan in Crete" (980).

While other readers have noted the way that the *Legend of Ariadne* undercuts the chivalric ethos, they have not noticed that Chaucer frequently does so by resorting to fabliau misogyny. The influence of obscene comedy is evident in a series of references to sexuality and the lower bodily functions that dot the legend. Most obvious is the mention of the "foreyne" (or toilet) of the young princesses, on which Theseus's prison borders. As Sheila Delany has noted, "if the princesses from their quarters can overhear Theseus lament, does it not follow that he in turn must overhear them when nature calls?"[86] The reference thus functions not only as a degradation of Theseus but also of the princesses themselves, drawing attention to their bodily functions, specifically their excrement, in a way that is strictly forbidden in the discourse of medieval romance. Women's excrement is, however, a not uncommon focus of the fabliau, where we see narratives like *La crote* (6.57) ["the Turd"], in which a wife tries to beat her husband at a guessing game regarding what each person has in his or her hands by taking hold of a piece of her own excrement or *La coille noire* (5.46) ["Black Ball"] in which a wife goes to the bishop to annul her marriage based on the blackness of her husband's testicles, only to have the case dismissed when he claims that his anatomical darkness is caused by her failure to wipe after defecating.

A fabliau-esque sexual rapaciousness in the *Legend*'s women is also implied at a number of points. Phaedra's 20-line speech describing how Theseus might escape the labyrinth is full of obscene sexual puns. Phaedra's description of Theseus's "wepen," her plan to make him "balles" (of twine, ostensibly), and her remark that she and her sister will thereby discover "if that he be a man" intimate male sexual anatomy and performance, while her description of the labyrinth as a "krynkeled" passageway with "queynte" turns calls up images of the female genitalia. [87] In addition, the two princesses are figured not as chaste aristocratic maidens, but as a pair of fabliau-style floozies, "at a loose end and ripe for amorous adventure."[88] In a variation on the fabliau that is very similar to the *Reeve's Tale*, Chaucer invests his princesses with an ambition for social advancement. The two spend an inordinate amount of time musing on the great social advantages that will accrue from rescuing a "kinges sone" (1953).[89] Impressed by Theseus' courtly speech and pledge of seven years' service in exchange for her help, Ariadne gloats in a whisper to her sister over the advancement the two can expect if they help this highly ranked young man:

> Now be we duchesses, both I and ye,
> And sekered to the regals of Athenes,
> And bothe herafter likly to ben quenes. (2127–30)

Diverging from romance heroines—who are often passive bystanders, or at best helpers, in male-dominated pursuits—Chaucer characterizes the princesses with the agency, greed, and talent for trickery that are typical of fabliau women.

Chaucer's focus in the *Legend of Ariadne* on a chapter of Theseus' history that medieval audiences regarded as highly blamable suggests that he intends it as a critique of Theseus and, through him, of aristocratic culture. In the end, however, this attempt is thwarted by obscene comedy misogyny. Certainly, the *Legend of Ariadne* certainly does not cast male nobility in a favorable light: the vacuity of Theseus' courtly pledges is exposed when he abandons Ariadne on Naxos, in favor of the better-looking Phaedra. However, because Phaedra and Ariadne are the tale's primary agents, and because its satire of "gentillesse" focuses primarily on them, the weight of obscene parody also falls primarily on them. In the *Legend of Good Women Ariadne*, the cultural force of a long tradition of comic tale telling whose humor depends on invoking misogynistic views of women as rapacious, immoral, and lascivious takes over, shifting the brunt of Chaucer's critique away from masculine aristocratic culture and toward courtly idealizations of feminine virtue. In the end, the *Legend of Good Women*'s *Ariadne* undermines the God of Love's views on feminine virtue, but does little to critique the principles that inform his tyrannical behavior.

The limitations of the *Legend of Good Women Ariadne* demonstrate that harnessing the subversive energy of the fabliau to a broad critique of aristocratic culture requires a writer to find ways of destabilizing the genre's misogyny. That Chaucer does precisely this in the *Canterbury Tales'* first fragment suggests that the *Legend of Good Women* may have been the place where he learned the lesson regarding "the master's tools" that Lorde describes. In the *Reeve's Tale*, Chaucer inverts the proposition of the *Ariadne*, making obscene comedy the dominant mode and using classical legend and romance discourse to alter and disrupt it. By interrogating obscene comedy from the inside out and retreating from its misogynist valence, Chaucer is able to clear the field, and marshal obscene discourse to a more direct critique of aristocratic culture.

A second and equally significant reason for Chaucer's interest in medieval gender politics in the *Reeve's Tale* is suggested by the parallels Chaucer draws in the prologues of both the *Reeve's Tale* and the *Legend of Good Women* between the plight of women in a violent masculine culture and that of subordinate men. The *Legend of Good Women* prologue is famous for its evocation of an intellectual being brow-beaten by a bullying aristocratic authority. Having been condemned by an angry God of Love for authoring works insulting to women because they fail to cleave to courtly love dictates of admirable femininity, "Chaucer" in the Prologue of the *Legend of Good Women*, agrees to write "a glorious legende/Of goode wymmen, maydenes and wyves" (F 483–84). The *Reeve's Prologue* features a similar scene of a subordinate male being forced into a particular style of tale telling by an aggressive male authority figure. As I have noted earlier in the chapter, the Reeve does not initially wish to tell a fabliau but is forced to do so by the Host, whose aristocratic-style authority is emphasized in Chaucer's description of him issuing his commands in a manner "as lordly as a kyng" (3900). Like Chaucer in the *Legend of Good Women*, the Reeve agrees to tell a tale in the mode required of him but registers his displeasure by ruining the pleasures it promises.

The fact that the Reeve's own will is violated in the prologue to a tale about the violations of female will indicates Chaucer's interest in the connection between women's subjection and that of subordinate men. Indeed, the fate of male subordinates is a constant theme in all of the Fragment-One tales, even as they seem on the surface to be primarily concerned with the control and administration of women: there is the plight of the imprisoned Palamon and Arcite; the manipulations and struggles of Absolon and Nicholas; and, finally, the struggle of the *Reeve's Tale*'s own clerks to distinguish themselves in the eyes of the Soler Hall authorities. When we examine Chaucer's portraits of Malyne and her mother, we can see that his interest in the women begins and ends at precisely the point where their plight intersects with that of subordinate men in aristocratic culture: in the assertion of the individual will and its quashing through intimidation and force. Whereas a woman's reflections on and reaction to sexual assault is a distinctly gendered experience, her experience of coercion in the face of violent male authority is not, and this is the object of Chaucer's focus in his portrayal of Malyne.

Discourse and Power: Language and Force in the *Reeve's Tale*

Although Foucault believes in discourse's capacity to change over time, he also emphasizes the limited ability of individual authors to alter discourse. While Foucault does not entirely deny the phenomenon of literary creativity, he abjures that it only exists within the discursive constraints that enable ideas and texts to be produced in a given society.[90] An awareness of the constraints Foucault describes is written into Chaucer's portraits of both the Reeve and "Chaucer the narrator" in the *Legend of Good Women*. Both "Chaucer" and the Reeve are figured as wishing to speak of other things but are forced to speak in ways that are deemed appropriate by those who exert power over them. If their attempts are mangled, indirect or unclear, their coercion by authoritarian governors demands that we consider how other meanings might be encoded in their works.

This is also an issue at work in Malyne's recitation of the courtly aube. Chaucer provides no justification for Malyne's courtly speech, thereby investing her aube with a tone of oddity and inappropriateness. The elisions and lack of logical justification invite us to read Malyne's aube in the same way that we read the Reeve's and "Chaucer's" articulation of their respective discourses—as scripts that are uttered not out of sincere belief but because they are demanded by those in power. Similarly, Chaucer leaves us wondering whether Malyne's words signify real affection for the clerk, or whether she utters them because she has no other choice.[91]

Chaucer's understanding of discourse's power to determine what can or cannot be said or done might also be taken as index of his own limitations as an author. If the Reeve's critique of the Knight is profound, when read in a certain light, it is also obscure. As I have noted in my discussion of Langland, obscene comedy has a masking function for medieval authors, making subversive work appear to be, on the surface, conformist and conventional. This obscurity and adherence to convention, however, also has its risks. While the lower-class, degraded world of the fabliau gives Chaucer a certain freedom to critique the failings of violent male authority in a way he would never have been able to carry out if his characters had been aristocratic, it also means that the tale can be marshaled to precisely the ends it is at pains to resist. For those un-attuned to literary subtleties, the tale can easily be read as just another fabliau burlesque, in which a family of peasants and two student buffoons have their social pretentions brutally upended in a manner that only accentuates their own degradation.

If the potential contained in the paradoxical and unstable nature of obscene comedy is a boon to a writer interested in interrogating the established social order, it is also his greatest limitation. The powerful associations that audiences have with obscene comedy mean that in spite of all an author's alterations and redirections, the discourse still retains the capacity to reassert the very status quo that he seeks to avoid. That dynamic cuts both ways, however, as we shall see in the following chapter. Here, we see Chaucer's fifteenth century heir, John Lydgate, attempt to use obscene comedy to bolster the legitimacy of male authority, only to author a work that gives women a greater voice in the public sphere than they had ever had before.

PART II

Fifteenth-Century Heirs

CHAPTER 3

The Henpecked Subject

Misogyny, Poetry, and Masculine Community in the Writing of John Lydgate

Although renowned for having written in just about every late medieval genre and mode, John Lydgate seldom composed the humorous tales of marital strife and adultery of which his "maister" Chaucer was so fond. While the perfidy of women is a favorite theme of Lydgate's, his exposition is rarely comic, tending instead toward the censorious tone of clerical misogyny.[1] It is one of the ironies of history that, in spite of his general distaste for the discourse, Lydgate's few ventures into obscene comedy are among the works and passages most admired by modern readers. His most extended obscene comedy piece, the *Mumming at Hertford*, has been called by various critics "a landmark in the history of English drama," an "unexpected triumph," and a work that "reveals a talent for humour and satire to which [Lydgate] all too rarely gave expression."[2] Long regarded as a derivative and unsophisticated work, in spite of its charm, the *Mumming at Hertford* has drawn a number of insightful readings over the past decade. Nevertheless, Lydgate's humor (or lack thereof) has rarely been subjected to systematic analysis or connected to any of his major concerns.[3]

Lydgate's avoidance of comedy has often been written off as a sign of his awkwardness or lack of talent as a writer, but this analysis is not terribly credible. Whatever one might think of Lydgate's abilities, surely lack of talent could not have been the deciding factor that turned him away from the formulaic humor of the fabliau and toward lengthy epics, saints' lives, and *specula principum* instead. Indeed, the more carefully one considers it, the more notable the absence of obscene comedy in the canon of this otherwise omnivorous writer appears to be. As a cleric, Lydgate was primed by both custom and education to indulge fulsomely in obscene comedy, which, as I have noted in the Introduction to this study, is a staple mode of communication in the medieval Church, appearing frequently in sermons, church architecture, and other forms of ecclesiastical writing. As an author of secular works, too, Lydgate ought to have been interested in fabliau-style narratives, given their popularity and the interest they held for his artistic paragon, Chaucer.

More notable still is the fact that Lydgate's few ventures into obscene comedy almost all occur in works of high profile that are closely associated with his career as laureate poet to the Lancastrians.[4] The *Mumming at Hertford* was commissioned by a courtier and presented to the young King Henry VI and his mother at Hertford Castle over Christmas. Obscene comedy is also a feature in two major works of Lydgate's laureate career. The *Troy Book*, commissioned in 1412 by the future Henry V when he was still prince of Wales, is punctuated with a series of asides in which Lydgate humorously plays out a fearful man/ aggressive woman scenario by reciting long misogynist passages and then appending them with ridiculously exaggerated praises of women created in supposed fear of his female audience's anger. A similar passage, as well as a portrait of Orpheus as the downtrodden husband of a shrewish Eurydice, appears in Book One of the *Fall of Princes*, a work commissioned by Henry V's brother Humphrey, duke of Gloucester.

Both Lydgate's avoidance of obscene comedy and his selective use of it in works of political import are a sign of the profound changes in the status of the discourse in England as a result of Langland's and Chaucer's innovations. Lydgate's commitment to upholding established powers is well known. He shows little interest in demanding that medieval elites attend to their duties (as Langland does) or in pulling the rug out from under their self-justifying ideologies, in the manner of Chaucer. Instead, Lydgate upholds the authority of king and Church. His allegiances in this regard align with those of earlier forms of obscene comedy, like the fabliau, the Latin elegiac comedies, and the sermon exempla of the twelfth through early fourteenth centuries. Lydgate's scrupulous avoidance in the early fifteenth century of a discourse that had once been the stock in trade of establishment writers reveals how profoundly Langland's and Chaucer's interventions had altered the political valence of obscene comedy, accentuating its semiotic instability and giving it subversive associations it had not previously had.

Nevertheless, even Lydgate is not inured to obscene comedy's political appeal. It is no coincidence that his few evocations of the discourse occur exclusively in his laureate texts, which are also works that engage with matters of politics and policy. Deliberately opposing Chaucer, Lydgate crafts his own version of obscene comedy, repeatedly emphasizing certain elements of it, while ignoring or redirecting others. These alterations help Lydgate formulate some of his most original and arresting political visions, allowing him to imagine an all-male political community unified across class and to promote royal authority in a way suited to the changed political realties of the fifteenth century.

As in the case of Langland, understanding Lydgate's obscene comedy requires that we re-examine some long-held assumptions about the nature of his work and politics. Primary among these is a reevaluation of Lydgate's misogyny. Although Lydgate's fondness for misogynist invective is well known and well acknowledged, it is generally written off as an uninteresting repetition of medieval commonplaces, rather than a dynamic entity that is an integral part of the poet's literary and intellectual agenda.[5] Nor have scholars given much credit to the notion that Lydgate's misogyny was anything unusual or remarkable in the eyes of his original audience.

In fact, neither assumption is true. Both misogyny and women's role in public life were subjects of considerable debate in the early years of the fifteenth century. Lydgate's career is contemporaneous with the most articulate and authoritative challenge ever to be issued against misogyny in the whole of the medieval period, in the person and writings of Christine de Pisan, a figure who presents a distinct threat to Lydgate not only because of her intellectual cogency but also because of her popularity among the Lancastrians. In addition, the royal court in the first decades of the 1400s includes a number of powerful and controversial women, like Joanne of Navarre (Henry IV's queen) and Catherine of Valois (wife of Henry V and later dowager queen during the minority of Henry VI).

Nor is Lydgate's misogyny simply rote or commonplace. It is, in fact, a purposeful and well-considered gambit, closely linked to his two most cherished enterprises: his mission to construct poetry as an authoritative public discourse and his desire to establish himself as laureate poet to the Lancastrian regime. A close examination of these projects reveals that both required Lydgate to assert and keep current a philosophy of male superiority and female perfidy. Misogyny is an integral part of Lydgate's attempt to create a community of male readers whose loyalties transcend the boundaries of rank. Moreover, as a monk, his authority is predicated on misogyny, since freedom from the malign influence of women is a key element in the monk's claim to objectivity and wisdom.[6] Finally, Lydgate's desire to present himself as a mediator in public affairs requires him to promote misogynist notions of women's duplicity and moral instability, since this role was very similar to the mediating function often accorded to noblewomen.

If we examine Lydgate's obscene comedy in the context both of his own career and of the waxing and waning of women's power in the first decades of the fifteenth century, we can see that it tends to emerge at those moments when Lydgate wishes to promote the hatred of women, but cannot do so unambigiously, either because anti-misogynist critiques are culturally ascendant or because there are certain powerful women he cannot afford to insult openly. In these cases, the semiotic instability of obscene comedy (most of the time so distasteful to Lydgate) becomes useful to him. In ironic and comical asides, Lydgate works to uphold his own authority and enforce an all-male community by appealing to obscene comedy characterizations of women as violent, dishonest, and irrational.

Also crucial to our understanding of Lydgate's obscene comedy is his desire to short-circuit middle-rank claims to entitlement. Like Christine's protofeminist stance and the rise of powerful Lancastrian women, the burgeoning middle ranks are a threat to the hierarchies that Lydgate wishes to uphold. In his attempt to come to grips with this problem, we see him turning to obscene comedy for the same reason that Chaucer and Langland turn to it, as a place whose mood of riotous inversion allows a writer to consider new forms of social and political relationships. While Lydgate is invested in upholding the privileges of medieval elites, he is not opposed to innovation. Well aware that the changed political and economic environment of the fifteenth century required new models of ruler-subject relations, Lydgate uses obscene comedy to reinvent royalty's relation to the common man.

In this respect, Lydgate's work is a fascinating early stage in the development of the household-state analogy that was to dominate political thought in the early modern period.[7] It has long been recognized that the early modern preoccupation with thinking about the king as a father and the father as a king represents a departure from medieval political paradigms. The exact evolution of this change has, however, remained obscure. Lydgate's obscene comedy represents an important missing link in that evolution. Drawn to the discourse's focus on the domestic, Lydgate breaks down the barriers obscene comedy erects between the court and the home, the lower ranks and the aristocracy, in order to establish a cross-rank homosocial community based on the shared problem of women. In doing so, he promotes a political imaginary based on a convergence between the power relations of the household and those of the state. In breaking with the medieval notion of the polity as an organically interdependent body, Lydgate predicts the early modern analogy of the household as a state in miniature and the king as father to his people.[8]

Lydgate's dedication to the established order may make him appear like an outlier in this study, which is otherwise concerned with works that interrogate the status quo. In this respect, Lydgate is, indeed, different. Nevertheless, he shares with the other writers of this study a political orientation in the sense that he wishes to influence and intervene in the power relations of his society. And, in spite of his establishment mentality, Lydgate is an innovator in his own right. As Larry Scanlon remarks of Langland's politics, the categories of "radical" and "conservative"—wherein an interest in social reform is aligned with a desire to break from the past—are ill suited to the political discourse of the later Middle Ages.[9] While dedicated to upholding established powers, Lydgate is nevertheless aware of the need to recast that power in new terms. Indeed, politically, Lydgate is perhaps the most innovative writer in this study in the sense that he portrays new political relationships more explicitly and concretely than any of the others.

Part I: The *Mumming at Hertford*'s Unique Version of Obscene Comedy

The *Mumming at Hertford* is a performance piece of some 250 lines in which a group of henpecked husbands appear before the king to complain of their shrewish wives. John Shirley's headnote to the *Hertford* text claims it was presented to the king at Hertford Castle at Christmas. The date of the *Mumming*'s performance is not certain, but most estimates place it during the Christmas season of 1427, when six-year-old Henry VI was likely in residence at Hertford Castle with his mother, Catherine of Valois.[10]

The Hertford performance begins with a long speech by a presenter introducing five "rustics" who come before the king on the evening before the New Year to complain about the shrewishness of their wives. The presenter introduces the husbands one by one, describes the abuses of their wives, then appeals to the king to modify the "Olde Testament" of women's right to have the "hyegher hande" (146, 144). In the second part of the *Mumming*, a single wife stands forward to defend herself and her cohort from the charges. The wife argues that women have the right to torment their husbands and appeals to the king to uphold the "statuyt" of women's mastery (213). In the *Mumming*'s final segment, the king promises to examine whether the husbands have any legal right to object but vows to uphold the wives' dominance over the next year. He concludes by warning that it is unlikely the husbands will find legal proofs for their right to "soueрayntee" over their wives (244).

Long admired for its comic appeal, the *Mumming at Hertford* has emerged as a focus of serious critical interest in recent years and has been the subject of a number of insightful readings.[11] Although these studies have rightly identified the *Mumming*'s fusion of political language, courtly setting, and domestic comedy as an arresting and original combination, they have tended to characterize Lydgate's project as a negative one, aimed at either rejection or containment of threats from subordinate members of his society.[12] I do not deny that containment and rejection are important to Lydgate in this text, but I also want to consider how these ends are achieved through a re-envisioning of hierarchical relationships that is actually quite innovative. In spite of his apparent dislike of it, Lydgate makes good use of obscene comedy in the *Mumming at Hertford*, exploiting its riotous, world-upside-down mood in order to imagine new political and social formations. Crucial to Lydgate's politics in the *Mumming at Hertford* is gender, an element of the work that has still not been fully explored. Although Lydgate explicitly presents household politics as the focus of the piece, gender has not been a subject of sustained interest in most of the recent analyses of the *Mumming at Hertford*.[13] In what follows, I want to take Lydgate at his word and think carefully about what his fusion of household and court tells us about misogyny and its role in the politics of the broader community.

In her study of Lydgate's attempt to create a public culture in England during the minority of Henry VI, Maura Nolan proposes that the Hertford performance represents Lydgate's rejection of what she calls "Chaucerian comedy." Reading the cultural transformations of this period as being carried out through literary form, Nolan argues that Lydgate rejects Chaucer's comedy as a mode whose optimistic move from "woe to wel" is inadequate to the tragic realities that arise in the wake of Henry V's death.[14] Nolan is right to note Lydgate's distaste for Chaucer's comedy, but I think she misunderstands the reasons for his dislike and overstates his rejection of it. A central problem in Nolan's analysis lies in the way she equates Chaucer's fabliaux with the definition of classical comedy that Lydgate outlines in the *Troy Book*. In fact, Lydgate never identifies medieval obscenity with classical comedy; nor does Chaucer, who consistently refers to his fabliaux not as comedy but as "harlotrye" (Chaucer, *Miller's Prologue*, 3184), a vocabulary that also follows the usage of William Langland.[15]

While the movement from "woe to wel" that Nolan describes certainly applies to classical and Renaissance theatrical comedy, it does not cohere with medieval obscenity. Neither Chaucer's fabliaux nor any of the other forms of medieval obscene comedy popular in the fifteenth century can be said to conclude on a harmonious note. Chaucer's *Miller's Tale* ends with the defeat of John and the scalding of Nicholas; the *Reeve's Tale* ends with the beating and humiliation of Symkyn the miller. The *Merchant's* and the *Shipman's Tales*, meanwhile, resolve on false harmonies, wherein the depredations of women are concealed and the patriarch continues in laughable ignorance. Indeed, the discourse's "'twas ever thus" philosophy rejects any notion of evolution or resolution. Instead, riot and inversion are given free play through the course of the narrative and then are either brought into submission by a senior male or, as is more often the case, continue on merrily, unabated. Moreover, if Lydgate's rejection of Chaucerian comedy is, as Nolan argues, the result of Henry V's death in 1422, it is difficult to understand why we do not see more of it in his early work and why he returns to it in the *Fall of Princes*, a poem written well after the king's demise.

As I have already noted, Lydgate's reasons for rejecting obscene comedy in the majority of his oeuvre likely had less to do with its innate unsuitability than with what it had become by the early fifteenth century, thanks to Langland and Chaucer. This general rejection makes the *Mumming at Hertford* all the more remarkable as Lydgate's one complete venture into the discourse. If, as Nolan proposes, the rejection of Chaucerian comedy were Lydgate's main purpose in writing the *Mumming at Hertford*, it is difficult to see why he felt compelled to articulate it in a piece that embodied the very object of his contempt. A more credible and likely conclusion is that Lydgate engages in obscene comedy in this particular instance because he finds a way to make it serve his intellectual and artistic purposes.

Reading the *Mumming at Hertford* in the context of obscene comedy reveals that Lydgate is selective and purposeful in his use of the discourse. Dominating the *Mumming* is the specter of the shrewish wife and the passive, long-suffering husband. All five of the Hertford women dispense beatings with little provocation. Beatrice Bittersweet serves her husband Robin the Reeve only lean gruel for supper and hits him if he complains; Cicely Sourcheer argues with her husband and beats him, as does "fierce" Parnell, who hits her husband Bartholemew over the head with a skimmer. The men, meanwhile, are uniformly browbeaten and passive. Not a single Hertford husband fights back against his wife.

Lydgate's portrait of unrestrained female aggression and total masculine submission is quite unusual, both in light of the *Mumming*'s supposed debts to Chaucer and in the context of fifteenth-century obscenity. Chaucer's fabliaux avoid the trope of the henpecked husband, favoring husbands who are dominant, even domineering.[16] In the obscene comedy of the fifteenth century, husbands may be dominated but tend to put up more of a fight than Lydgate's beaten creatures.[17] The husband of the fifteenth-century English *Tale of the Basin* begins as a passive sufferer but eventually rouses himself, with the help of his brother, to assert control over his domineering wife.[18] In the French farces of the fifteenth century, likely known to Lydgate from his travels in France, even the most henpecked of husbands show more verve than Lydgate's men. In the *Farce des Drois de la Porte Bodès*, a piece remarkably similar to the *Mumming at Hertford* in many respects, the husband of a disobedient and violent wife suffers in the style of Lydgate's men.[19] In the *Farce des Drois*, however, the husband's verbal and physical aggression are equal those of his wife. Indeed, it is he who initiates the fight.[20]

In spite of Lydgate's investment in female domination, one significant medieval symbol of it is strangely absent from the *Mumming at Hertford*.[21] While adulterous wives are omnipresent in fifteenth-century comedy and predominate in the work of Chaucer, Lydgate declines to portray them here.[22] This is remarkable not only in light of obscene comedy but also in the context of Lydgate's other work, in which he shows himself more than capable of dwelling on female sexual perfidy.[23]

Of particular interest is Lydgate's use of Chaucer in the *Mumming*. In certain respects, the performance comes off as a slavish imitation of Chaucer, and this is certainly how it was perceived for many years. Lydgate names the Wife of Bath and often includes lines that are identical or very similar to lines in Chaucer's obscene comedy. The work is not, however, as deferential to the master as is it might initially appear to be. In fact, Lydgate's use of Chaucer is highly selective, including only those portions of Chaucer's poetry that support Lydgate's own vision of obscene comedy as a showcase for female aggression and male passivity and ignoring those elements of Chaucer that challenge or reform the discourse's misogyny. Nolan proposes that Lydgate announces his rejection of Chaucer in the *Mumming at Hertford*, but I would propose that his purpose here is more subtle, involving an attempt to invest his own misogyny with greater authority by remaking Chaucer in a Lydgatean mold.[24]

If we examine Lydgate's references to the Wife of Bath in the the *Mumming at Hertford*, we can see that they focus primarily on the wife's shrewish abuse of her first three husbands. Lydgate has his own wife cite Chaucer's lady as one who "Cane shewe statutes moo þan six or seven / Howe wyves make hir housbandes wynne heven" (168–70); he recycles the Wife's reference to the Dunmowe bacon (186–87; compare *CT* 218) and expands considerably on the legal discourse the Wife uses to describe her tactics in her first three marriages.[25] And yet Lydgate makes no reference to the Wife's interest in sexuality or to her use of sex as a tool of manipulation; nor does he show any interest in the classical and early Christian traditions of misogyny that dominate so much of Chaucer's text. Not a single reference to Jerome's *Adversus Jovinianum* or Theophrastus's *Book of Marriage* appears in the whole of the *Mumming of Hertford*, a remarkable omission given Lydgate's fondness for authoritative misogyny. Also unacknowledged is Chaucer's attempt to move beyond an oppositional model of gender relations at the conclusion of the *Wife of Bath's Prologue*, when the Wife and Jankyn negotiate a power-sharing agreement in their marriage.

Lydgate's decision to situate his obscene comedy in the king's court is also notable for its divergence from Chaucer's fabliaux. Chaucer's comedy (and most fifteenth-century English tales of marital strife) take place in a hermetically sealed domestic universe that has little or no contact with public institutions of governance.[26] Chaucer's fabliaux entertain courtly audiences, but no king, duke, or prince enters their narrative environs, and no Chaucerian husband takes his grievances to a court of law.[27]

It is quite possible that Lydgate's interest in the law in the *Mumming at Hertford* was inspired by French farce, a genre known for its inclusion of courtroom scenes and legal language in comedies of domestic strife. The earliest manuscripts of French farces date from the latter half of the fifteenth century and thus might appear to have been authored too late to influence Lydgate. Farces are, however, notoriously difficult to date, and the scholarly consensus is that many farces were being played long before the dates of their earliest extant manuscripts.[28] Most notably, records from the royal court of Paris show payments for the performance of farces dated 1388, 1409, and 1415.[29] Lydgate may possibly have seen a farce during his sojourn in France with the Duke of Bedford from approximately 1426 to 1429.[30] There is a record of the Basochiens, the French association of legal clerks responsible for many of the farces, performing the "Mystery of the Old Testament" during the duke of Bedford's entry into Paris as regent for Henry VI in 1424.[31] One wonders what other dramas they might have performed for the duke during his time in France. Certainly other parts of Lydgate's oeuvre show the influence of French obscene comedy. *Bycorne and Chychevache*, a short poem concerning patient husbands and unruly wives, was likely inspired by what Lydgate saw or heard in France.[32]

Lydgate gives farce legalities his own unique spin when he has his Hertford couples submit their dispute not to an anonymous judge, as is the case in farce, but to the king himself. This royalist orientation accords with Lydgate's interest in promoting the king's authority. It also represents a marked change in the relationship between the elites and the lower orders. Whereas obscene comedy takes for granted that the marital problems of the third estate are not a concern for elites, other than as a source of amusement, Lydgate's piece proposes that elites ought to be regulating the lower-order household and taking its concerns seriously.

Another notable divergence from obscene comedy lies in Lydgate's treatment of the henpecked husbands in the *Mumming at Hertford*. In the farce, the fabliau, and fifteenth-century English comic tales, weak husbands are the butt of the joke, ridiculed for their inability to exert appropriate masculine control over family and household. The husband of the *Farce des Drois de la Porte Bodès* is a laughingstock for having been beaten in a physical contest by his wife. In the *Tale of the Basin*, a submissive husband, aided by his priest brother, comes up with a plot to humiliate his adulterous wife. After doing so, he returns to his position of dominance in the marriage, and he and the wife live happily ever after "withowt stryfe" (221).[33]

The ridicule of male weakness and affirmation of forceful husbandly behavior is absent from Lydgate's *Mumming*, which neither punishes nor admonishes the henpecked husbands. No character in the Hertford *Mumming* ever denigrates the husbands or suggests that they should display more assertiveness in controlling their wives. Nor does the presenter or anyone else in the *Mumming at Hertford* (except the unruly wives themselves) ever offer up retributive violence as a solution.

Instead of punishing his Hertford husbands, Lydgate deploys a misogamist discourse that characterizes marriage as an innately corrupt institution that can never be altered by *any* man, no matter how forceful or physically powerful. Even Bartholemew the Butcher, the one Hertford husband who exhibits the hallmarks of dominant masculinity [he is a "stoote and bolde" man with a "broode knyff" and a belly "rounded lyche an ooke" (91, 93, 99)], is impotent before the power of his ladle-wielding wife Pernell, who can defy "His pompe, his pryde, with a sterne thought, / And sodeynly setten him at nought" (97–98). The king himself affirms that misery in marriage is intrinsic to the institu-

tion, when he remarks in his concluding comments that "whoo is wedded
lyueþe euer in seruage" (250).

The Mumming at Hertford *and the Legal Regulation of the Shrew*

Lydgate's sympathetic treatment of the henpecked husbands and his subjection
of household politics to royal judgment suggest that the unruly woman ought
to be subject to state authority. Unlike the farce, which invites its audience to
laugh at the ludicrous notion that domestic disputes might be regulated by the
law, Lydgate's *Mumming* treats it as a valid possibility. The husbands are not
ridiculed for their inability to control their wives, and the king himself takes
the husbands and their problems seriously.

The *Mumming*'s comic use of legal language repeatedly draws audience
attention to the absence of legal regulation for female unruliness. The notion
that men could appeal to the king to alter some kind of "statute" allowing
wives to annoy and beat their husbands is funny because *there are no statutes*
regulating domestic behavior. Instead, the *domos* operates according to its own
unwritten law that, in its promotion of women, is at odds with the covenants
governing the rest of society. In spite of the ironic respect that all of the *Mumming at Hertford*'s characters display toward these fictional domestic "statutes,"
Lydgate's presenter is careful to draw our attention to their horrid unnatural-
ness. As the presenter tells the king when he begs his majesty to alter the "Olde
Testament" of wives' rule,

> For it came neuer of nature ne raysoun,
> A lyonesse toppresse þe lyoun,
> Ner a wolfesse, for al hir thyraunye,
> Ouer þe wolf to haven þe maystrye. (1151–54)

Lydgate's attempt to figure female behavior as an issue of public concern
is notable for the way it reflects trends that historians have observed in
fifteenth-century courts. Marjorie McIntosh's study of juries convened in the
courts of England's market towns shows a gradual rise between the late fourteenth and the end of the sixteenth century in concern over social misbehavior
not explicitly forbidden by law.[34] The most common offense reported by juries
in the first half of the fifteenth century is scolding, a charge that could denote
either argumentative speech or the spreading of malicious gossip. Scolding is

an overwhelmingly female offense from the later fourteenth century through the 1510s.[35] During this period, the great majority of those presented for scolding—between eight and nine tenths of the total—were women.[36]

A similar trend toward characterizing the unruly woman as a serious, rather than a comic, problem has been observed in the literature of the later fifteenth and early sixteenth centuries. In his survey of antifeminist satire from the early Middle Ages until 1568, Francis Utley notes that the last sixty-eight years of the survey account for over half the antifeminist pieces he catalogues. Like Lydgate, these later writers invest the stock figures of obscene comedy with a tone of increasing seriousness, creating an environment in which obscene comedy loses its humor and becomes more literal.[37]

Emasculation Nation: Henpecked Husbands and the Ideal Subject

Lydgate's selective evocation of obscene comedy and his attempt to configure the unruly woman as a social problem are part of a broader initiative in the *Mumming at Hertford* aimed at exploiting misogyny in order to reassert royal authority and quell burgeoning middle-rank claims to political entitlement. Seen in light of the fractious relationship between English elites and their subjects in the seventy-five years following the Black Death, the *Mumming at Hertford* emerges as a politically innovative piece. Converting aristocratic contempt for the lower orders' supposed lack of forceful masculinity into sympathetic commiseration, Lydgate founds a new model of subject-ruler relations based on shared misogyny and locates, in the obscene comedy trope of the submissive and downtrodden husband, a model of the ideal male subject.

Historians have long observed that the late fourteenth and fifteenth centuries see an increasingly aggressive insistence on the part of the middle ranks to have a say in the governance of a variety of different spheres. This movement is most conspicuously witnessed in the numerous outbreaks of rebellion in the period, including the revolutions of 1381 and 1450, and significant popular insurrections in 1377, between 1399 and 1405, in 1414, and in 1431. Perhaps even more significant, though, is the growing political activity and sense of entitlement exhibited among the lower orders on a daily basis. John Watts notes that, in England in the late fourteenth and fifteenth centuries, "for the first time, the confident use of public speech and action by lower social groups was a recurring and recognized feature of the political scene."[38] Lower-rank individuals, moreover, "possessed numerous means of political organization and many reasons to engage in it. As office holders, tax payers, . . . representatives of the community of the vill, attenders at country courts—so voluble and confident that some of them had to be formally excluded from the parliamentary franchise in 1429; as petitioners to the king, his chancellor, his parliaments, as jurors and oath-helpers, as militiamen and coast guards, as constables and churchwardens, the upper ranks of the peasantry . . . were in contact with the world of government."[39] This new political entitlement sparked numerous microconflicts between the lower orders and the elites over liberties, privileges, and rents. Everyday acts of resistance by peasants and middle-rank people against their secular and monastic landlords were omnipresent in England during the later medieval period, producing what David Rollison calls "a tremendous pressure from below" that substantially changed English political culture between the fourteenth and the seventeenth centuries.[40]

An outstanding instance of this persistent low-level resistance can be found in Lydgate's own home of Bury St. Edmunds, where a series of lawsuits in the fifteenth century bears witness to an ongoing conflict between the townspeople and the abbey.[41] Rich from the Suffolk wool trade, the townspeople of Bury were anxious to throw off the financial burdens and other restrictions imposed by their monastic landlord. Their desires clashed with the Abbey of St. Edmunds, which resolutely enforced its economic monopolies and tithes. This conflict resulted in what Robert Gottfried calls "a bitter struggle which encompassed nearly every aspect of the history of late medieval Bury."[42]

While Chaucer seems to accept and even to advocate this burgeoning middle-rank confidence in his portrait of the Host and the guildsmen of the *Canterbury Tales General Prologue*, whom he describes as wise and worthy to govern as marshals and aldermen (I 371–72, 751–52), Lydgate seeks to obliterate it. Although the presenter describes the husbands as "poure lieges" (4), "sweynes" (rustics) (6), and "hynes" (farm laborers or servants) (25), the men's occupations associate them more with the middle ranks than the rural peasantry. There is Hobbe the Reeve, whose occupation associates him with leadership. There are also Bartholemew the Butcher and Colin the Cobbler, two crafts associated more closely with late medieval towns and villages than with isolated rural areas. Similarly, the wives' names associate them less with peasant wives than with market-oriented urban women. "Tybot Tapister" is an alewife and "Phelyce . . . þe wafurer" is a baker (128).

By characterizing middle-rank men as peasants, Lydgate engages in a form of political degradation also practiced by the chroniclers of the 1381 rebellion, who referred to the rebels as "rustics," "servants," and "mobs," despite the fact that many of them were middle-rank community leaders.[43] Casting the husbands as ineffective domestic leaders also a denigrates their political status since, in the later Middle Ages, a man's legitimacy as a community leader was closely associated with his ability to be a dominant partner in marriage and a leader of his household. In the bourgeois communities of fifteenth-century London, a man's reputation and status depended on "his ability to protect and control his dependents and to represent them in the political arena."[44]

In the *Mumming*'s husband-wife debate, Lydgate's references to landlord-tenant conflict turn the domestic incompetence of middle-rank men into a justification for their political disenfranchisement. The husbands frequently use vocabulary that identifies them with town and city dwellers. For instance, they beg the king for "fraunchyse and also liberte" (138). The word "franchise" could denote a whole variety of privileges, but, when used in conjunction with "libertees," it is most likely to be associated with the rights given to burgesses by the lord to ease trade.[45] Thus *The Little Red Book of Bristol* declares no person may hold a house or a shop in the city "vnto he be accepted free burgeys to *the libertees and franchise* of Bristow" (italics mine).[46]

The wives, meanwhile, are often described in terms that associate them with lordship. They claim mastery by "prescripcyoun, / Be long tytle of successyoun" (203–4), echoing the language by which landlords justified their privilege. The wives also evoke the aristocratic practice of trial by combat when they vow that, if chiding does not work, they will prove their rights "in chaumpcloos by bataylle" (166). The beatings Parnell bestows on Bartholemew are figured according to the language of wages. She faithfully pays him his "quarter sowde" (a word denoting wages paid four times a year) "And his waages, with al hir best entent" (112).

One might assume that identifying aristocratic landlords with unruly women would work to the advantage of middle-rank claims, suggesting that the landlords ought to defer, just as the wives should. In Lydgate's construction, this is not the case. The king claims he is unable to change the statue justifying wives' power in the household. The husbands' inability to do so themselves, meanwhile, bears witness to their incompetence as leaders and their need for paternalistic rule.

If Lydgate's portrait of the husbands undermines their claims to political enfranchisement, his newly sympathetic attitude to the henpecked husband seeks to celebrate middle-rank male passivity. Revealing a keen awareness of the way that notions of appropriate masculinity in the household inform men's behavior in the political sphere, Lydgate seeks to celebrate the husbands' passivity as a way of creating a deferential middle-rank male subject. If men are not enjoined to assert dominance in the household, Lydgate's logic goes, they will not be inspired to dominate in the political sphere either. Instead, the king will dominate in both areas.

By characterizing the wives' unruliness as a problem requiring a political resolution, Lydgate adapts the old feudal model of lower-order labor in exchange for higher-order protection to the social and economic realities of the fifteenth century. In the more politically stable, mercantile world of the later Middle Ages, the warrior's protection is increasingly obsolete. Lydgate's vision of dangerously unruly women replaces "the enemy without" that justified the old feudal system with an "enemy within." Rather than the incursions of wild animals or outsiders, the new source of misery and suffering for the lower ranks comes from within their own households, in the form of violent, ungovernable women. It is worth noting how this characterization of women aligns with the Lancastrian campaign to situate Lollardy as a dangerous internal threat. As Strohm notes, Henry IV and V "are the first English kings to grasp the sense in which orthodoxy and legitimacy might be defined and dramatized via the creation of a decidedly unorthodox and illegitimate group internal to the realm."[47] The defense offered by elites in Lydgate's new paradigm is not military action but a succor founded on conversation and exchange of information. In the old elite obscene comedy, the domestic trials of lower-rank men exist only to be laughed at. In Lydgate's new version, the perfidy of women becomes the foundation of new bonds between men of all social ranks, allowing them to unite across social differences in a community of mutual understanding.

Lydgate bolsters his new vision with portraits of idealized deferential subjects, replacing the middle-rank threat to elite authority with a fantastical vision of submission.[48] Not a single peasant in the *Mumming at Hertford* questions or resists the presenter or the king, not even to be corrected as an instructive example. The husbands (in the voice of the presenter) end their complaints by "Lowly beseching in al hir best entent, / Vnto Your Noble Ryal Magestee" (136–37). This fantastically deferential behavior represents the same idealized portrait of ruler-ruled relations promised by Flora in the May Day *Mumming at Bishopswood* that Lydgate presents to the sheriffs of London:

> Lordes to regne in Þeire noble puissance,
> Þe people obeye with feythful obeyssaunce.
> Of alle estates Þere shal beo oone ymage,
> And princes first shal ocupye Þe hede. (48–51)

As Claire Sponslor notes of Lydgate's London mummings, the *Mumming at Hertford* emphasizes "a reciprocal relationship premised on loyal service on the part of subordinates and beneficent paternalism on the part of the ruler."[49]

In this amicable relationship, the poet plays a central role as mediator. It is only through the verse mediation of the presenter that the men are able to speak to the king and he to them.[50] In this respect, the *Mumming at Hertford* partakes in what David Lawton sees as Lydgate's larger project to establish poetry as a public sphere of discourse "parallel to and connected with the structures of power" and to justify that role by presenting poetry as a source of stability and moral authority that can "create continuity and unity where in the actual center of power there is instability and 'dyuision'."[51]

The Mumming at Hertford *and Catherine of Valois*

Commentators have often puzzled over the relationship between the unruly wives of the *Mumming* and the controversial figure of Henry VI's mother, the widow of Henry V, Catherine of Valois, who would very likely have attended the *Mumming*'s performance at Hertford castle (indeed, the castle belonged to her). Widowed in 1421, Catherine had embarked on an affair with the clerk of her wardrobe, Owen Tudor, possibly as early as 1425. The relationship occasioned discomfort among members of the government, who were concerned about the influence a stepfather might exercise over the young Henry VI.[52] By the earliest possible date of the *Mumming at Hertford*, 1427, Catherine's affair with Tudor was well known. Indeed, the Parliament of 1427/28 had reacted to news of it by passing an act declaring that anyone who married a queen-dowager without the king's assent would be deprived of his lands and possessions during his lifetime.[53] Noting the parliamentary act and the fact that one of the *Mumming*'s misogamist declarations makes reference to azure and gold, the colors of the French royal arms, Richard Firth Green concludes that the *Mumming at Hertford* is a "clumsy piece of contemporary satire" directed against Catherine.[54] In a similar vein, Claire Sponsler reads the *Mumming*'s theme of female unruliness as a warning to Catherine not to overstep her bounds as dowager queen.[55] Derek Pearsall, however, rejects the notion that Lydgate's *Mumming* aimed to reprove Catherine, pointing out that she "was a wealthy woman in her own right and exerted considerable power as the king's mother and the living embodiment of his claim to the dual monarchy" and that no-one, least of all Lydgate, would be making digs at her.[56]

In fact, the Hertford *Mumming* does attempt to undermine Catherine, but in a more attenuated way than Firth or Sponsler imagine. The *Mumming*'s portrayal of unruly women cannot by itself be interpreted as an insult to the queen. Reading the *Mumming* in this way overlooks the conventional status of obscene comedy in medieval culture and the firm division it traditionally asserts between the aristocracy and the lower ranks. It was common in Catherine's era and before for upper-rank women to form the audience for works in which lower-rank women were denigrated. Certainly upper-rank women were affected by obscene comedy misogyny, but the rigid class distinctions of medieval society meant that its influence would have been indirect.

Indeed, the history of the farce in France suggests that the subject matter of the Hertford *Mumming* may have been chosen as a particular compliment to Catherine, recalling works popular in her home culture. Records from the royal court in France reveal that farces were played before Catherine's own parents, Charles VI and Isabeau of Bavaria, on at least three occasions. Apparently, the taste for obscene comedy belonged as much to the queen as to the king, since one record specifies an exclusive performance before Isabeau, detailing a payment made to one "Jehannin Cardon, actor, for him and six of his companions who had played before the said lady [Queen Isabeau] several farces and plays."[57] Catherine may well have enjoyed these performances with her parents (all the extant records of farces at the French court antedate Catherine's departure for England in 1420).

The notion that the *Mumming at Hertford* may have been designed, at least on the surface, to please Catherine also accounts for its strange excision of female adultery. Given the context of Catherine's well-known affair with Owen Tudor, a mention of sexual misbehavior may well have been read in the satiric or monitory terms that Green and Sponsler envision and that Pearsall believes would have been beyond the pale. Certainly, eliminating this element while retaining other forms of unruliness would have been a wise move on Lydgate's part to avoid offending the powerful mother of the young king.

On a subtler level, however, the *Mumming at Hertford* does indeed repudiate Catherine by robbing her of her role as mediator. While historians have noted the gradual disempowerment of queens as independent political agents through the later Middle Ages, royal women retained their role as intermediaries.[58] The role may appear symbolic, but it was, according to Theresa Earenfight, "a very effective form of queenly power."[59] Chroniclers and poets celebrated the queen's role as an intercessor who could appeal to her husband for mercy on behalf of lower-order subjects or prisoners. The most famous instance of this in the fourteenth century is Philippa of Hainault's plea to Edward III in 1347 to spare the lives of six burghers of Calais after Edward vowed to execute them in retribution for English deaths during the siege of Calais. According to Froissart's account, the heavily pregnant queen

> se jetta en genouls par devant le roi son signour et dist:
> "Ha! très-chiers sires, puis que je apassai par deçà la mer en
> grant péril, ensi que vous savés, je ne vous ai requis, ne don
> demandet. Or vous prie-je humlement et requier en propre
> don que pour le Fil à sainte Marie et pour l'amour de mi,
> vous voelliés avoir de ces sys hommes merchi."

> [threw herself on her knees before the king her lord and
> said, "Ah my dear lord, since I passed over the sea in great
> peril, as you well know, I have asked nothing of you, nor
> demanded any favor. Now I pray you humbly and ask of you
> a favor for the son of the blessed Mary and for your love
> of me, that you show a merciful disposition to these six
> men."][60]

The tradition of queenly intercession continues in England through the late fourteenth and early fifteenth centuries. On her arrival in England, the citizens of London petitioned Richard II's queen, Anne of Bohemia, urging her to act as intercessor for them with the king. An epitaph of Anne, probably composed during the reign of Henry V, emphasizes her role as nurturer and mediatrix: "always inclined to give offerings to the poor, she settled quarrels and relieved pregnant women . . . offering solace to widows, medicine to the ill."[61] Although Henry IV's second wife, Joanne of Navarre, was eventually imprisoned on charges of sorcery, she too was a famed mediatrix, both during her first marriage to John V of Brittany and during her tenure as Henry IV's queen, when she "quickly established a high profile for merciful interventions."[62] Catherine herself had been asked to intercede on several occasions. She was appointed arbiter to resolve a quarrel between the dukes of Gloucester and Burgundy in 1425 and had intervened with her husband for the release of James I of Scotland (then a prisoner of Henry V) during her coronation feast in 1421.[63]

The invisibility of the queen in the *Mumming at Hertford* is a necessary prerequisite for the role that Lydgate wishes to accord to himself. Her absence allows Lydgate to situate the poet-like "presenter" as the figure who mediates and settles quarrels. Thus, the mumming works in a subtle manner to limit the power of aristocratic women, constructing a cross-class male alliance in place of the class-based identities of the past, which positioned women of the ruling orders over male members of the lower ranks.

Women's Political Engagement in the Mumming at Hertford

Lydgate's merging of lower-rank family and royal court in the *Mumming at Hertford* is also remarkable for the way it seems to predict the household-state metaphor that was to become prominent in early modern political theory. This is markedly different from the organic metaphor of the body politic.[64] First articulated by John of Salisbury in the twelfth century and repeated many times by intellectuals throughout the medieval period, this model envisions the king as the head of the body, with the knights as the arms and hands, and the people symbolized by the legs and feet.[65] In this model, women and the household are invisible, subsumed within a rank-based vision of political relations.

The way that Lydgate imagines the relationship between the family and the state, however, is markedly different from that of early modern theorists. Early modern political theory uses analogy to construct the family as a model of the state in microcosm (or to understand the state as a model of the family in macrocosm). According to this vision, the family and the state are separate units, mutually enforcing one another. Lydgate's family-state imaginary does not separate out the family from the state, but rather merges the two into a whole whose organic integration resembles the traditional medieval concept of the mystical social body. Instead of using familial obedience as a *model* for the appropriate behavior of citizens in the commonwealth and leaving the family as a closed unit whose political representation is limited to husbands and fathers, Lydgate opens the family to public supervision, characterizing it as a unit directly linked to the very highest echelons of public authority. Where early modern political theory gives us "every man is a king in his own household," Lydgate gives us "every man can *have* the king in his own household."

Lydgate intends for this configuration to bolster the authority of the king and in many respects he is successful. By configuring lower-order people appealing to the king for help in their domestic affairs, Lydgate implicitly gives the king authority over family law. In this respect, the *Mumming at Hertford* engages in a project similar to the one Larry Scanlon identifies in the *Fall of*

Princes: that of broadening aristocratic authority by extending it into areas that were commonly the provenance of the Church.[66]

At the same time, bringing the king into the household has some unintended consequences. Although Lydgate wishes to establish the king's authority over the *domos*, he is squeamish about subjecting him to the very female unruliness that originally justifies his entry. Thus, while the wives are said to be fearsome specters of irrational aggression, in the *Mumming* itself they are model subjects: nonviolent and deferential to both presenter and king. In this respect, Lydgate integrates women into the political sphere to an extent not seen in either medieval or early modern political theory.

Given the plentiful evidence in the *Mumming at Hertford* and elsewhere in his oeuvre for Lydgate's misogyny and desire to shut women out of public discourse, this integration is almost certainly unintentional. It is worth noting, however, for what it tells us about the dangers inherent in Lydgate's method of uniting the civil and domestic. While the early modern analogy keeps family and state in clearly separate spheres, Lydgate's vision does not. By introducing a paradigm that breaks down the boundaries between king and household, Lydgate is forced to integrate women into the polity much in the same way that they are already integrated into the family unit.

Part II: Obscene Comedy in Lydgate's Laureate Poetry

While the *Mumming at Hertford* is Lydgate's most conspicuous work of obscene comedy, the discourse also inflects two of his most celebrated poems, the *Troy Book* (1412–20) and the *Fall of Princes* (1431–39). While Lydgate's use of obscene comedy may be more subtle in these poems than in the *Mumming at Hertford*, it is nevertheless just as significant in terms of the cultural and political work it performs. The ends to which Lydgate deploys obscene comedy in these two poems are, moreover, very similar to those we see in the *Mumming at Hertford*: creating an all-male community across ranks, based on a shared misogyny, highlighting the role of the male poet in this community, and defusing the threat of powerful women. While Lydgate deploys obscene comedy in the *Troy Book* and the *Fall of Princes* for similar purposes, his manner of evoking the discourse differs quite significantly between the two works, reflecting changes in women's influence and in attitudes toward misogyny between the *Troy Book*'s creation during the 1410s and the writing of the *Fall of Princes* two decades later.

The *Troy Book* is a translation of Guido delle Colonne's *Historia Destructionis Troiae*. The future Henry V commissioned the work in 1412, when he was still prince of Wales. Lydgate completed it in 1420. The poem contains a number of ironic asides, wherein Lydgate narrates extended passages condemning women's perfidy, then steps outside his role as "translator" to bewail the misogyny of his original source, often in exaggeratedly fearful or deferential terms. These asides occur in three sections ranging from 60 to 150 lines in the *Troy Book*. They are remarkable because they do not occur anywhere else in Lydgate's oeuvre, with the exception of a single brief passage in the *Fall of Princes* and another in *Reson and Sensualyte*.

The first of Lydgate's ironic asides in the *Troy Book* occurs in Book One when, after telling of Medea's desire for Jason, the narrator veers off into a misogynist diatribe of more than twenty lines on the horrors of women's falsity and "doubleness." Women, the passage tells us, can hide their lusts under an honest exterior but beneath the "floures depeint of stabilnes, / The serpent dareth of newfongilnes" (I.2091–92). Women may speak fair words, but we should not believe them, "For what thing be most unto ther pay / Thei wil denye and rathest ther swere nay" (I.2095–96). The invective is then interrupted in what we presume to be the voice of Lydgate himself, decrying "Guido" for writing so insultingly of women and expressing sorrow over his obligation to translate such slander:

> Thus liketh Guydo of wommen for t'endite.
> Allas, whi wolde he so cursedly write
> Ageynes hem or with hem debate?
> I am right sory in Englische to translate
> Reprefe of hem or any evel to seye; (I.2097–2101)

He himself, Lydgate tells us, would rather die for women's love. Therefore, he asks women to "take in pacience" his translation, since he knows that every one of them is good and perfect (I.2103; 2105). Indeed, he continues, "To rekne alle, I trowe ther be nat on/But that thei ben in wille and herte trewe" (I.2106–7). This is followed by an additional twenty-eight lines in which Lydgate continues to condemn Guido's misogyny and issues the rather specious argument that, if women are indeed fickle, they should not be blamed since some men behave in the same way and that it is of no account if women have more than one lover.

In fact, the elaborate misogynist passage on women's doubleness is all Lydgate's own, the tremulous fidelity to Guido and reluctance to translate an elaborate poetic fiction created by none other than the "translator" himself. Guido's original contains only a single sentence of misogynist condemnation, when he remarks of Medea's seduction of Jason that "it is always the custom of women, that when they yearn for some man with immodest desire, they veil their excuses under some sort of modesty."[67]

Lydgate creates a similar fiction in Book Two, when he interrupts the story of Paris and Helen to issue a misogynist condemnation of women's lusts. In this case, Lydgate's addition actually inverts Guido's original. After a brief mention of the "eager appetite of changing desire, which is wont to seize the hearts of women," Guido's original passage focuses on men's unscrupulous seduction of young girls.[68] In Lydgate's version, the description of masculine corruption is left out, and it is the women themselves who are the seducers. Nevertheless, Lydgate concludes with another condemnation of Guido for having "seyn ille" (II.3557) of women. Translating it is against Lydgate's will since "To alle women I am so moche bounde: / Thei ben echon so goodly and so kynde" (II.3562–63). Indeed, Lydgate pretends to be so overwhelmed by Guido's ill words that when he reads them "my herte quoke, / And verrailly my wittis gonnne faille, / Whan I ther-of made rehersaille" (II.3566–68).

In Book Three of the *Troy Book,* five sentences in Guido regarding women's fickleness are turned into eighty lines on women's falsity that end in a description of men's suffering in marriage and the conclusion that "Wherefor, my counseil is to both two: / Cast of the bridel, and lightly lete hem go" (III.4341–42). This is followed by another of Lydgate's impassioned denials of responsibility ["Thus techeth Guydo, God wot, and not I!"] and another exaggeratedly emotional repudiation regarding the justice of Guido's remarks ["Inwardly myn herte I felte blede, / Of highe dispit, his lausis for to rede" (III.4351–52)].

While none of these passages are conventional pieces of obscene comedy, they evoke its tropes nonetheless. Notably, their pattern of emphasis is similar to that of the *Mumming at Hertford.* In each passage, Lydgate invites his readers to imagine women responding angrily (and perhaps violently) to misogynist statements; he configures himself as a tremulous poet who fears women and attempts to pacify them while remaining honorably loyal to his source. In the figure of the apologetic poet and his imagined audience of angry females, we have, once again, the domineering women and henpecked men of the Hertford mumming, as well as that work's attempt to associate women with irrational violence and men with conciliatory and peaceable behavior. The passages, as other readers have recognized, are meant to be funny, engaging in a humorous irony that reasserts the very misogyny the narrator claims to deny, since his fear of the angry women ironically refutes the portrait of sweet and docile femininity he cites in attempting to correct his source.[69]

The *Troy Book* asides are also notable for a circumlocution on the subject of misogyny that is at odds with the straightforward declarations against women elsewhere in Lydgate's oeuvre and for the fact that they evince a humorous irony that is also rare in his work. One must ask, why *did* Lydgate express his misogyny using humor and irony at this particular juncture? The reason, I propose, lies in the high status of certain powerful women in early fifteenth-century England, as well as in the cultural capital that criticisms of misogyny had gained at this time. Two cultural phenomena that Lydgate never mentions in the passages themselves, but that strongly influence their creation, are the cultural ascendency of Christine de Pisan and a number of significant aristocratic female mediators, in particular, Henry IV's queen, Joanne of Navarre. In an approach that is similar to his treatment of Catherine of Valois in the *Mumming at Hertford*, Lydgate renders these women invisible in the text itself and yet structures his writing in a deliberate attempt to defray their power.

Christine de Pisan

By the time Prince Hal commissions the *Troy Book* in 1412, Christine de Pisan had achieved considerable cachet in English aristocratic and literary circles. Henry IV and others admired her *Epistre d'Othea* (1399), a work in the "mirror of princes" tradition that takes the form of a letter of advice from Christine's own fictionalized goddess of wisdom, Othea, to Prince Hector of Troy. Forty-five English manuscripts of the work survive, indicating an enviable popularity and dispersion. Henry IV was so impressed with the *Epistre* that he attempted to persuade Christine to come to England, even going so far as to detain her teenaged son, whom he released only when Christine provided Henry with an *Othea* manuscript, appended with verses dedicated particularly to him.[70] Another of Christine's works, the *Epistre au Dieu d'Amours* (1399), was also prized by the Lancastrians, having been translated into English in 1402 by Thomas Hoccleve at the behest of Henry IV's brother Humphrey of Gloucester.[71] The work is one of Christine's notable statements in women's defense, featuring Cupid railing against clerical misogyny and alleging that male adherents of courtly love are more interested in seduction than in honoring women. Lydgate is also likely to have known the *Querelle de la Rose*, the epistolary argument regarding the merits of the *Roman de la Rose* that Christine carried out with a number of French writers and clerics in the early years of the fifteenth century and that she had collected and presented to Isabeau of Bavaria, the mother of Catherine de Valois (who married Henry V in 1420, just as the *Troy Book* was nearing completion).[72] These letters criticize the *Roman de la Rose* not only for its obscenity but also for its negative depictions of women and its courtly emphasis on the arts of seduction.

Christine's status, particularly the way that she exploited her gender identity to achieve authority, represented both an inspiration and a threat to Lydgate. As Jennifer Summit has perceived, Christine's presentation of female counselors as writers outside the court or monastery appealed to the fifteenth-century men who made up a secular administrative class of "gentleman bureaucrats."[73] While Lydgate was a monk, his ambition to exercise political influence meant that he too sought to occupy the new secular space of Christine's imagination. Expanding on Summit's theory, Robert Meyer-Lee has said that the source of Christine's appeal to Henry IV and other Lancastrians lay in her construction of herself as an author outside the traditional centers of power whose very outsider status gave her a special insight and an ability to comment on those powers. This marginality made her praises of royalty particularly valuable, since the affirmation of an independent authority confers more legitimation on kings and princes than the praises of a hired lackey.[74] Like Christine, Lydgate's emphasis on his status as a monastic historian sought to access the authority of the outsider, separate from the realm of power but knowledgeable about it.[75]

If Christine provided a model for Lydgate, both her gender and her invectives against misogyny threatened to undermine his status. Lydgate's claim to authority was, like Christine's, dependent on notions of gender. Whereas Christine's identity depended on refuting misogyny, however, Lydgate's depended on affirming it. Dyan Elliott has described how the Church's twelfth-century attempt to construct clerics as a class of individuals superior to the laity was dependent on misogynist notions of women's perfidy. By enforcing clerical celibacy and emphasizing misogyny, the Church was able to set clerics in a special class above laymen, based on their freedom from women's malign influence.[76] As a man who had not only forgone married life but lived isolated from women, the monk's authority was even more grounded in misogyny than the authority of the regular clergy. Thus, an attack on misogyny such as that issued by Christine was also an attack on the special basis of Lydgate's own authority as a political commentator.

Extending Obscene Comedy Misogyny to Noblewomen

As I have noted in my discussion of the *Mumming at Hertford*, the aristocratic female mediator is also threat to Lydgate's construction of the public male monastic poet. In this area too, the early fifteenth century produced a formidable character in the person of Henry IV's queen, Joanne of Navarre. Although she was eventually placed under house arrest on charges of sorcery, Joanne was famed as a mediatrix for much of her life. In 1412, she was at the height of her influence in the Lancastrian court, both as a mediator between Henry and his subjects and between the king and his son. This latter role was particularly detrimental to Lydgate in the 1410s, since the *Troy Book* itself was intended to reconcile the king and his son.[77]

The importance of misogyny in Lydgate's construction of his poetic identity at this juncture in his career is witnessed in the fact that the *Troy Book*'s misogynist passages always appear at precisely the points where he distinguishes himself from his continental source. Lydgate's "critiques" of Guido's misogyny are virtually the only places in the *Troy Book* that he differentiates himself from Guido and establishes himself as a separate poetic entity.[78] In this way, we see Lydgate aligning an appeal to misogyny with his own authority as poet and interpreter of continental poetry for an English audience.

If misogyny was essential to Lydgate's poetic authority, however, asserting it in the 1410s was no simple matter. Christine's prominence and her attacks on clerical misogyny meant that, if Lydgate issued a straightforward declaration, he risked being dismissed as one of Christine's bitter clerics, a man whose very investment in misogyny was evidence of his moral corruption and alienation from the realities of the secular world. In a society increasingly populated by educated men attempting to assert their own importance against "the Latinate, scholastic settings of the medieval monastery and university,"[79] Lydgate could not afford to do anything that might have associated him with monkish otherworldliness.

In this situation, the ambivalent quality of obscene comedy was Lydgate's only option, allowing him to assert misogyny while seeming not to do so. The effectiveness of his approach becomes clear if we examine the structure of the *Troy Book*'s ironic passages. First, Lydgate the "translator" recites a long misogynist passage that provides an excellent review of the theory's basic tenets. Lydgate then "disavows" the passage with a condemnation of the original author and a recitation of women's virtues. That recitation, however, is so ridiculously exaggerated that it drives the audience back to the negative stereotypes of women so recently outlined.

Thus Lydgate plays on obscene comedy's status as an anti-courtly mode whose portraits of women provide a corrective to idealized courtly fictions. Although Lydgate in general dislikes the obscene comedy celebration of renegade behavior, in this case it works in his favor, allowing him to counter Christine's popular anticourtly stance with one of his own and countering her image of the bitter misogynist cleric with the image of the misogynist poet as clever truth teller, pulling the rug out from under courtly fictions. The truth claims of obscene comedy also allow Lydgate to create the same kind of homosocial community that he creates in the *Mumming at Hertford*. Drawing on the fabliau-style claim that misogyny represents the raw, unvarnished truth, Lydgate's *Troy Book* asides reward the male audience by making them feel like members of a special group who have privileged access to the reality that lies behind social fictions. "Politeness may demand that I defend women against the depredations of Guido," the subtext of Lydgate's asides goes, "but my male audience knows the reality that underlies this, a reality so obvious and so common to all men that it requires no further extrapolation than a simple gesture." In this way, Lydgate is able to spin straw into gold, converting Christine's interrogation of misogyny from a threat to a circumstance that only makes this special community of male knowers more discerning and unique.

Lydgate's fictionalizing of Guido is effective whether the audience members recognize it or not. For those unfamiliar with Guido's original, the belief that such misogyny exists in Guido endows it with greater authority. For those who know the original (surely a group that would have included Duke Humphrey himself), recognizing Lydgate's embroidering of his source only deepens the sense of special insider status fostered by the text's ironic misogyny.

Also crucial to Lydgate's misogyny in the *Troy Book* is the obscene comedy trope of woman as angry shrew. Although Lydgate never says as much outright, his repeated fear in the *Troy Book* asides that women will be upset—and his showy attempts to placate them—conjure up a vision of an angry (and potentially violent) female audience. As a rhetorical tactic opposing Christine, this maneuver is brilliant, attacking her in precisely the place she is most vulnerable. Christine's anti-misogynist writings show her to be well aware of the cultural taboos pertaining to self-assertion. These taboos mean that any woman attempting to criticize misogyny risks being dismissed as an angry shrew.[80] Cognizant of this danger, Christine is at pains to deflect it by uttering her critiques of misogyny in the voices of men or of allegorical female figures. In the *Epistre au Dieu d'amours*, it is the God of Love who criticizes misogynist discourse. In the *Book of the City of Ladies*, Christine figures herself as a sad and confused reader of misogynist texts whose negative vision of women is corrected by three allegorical ladies.[81] By emphasizing women's angry response to the *Troy Book*'s misogyny, Lydgate brings the full force of misogynist discourse to bear on Christine in precisely the way she had sought to avoid.

Lydgate's figuration of woman as shrew in the *Troy Book* asides also works to defuse the power of the aristocratic female mediator. Like the refutation of Christine, this is a tricky assignment for Lydgate: while undercutting the power of a mediatrix like Joanne of Navarre was important to Lydgate's construction of an all-male political community, he could not openly insult her. The trope of the fearful poet and the angry female audience allows Lydgate to undermine Joanne's power without ever seeming to do so. Although elite women are never directly identified as the angry female audience members, the implication must be that they are, for who else might be found in the female audience of a piece commissioned by a prince? And while Lydgate on the surface defers to women, he nevertheless identifies them with anger and aggression in ways that undercut their claims to peaceable mediation.

As in the *Mumming at Hertford*, Lydgate's obscene comedy in the *Troy Book* asides is very strictly controlled. His manner of evoking ironic humor in the asides, then quickly cutting it off before it fully blossoms, has been taken as evidence of a humorless authorial clumsiness. If, however, we understand obscene comedy as a discourse marked by semiotic instability, then these truncated ventures make a good deal of rhetorical sense. Unwilling to give the discourse free play in ways that might lead to the inversion of the very misogynist principles he seeks to inculcate, Lydgate cuts it off the minute it has served his purpose. If this truncation makes the work less satisfying as a piece of literature, it nevertheless ensures its effectiveness as a piece of rhetoric.

The Fall of Princes—*Obscenity and the English National Community*

The *Fall of Princes*, begun almost two decades after the *Troy Book*, reveals an author much more comfortable with making straightforward assertions of misogyny. In the Prologue, Lydgate remarks, without the cover of ironic humor, that his "maister Chaucer" (275) was unable to find nineteen good women to fulfill the queen's request in the *Legend of Good Women*:

But for his labour and [his] bisynesse
Was inportable his wittis to encoumbre,
In al this world to fynde so gret a noumbre.
   (Prologue, 334–36)[82]

The source of Lydgate's new boldness in the *Fall of Princes* can be found in the decline of women's power and cultural authority in the 1430s, as opposed to the 1410s. By 1431, when Humphrey of Gloucester commissions Lydgate to translate the *Fall of Princes*, Christine de Pisan is no longer a threat, not only because of her likely death by this date, or because we are now three decades removed from Henry IV's intense interest in her, but because she had alienated the Lancastrians by taking the French side in the Hundred Years War.[83] Joanne of Navarre is still alive, but sidelined due to her conviction on charges of sorcery and the death of her fond stepson, Henry V.[84] Catherine of Valois is also defused as a threat by this time, having likely given birth to her first child with Owen Tudor by 1431.[85] Henry VI, meanwhile, is still a child and without a queen.

    An ironic aside like those of the *Troy Book* appears only once in the *Fall of Princes*, in Book One when, after narrating the death of Hippolytus due to Phaedra's accusation of rape, Lydgate informs us that "Bochas" enters into "an exclamacioun / Ageynes women" (I.4720–21) that describes their doubleness and their bestial insatiability. Lydgate decries the passage, assures us that Boccaccio means only the women born in Crete, and praises Englishwomen in exaggerated terms:

For women heer, al doubilnesse thei lete,
And haue no tech off mutabilitie,
Thei loue no chaungis nor no duplicite
For ther husbondis, in causis smal or grete,
What-euer thei sen, thei can nat countirplete. (I. 4727–32)

The passage continues for several lines in the same mode, the narrator noting that he speaks of *all* Englishwomen, not just one, who are "professid onto lowlynesse" and silence (4743). Of this, the narrator says, all true husbands can bear witness:

For weddid men, I dar riht weel expresse,
That haue assaied and had experience,
Best can recorde off wifli pacience. (I. 4744–46)

As we can see, the *Fall of Princes* passage exploits the same association between obscenity and truth that we see in the *Troy Book* and invites men into the same kind of knowing homosocial community. Much more emphatic in the *Fall of Princes*, however, is the stress on national identity. While nationality is always implicit in the *Troy Book* asides, because they are an English poet's evaluation of his continental source, the *Fall of Princes* brings nationalism to the fore, making the homosocial community Lydgate builds through obscene discourse an exclusively English entity. Lydgate claims that Boccaccio does not refer to Englishwomen, but, of course, the implication is just the opposite: the audience is to assume that women of "this countre" are exactly the same as those Boccaccio has described. English*men*, however, are not like other men but are distinguished by their canny ability to read between the lines of courtly deference to the reality of women's sameness. In doing so, Lydgate both encourages a notion of national identity and specifies that only men can be included in the English national community.

The connection between obscene truth and English sincerity is also made elsewhere in the *Fall of Princes*. In one of the few places in Lydgate's oeuvre where he castigates a man for his weak behavior toward his wife, Lydgate describes how Candalus foolishly displays his wife's nudity before one of his knights, Gyges, thereby leading to their adulterous liaison. It is an occurrence Lydgate articulates in obscene terms. Gyges, Lydgate writes, "To speke pleyn Inglissh, made hym a cokold." The poet then highlights his own obscenity by ironically disavowing it:

> Alas, I was nat auysid weel beforn,
> Oncunnyngli to speke such language;
> I should ha said, how that he hadde an horn,
> Or souht sum tee[r]me with a fair visage
> Texcuse my rudnesse off this gret outrage,
> As in sum land Cornodo men them call,
> And summe afferme how such folk ha[ue] no gall.
>   (II. 3360–67)

Here we see the very obscenity of the word "cokold" being characterized as proof of its truth. To speak obscenely is to speak "oncunnyngli," without guile, surely an honorable quality in Lydgate's political ethos of avoiding "doubilnesse." Moreover, it is the English language, "pleyn Inglissh," that has the capacity to identify truth without the polite metaphors of the Italian term

"Cornodo." Thus Lydgate locates misogyny at the core of English national identity by linking it with the quality of forthrightness.[86]

Orpheus and Obscene Comedy in the Fall of Princes

The *Fall of Princes*, Book One, includes another fascinating evocation of obscene comedy in Lydgate's retelling of the Orpheus legend. Lydgate begins by following his primary source, *Des Cas des Nobles Hommes et Femmes* by the French court writer, Laurent de Premierfait. He tells the traditional tale of how Orpheus's attempt to rescue Eurydice from the underworld is frustrated by his excessive devotion, which causes him violate Hades' injunction not to look back at Eurydice as he leads her to the land of the living. At this point, Lydgate departs from his source to create a scenario of his own invention. After noting Orpheus's loss, Lydgate remarks that there are some husbands who, if a sudden look had lost them their wives, would have put up with it very patiently and thanked God:

> that broken was the cheyne
> Which hath so longe hem in prisoun bounde,
> That thei be grace han such a fredam founde. (I.5808–10)

Although Lydgate's Orpheus is initially grieved by the loss of his bride, he soon realizes his own good luck. He decides never to marry again and goes on to give "counseil ful notable" to other men, advising bereaved husbands not to make the mistake of remarrying, for

> Oon hell is dreedful, mor pereilous be tweyne;
> And who is onys boundyn in a cheyne,
> And may escapen out of daunger blyue
> Yiff he resorte, God let hym neuer thryue! (I.5835–38)

Lydgate's version represents a rather shocking take on the Orpheus legend, given its status in the Middle Ages as an inspiring testament to the power of romantic love.[87] Taking into account the legend's reputation, it is worth asking why Lydgate would choose to characterize Orpheus as a henpecked husband and Eurydice as a shrewish wife when classical legend and biblical narrative offer up such a rogue's gallery of bona fide female monsters whose perfidy requires no divergence from tradition. Already, the *Fall of Princes*, Book One, includes the tales of Medea, Phaedra, Pasiphae, and Delilah, women whose "doublenesse," rage, and lust cause the destruction of prince and polity. Why, given the more-than-adequate horridness of these women, should Lydgate wish to remind us of the unruly wives of obscene comedy, whose misbehavior occurs on such a smaller scale?

The answer lies in Lydgate's desire to break down the boundaries between domesticity and public life and to unify men of all ranks on the basis of a shared misogyny. In light of this agenda, Eurydice's status as a valued aristocratic woman is exactly what makes her a good candidate for obscene comedy treatment. As we have seen in the *Mumming at Hertford* and the *Troy Book*, Lydgate is anxious to undo the higher status accorded to aristocratic women and make unruliness a quality shared by *all* women that in turn functions as a point of commonality for *all* men. In accord with the more misogyny-friendly environment of the 1430s, Lydgate is more explicit in the *Fall of Princes* than he is in the *Mumming at Hertford* and the *Troy Book* about extending unruliness to all women. While the queen is simply invisible in the Hertford piece, in the Orpheus episode she is, quite literally, one of the unruly women. This is a marked step forward, even if Eurydice's status as a classical legend queen still allows for a certain degree of separation between her and high-ranking medieval women.

The fusion of classical legend and obscene comedy in the Orpheus story also unifies domestic and public governance in a manner that, again, follows the agenda we see in the *Mumming at Hertford*, but it does so more explicitly. When one considers why Lydgate invokes wifely unruliness when the more horrifying examples of Medea, Phaedra, and company are so close to hand, one must note that these women's crimes occur on a grand historical scale that has little relation to the quotidian lives of nonaristocratic men. Certainly household politics inflect the tales of classical legend, but they are not posed in such a way as to invite parallels between the doings of kings and those of lower-rank people. By making Orpheus a married man who suffers in terms identical to peasant or bourgeois men, Lydgate breaks down the distinction courtly love imposes between the erotic lives of commoners and those of aristocrats. Because all women are similarly troublesome, all men suffer similarly, no matter what their rank. While the *Mumming at Hertford* demands that the aristocracy give the henpecked commoner a sympathetic hearing, the Orpheus episode takes male bonding a step farther by making the king a cosufferer. The destruction of courtly love is, thus, the prerequisite to cross-rank unity. Once the aristocratic heterosexual bond is broken, Orpheus is free to speak across rank and status to all "husbondis that han endurid peyne" and provide leadership for them in their own struggles (5833).

The Orpheus tale embodies, in sexual and domestic terms, the same pattern of identification between king and commoner that Larry Scanlon identifies in the form of ethics the *Fall of Princes* promotes. Scanlon has described how the *Fall of Princes* invites its lay audience "to identify their moral status with that of the prince, in a way that . . . earlier compilers of *Furstenspiegel* expected mainly of the court."[88] By heeding the examples of princes and putting themselves in his place, the laity "become morally self-corrective and self-regulative."[89] Similarly, by making the prince a husband in the manner of a bourgeois or peasant husband, Lydgate invites his noncourtly audience to follow the king in matters domestic as well as political.

As he does in the *Mumming at Hertford*, Lydgate selectively cites Chaucer in the Orpheus passage in order to make it appear that Chaucer shares his distrust of women. It is notable that the Orpheus episode's references to Chaucer are taken from his most unambiguous misogynist and misogamist passages. Those familiar with Chaucer's *Lenvoy a Bukton*—a work whose tone of man-to-man admonishment is already very similar to Lydgate's Orpheus—could not fail to recognize its trope of the unbreakable chain ["the cheyne / Of Sathanas on which he gnaweth evere" (*Bukton* 9–10)] in Lydgate's evocation of the irons at which wedded men fret, and "Which with no file may nat be broke assonder" (5817). Nor could they fail to hear, in Orpheus's exclamation against marriage, Chaucer's own outcry against men who would marry again: "God let him never fro his wo dissevere, / Ne no man him bewayle, though he wepe" (*Bukton* 15–16). When Lydgate remarks that any man who is freed from marriage "Will neuer his thankis come in the snare ageyn" (I.5831), he echoes the declaration of Chaucer's Merchant when he says that, if he were freed from his bond of marriage, "I wolde nevere eft comen in the snare" (*MerPro* 1227).

Lydgate and the Problem of Violence

It is clear that Lydgate intends his writing to speak to historical problems. This is witnessed not only in the pretentions inherent in the concept of "public poetry" but also in the way Lydgate's writing persistently crosses the boundary between the fictive and the historical. This boundary crossing is implicit in the form of the *Mumming at Hertford*, since the mumming as an art form breaks down the division between poetry and lived experience by mixing actors with historical figures. It is also implicit in Lydgate's *Troy Book* asides, which, ostensibly, speak about real women and address real male audience members.

As I have been arguing throughout this chapter, part of Lydgate's bid for historical influence lies in his attempt to create a new model for upper- and lower-rank relations. In spite of this ambition, however, his imaginings remain more fantastical than practical. The king-commoner relation of the *Mumming at Hertford* projects onto its "hines" a passivity that is at odds with their historical confidence and aggression. Although this passivity might represent a wish fulfillment for an aristocracy threatened by popular resistance, its unrealistic representation of the lower orders means that it offers little in the way of a workable political model. The *Mumming* offers even less to middle- and lower-rank men, first, because its vision of their total subjection conflicts with medieval notions of masculinity and, second, because their appeal to the king results in no material change in their circumstances.

Why does Lydgate fail to come up with a cogent model of political relations? One answer to this question would default on Lydgate's famed maladroitness as an author and thinker but, as I have been arguing throughout this chapter, that label is misapplied to a writer who frequently shows a keen political and literary sense. I would like to suggest instead that the root of Lydgate's nonsensical political theory lies in his aversion to violence.

Lydgate's dislike of violence has long been noted in discussions of his public poetry.[90] That same aversion defines Lydgate's attitude to obscene comedy, constituting his most profound divergence from the discourse. There is no distinction in Lydgate's writing, as there is in obscene comedy, between disruptive and constructive violence, between the riotous aggression of the shrew and her husband's rightful exercise of authority through the stick or the fist. For Lydgate, all violence is negative.

Lydgate wishes to marshal obscene comedy to the creation of a real-world political theory, but he fails because he refuses to admit what obscene comedy acknowledges without shame or ruth: that hierarchies are only enforced by violent coercion. The unresolved conflict between Lydgate's dedication to the traditional order and his squeamishness about the violence necessary to enforce it means that his political theory can never be anything but nonsensical. The logically coherent response to middle- and lower-rank demands for political enfranchisement from a writer invested in aristocratic dominance would be the one issued by many chroniclers during the 1381 rebellion: a characterization of the protestors as animalistic and irrational in a way that justifies the use of force against them. Lydgate's desire to secure upper-rank dominance and his reluctance to advocate a violent assertion of that dominance results in his fantastical image, in the *Mumming at Hertford*, of passive and peaceable "hines."

The same problem emerges in Lydgate's treatment of misogyny. Like any system of thought that creates and stigmatizes an "other," the ultimate function of misogyny is to promote a social hierarchy and to justify the coercive violence necessary to maintain it. This is something obscene comedy takes for granted: "Women are liars, sex maniacs, and shrews," says obscene comedy, "and because of that, they must be beaten into submission." Lydgate wishes instead to use misogyny to create a sexual "other" who will encourage the unity of men across ranks. "Women are liars, sex, maniacs and shrews," Lydgate says, "and that is why men must come together." But what, then, ought to be done with the women? This is where Lydgate runs into trouble, because the misogyny he promotes provides an answer (beat them into submission) that he cannot advocate.

For this reason, obscene comedy misogyny works best for Lydgate when it is nonnarrative, as it is in the asides of the *Troy Book*. Here, the shrews can be left as specters, with no obligation on Lydgate's part to recommend what should be done with them. The times when Lydgate ventures into narrative, in the *Mumming at Hertford* and the tale of Orpheus in the *Fall of Princes*, the impossible conflict between his promotion of misogyny and his aversion to violence results in nonsensical conclusions that fail to provide a workable model of domestic or political relations. The *Mumming at Hertford*, as many have noted, ends strangely, in the king's mysterious and seemingly weak refusal to issue judgment. The conclusion that logic dictates from a writer so firmly entrenched in misogyny would be for the king to say that women must be subject to their husbands, that the husbands must force them into this subjection, and that the king himself will step in to enforce the husbands' authority if necessary. Lydgate's nonviolence will not, however, allow him to sanction such a conclusion, so he defaults on a provisional ending that *delays* judgment in the future, thereby allowing him to exploit misogyny for its power to unify men across ranks without having to confront its logic of violence. This is also why Orpheus's death is very convenient in the *Fall of Princes*. Like the king in the *Mumming at Hertford*, Orpheus is a leader who emphasizes women's degeneracy but is never called on to do something about it, because his death at the hands of the Maenads intervenes.

It is notable that early modern political theories relating to family and state do not share Lydgate's aversion to violence. As I have already noted, Lydgate's attempt to bring the obscene comedy household into the public sphere has much in common with the early modern analogy of family and the state: both seek to connect state and household in some kind of interdependent theoretical framework; both do so as part of an attempt to bolster a centralized monarchical authority; both literalize the unruly woman, making her less a figure of fun and more of a social problem. Like Lydgate's theories, the early modern emphasis on paternal authority also goes hand in hand with misogyny. Early modern culture is well known for its misogynist vein. Joseph Swetnam's *The Arraignment of Lewd, Idle, Forward, and Unconstant Women* goes through ten editions between 1616 and 1634; from 1562 onward, the Crown orders that the "Homily on Marriage," a homily that recites the inferior status, rights, and character of the wife, be read out every Sunday in church.

The early modern household-state analogy succeeds better than Lydgate's theories because, unlike Lydgate, early modern thinkers are willing to promote and advocate coercive violence, making it the basis on which a political bargain between the upper and lower orders of society is built. Lawrence Stone records the way this analogy not only imagines the household as a state in miniature but also advocates authoritarian dominance by the husband and father over women and children in the nuclear family, making him "a legalized tyrant" in the home.[91]

This makes early modern theory politically viable in a way Lydgate's vision is not, because it has something to offer the two interested parties: royal authority and nonaristocratic men. While Lydgate understands that the family must play a key role in the reconfiguration of medieval social formations away from a lordship-based model to a more centralized model focused on the king, he does not provide any reward to nonaristocratic men for their new loyalty. The early modern family-state analogy does offer a reward to these men in the form of a power trade-off: nonaristocratic men are asked to defer to absolutist authority in public life but are rewarded with state support for absolute authority within the household.

In spite of its failures and incoherence (indeed, because of them), Lydgate's work has something significant to tell us about the role of obscene comedy in the history of Western political thought. The fact that his model is so very similar to the early modern family-state analogy, and that he draws on obscene comic discourse in creating that model, shows the influence of this seemingly trivial and entertaining mode not just on ideas of marital relations, sexuality, and domestic life, but on political life as well. Although obscene comedy has never been identified as an influence on the early modern family-state metaphor, Lydgate's work indicates its importance. If the family was to come under new public consideration, its literary modes would come with it as well, powerfully influencing the way thinkers and writers imagined the family's role in a postfeudal world.

CHAPTER 4

"Ryth Wikked"

Christian Ethics and the Unruly Holy Woman
in the *Book of Margery Kempe*

Anyone who has discussed the *Book of Margery Kempe* in a college classroom knows that many readers find it funny.[1] Episodes like Margery's conversation with her husband on the road to Bridlington, her arguments with the archbishop during her trial at York, and her imprisonment in Beverly (in which her "good talys" inspire the local women to bring her an illicit pot of wine) are all likely to prompt laughter.[2] The *Book*'s humor has been recognized since, quite literally, the moment of its discovery. In her letter to the *Times of London* after the sole extant manuscript of the *Book* was brought to the Victoria and Albert Museum in 1934, Hope Emily Allen remarks that Margery's "earnest desire to set everything down just as it happened brings us many narratives full of unconscious humour."[3]

Readers have continued to remark on the *Book*'s humor, noting that it is "comic" or "very amusing, in places hilariously funny" or that it contains "hilarious overtones."[4] Yet comedy has rarely been a focus in Margery Kempe scholarship. Unlike the humor of other medieval authors, which is usually taken as a mark of sophistication, the humor of the *Book of Margery Kempe* is most often regarded as something of an embarrassment. Although critical perspectives on Margery and her adventures have changed radically since the 1930s, Allen's portrait of a naïve author, unaware of her own hilarity, remains unaltered. The *Book*'s humor is "unfortunate," to be enjoyed illicitly and in a way that "does not distract us from [the *Book*'s] solid worth."[5] Even feminist readers—otherwise strong proponents of a self-conscious and sophisticated author—have been reluctant to take up the subject of the *Book*'s comedy.

Feminists have argued persuasively for the author's studied engagement with hagiography, affective piety, virginity, and other elements of late medieval religious practice, but have remained largely silent on the subject of humor.[6] One feminist critic has made humor a point of analytic interest, but even in this case the *Book* is not treated as a comical text.[7] Professing her reluctance to credit Margery "with calculated and deliberate self-fashioning," Karma Lochrie focuses instead on the performative aspects of the mystic's laughter.[8]

Almost all the *Book*'s humor is rooted in the tropes, characters, and narrative patterns of obscene comedy. Margery's combativeness, her frequent conflicts with (and victories over) male authority figures, and the text's persistent interest in marital power struggles, adultery, and sexual misbehavior all recall the adventures of fabliau wives and other unruly female protagonists of drama, tales, and art. These parallels have not gone entirely unnoticed. Readers have remarked on Margery's close resemblance to various obscene comedy females, like Chaucer's Wife of Bath, the uxor of the biblical drama Noah pageants, and the fabliau wives.[9] But again the matter of self-conscious authorship has been dismissed. Those noting the parallels do not discuss the work's engagement with a long-standing literary tradition but rather note the similarities between the unruly women of medieval fiction and their supposed historic counterparts.

And yet it strains credibility to imagine that a fifteenth-century author could have written about the adventures of a loud, assertive, middle-rank wife in ignorance of the close resemblance her stories bore to a popular and widespread discourse. Even if one takes the *Book* at its word and believes it to be the product of an illiterate townswoman (although this is in no way a foregone conclusion), obscene comedy would have been hard to avoid. Obscenity is omnipresent in late medieval religious culture, appearing not only in the English biblical drama, which a fifteenth-century resident of Lynn was likely to have seen, but also in church architecture and sermon exempla.[10] Indeed, Margery's own beloved St. Margaret's Church in Lynn includes a sculpture of a woman in a scold's bridle and other obscene comic figures.[11] Moreover, fifteenth-century women, even those in the middle ranks, would also have had access to secular obscene comedy. Nicola McDonald has recently argued that the range of texts to which women were exposed (either as readers or auditors) was likely to have been far more broad than the pious works that testamentary evidence has identified as feminine reading. Noting that the very "household miscellanies" in which we find pious texts also include a variety of other works, McDonald argues that women were likely to have read social criticism, complaint, vulgar comedy, and erotic verse.[12] Certainly records of the distribution of Chaucer's *Canterbury*

Tales in the fifteenth century—which included members of the urban bourgeoisie—suggest that a woman of Margery's status could have known of Chaucer's Wife of Bath and of his fabliaux.[13]

In this chapter, I read the *Book of Margery Kempe* as a text that self-consciously uses obscene comedy for specific rhetorical purposes. In doing so, I propose that the *Book*'s humor should not be set aside with embarrassment by those interested in reading it as a significant document in the history of gender or of Christianity. In fact, comedy is an essential part of the *Book*'s engagement with both of these issues.

In spite of its secular protagonist and its preoccupation with social life, the *Book of Margery Kempe* is, of all the texts examined in this study, the one most exclusively focused on matters pertaining to the institutional Church. While Langland is often identified as a Church-oriented author, he expends a considerable amount of time and energy on evaluating secular authority as well. Not so in the *Book of Margery Kempe*, which only considers secular powers as they relate to the Church. The *Book*'s author (or authors) is particularly interested in pointing out how the Church's anti-Lollard campaign is at odds with the foundational Christian values of compassion and humility. By casting its protagonist both as an unruly woman and as a mystic of legitimate talents, the *Book* critiques the Church for confusing heresy with violations of social norms and persecuting those whose visionary gifts it should respect. Like William Langland, the author of the *Book of Margery Kempe* is at pains to remind readers of the limits Christianity places on human authority.[14] And, also like Langland, the *Book*'s author exploits the unruly woman both to pose questions of that authority and to provide the author with an avenue of retreat in which potentially dangerous criticisms can be dismissed as the symptoms of a ludicrous and degraded discourse.

However, the *Book* differs from *Piers Plowman* (and indeed from every other text under consideration in this study) in the depth and intensity of its concern with gender. Gender in the *Book of Margery Kempe* is not just a metaphor but the very ground on which its critique of the Church's anti-Lollard campaign is built. Of course, gender has long been a focus in Margery Kempe scholarship, but the *Book*'s engagement with that subject cannot be fully understood if we do not also appreciate its engagement with obscene comedy. Unlike the other texts in this study, the *Book of Margery Kempe* revises the gender politics of obscene comedy in ways that are specifically aimed at women's interests, rather than the interests of social justice (as is the case in Langland's *Piers Plowman*), the struggles of subordinate men (a dominant concern in Chaucer), the preservation of established powers (as we see in Lydgate's work), or in the development of class politics (as in the biblical drama).

The chapter is divided into four sections. The first section addresses the tendency, still predominant in Margery Kempe scholarship, to root the *Book* in historical reality and the barriers that this approach presents to a full understanding of the *Book*'s engagement with obscene comedy. Section 2 examines a series of comical encounters between Margery and various clerics, as well as one of *Book*'s most remarkable portions—a self-contained unit that I call "the trials segment" that I propose may well be a fictionalized or engineered account. These passages illustrate how, in its humorous portrayal of clerics who dismiss Margery on the basis of her unfeminine behavior, the *Book* argues for women's spiritual entitlement, regardless whether they conform to social norms of gender. Section 3 examines several episodes in which Margery is accused of sexual misbehavior, showing how the *Book* often ventriloquizes obscene comedy misogyny to refute its tendency to associate women with immoral sexual behavior. The fourth and final section of the chapter discusses the *Book*'s refutation of fabliau-style depictions of marriage by examining the two major comic episodes involving Margery and her husband. Here, I note how the *Book* revises obscene comedy notions of marriage in ways that accord with the principles of companionate marriage said to be emerging in northern Europe during the later Middle Ages.

History and Rhetoric: Creating a Space for Obscene Comedy

One of the major stumbling blocks to a full understanding of obscene comedy in the *Book* is the tendency, still dominant in Kempe scholarship, to assume that the *Book*'s content is based in historical reality and that Margery is a sincere and transparent historical subject. Although interrogations of the *Book*'s facticity by Lynn Staley and others are now decades old, these assumptions are still the default paradigm for most treatments of the *Book*, even those that acknowledge that its connection to historical reality is tenuous.[15]

While the *Book* advertises itself as a spiritual memoir based in historical fact, there is no evidence to corroborate its veracity. The absence of historical corroboration was noted by the *Book*'s first editor, Sanford Meech; was later independently confirmed by Lynn Staley (in a landmark study that argued for the importance of reading the *Book* as fiction); and has been reaffirmed most recently by the historian Sarah Rees Jones.[16] Much has been made of the single corroboration that does exist: the fact that one Margery Kempe was admitted to the Guild of the Trinity in Lynn in 1438. As Rees Jones has noted, however, nothing other than the name links this person to the protagonist of the *Book*.[17] The *Book*'s own history of its creation—involving illegible writing, two anonymous scribes, and several years of negotiations—is, in the words of David Lawton, "complex, circumstantial, and wantonly obscure."[18] It is highly unusual, moreover, that the *Book* never provides the second scribe's name and qualifications, given the medieval tradition of naming the holy woman's biographer.[19]

Nevertheless, it is not my goal in this study to do away with the possibility that the *Book* might be grounded in historical reality in some way. Rather, I wish to emphasize the profound lack of evidence upon which to base *any* theory of the *Book*'s production and to argue against attempts to limit what can be interpreted from the *Book* based on assumptions regarding the nature of its creation. As Ruth Evans has argued, we must "respect the Book's singularity, and not reduce either text or protagonist to what is immediately familiar and comprehensible."[20]

Numerous other possibilities for the *Book*'s production exist that are just as likely as the one that roots it in historical reality. The *Book* might, as Staley proposes, have had a literate female author who used the trope of the scribe to protect herself from accusations of heresy, or, as Rees Jones suggests, it might not have been authored by a woman at all but have been written by a male cleric for the correction and edification of his colleagues. Alternately, the *Book* might have been dictated by a woman but altered by its scribe or scribes, including both the scribes and copyist of whom we know and others whose existence is not recorded in the single manuscript left to us.[21]

The possibility of scribal intervention into an original document or oral narrative is a compelling one, given the *Book*'s obscure textual history. The single extant manuscript of the *Book* is not the original that the narrator describes, but a copy made around the middle of the century by a scribe who signs himself "Salthows." Just on the evidence of the manuscript alone, there are four different individuals who might have influenced the text: Margery; her first scribe, who dies before he can complete his task; the second scribe, who finishes the text; and Salthows. There may well have been an even greater number of mediators than this, if there are any intervening manuscripts between the second priest's final copy and Salthow's.

Sanford Meech was quick to recognize that the phonology, morphology, and spelling of the manuscript are very consistent—even though the *Book* records itself as having been copied by two scribes. This led Meech to conclude that one of the *Book*'s scribes must have altered the original text to conform with his own practices. Meech did not believe that those changes were anything but technical, but, if a scribe was capable of altering a matter as basic and pervasive as language, it follows then that he, and other intervening scribes, may also have altered content. If we imagine that the text has some provenance in oral narrative, it is not out of the realm of possibility to imagine the original amanuensis, or some later scribe, embroidering on or adding to a holy woman's original story.[22]

The possibility of scribal additions to the *Book* becomes even more plausible if we examine the textual history of *Piers Plowman*, a work whose episodic and discontinuous narrative is similarly inviting to the aspiring supplemental author. In a study of Langlandian reading circles, Katherine Kerby-Fulton and Steven Justice observe how Langland's scribes "regarded his text as a living organism, which, owing to the fluidity of manuscript transmission, lay hostage to anyone's zeal for communal authorship."[23] Indeed, some scribes embroider Langland's original so skillfully, that it is very difficult to distinguish master from disciple. According to Justice and Kerby-Fulton, scribes even felt free enough to take humorous liberties with their texts. The author of the Z-text manuscript of *Piers* injects humor into Langland's allegorical idiom. The scribe satirizes Will's willingness to go with any guide figure by having him glibly offer to follow Hunger, Fever, and Death.[24] If such cheeky riffing could be carried out on a text as revered and popular as *Piers Plowman*, then it is unlikely that anyone would have hesitated to alter the text of an obscure holy woman for his or her own purposes.

Within the paradigm that takes a historical Margery for granted, there has been considerable discussion, over the years, of Margery's relationship with her scribe and of the extent to which the scribe might have intervened to alter her oral narrative.[25] It is a fascinating index of obscenity's close association with historical reality in the minds of modern critics that all of these discussions assume that the scribe would have been the force of reason, who tamed or rendered more conventional the outrageous Margery. It has never been suggested that the scribe might *himself* have been responsible for Margery's outrageousness and that the real Margery Kempe might have been far less outlandish than the Margery of the *Book*. Yet medieval literary history indicates that the scribe's creation of an unruly female is a perfectly likely scenario. As the fabliau wives, Chaucer's Wife of Bath, Langland's Dame Study, and Lydgate's Hertford wives attest, English male writers frequently created characters like Margery throughout the high and later Middle Ages.

Even if we do choose to believe that the *Book* is grounded in historical reality, we should not allow assumptions about Margery's sincerity to forbid us from reading it as a rhetorical text. It is by now a well-accepted principle in the study of autobiography that such texts are not transparent records of reality, but constructions that make rhetorically driven choices about narrative, commentary, and characterization. The possibilities extend farther than this. If one can narrate real-life occurrences according to certain tropes, one can also live them according to those same tropes. It is possible, in other words, for historical personages to adopt—episodically or long term—characteristics derived from literary discourses. Thus we may also consider the possibility that Margery self-consciously played the role of the unruly woman during her encounters with historic individuals with the idea in mind of eventually retelling or textually recording those scenes in narratives directed to specific rhetorical ends. It is worth noting in this context that most performance art of the fifteenth century—court entertainments, dances, mummings, biblical drama, and royal ceremonies—mixed fiction and reality. Additionally, some of these involved role playing that included female unruliness. In the Hocktide ritual observed in English parishes in the fifteenth century, for instance, female members of the parish chased men, tied them up, and released them on the payment of a forfeit.[26]

Although the theories of authorship for the *Book of Margery Kempe* are both various and impossible to verify, all of them invite us to make a clear distinction between author, protagonist, and narrator, rather than collapsing them into a single entity as has so often been the case in Margery Kempe studies. This distinction, rather than any particular theory of authorship, is the most crucial prerequisite to a study of the *Book*'s obscene comedy. Feminist resistance to the *Book*'s humor is understandable if we read it as a transparent text, since Margery often appears as the butt of the joke. If, however, we can understand Margery as a fiction, then we can acknowledge her resemblance to obscene comedy women without feeling that we are rewriting medieval misogyny onto a rare female voice from the past. We can, in other words, acknowledge that Margery the character is "vain" and "petty" and ridiculous without having to abandon a feminist reading of the text.[27]

In her study of the *Book*, Staley differentiates between author and protagonist with the terms "Kempe" and "Margery." Staley's designations, while helpful, are somewhat limiting in that they assume that the author is a singular personage (when the *Book* may have been the result of collaboration) and propose that character and author are necessarily related entities (like Chaucer and "Geoffrey") when, in fact, they may not have been. Thus, in this chapter, I will designate the central character by the name "Margery" and the *Book*'s author according to that term, assuming that it can also encompass the possibility of multiple authors as well as the governing intelligence behind a role-playing performance.

Sanctity and the Problem of Margery's Unruliness

It is undeniable that Margery Kempe the character is intensely focused on establishing herself as a legitimate visionary. Many critics have assumed that this is the author's sole rhetorical purpose as well, some even going so far as to argue that the *Book* is a document aimed at canonizing Margery.[28] If the author's solitary aim were to establish Margery's religious authority, however, we would expect the *Book* to present her as an exemplar of spiritual living. In her analysis of the *Book* in the context of works by and about other medieval holy women, Rosalyn Voaden notes that hagiographic texts and books of revelations represent the visionary or saint according to established models: "There was no ambivalence about the subject's virtue, or about the authority of the text."[29] Yet the *Book of Margery Kempe* is packed full of details about Margery's unruliness and airs a whole variety of calumnies lodged against her (many of them sexual in nature).

The *Book*'s catalogue of obscene behavior is particularly intense at precisely the place where we would least expect it in a holy biography, at the *Book*'s outset, when most biographers are at pains to illustrate the innate piety of their subjects with tales of self-denying and virtuous childhoods. In his *Life of Marie d'Oignies*, Jacques de Vitry begins by describing Marie's disinclination for things of this world and her dedication to prayer: "Adeo enim ab infantia cum ea crevit miseratio & pietas, & quasi naturali affectione religionem diligetbat" [Thus mercy and righteousness grew in her from her infancy and she loved the ascetic life as if with a natural affection"].[30] The first dozen chapters of Margery's book are very different. They begin with her sexual initiation and include such unflattering episodes as Margery's desire to commit adultery with the man in St. Margaret's Church (29), the tale of her pride and wearing of extravagant gold tippets (24), her failed career as a brewer, a profession closely identified with female unruliness in the later Middle Ages (24), and the tale of her argument about married chastity with her husband on the road to Bridlington (37).[31] These pages also cast Margery in the unbecoming role of the termagant. During her postpartum episode of insanity, Margery slanders her husband and her friends and speaks "many a reprevows worde and many a schrewyd worde" (22).

One might argue that the *Book* is following the Magdalen pattern of "the fallen woman redeemed" or the Augustinian model of "the sinner reformed." And yet no other medieval biography of a holy woman portrays its heroine in these terms. While the biographers of other medieval holy women may record instances of disobedience, these tend to be passive forms of resistance carried out in the interests of asserting an ascetic spirituality—like Marie d'Oignies' rejection of her parents' offers of fine clothing.[32] They do not feature the self-interested agenda of pride and vanity that motivates Margery's initial defiance of her husband and her entry into business. Nor does Margery's early unruliness conform to a conversion model, since she is just as obstreperous after her conversion as she was before.

Margery's conflicts with authority figures are also at odds with the tradition of *discretio spiritum* that defined the visionary careers of medieval holy women. According to this tradition, the holy woman must be externally authorized and directed by figures of ecclesiastical authority. She must be obedient and deferential to the Church and must not appear to act in her own right: "She is constructed as passive, obedient, and submissive. . . . Her own will and desire are absent. She is a channel for the divine word, an instrument of divine will."[33] While holy women like St. Bridget might reprove ecclesiastical authority, they do so in the voice of God, not in their own interests or to further their own agenda as Margery does during her trial before the archbishop of York, when she resists the archbishop's command to leave the diocese in favor of her own travel agenda, which involves taking leave of her friends in York, speaking "wyth good men," and consulting with her confessor in Bridlington (126).

And yet it is equally clear that the *Book*'s author wants us to see Margery as a serious mystic. Even as it charts Margery's obscene behavior in detail, the *Book* also provides compelling evidence of divine inspiration. Among the miraculous occurrences cited in the first part of the *Book* are the second scribe's sudden ability to read the "ill formed" letters of the first scribe (20); Margery's escape from the falling stone and beam in St. Margaret's Church, which no less an authority than the White Friar, Master Allen, is quoted as deeming a "gret myracle" (36); and her knowledge of the lecherous monk's sins (40). Even as the *Book* is unstinting in its depictions of Margery's bad behavior, it also quotes the Dominican anchorite who remarks, after hearing of her visions, "Dowtyr, ye sowkyn evyn on Crysts brest" (31).

If we equate author and protagonist, we cannot help but conclude that the *Book* is a rhetorical failure, since its catalogue of the sexual and moral failings of its holy heroine was unlikely to garner her a following in late medieval religious culture.[34] If we separate author from protagonist, however, and think about Margery's unruliness as a characteristic deliberately juxtaposed with her spirituality for a particular purpose, a different picture emerges. Thinking about Margery's obscenity as a rhetorical technique allows us to see the *Book*'s abiding concern with the issue of tolerance in late medieval Christianity and its interest in exploring how the faithful (clerics in particular) should distinguish divine law from social norms in evaluating visionary women.

The opposition of worldly and divine prerogatives is a well-known conflict in Christianity. Christ's birth as the son of a carpenter bears witness to God's disregard for the hierarchies of the human world, as do Christ's repeated declarations, in the Gospel of Matthew and elsewhere, that in the heavenly kingdom "many that are first, shall be last: and the last shall be first."[35] The contradictory treatment of female visionaries in the medieval Church—wherein the visionary is at once honored as a vessel of God and forced to submit to human male authority—embodies precisely this conflict. In Margery's fifteenth-century England, the struggle to reconcile divine prerogative with social norms of gender had acquired fresh poignancy for a number of reasons. First among these was the role that gender played in the debate over Lollardy. Both the Lollards and their opponents accused one another of promoting sexual corruption and disrupting the natural gendered order that placed women under male authority.[36] In addition, as I have noted in my discussion of Lydgate's *Mumming at Hertford*, social authorities in the fifteenth century were showing increasing concern over disobedient women. Records of public courts held in villages, market centers, and hundreds show that, beginning in the late fourteenth century, there was a growing attempt to regulate a variety of minor offenses perceived as being injurious to the public peace. The most prominent among these was scolding, "an overwhelmingly female offence from the later fourteenth century through the 1510s."[37] Concerns over these forms of misbehavior appear particularly early and are particularly keen in Margery's own region of East Anglia.[38]

That the *Margery Kempe* author is aware of God's prerogative to choose his own emissaries, without regard for the opinions of human beings, is witnessed in the text's repeated references to precisely that fact. When the vicar of St. Stephen's Church of Norwich affirms Margery's spiritual gifts, he declares that she is "indued wyth grace of the Holy Gost, *to whom it longyth to enspyr wher he wyl*" (52, italics mine). Later, the narrator tells us that, when the priest scribe turns away from Margery after hearing the famous friar preach against her weeping, his faith in her is restored after reading of Marie D'Oignies' tears. Once the scribe reads of the spiritual gifts of this lowly woman, the narrator recounts, "Than knew he wel that God *gaf hys grace to whom he wolde*" (149, italics mine) and renews his allegiance to Margery.

The unruly mystic is an inspired choice for an author interested in asserting the difference between modes of behavior acceptable in the human world and those approved by God, since her character is founded upon a defiance of gender norms. In a number of encounters between Margery and various male clerics, the *Book*'s author exploits Margery's comic energy and the narrative trajectories of obscene comedy to denigrate clerics who insist on applying worldly categories to the divinely inspired Margery. The men who condemn or attempt to control Margery in these passages not only are characterized as hypocritical and unkind, but become laughingstocks in the manner of obscene comedy bozos.

Inevitably, these naysayers are sucked into the comic momentum that Margery carries with her everywhere she goes, becoming the kinds of petty, foolish individuals who fully deserve to get their comeuppance from an uppity woman. There is, for instance, the monk who "despised her and set her at naught," who becomes intrigued by the "good words" Margery shares at table but still refuses to accept her as a holy woman unless she can tell him whether he will be saved and what his sins are (39). This lack of faith lands the offending monk straight in the middle of a fabliau plot, as Christ informs Margery that the monk has engaged in the sin of lechery with married women (40). Similarly, the old monk who takes hold of Margery in the church at Canterbury, wishing her "closyd in an hows of ston that ther schuld no man speke wyth the," finds himself playing the role of patsy in a "world upside down" inversion of rank and power. Although the old monk was a man of status and wealth in his secular life, a treasurer to the queen and "gretly dred of mech pepyl," the unlettered Margery gets the better of him, telling an exemplum that converts his insults to an honorable martyrdom wherein Margery endures the "shame, scorn, and despite" of the world for Christ's love (41). The episode makes a meaningful theological point when it figures the monk's power as deriving from wealth and coercion rather than the spiritual authority of the gospels.[39] That point, however, is made comically, rather than polemically. We learn to dismiss the old monk because we laugh at him for being sent up by a woman, who should be his inferior.

Margery herself is not dignified in these passages. She does not appear in a manner befitting a spiritual woman, bickering with various clerics instead of patiently enduring the slings and arrows of religious persecution. But that, as I have been arguing, is precisely the point. It is the holy spirit's prerogative "to enspyr wher he wyl" (52), meaning not only that an unlettered woman like Margery can best a high-ranking intellectual in a contest of wit, but that this same woman's unruly behavior cannot be used to dismiss her spiritual gifts.

A contrasting series of encounters with high-ranking clerics affirms that Margery's violation of feminine conduct should not be used to dismiss her spiritual message. In meetings with Archbishop Arundel of Canterbury and the bishop of Worcester, Margery is her usual fractious self. She enters her conference with Arundel complaining about the swearing of his clerks, and she takes the bishop of Worcester to task because his summons "was to hir gret noye and hynderawns" (112). Yet both men are models of tolerance in their dealings with Margery. After listening to Margery's revelations of her "dalyawns," Arundel expresses gladness "that owyr mercyful Lord Cryst Jhesu schewyd swech grace in owyr days" and grants her the right to chose her own confessor and receive communion every Sunday. Nor is Arundel defensive about the matter of the swearing clerks, but "Ful benyngly and mekely he suffred hir to sey hir entent and gaf a fayr answer" (49). The bishop of Worcester gives a courtly response to Margery's criticism of him, denying that he ever summoned her and begging her not to be angry with him (112). As a result, both men are lifted safely above the obscene comedy mêlée, leaving their conferences with Margery with dignity and reputation intact. In this manner, the *Book* uses obscene comic discourse to identify tolerance of Margery with effective male leadership and to associate attempts at censure and control with a bumbling masculinity whose very aggressiveness guarantees the failure of its authority.

It is notable that, even as these passages draw on obscene comedy, they alter it substantially by reversing the discourse's logic. Traditionally, obscene comedy tends to praise forceful and controlling men and ridicule those who are credulous and tolerant. Narratives that approve of violent male responses to female unruliness are common in sermon exempla. A man in one exemplum marries a shrew, then tames her by killing his dog, cat, and horse before her eyes when they fail to obey his commands.[40] Another exemplum features a husband who kills his disobedient and adulterous wife with a box of poisoned sweets. In yet another, a husband catches his adulterous wife with a priest and tonsures her.[41] Although brutal violence is more rare in the fabliau than in sermon exempla, many fabliaux denigrate men who trust women implicitly and praise those who assert forceful control. "A mol pastor chie los laine!" (4.34.296) [When the shepherd is weak, the wolf shits wool] opines the author of *Berengier au lonc cul* (4.34), a tale in which a cowardly knight is bested by his wife. The fabliau *La sorisete des estopes* (6.66)—in which a foolish man is tricked by his adulterous wife—concludes with the following statement:

> . . . fame set plus que deiable
>
> . . . .
>
> Qant ele viaut om decevoir,
> Plus l'en deçoit et plus l'afole
> Tot solemant par sa parole
> Que om ne feroit par angin.(6.66.214; 218–21)

> [Woman knows more than the devil. . . . When she wants to fool a man, she tricks him and makes him more crazy, solely by her speech than a man can do by schemes.][42]

In the *Book of Margery Kempe*, however, it is the men who distrust Margery and attempt to control her who appear comically ineffective and stupid, while those who tolerate her rise magisterially above the fray.

The Trials Segment and the Lincoln-Arundel Segment

Margery's encounters with Arundel and Worcester are part of two unique and fascinating portions of the book that I term "the trials segment" and "the Lincoln-Arundel segment." The Lincoln-Arundel segment consists of two consecutive chapters (15 and 16) that narrate Margery's attempt to gain the official blessings of the two clerics. The trials segment—which runs from Chapters 45 through 55—is a remarkable interlude encompassing eight different episodes in which Margery is either arrested, called to appear before religious authorities, or examined for heresy. Included in this segment are Margery's appearance before the bishop of Worcester; her arrest and imprisonment by the mayor of Leicester and interrogation by the steward of Leicester; her trial before the abbot of Leicester; her interrogation at the York Minster chapterhouse; her trial before the archbishop of York; her arrest and imprisonment by the Duke of Bedford's men; her second appearance before the archbishop of York in Beverly; and her final arrest for Lollardy on the banks of the Humber.

Most accounts of this portion of the *Book* assume that it is factually based.[43] However, for anyone willing to entertain the possibility that the *Book* in its present form was created by multiple authors, who added to or embroidered upon an original document, or that its events may have been choreographed in ways the text does not admit, the Lincoln-Arundel segment and the trials segment are highly suggestive, since both contain features not seen anywhere else in the *Book*. Of the *Book*'s ninety-nine chapters, high-ranking clerics and individuals associated with Henry V are mentioned *only in these thirteen chapters*. The bishop of Worcester; the archbishop of York; the duke of Bedford; Lady Westmoreland, Joan de Beaufort and her daughter Lady Greystoke; the bishop of Lincoln; and Archbishop Arundel are all mentioned *only* in these sections of the *Book*.[44] These segments also contain all but one of the eight accusations of Lollardy in the *Book*.[45] Six of the eight accusations of Lollardy occur between Chapters 45 and 55. An additional one occurs in Chapter 16, outside Archbishop Arundel's palace in Lambeth, when the woman in the pilche wishes that Margery was "in Smythfeld" (48), the location where the first two Lollards were burned: William Sawtre of Margery's own parish, in 1401 and John Badby in 1410.[46]

The concentration of Lollard references and heresy trials in these thirteen chapters presents a challenge to those who wish to see the trials as being grounded in historical reality. If the *Book* were, in fact, a true account of unchoreographed events over thirty or more years in the life of an unconventional religious woman during the most intense decades of the English Church's anti-Lollard campaign, one might expect to find such accusations and interrogations scattered at various points. We cannot, furthermore, account for the grouping by saying that it reflects the associative patterns of oral narrative, since Margery's trials and arrests are characterized as occurring during a relatively brief period and follow chronologically one upon the other.

It is also worth noting that the Lincoln-Arundel segment contains two of the *Book*'s most notable textual inconsistencies. While Chapter 21 mentions Margery's being with child, Chapter 17 tells us of Christ's promise to Margery that she should have no more children, prompting the scribe to advise readers to read Chapter 21 before Chapter 17. And it is during the account of Margery and her husband's interview with the bishop of Lincoln that the narrative voice makes a unique slip from third- to first-person. Immediately after Margery and her husband take their vows of chastity before the bishop, the narrator goes on to say that "the Bysshop dede no mor to us at that day, save he mad us rygth good cher and seyd we wer rygth welcome" (47).[47] Also remarkable is the fact that none of the events in the trials segment are ever mentioned again in the *Book*, either by Margery or by anyone she meets, which is strange, given the intensity of the experience and the way the rest of the *Book* characterizes the operation of rumor, with many individuals siding against Margery or refusing to meet with her because of what they have heard about her.

If we read the *Book* as a rhetorical text that creates scenarios and characters for particular effect, we can see that the trials segment displays a deep concern with the social and religious consequences of the English Church's anti-heresy campaign.[48] As Ruth Nisse Shklar notes in her account of the trials, Margery, in these episodes, "not so much proves her legitimacy as questions the processes of legitimation themselves."[49] As in the other obscene comedy episodes of the *Book*, the question of how one ought to distinguish between worldly standards and Christian ones is prominent in the trials segment. Unlike other portions of the *Book*, however, the trials segment links unjust treatment of Margery directly to the Church's anti-Lollard campaign. Over and over again, the trials segment characterizes the Church's crackdown on Lollards as having fostered an uncontrolled paranoia about heresy that leads both secular and Church officials to advocate unjustified violence and to abrogate the Church's own due process.

It is remarkable that the trials segment, in spite of its variety of character and locale, essentially repeats the same sequence of events over and over again. In each trials segment episode, Margery's violation of gender norms prompts accusations of heresy, accompanied by threats of violence; she is then brought to trial, wherein official examinations prove that her offenses are irrelevant to the question of heresy, and she is released. Thus, the trials segment promotes a strict definition of heresy as a violation of the Articles of the Faith and repeatedly defends that definition as being distinct and separate from violations of social norms or sexual morality. This is a notable position for an author to advocate during a period famous for its ideological merging of heresy and other crimes, including treason, sexual sin, and defamation.[50]

Noting the *Book*'s positive depictions of bishops, Sarah Rees Jones argues that it affirms episcopal authority during a time when that authority was being challenged by secular officials, the laity, and the divisions and weaknesses of the lesser clergy, portraying the episcopacy "as triumphing over potential heretics, through their frequent assertion of Margery's orthodoxy," and asserting "episcopal willingness to accept and acclaim new forms of devotion." If we were to describe the *Book*'s surface message, we would have to agree with Rees Jones. However, I think the *Book*'s largely negative portrait of the Church's anti-Lollard campaign leads us to question how sincere its support for Worcester

and Arundel actually is. It is ironic, to say that least, that the *Book* portrays
Arundel as a model of compassion. Arundel was the leading proponent of the
anti-Lollard campaigns, who lobbied to legalize the burning of heretics, who
himself presided over the trials of those who were burnt, and whose *Constitutions* are famous for their unprecedented crackdown on lay religiosity.[51] The
archbishop's tolerant response to Margery stands in marked contrast to the
portrait of him in the account of his examination of William Thorpe, wherein
he becomes enraged at Thorpe's refusal to submit to his authority: "But I say to
thee, lewd losel! Either thou quickly consent to mine ordinance, and submit
thee to stand to my decrees, or, by Saint Thomas! Thou shalt be disgraded and
follow the fellow in Smithfield!"[52]

    As I shall be discussing in more detail below, the trials segment issues some
rather striking critiques of precisely the programs over which Arundel presided
and that clerics like the bishop of Worcester encouraged. Although the *Book*
issues no direct criticism of episcopal leadership, it also does nothing to prevent
its audience from connecting the bad behavior of members of the laity and
lesser clergy to the episcopal policies that promoted hysteria over Lollardy.
Given this fact, it is possible that the *Book*'s deference to these two senior clerics has more to do with setting up a bulwark against possible repercussions
resulting from the *Book*'s criticism of the anti-Lollard campaigns than it does
with a sincere promotion of Arundel and Worcester.

The Trials Segment

LEICESTER

Margery's first arrest in the trials segment happens at the hands of the mayor of
Leicester. Although he arrests Margery for heresy, accusing her of being "a fals
loller, and a fals deceyver of the pepyl," the mayor is not actually interested in
Christian doctrine, as he should be if he is attempting to detect for heresy
(114). Instead, he is concerned over the fact that Margery, a married woman
and a mother, is wearing white. The import of Margery's garb, for the mayor,
does not lie in its defiance of religious doctrine but in what it suggests about
Margery's attitude toward marriage. During her examination before the abbot
at the Church of All Saints at Leicester, the mayor punctuates his demand to
know the reason for her white clothing with the accusation that "thow art
comyn hedyr to han awey owr wyvys fro us and ledyn hem wyth the" (117).

Margery's white clothes are a frequent subject of debate during the trials segment. The mayor's characterization of her wardrobe choice in this passage as an act linked to a kind of obscene disruption of the sexual order is revealing. Ostensibly, Margery is not participating in an act of sexual obscenity by putting on white clothes, yet the mayor thinks she is. The problem seems to lie in the fact that she is adopting a virginal symbol when she is not, in fact, a virgin.[53] The obscenity of wearing white, then, is not so much a sexual violation as a violation of hierarchies in the sense that wearing white involves making a claim to a higher spiritual status to which Margery, as a married woman and mother, should not be entitled. Notably, the claim to special status applies not only to white's associations with virginity but to all of its other associations in fifteenth-century England (with radical continental piety, with the elect in heaven, and with a variety of "carefully defined moments of transition").[54] As I have noted in the introduction to this study, transgressions of hierarchies are often as obscene in medieval culture as sexual transgressions and are often, as the mayor's sexual suspicions of Margery indicate, associated with sexual transgression.

The trials segment is fascinating because it in no way accepts Margery's obscenity as just cause for her religious persecution. Instead, the *Book* uses debates over the wearing of white to illustrate how various authorities lack a clear understanding of the difference between violations of social norms and violations of Christian doctrine—between, that is, obscenity and heresy. This is the case with the mayor of Leicester's accusations over Margery's white garb. The abbot and his clerks, following the dictates of canon law, examine Margery on the Articles of the Faith. She is found to be perfectly orthodox and thus not vulnerable to prosecution by the Church courts. The trial indicates that Margery's white clothes, as offensive as they may be to some people, have nothing to do with heresy, a fact that is underlined when the mayor disputes the clerks' favorable judgment of Margery and is told, "Sir, she answeryth [the Articles of the Faith] ryth wel to us" (117).

Margery's encounter with the mayor also touches upon several issues relating to the Church's anti-Lollard campaign. As a secular official attempting to prosecute a doctrinal crime, the mayor takes a role that would have been quite new for secular authorities in the fifteenth century. Traditionally, the enforcement of religious orthodoxy had been reserved to Church officials. Since the late fourteenth century, however, the Church had been progressively encouraging increased lay involvement in the prosecution of heresy.[55] The passage of *De Heretico Comburendo* in 1401 was a watershed moment, giving lay powers an unprecedented role in punishing spiritual crimes.[56] In 1414, parliament made heresy hunting a normal duty of the chancellor, treasurer, justices, and all local officials, who were now to be sworn to this obligation as part of their oaths of office.[57] The rationale was that involvement of lay officials would limit the spread of heresy by allowing the Church to root it out sooner. The Leicester episode, however, shows a different side of the matter. The mayor's ignorance of canon law, and his inability to distinguish between heresy and secular violations, seems deliberately calculated to highlight the problems involved in employing secular forces to enforce Church doctrine.

The episode also invites the *Book*'s readers to see how the involvement of secular powers in the anti-Lollard campaign threatens to blur the boundaries between secular and religious authority. The law gave secular officials the power to arrest individuals on the suspicion of heresy, but it was up to Church courts to determine whether such a violation had actually occurred. The encroachment of secular authorities on ecclesiastical ground was a danger of which English authorities were aware, as is revealed by the stipulation in the 1414 statute that the cognizance of heresy, errors, and Lollardy pertains only to judges of the Church and not secular judges.[58] The mayor in these scenes does not respect the limits of his authority, presuming to judge doctrinal matters on his own and calling Margery a "fals loller" before she has even been brought to trial (114). Margery herself, meanwhile, emphasizes the Church's exclusive power to interpret and administer Christian doctrine. When the mayor demands to know why she goes in white, Margery tells him that he "is not worthy to know it," but that she will explain her wearing of white "to thes worthy clerkys wyth good wil be the maner of confessyon" (117).

The Leicester episode also suggests that *De Heretico Comburendo*—the 1401 act that allowed English authorities to punish heretics with burning—has sparked a lamentable rush to violence among laypeople that is at odds with the canon law's circumspect approach to punishing heresy. During Margery's imprisonment in Leicester, she learns from two pilgrims that "yyf the meyr myth han hys wil, he wolde don hir be brent" (116). As we consider this scene's effect on the *Book*'s fifteenth-century readers (particularly its clerical audience), we should note the strong emphasis on mercy in canon law as it pertained to heresy. The canonist Gratian was keenly aware of the indeterminacy of human judgment on matters of faith, writing that "many are corrected, like Peter; many tolerated, like Judas; while many are not known until the coming of the Lord, who will illuminate the secrets of the darkness."[59] Cognizant of human limitations in the judgment of spiritual legitimacy, canon law instructed that judicial procedure in matters of heresy should be bound by the compassionate imperative of *equitas canonica* to find a middle way.[60] Traditionally, a simple conviction of heresy was not enough to merit death, a punishment reserved only for unrepentant and lapsed heretics.[61] While it is true that these canonical principles had already been violated many times over on the Continent, we should keep in mind that a tradition of tolerance did exist in the Church and was advocated by the Church's own law.[62] That such principles still held sway among many English clergy, even amid the anti-Lollard campaign, is witnessed in the fact that only a small minority of heresy cases tried in England between 1414 and 1522 (33 of 545) actually resulted in execution.[63]

The trials segment frequently exploits the tropes and narrative trajectories of obscene comedy to increase the rhetorical power of its critique of the anti-Lollard campaign. The scenes in which the mayor becomes increasingly furious as Church officials refuse to support his view of Margery as a heretic—and those in which the clever Margery takes control, winning clerical officials to her side—draw on the humor of incongruity that we frequently see in obscene comedy, wherein those on the lower end of the social hierarchy best their social superiors in contests of wit. Particularly germane to Margery's status as a woman in middle age in these scenes is obscene comedy's tendency to feature clever old women who overcome men with their superior knowledge and capacity for trickery. This is the plot of the earliest extant piece of English obscene comedy, *Dame Sirith*, which narrates the tale of an old bawd who leads a young wife into adultery with a young clerk after convincing the wife that she will turn into a dog if she does not indulge him.[64] One Old French fabliau even features a clever old woman swindling a bishop in an ecclesiastical court. In *Le prestre qui ot mere a force* (5.41), an old woman complains to the bishop about her son's poor treatment of her and manages to trick the bishop into sending her off as the mother of another priest, whom the bishop orders to care generously for her on pain of death, in spite of the innocent man's outraged protestations.[65]

Although it may initially seem at odds with the serious thematic concerns of the episode, the comedy of Margery's trial at Leicester is essential to communicating the meanings I have discussed above. The rhetorical power of the Leicester episode depends on the audience being able to question secular authority and to sympathize with Margery in her violations of social decorum. Achieving this effect, however, would have been a challenge for a medieval author writing in any discourse other than obscene comedy. The patriarchal nature of medieval culture and the respect for social authority evinced in so many medieval discourses would have disposed the audience to respect the mayor's authority and condemn Margery for her social infractions. Casting the episode as obscene comedy helps the author divert this response by drawing on obscene comedy's celebration of "the world upside down." Gaunt's remark that the fabliau "likes nothing better than destabilizing the categories medieval culture used to rationalize its social order and the internal hierarchies upon which it rested" applies to the discourse as a whole.[66] Thus, obscene comedy encourages audiences to go against the cultural grain and side with the renegade figure.[67] It is acceptable, in the comic spirit of the discourse, to characterize social authorities as stupid and laughable and to enjoy their downfall at the hands of clever subordinates.

THE YORK TRIAL

The second phase of the trials sequence—Margery's examination at York minster and subsequent hearing before the archbishop of York—replays many of the elements of the Leicester episode. Here, once again, the impetus for concern over Margery's orthodoxy lies in her violation of gender conventions. The first question the doctor at York minster asks Margery concerns the location of her husband and whether he has given her leave to travel about the country alone. When Margery comes before the archbishop of York, Henry Bowet, his first question interrogates Margery about her wearing of white and its relation to her sexual status: "Why gost thu in white? Art thu mayden?" (124). Like the Leicester episode, the York episode links the Church's anti-Lollard campaign with the abrogation of due process. As Margery enters Bowet's court, members of his household call her a Lollard and a heretic, threatening her with burning before she has even been examined. As in the trial at Leicester, such accusations are proven to be groundless as Margery answers the Articles of the Faith with perfect orthodoxy.

In the York trial, however, the author takes his or her examination of the Church's obsession with heresy a step farther. Contained within the York trial is an extended discussion that takes up the Lollard sponsorship of lay preaching and considers how officials' obsession with stamping out Lollardy has led them to violate the Church's own doctrine.[68] In doing so, the episode reminds its audience that lay speech is a legitimate part of orthodox spirituality and reveals how Church officials' failure to understand the difference between orthodox and heretical speech is leading to the persecution of innocent lay people.

Obscene comedy is a crucial part of the author's technique in the York trial. Like the Leicester episode, the York trial's trajectory follows the discourse's "world upside down" paradigm as the irrepressible Margery takes on the archbishop and various clerks in a battle of wits and emerges triumphant. A brief summary of Margery's argument with the archbishop shows how the *Book*'s author draws on obscene comedy tropes of feminine unruliness and bumbling masculine authority to underline the problems in the Church's obsession with Lollardy.

Having examined Margery in the Articles of the Faith, the archbishop declares her to be orthodox and asks his clerks what to do with her. His clerks acknowledge that Margery is orthodox but say that they want her to leave the diocese because the people have great faith in her "dalyawnce" and they fear she will "prevertyn summe of hem" (125). The archbishop then remarks to Margery, "I am evyl enformyd of the; I her seyn thu art a ryth wikked woman." In response, Margery turns the proposition on its head, informing the archbishop that she hears the same thing about him: "Ser, so I her seyn that ye arn a wikkyd man. And, yyf ye ben as wikkyd as men seyn, ye schal nevyr come in hevyn les than ye amende yow whil ye ben her" (125). The rumors of his own perfidy upset the archbishop, and he responds "ful boistowsly, 'Why, thow, what sey men of me?" To which Margery issues the cagey reply that "Other men, syr, can telle yow wel anow" (125). The frustrated archbishop then seeks to secure a promise from Margery that she will leave his diocese. She refuses and asks leave to go into the city to say goodbye to her friends. The archbishop gives her one or two days, a time she finds too short. Finally, the archbishop warns her not to teach or reprove the people in his diocese. Margery refuses this request as well, saying she will not do so until the pope and Church forbid people from speaking of God (126).

The passage invites its audience to laugh at the archbishop for the same reasons that the fabliau invites its audience to laugh at the unruly woman's husband: because he cannot control his female subordinate. The rhetoric directing the comedy of the York trial, however, is not the the fabliau rhetoric underlining the perfidy of women and the need for masculine control, but a theological rhetoric regarding the permissibility of lay speech about God. Like the other obscene comedy encounters in the *Book*, this one inverts the discourse's logic, making the archbishop's attempts at control, and his lack of faith in Margery's rectitude, the mark of his failed authority. In refusing Bowet's demand that she neither teach nor reprove, Margery draws attention to the fact that no orthodox religious authority forbids it, vowing that she will speak of God "unto the tyme that the pope and holy chirche hath ordeynde that no man schal be so hardy to spekyn of God, for God almythy forbedith not, ser, that we schal speke of hym" (126). Margery then affirms the truth of her statement though an appeal to the Bible itself, citing a passage from Luke 11:27, wherein a woman calls out to Christ "wyth a lowde voys," blessing the womb that bore him, and Christ responds by saying, in Margery's rendering, "Forsothe so ar thei blissed that heryn the word of God and kepyn it."[69] True to its orthodox doctrinal stance, the *Book* does not advocate preaching by women, but by citing Luke it counters the ecclesiastical court's resistance to *any* female religious speech by showing that female speech alone (even if it is loud and public) is not forbidden.

The distinction between preaching and teaching is re-enforced when a clerk of the archbishop's responds to Margery's citation of the Bible by citing Paul's strictures on women's preaching. Margery denies having preached on the basis that "I come in no pulpytt," thereby providing women with considerable latitude to speak of God as long as they do not presume literally to occupy the established space of the preacher (126). As artificial as it might seem, the distinction is not original to the *Book*. The author of a fifteenth-century treatise, *Speculum Christiani*, makes the pulpit into a similar boundary marker between preaching and lay teaching.[70]

Through all of this, the unruly woman's voice and stance plays an important role in enabling the *Book*'s doctrinally based critique of the anti-Lollard campaign. As I have noted in my discussion of Langland, the unruly female voice articulates a resistance to authority whose aggression is unmatched by any other medieval discourse. There are few voices—male or female—anywhere in medieval literary culture that attack social authority with the assertiveness that we find in the voice of the obscene comedy woman. One might say that, in its trial setting, the battle between Margery and the archbishop also recalls the pagan trials of the virgin-martyr saints and that it is to this tradition that we owe Margery's antiauthoritarian voice. It is certainly true that one of the only other medieval discourses to offer up an aggressive female voice is the discourse of hagiography, and there is no reason to deny its influence here. The saints' legends, however, are not often funny. It is in the humor the *Book* associates with the unruly Margery's voice (as well as the fact that Margery is a middle-class, married woman, rather an aristocratic maiden in the tradition of the virgin martyr legends) that the influence of obscene comedy leaves its mark.[71]

The York trial enacts a further critique of the Church by suggesting that those clerics obsessed with unlicensed preaching are guilty of their own spiritual infractions. It is both humorous and intriguing that Margery counters Bowet's accusation regarding her wickedness with the observation that Bowet himself has a reputation for evil (125). The subject is never explored fully. After a clerk interrupts the exchange, we hear no more of Bowet's sins. One wonders, however, whether this passage had a specific referent for the *Book*'s fifteenth-century readers and what that referent might have been. Bowet was famed for his prosecution of Lollardy and had aided Arundel in the trial of one of the first victims of *De Heretico Comburendo*, John Badby, in 1410. Would this perhaps have been regarded as wicked by sympathetic readers, given the *Book*'s other criticisms of the anti-Lollard campaign? Or could the accusation relate to Bowet's famously luxurious lifestyle (involving a household that consumed eighty tuns of claret yearly)? Or perhaps to events relating to some of his many secular responsibilities during the reign of Henry IV? Or to the fact that he had been declared a traitor and banished during the reign of Richard II?[72] Whatever the original inference might have been, it is certain that Margery's words leave a lasting doubt as to Bowet's moral authority, for, even if the *Book* does not support Margery's accusation with evidence, it also does not refute it.

Clerical morality is again at issue in the obscene tale Margery tells during her second trial before the archbishop of York. When a doctor of the Church accuses her of telling "the werst talys of prestys that evyr I herde" (127), Margery volunteers to narrate it. In this tale, a priest sees a bear eating the flowers of a pear tree and voiding "hem owt ageyn at the hymyr party." He asks an old man, described as "a palmyr er a pilgrime," to interpret it (127). The old man tells him that the excrement symbolizes the priest himself, who preaches and administers the sacraments but does not himself live virtuously. It is notable that this exemplum also touches on the same theme of God's capacity "to enspyr wher he wyl" (52) that is emphasized elsewhere in the book." In spite of his clerical status, the priest does not understand the meaning of what he has seen. It is the old man (an unbeneficed individual) who, "schewyng hymselfe the massanger of God," is able to interpret the meaning of the vision (127).

THE BEDFORD EPISODE

In the final extended episode of the trials segment, Margery is apprehended by the Duke of Bedford's men, imprisoned, and brought for a second trial before the archbishop of York. As in the other two episodes, the Bedford episode illustrates that accusations of heresy are sparked not by doctrinal infractions but by Margery's refusal to conform to norms of appropriate feminine behavior. Having arrested her as "the grettest loller in al this cuntré," the Duke of Bedford's men question Margery's desire to travel about as a lone woman, advising her to "forsake this lyfe that thu hast, and go spynne and carde as other women don" (129). Margery is also accused of disrupting gender hierarchies in marriage when, during her second examination before Bowet, the Friar Preacher asserts that she advised Lady Greystoke to leave her husband (133). In yet another confusion of social and doctrinal violations, the friar assumes that Margery's defiance of gender hierarchies is sufficient to have her punished as a heretic. Having outlined Margery's supposed advice to Lady Greystoke, the friar concludes that Margery "now hast seyd inow to be brent for" (133). As in all Margery's trials, the Bedford episode demonstrates that violations of social norms have nothing to do with heresy.

In the Bedford episode, we see the *Book*'s author issuing his or her most direct and far-reaching critique. Unlike the other episodes, which focus on clerical officials and low-ranking secular authorities, the Bedford episode mentions high-ranking members of the secular elites by name. The Duke of Bedford, whose men seize Margery at the episode's outset, was one of the most powerful personages in the land, a brother of Henry V who, at the time of the *Book*'s creation, was senior regent of Henry VI's minority and the leader of England's ongoing war in France. Also mentioned is Lady Westmoreland, the mother of Lady Greystoke, whom Margery is accused of corrupting. This was Joan de Beaufort, the daughter of John of Gaunt, and thus the sister of Henry IV and aunt of Henry V. Although the text casts Westmoreland in a positive light (Margery seems to have received sympathetic treatment from the lady and her daughter), its treatment of Bedford is more ambivalent. The criticism of the duke is not direct—the man himself never appears, and we are uncertain to what degree his men carry out his orders and to what degree they act on a flawed mandate of their own. Nevertheless, the mere involvement of such a high-ranking personage in what is ultimately shown to be a flawed attack on a doctrinally orthodox holy person is a bold enough move considering the political context.

More than any other part of the trials segment, the Bedford episode underlines the paranoia and violence sparked by the Church's anti-Lollard crackdown. Threats of burning abound here, appearing more than anywhere else in the *Book*. When Margery arrives in Hesle, "men callyd hir loller, and women cam rennyng owt of her howsys wyth her rokkys, crying to the pepil, 'Brennyth this fals heretyk'" (129). In the archbishop's court, the Friar Preacher not only decides that Margery's words to Lady Greystoke are enough to be burnt for, he also remarks that she would have been burnt at Lynn if his order had not been there (131). After Margery is found to be free of heresy, the archbishop's steward "and many mo wyth hym" advise him to let Margery go this time, but if she ever returns "we schal bren hyre owrself" (133).

The Bedford episode is also remarkable for the way it underlines the Church's subjection to secular powers. During the second trial, the archbishop dismisses the Friar Preacher's accusations against Margery, telling him that what he has described is not heresy. The friar agrees, but maintains that the Duke of Bedford is angry with her and "wyl han hir" (132). This is enough for the archbishop to capitulate. Declaring that he would not want the Duke of Bedford angry with him, the archbishop agrees to keep Margery for another day in spite of the fact that he has cleared her of heresy. While the deference of the fifteenth-century English Church to secular authority is not news to any student of English medieval history, it is nevertheless remarkable to see a contemporary source outlining that power relationship so explicitly and in a way that is so unflattering to high-ranking ecclesiastical officials.

It is no coincidence that the passages containing the *Book*'s most stringent critiques of secular authority also feature its most outrageous obscene comedy. As well as the comical trial scene I have described above, the Bedford section is also punctuated with the riotous episode of Margery's imprisonment in Beverly. Carried to Beverly by the Duke of Bedford's men and imprisoned in a "chambyr," Margery nevertheless refuses to be silenced, telling "good talys" from the window of her prison to all who will hear her. Margery's speech so affects the women gathered to hear her that they put a ladder up to her window to bring her a pot of wine, advising her to hide the pot when she is finished so the jailer will not know (130).[73] Riotous defiance of male authority is again on show during Margery's triumphant exit from the archbishop's court, having been cleared of all heresy charges, bearing the archbishop's letter in her hand, and laughing in the face of a furious steward of Leicester (134).

As in Langland's *Piers Plowman*, obscene comedy in the trials segment of the *Book of Margery Kempe* functions as a blind behind which the author can issue potentially dangerous critiques of the powerful, in particular secular authorities. To return once again to the theories of James Scott, obscene comedy in these passages allows the *Book*'s author an "avenue of retreat" away from his or her critiques to a more innocuous meaning.[74] If we assume that the *Book* was written in the late 1420s or early 1430s, then the atmosphere of repression relating to any writing on religious or Church matters would still have been severe. The period, in fact, saw a resurgence of repression relating to Lollard activities, with the Norwich trials in the late 1420s and the uproar over a Lollard insurrection in Abingdon in 1431.[75] If Margery is funny in these passages, if she draws audience sympathy as she combats various stuffed-shirt authority figures, it nevertheless remains true that she is not authoritative or respectable herself. While Margery's status as a ludicrous comic figure might seem to undermine the *Book*'s critiques of secular and ecclesiastical authority, in the fifteenth century's climate of political repression, it actually enables them, allowing an "avenue of retreat" wherein the questions she poses of institutions and powerful figures can be dismissed as the ranting of a degraded obscene comedy woman.

One can perceive the very different political and ethical valence that the unruly Margery injects into these scenes if one imagines how they would have appeared if they concerned the persecution of a woman like Marie d'Oignies and were written by a high-ranking cleric like Jacques de Vitry. Such a narrative would read as a ringing condemnation of all involved, something that undoubtedly would have been very dangerous in the first half of the fifteenth century. An account of an unruly holy woman by a near-illiterate and anonymous cleric is much safer, even if it airs the same concerns, because it lacks the authority that would inhere in a more conventional hagiographic narrative.

Compassion and Subordinate Rebellion in the Trials Segment

One of the most remarkable features of the *Book of Margery Kempe* is its emphasis on the importance of compassion. Compassion is the dominant theme of the visions, which repeatedly show Christ and God comforting and loving Margery, even when she sins. The importance of compassion is quite clearly set out in the opening proem, whose first sentence tells us that the *Book*'s primary goal is a compassionate one, to extend comfort to "synful wrecchys" so that they can understand the "hy and unspecabyl mercy" of Christ (17). The second sentence of the proem elaborates that compassion is important not only for what it gives to others, but also for what it brings back to the compassionate. All Christ's works, the proem tells us, are for our example and instruction and "what grace that he werkyth in any creatur is ower profyth *yf lak of charyté be not ower hynderawnce*" (17, italics mine). Thus, "charity" (a term closely associated with benevolence and mercy in medieval thought) is salient not just as a moral value but because it opens our minds to the word of God.[76] The word "compassion" itself, which recurs many times in the *Book*, is a relatively late term. As a word that denotes one's feeling for the suffering of another, it appears for the first time in 1340. That new sense of the term, as Sarah McNamer has observed in her study of compassion in late medieval culture, is witnessed in the *Book of Margery Kempe*.[77]

The *Book* repeatedly suggests that compassion and tolerance, rather than control and discipline, are the appropriate responses to the unconventionally holy, as long as they remain doctrinally orthodox. From one angle, it might seem that the *Book* is rather elitist, in the sense that it is often the highest-ranking officials who best embody its ethical values, while those who come in for the most blistering treatment for their ignorance and cruelty are the mid-level officials like the mayor of Leicester, the steward of Leicester, the Friar Preacher, and various other monks and priests.

The *Book*'s apparent elitism is, however, qualified by a couple of significant details in the trials and Lincoln-Arundel segments. While it is true that the excesses associated with the anti-Lollard campaign are expressed primarily by mid-level officials, it is nevertheless significant that such excesses always occur in close proximity to the high-ranking clerics who were well known for their dedication to rooting out the Lollard heresy. It is in front of Arundel's palace at Lambeth that a townswoman tells Margery she wishes she were being burned at Smithfield. It is when Margery is being brought to the archbishop of York's court that men call her a Lollard and women demand that officials burn her as a heretic.

There are two possible readings of these juxtapositions. One reading would say, as Sarah Rees Jones does, that the passages affirm episcopal authority by showing how the lower orders of society are guilty of an excess that is only controlled by the superior rationality and wisdom of high-ranking clerics. Alternately, however, we might say that these juxtapositions invite us to read back from lower-order excesses and locate responsibility for their madness in the leaders who created such policies in the first place. We should not underestimate the lure of the second reading, particularly in the case of clerics like Arundel, the bishop of Worcester, and the archbishop of York, all of whom were well-known for their active pursuit of Lollards. Indeed, as Lynn Staley has remarked, in spite of the fact that the scenes with famously anti-Lollard prelates are ostensibly meant to affirm Margery's orthodoxy, "they seem, instead, to recall England's history of dissent, a history of the divisions between the prelates of the English church and some of the English."[78]

Also relevant is the trials segment's representation of subordinate rebellion. A number of times in these pages, Margery's rebellion "goes viral," spreading to subordinates who, in sympathy with or admiration for Margery, begin themselves to resist the commands of social and religious authority. This, too, is a common feature of obscene comedy, which often depicts renegade women leading subordinates in outrageous rebellions against senior males.[79] As is so often the case in the *Book of Margery Kempe,* the moral valence of these scenes is reversed from its obscene comedy trajectory. While the rebellion of subordinates in genres like the fabliau is most often carried out in the interests of greed or lust, subordinates in the trials segment rebel by asserting the Christian values of mercy and compassion against an unjust officialdom. Thus, the jailer in Leicester resists the mayor's command to imprison Margery because it would mean exposing her to the risk of sexual assault. He is described as "havyng compassyon of hir wyth wepyng terys" (114). The "good folke of Leicetyr" who escort Margery out of town regret her harassment by the courts and promise that, if she ever returns to the town, she will have better comfort among them (119). The "seculer pepil" beg the judge at York minster not to imprison Margery while she awaits trial before the archbishop and put themselves forward as surety for her (91). Finally, there are the women who tend to Margery during her imprisonment in Beverly. Their behavior is cast according to the obscene comedy emphasis on women's talent for lying and trickery (they advise Margery to hide the pot of wine and the cup they have given her so that the jailer will not see them), but their actions are directed toward a compassionate care for Margery's thirst and a resistance to harsh punishment. "Alas, woman, why schalt thu be brent?" they ask, after hearing Margery's "good talys" (130).

Sarah McNamer's recent study allows us to link the *Book*'s affective piety to its promotion of compassion and its opposition to violence. Affective piety encouraged its adherents to cultivate pity for Christ in his suffering on the cross. As a result, McNamer argues, affective piety exposed the horrific consequences of violence and gave rise to a current of protest against ethical systems that accepted violence as a legitimate means to an end.[80] While the *Book* promotes compassion consistently throughout its narrative, it is only in the trials segment that it politicizes compassion. While other parts of the book tend to characterize bad behavior or unjust responses to Margery according to a more generalized theory of a "fallen world," in which few can hear the word of God, the trials and Arundel-Lincoln segments characterize injustice as an institutional phenomenon—the outcome of specific official policies and doctrines.[81]

Revisions of Obscene Comedy Tropes of Female Sexuality

Sexual misbehavior is the only misdeed other than heresy of which Margery is persistently accused. This pairing is not unusual, since the two crimes were often conflated in the fifteenth century. As in the case of the heresy accusations, the numerous scenes wherein Margery is accused of sexual misdeeds and defends herself draw extensively from obscene comedy. In this instance, however, the author does not just appropriate elements of obscene discourse but instead ventriloquizes some of its misogynist assumptions to challenge the discourse's tendency to equate unconventional female behavior with sexual corruption. While the *Book* cleaves quite faithfully to the Church's policies on sexual behavior—acknowledging that celibacy is a higher spiritual practice than married sexuality and that adultery and fornication are grave sins—it disputes the assumption that women are more sexually corrupt than men and that unconventional female behavior is necessarily indicative of a taste for sinful sex. These assumptions, the *Book* demonstrates, lead Christians to condemn innocent women and ignore the sins committed by men.

As I have noted throughout this study, the identification of women with sexual corruption is pervasive in obscene discourse. Tales of women's adultery qualify as a subgenre of the fabliau, which often features an innocent husband being pitted against an adulterous wife, possessed of an inexhaustible sexual appetite.[82] The obscene stone and wood carvings that bedeck medieval churches frequently evince similar themes. This medium is germane to the *Book of Margery Kempe*, which exhibits a close familiarity with the churches of medieval Europe. Carvings of monstrous-featured women exhibiting their vulvas are often found in churches along the pilgrimage routes Margery travels—in the churches of the British Isles, northern Spain, and western France. A number of the churches that feature obscene carvings are located in cities that Margery herself visits in the *Book*: the cathedral in Lincoln features a *femme aux serpents* (a sculpture of a naked woman with a pair of serpents feeding on her breasts); the cathedral in Bridlington features an exhibiting female; Ely Cathedral also contains a female exhibitionist figure; and the Cathedral of St. James in Santiago features two *femmes aux serpents* and a female exhibitionist. Finally, Margery's own St. Margaret's Church in Lynn features sculptures of a female mouth puller (closely associated with female exhibitionism, given the medieval equation between mouths and vulvas), a woman in a scold's bridle, and female feet-to-ears acrobats (also closely associated with the exhibitionist carvings due to the acrobats' exposure of the genital and anal areas of the body).[83]

Of particular relevance to Margery's situation is the obscene comedy trope of the lascivious woman who hides her illicit desires behind protestations of modesty. In one popular tale that appears as both a fabliau and a sermon exemplum (and was likely well known in East Anglia, since the N-Town plays make reference to it), an adulterous wife evokes a kind of immaculate conception when she tells her husband that a child born while he was away from home was conceived by means of a snowflake.[84] Margery's accusers often assume that her piety hides a similar corruption. The monk of Norwich accuses Margery of using pilgrimage as an excuse for adultery, and various individuals accuse Margery and her husband of failing to keep their pious vows of chastity.

Also relevant to the *Book* is obscene comedy's tendency to characterize older, postmenopausal women as especially obscene. Old women were, as Jan Ziolkowski has noted, the "truck drivers" of the middle ages, regarded by many moralists as "likely to employ dangerous speech pertaining to sexual organs, sexual acts, and immorality."[85] Older women's sexual knowledge, combined with their higher levels of independence and the authority vested in them by virtue of their age, worried many moralists, who were concerned about old women's capacity to lead younger women into bad behavior. In fabliaux, in Latin elegiac comedy, and in English tales, elderly women are often figured leading young women into sexual sin.[86] We can see this obscene comedy character being adumbrated in the mayor of Leicester's accusation that Margery has come to Leicester to "han awey owr wyvys fro us and ledyn hem wyth the" (117). Similar presumptions are evident in the accusation delivered by the suffragen of the archbishop of York that Margery counseled Lady Greystoke to leave her husband.

Even as we read the calumnies lodged against Margery, however, we always know that Margery is innocent. We have been with her on her pilgrimage to Rome and Jerusalem and know that the monk of Norwich's accusation is groundless. The mayor of Leicester's allegation regarding Margery's intention to carry off the town's wives is preceded by a tale of Margery's blameless worship of holy objects at a Leicester church (118). The archbishop of York's investigation of the Lady Westmoreland incident reveals that Margery spent her time at that lady's home telling pious exempla.

By ventriloquizing obscene comedy misogyny and showing how it results in a variety of hardships for Margery—arrest, withdrawal of spiritual mentorship, censure—the author asks us to see how the discourse punishes innocent women. In doing so, the *Book* draws its readers' attention to a social problem whose historical importance has recently been discussed by Judith Bennett. In attempting to determine why women's participation in the ale industry declined so precipitously from the fourteenth to the sixteenth centuries, Bennett cites economic factors but posits that late medieval literature also contributed to the decline of women in brewing by associating alewives with dishonesty and sexual wantonness. These texts, Bennett argues, affected women brewers by socially marginalizing them and encouraging towns concerned with disorder in alehouses to link that disorder to the presence of women in the industry.[87]

If the *Book of Margery Kempe* only demonstrated the injustice of obscene misogyny by creating a narrative in which it harmed a chaste married woman, spotless in thought and deed, its resistance to obscene discourse would be significant but limited. It would not challenge the basic polarities by which medieval culture categorized women. This is the case with Johannes von Marienwerder, whose biography of Dorothea of Montau opposes the accusations of sexual obscenity made by members of Montau's community with the impeccably chaste sexuality of Montau herself.[88] The author of Margery Kempe's book goes much farther and does something much more interesting, reconstructing the category of the spiritually virtuous to include women who may have had sinful thoughts and outsized sexual desires in their pasts. These women, the *Book* proposes, can be admitted to the ranks of the holy as long as they struggle against their impure thoughts and as long as they do not behave obscenely in the present. In this way, the *Book*'s author maps out a more human (and humane) middle ground between the depraved sex maniacs of the fabliau and the utterly pure holy women of tale and legend.

As every reader of the *Book of Margery Kempe* knows, Margery is regularly dogged with impure desires. The author's conviction that such desires should be accepted as the legitimate struggles of a religious person is signaled by the very early inclusion of scenes of sexual temptation. Barely fourteen pages into the *Book*, we learn that two years after her spiritual awakening, Margery is beset by three years of "temptacyons" (28). In the most spectacular of these, Margery, while attending evensong at St. Margaret's Church, conceives of a lust for a man "whech she louyd wel" (29). The man propositions her, and Margery is so strongly tempted "for to syn wyth him" that at last she propositions the man herself (29). In one of the *Book*'s most notorious episodes, Margery, beset with "fowle thowtys and fowle mendys of letchery and alle unclennes" imagines various men of religion—"preystys and many other, bothyn hethyn and Cristen . . . schewyng her bar membrys unto hir" (142). When the Devil tells Margery that she must "be comown to hem all," she thinks that she will do it and that "thes horrybyl syghtys and cursyd mendys wer delectabyl to hir" (143).

Undoubtedly, these scenes are funny. As in previous episodes, however, the *Book* uses obscene comedy to force readers to interrogate their own laughter. One wants to laugh at Margery because she is pursuing a holy status wherein absolute sexual purity is the prerequisite and yet confesses to wildly explicit sexual visions. But Christ, the *Book* tells us, forgives Margery. Christ does not laugh, so why should we? What, indeed, is so outrageous about a woman confessing sinful thoughts when such confessions are a well-accepted trope in the narratives of male religious authorities like St. Augustine?

In a manner that is quite similar to Langland's Will, the *Book* has Margery diverge from the unapologetic rebellion of the obscene comedy subordinate by revealing her capacity for guilt and shame. This suggests that women can both experience obscene desires *and* have a moral self that regards such impulses with horror, thereby redeeming them in the same way that men are redeemed for controlling their desires. It is also worth noting that, while the portrayals of female desire in works like the fabliaux always construe lasciviousness as an innate element in the female personality, the *Book* always figures Margery's obscenities as coming from outside her authentic self. The snare of temptation at St. Margaret's Church is laid by the devil (29), and the visions of the bare-membered men are said to emanate from the same source. They are delectable to Margery "ageyn hir wille" (143).

The fact that temptations exist is less relevant than the fact that Margery's moral self can always be counted on to overcome them. In this she is, again, markedly different from the women of obscene comedy, who have no internal-ized control over their lasciviousness and must always be monitored from the outside, by their husbands. Not so for Margery, who responds to her shaming in St. Margaret's Church by increasing her religious observances: she is shriven many times and "dede hir penawns whatsoevyr hir confessowr wold injoyne hir to do, and was governed aftyr the rewelys of the Chirch" (30). Similarly, after the vision of naked men, "sche was schreuyn and dede al that sche myth" (143). Eventually, in both cases, Jesus has mercy on Margery and relieves her from her temptations. By showing Christ continuing to support Margery despite these lecherous visions, the *Book* indicates that Margery's holiness is located in her fight against temptation, rather than her lack of sexual desire.

As in the trials segment, the sexuality debates juxtapose Christian humil-ity, mercy and compassion with the assertion of exclusionary categories that are rooted in contemporary social mores rather than Christian doctrine. The *Book*'s author emphasizes the conflict between Christ's ministry and the medi-eval discrimination against married women by repeatedly referring to passages from the gospels that describe Christ's merciful treatment of remorseful, sexu-ally fallen women. In a series of conversations with Christ, Margery voices the predominant medieval view regarding the irredeemable impurity of wives, and Christ responds by citing the various passages from the gospels and saints' lives in which such women are redeemed, like the woman "takyn in avowtre" (73, 234), Mary Magdalene, and Maria of Egypt, the prostitute- turned-hermit who is canonized for her piety (59, 234).

The *Book*'s attack on the gendered associations of obscene behavior also includes several episodes that showcase men's capacity to engage in sinful sexual behavior and that position women as the guardians of sexual morality. When Margery correctly names lechery as the sin of the doubting monk, she converts him to a blameless life (40). Later, Margery affects a similar conversion of another sinful man, this time her son, who goes over the sea as a merchant and falls into "the synne of letchery" despite his mother's warnings that he should "kepe thi body klene at the lest fro womanys feleschep tyl thu take a wyfe aftyr the lawe of the Chirche" (207). The son becomes ill with a disfiguring disease that he ascribes to his lecherous behavior, loses his job, and returns to his mother in desperation, asking her to pray for the removal of the disease. Margery, "wyth scharp wordys of correpcyon," agrees (208). The son recovers and marries soon after. Margery "thankyd God wyth al hir hert, supposyng and trustyng he schulde levyn clene & chast as the lawe of matrimony askith" (208).

The most unusual facet of the *Book*'s treatment of men and obscenity lies its portrayal of men who use obscene language as a form of intimidation. This aspect of the *Book* should be noted, for its position is markedly different from other medieval writings on the perils of obscene speech. In an essay on lewd speech, Ruth Mazo Karras surveys a variety of clerical writings from England. Noting that, in general, concern about obscene speech is not intense, Karras remarks that the clerical writings that do express an interest in it have an outlook that is very different from feminist theorists like Catherine MacKinnon. While modern feminist thought on obscenity is concerned with the performative effects of obscene speech as a form of violence against women, medieval authors worry about obscenity as a sign of an interior state. Medieval treatises like *Handlyng Sin* worry about filthy words both as a sign of a sinful heart and a cause of sin in oneself and others.[89]

Attitudes in the *Book of Margery Kempe*, however, appear much closer to twentieth-century feminist interpretations that identify obscene speech as a form of intimidation used by one socially empowered group, men, against a socially disempowered one, women. During Margery's encounter with the steward of Leicester, the steward uses obscenity to humiliate Margery in order to extract information from her. After Margery's arrest, the steward takes her from her prison and interrogates her in front of a group of priests. He accuses her of lying, then asks her many questions, but cannot find anything incriminating

(115). Having failed in this attempt, he then takes Margery by the hand and leads her into his chamber where he "spak many fowyl rebawdy wordys unto hir, purposying and desyryng, as it semyd hir, to opressyn and forlyn hir" (115). The author's description illustrates that the purpose behind the steward's lewd speech is not so much sexual as it is a power play aimed at extracting the truth from Margery regarding her visions. The steward's repeated failures to overpower Margery result in an increase in his sexual harassment: "seyng hir boldenes that sche dred no presonyng, he strogelyd wyth hir, schewyng unclene tokenys and ungoodly cuntenawns," whereby he frightens her so much that she reveals to him "how sche had hyr speche and hir dalyawns of the Holy Gost and not of hir owyn cunnyng" (115). The steward's use of obscene language and gesture is intended to intimidate. Margery reads from his behavior a threat of sexual violence ("purposyng to oppressyn and forlyn hir") that can only be carried out because he is a man in a position of authority and she is a woman alone in his city without male friends or associates.

The *Book* also inverts the obscene comedy trope of the law-abiding man and the riotous, immoral woman. While men are often figured as the sources of lewdness and obscenity in the *Book*, the women Margery encounters are often figured as a force of sexual order. When the steward initially arrives to interrogate Margery, her jailer is not home, and the wife "wolde not late hir gon to no man, Styward ne other" (114). When the priests harass her, Margery goes to the good wife of the house and asks the wife to give her two maidens to sleep with at night (220). When Margery travels to Calais with a friar, she looks to women along the way to protect her from rape. And when the narrator remarks that Margery "durst trustyn on no man," the statement is gender specific: "therfor sche went to bedde gladlich no nyth les than sche had a woman er tweyn wyth hir" (224).

Compassion and Companionate Marriage: The Bridlington Episode and John's Old Age

Few portions of the *Book of Margery Kempe* show more indebtedness to obscene comedy than those depicting Margery's conflicts with her husband. As is often the case with medieval literary obscenity, these passages appeal to modern readers and are among the *Book*'s most popular and anthologized segments.[90] Many have assumed that the *Book*'s attitude to earthly marriage is negative since it often depicts Margery longing to be free of the sexual and social obligations of marriage. Once again, however, if we separate author from protagonist, a different picture emerges. In the context of the *Book*'s extended critique of contemporary society and its failure to embody Christian values, Margery's marriage emerges as an exemplar for how social authority should deal with nonconformist, spiritually gifted women. Unlike so many other male authorities in the *Book*, John does not reject or abuse Margery for her failure to obey him or to lead a conventional woman's life dedicated to caring for husband and family. Instead, he negotiates with her, treating her with compassion and respect even when their needs conflict and she challenges his authority. In many respects, John's behavior aligns with the principles of companionate marriage that historians have seen developing among the middle ranks of northwestern Europe in the later medieval and early modern periods. Although the couple's arguments might initially appear to be the nadir of their relationship, they are actually the locus of the *Book*'s attempt to revise the notion that husbands and other authorities must enforce total domination and control in their governance of women. By juxtaposing John's more moderate approach with the severe reactions of male ecclesiastical figures, the *Book* suggests that the principles of companionate marriage accord better with Christian doctrine than the authoritarian attitudes exhibited by many male ecclesiastics in the *Book*.

Emerging in the late medieval and early modern period among the shopkeepers, artisans, yeomen, merchants, and professionals of northwestern Europe, a companionate notion of marriage envisions it as a partnership among equals, made for the purposes of friendship and mutual aid. In this model, greater autonomy is granted to wives and patriarchal authority is moderated in favor of a power-sharing relationship between husband and wife.[91] This new vision contrasts with an older, hierarchical notion of marriage, in which unions are used primarily to cement bonds between men and in which women's desires are of little account.

As Emma Lipton has noted, the *Book*'s depictions of marriage often characterize it in companionate terms. With the exception of the sexual oppression symbolized by John's insistence on married sex in spite of Margery's resistance (which Lipton regards as a trope taken from hagiographic literature), the Kempe marriage is affectionate and mutual.[92] What we see growing out of this mutuality is precisely the kind of compassion and humility regarding the unconventional female visionary that is so often lacking among the *Book*'s ecclesiastical authorities. John's "compassyon" is a repeated refrain throughout the text. When Margery is cured suddenly after her postpartum madness, she requests the keys of the buttery. The household staff counsels against doing so, but her husband "evyr

havyng tendyrnes and compassyon of hir" commands that she be given the keys
(23). Other portions of the *Book* show John remaining loyal to Margery with a
courage matched by few other men in the *Book*. When Margery travels about
England, the narrator tells us, her husband goes with her "for he was evyr a good
man and an esy man to hir" (45).

When she is harassed and threatened with burning, he leaves her alone
out of fear for a time, "yet he resortyd evyrmof ageyn to hir, and had compassyon of hir" (45). John's loyalty is juxtaposed with the disloyalty of many of
the supposedly spiritual individuals who abandon Margery. One man deserts
Margery in spite of the fact that he was "holdyn so holy a man . . . and evyr hir
husbond was redy whan alle other fayled" (45–46). The *Book* locates the
source of John's loyalty to Margery in the same willingness to prioritize divine
revelation over social convention that it promotes so forcefully in other passages. When Margery wishes to go traveling to holy sites, she must ask her
husband permission, and he gives it willingly, "fully trostyng it was the wyl of
God" (36).

The legitimacy of John's approach is affirmed by Margery's spiritual
visions, in which Christ himself adheres to companionate principles of marriage.[93] Shortly after her marriage to the Godhead, Christ explains to Margery
his total acceptance and love of her. He, Christ says, should not be ashamed of
Margery as other men are; indeed, he would take her by the hand among the
people, "For it is convenyent the wyf to be homly wyth hir husbond" (94).
Christ's marriage metaphor articulates a love that trumps the social hierarchies
that oppress Margery in her earthly life. Even if the husband is a great lord and
the wife is lowly, "yet thei must ly togedir and rest togedir in joy and pes" (94).
The duties and obligations of marriage are also used in a later vision to articulate Christ's abiding loyalty to Margery. Christ tells Margery to love him and
that he will provide for her: "And thow alle thy frendys forsake the, I schal
nevyr forsakyn the. . . . And I schal ordeyn for the, dowtyr, as for myn own
modyr and as for myn owyn wyfe" (153).

Margery's and John's disputes would seem to characterize them as
degraded and ludicrous characters, but in fact their arguments revise the discourse of obscene comedy much in the manner that we see it being revised in
Margery's conflicts with ecclesiastics elsewhere in the *Book*, working to reverse
the discourse's affirmation of dictatorial authority in favor of a power-sharing
approach. This is something we also see in the obscene comedy pageants of the
biblical drama (the subject of Chapter 5 of this study), but the *Book*'s revisions
go much farther in promoting female autonomy than the biblical drama, which

ultimately affirms patriarchal authority in ways that the *Book of Margery Kempe* does not.

In the first episode, which occurs as the couple travels together on the road to Bridlington, John asks Margery a hypothetical question: if a man threatened to smite off his head with a sword if John did not "comown kendly" (have sex) with Margery, would she allow him to "medele" with her? Margery answers that "forsothe," she would rather have him slain (37). John then accuses Margery of being "no good wyfe" (37). When John offers Margery a celibate marriage in exchange for paying off his debts and eating dinner with him on Friday nights, Margery must rush off to consult with Jesus, who assures her that her Friday night fasting may be given up (38).

In one sense, it appears as if Margery and her husband are the butt of a joke in this episode. Margery appears to embody all the resistant energy of the disobedient wife, while John shares in the defeat and exasperation of the fabliau husband. The couple is laughable for their mutual animosity and the lack of distinction they make between matters of the spirit and lowly quotidian concerns like the paying of debts and the eating of dinner. However, while the "road to Bridlington" argument recalls obscene comedy in many respects, it also revises it. Margery's expressions of pain and dread render her far more vulnerable than the average fabliau woman, allowing us to see how she suffers under the restrictions placed on married women. When she thinks about sexual relations with her husband, Margery has "gret sorwe and gret dred for hyr chastite" (37–38). When Margery realizes the conflict between her Friday fasts and the bargain her husband wishes to strike with her, she prays "wyth gret habundawns of teerys" (38). For his part, John does not react in the manner of a fabliau husband by attempting to impose control over his unruly wife through stratagems or violence. Instead, he negotiates with his wife in a way characteristic of the power-sharing approach of companionate marriage, telling her, "grawnt me my desyr, and I schal grawnt yow yowr desyr" (38). The couple's negotiation is quite remarkable in its vision of equality: the two negotiate as equals, and there is no assertion of male authority on John's part. While Margery defers to masculine dominance in the figure of Jesus, there is no deference in her relationship with her earthly husband. In characterizing the couple's negotiations in this way, the Bridlington episode cuts a middle way between the fabliau extremes of the contemptibly uxorious husband and the admirably violent authoritarian. John is no pushover (he will not agree to chaste marriage unless Margery also grants his desires), but he is no dictator either. The negotiation is characterized as being very successful, ending in an accord—wherein the couple eats and drinks together "in gret gladnes of spyryt" (39)—that is uncharacteristic of the marital battles of obscene comedy.

John's response provides a foil for the way that male authority figures treat Margery in the trials sequence. Like the men in the trials sequence, John confronts a woman who does not defer to male authority. While Margery officially cleaves to the doctrine of female obedience in certain respects (she always asks John's permission before traveling and will not refuse him sex without his consent to a spiritual marriage), her preference for his death over sexual intercourse and her threat that Christ will "slay" John next time he touches her run radically counter to models of female deference in marriage.[94] But John's solution is far different from those of the men who respond to Margery's nonconformity by seeking to imprison her, kill her, or close her in a house of stone.

By juxtaposing Margery's conflicts with John and her conflicts with ecclesiastical authorities, the author uses the couple's companionate marriage to instruct other institutions, attempting to diffuse the more democratic notions of governance that grow up in bourgeois marriage arrangements to other sectors of medieval society.[95] Obscene comedy is crucial in enabling the *Book*'s author to carry out this project. If companionate marriage is the message, obscene comedy is the vehicle through which the message is conveyed. By invoking obscene comedy in Margery's marriage and her encounters with Church authorities, the author is able to put into communication two realms—the ecclesiastical and the marital—that are traditionally separated in medieval thought.

In the second of the *Book*'s notorious marital conflicts, Margery is dismayed to find herself bound to wifely duties after a now-elderly John falls and injures himself. Neighbors, outraged that Margery does not "keep" her elderly spouse, say that, if he dies, she should be held responsible. This inspires Margery to pray that he live another year in order that she can be delivered from slander. God asks Margery to keep the old man, and she does so, complaining extensively about the cost, time, trouble, and loss of contemplation that the situation occasions. Here once again, Margery seems to be cast in the role of bad fabliau wife. Like the wife of *Sire hain et dame anieuse* (2.5), who seems to exist only to frustrate her husband's desires, caring little for his health and well-being, Margery does not happily or willingly aid her sickly husband. The incongruity is particularly keen (and particularly humorous) in Margery's case because it stands in radical opposition to her loving and dutiful attitude to Christ. Like the Bridlington episode, this passage juxtaposes high spiritual principle with quotidian (and obscene) detail, giving a detailed account of how John became childish in his old age and "voydyd his natural digestyon in hys lynyn clothys ther he sat be the fyre er at the tabil, whethyr it wer, he wolde sparyn no place" (173).

There is more to this episode, however, than the simple obscene comedy portrait of an unloving wife. Margery resists marital duties not out of antipathy to her husband but because she wishes to pursue her spiritual contemplation. As in the case of the Bridlington episode, these details allow us to see how women are constrained by what their culture demands of them. Moreover, Margery ultimately comes around to the charity and compassion that are so highly valued in the *Book*. In spite of her initial dislike for the task, Margery does a very good job, caring for the old man as she imagines she would have done for Christ himself (173).

Margery and John's marriage is not flawless. There is no doubt that it fails to meet the standard of total compassion and love set by Christ's relationship with Margery. However, it is in these very imperfections that its significance lies. In the *Book*'s measure, marriage is like any other earthly relationship in its inferiority to the divine because it involves human beings with all of their ambitions, desires, and conflicting needs. Nevertheless, in its ability to encompass these typically human imperfections, the *Book* presents bourgeois marriage as an institution that is superior to the other institutions in its society, most notably the Church. Unlike the Church—which the *Book* shows being distorted in its attempt to crack down on difference—Margery and John can cope with difference while still remaining bound in an alliance that provides compassion and care to its members. The *Book* shows us that the durability of the union, which lasts until John's death, lies precisely in its mutuality and refusal of strict hierarchies.

In its emphasis on marriage as an institution whose durability and compassion are superior to the Church, the *Book of Margery Kempe* resembles *Piers Plowman*, which also features a married couple whose bond endures through conflict. As we shall see in the following chapter, the biblical drama of the late fourteenth and fifteenth centuries also exploits the conjugal focus of obscene comedy to assert a middle-rank notion of companionate marriage. This vision, however, is more patriarchal than that which we see in the *Book*, enforcing masculine authority in the household, even as it gives women more latitude. In its depiction of equality, and its desire to bring that egalitarian spirit to the Church, the *Book of Margery Kempe* stands alone.

CHAPTER 5

Women's Work,
Companionate Marriage,
and Mass Death in the Biblical Drama

Obscene comedy is ubiquitous in the biblical drama of late medieval England: Noah and his wife insult and beat each other; an elderly Joseph accuses his young wife of adultery; the mothers of the murdered children in the "Massacre of the Innocents" plays beat Herod's soldiers with distaffs, and Mak and Gyll squabble over domestic duties in the *Second Shepherd's Play*. The discourse's influence extends across both geography and time, from the northern York cycle to the East Anglian N-Town plays, from works likely produced in the late fourteenth century to those created in the early 1500s.[1]

From the earliest days of medievalist scholarship, the scenes of battling husbands and wives have sparked interest. In 1814, an auction catalogue description for the single manuscript of the Towneley plays lists the pageants and makes no other comment on their content except to note that the *Noah* pageant includes "a ludicrous and quarrelsome dialogue between Noah and his Wife" and that the Last Judgment features "many quaint and humourous dialogues of devils."[2] In modern scholarship, critical analyses of the *Noah* plays and the *Second Shepherd's Play* dwarf those of any other pageant, even those, like the York *Crucifixion*, that are widely admired and anthologized.[3]

In spite of its perennial appeal, the obscene comedy of the biblical drama raises difficult questions for the modern critic. How does one explain why not just one but four different versions of the Noah pageant include the extrabiblical scene of Noah and his wife quarreling as the flood waters swirl around them? Why were the creators of the Innocents pageants inspired to inject a ludicrous battle of the sexes into a scene of child murder? And how does one reconcile the scenes in which Joseph's rages over Mary's "adultery" with the reverence accorded to the Annunciation?

Various explanations of the drama's comedy have been issued over the years, but none has provided a fully cogent reading of its function. The drama's first modern critics concluded that the plays were simply bad art created by amateurs for unrefined audiences who required the sugar of comedy on the pill of biblical teachings.[4] Subsequent New Critical analyses attempted to recoup artistic legitimacy for the biblical drama by reading its comic segments typologically. Most notable among these were readings that interpreted the marital battle of the Noah pageants as a metaphor for the recalcitrant sinner's resistance to God. This theory, however, is compromised by the fact that Noah's own flaws make him an unlikely stand-in for the divine.[5] Beginning in the 1980s, a new phase of criticism issued socially oriented interpretations of the pageants as ritual rather than art. These readings associated the comic pageants with popular carnivals celebrating the overturning of social hierarchies and characterized them as "release-valve" transgressions whose subversions were contained by the orthodox tone of the cycles as a whole.[6] While the social purview of the drama-as-ritual analyses seemed to offer a more promising ground on which to understand the pageants' obscene comedy, they actually restricted interpretation since, as Ruth Evans has noted, a notion of the pageants as ritual defines them as static entities, rather than as places where meaning can be contested.[7]

Recent years have seen a remarkable growth in feminist analyses of the biblical drama. Interestingly, these analyses have often focused on the obscene comedy pageants, including the Noah plays, the *Second Shepherd's Play* and the "Massacre of the Innocents" pageants.[8] The majority of feminists, however, continue to read the plays' obscene comedy as a static appropriation of a misogynist tradition.[9] Theresa Coletti credits some obscene comedy pageants with a critique of misogyny, but only when they juxtapose the unruly woman with biblical women of impeccable virtue, such as occurs in the "Troubles of Joseph" pageants, when Joseph suspects the Holy Virgin of adultery. She does not credit the unruly women themselves as being anything more than expressions of "a familiar festive type."[10] Christina Fitzgerald provides an insightful reading of the York and Chester Noah pageants as expressions of "the frustrations and fantasies of being male in the Middle Ages," but regards the unruly women of the Wakefield plays as "farcical and stereotypical."[11] Jane Tolmie, meanwhile, delivers an astute analysis of Mrs. Noah in the Towneley, Chester, and York pageants, but ultimately concludes that the plays reflect "a culture in which women's dissenting voices are created in order to be suppressed, and moreover suppressed with physical force."[12]

One of the greatest hindrances to a full understanding of obscene comedy in the biblical drama is the assumption that it must perform an identical function in every cultural iteration. In many analyses of the plays, the identification of a fabliau-like character—or a trope from a popular festival like Hocktide or St. Distaff's Day—has been taken as an answer in and of itself.[13] In fact, such identifications raise more questions than they answer since the semiotic instability of obscene comedy means its thematic valence can vary significantly. This is even more true of performance-based comedy than it is of written forms or those depicted in the visual arts. As Simon Dentith has remarked, carnival ritual does not have "one univocal social or political meaning" but provides "a malleable space, in which activities and symbols can be inflected in different directions."[14] Similarly, in a recent study of festive practices in medieval England, Chris Humphrey argues that "the view of festive misrule as a static, self-contained and slightly provocative set of customs is unrepresentative of the evidence . . . we should prefer instead a view that perceives it as a dynamic and interconnected practice whose tone could vary enormously."[15]

This chapter examines biblical drama comedy in the context both of its own social environment and of obscene comedy in Europe, demonstrating how biblical drama authors appropriated, revised, and repurposed the discourse in ways that spoke to their particular political, economic and social concerns. The obscene comedy pageants may, at first glance, appear simply to repeat the discourse's misogyny. If, however, we view them in the context of other fifteenth-century iterations of obscene comedy—including misericords, tales, lyrics and other forms of drama, like the French farce—we can see that they often diverge quite radically from the discourse's gender politics.

Most notable is the way that many pageants depart from the obscene comedy principle that an assertive and independent woman is a threat to the social order, instead characterizing her as a useful member of her family and community. In the Noah pageants and the Towneley *Second Shepherds' Play*, in the "Troubles of Joseph" episodes, and in the "Massacre of the Innocents" plays, misogynist notions of assertive women are revised, and presumptions about women's dishonesty and sexual lasciviousness are questioned. In this respect, the pageants reflect the move to a companionate model of marriage that historians have identified with the middle ranks during the late medieval period.[16] Even more remarkable is the fact that the drama's authors appear to have been cognizant of the fact that that their changes are emblematic of middle-rank perspectives, since the pageants display an awareness of gender norms as socially constructed entities that vary across the different ranks of medieval society.

The pageants' divergences from obscene comedy gender norms are often not only directed at a re-evaluation of marriage or women's status, but facilitate an assertion of a middle-rank identity and middle-rank values against those of secular and ecclesiastical elites. Most notably, the biblical drama often turns to obscene comedy at moments when it depicts mass death. The Noah story and Herod's "Massacre of the Innocents"—the two narratives most likely to be infused with obscene comedy in the biblical drama—are also those that concern large-scale death. These pageants use obscene comedy to assert a human and humane reading of human suffering and to critique the violence and injustice of medieval elites.

Like William Langland and the author of the *Book of Margery Kempe*, the creators of the biblical drama use the unruly woman to issue criticisms of elites that would have been impossible in any other medieval discourse. Exploiting the anti-authoritarian force of her voice and personality, the pageants are able not only to interrogate elite values and ideologies but even to portray physical attacks on them (as in the assaults of the Innocents pageants' unruly mothers). Like Langland and the *Margery Kempe* author, the creators of the biblical drama are also aware of the unruly woman's value in providing an avenue of retreat from the social criticisms issued in her voice or person, her heritage in misogynist comedy furnishing an alternative, innocuous reading at those points when the criticisms are most intense.

To argue for the pageants' revision of the unruly woman is not in any way to deny their patriarchal orientation. There is no doubt that the biblical drama is written from a male perspective and was performed in productions dominated by men. What makes the gender politics of the biblical drama so fascinating, however, is the fact that they combine a patriarchal outlook with an interrogation of dominant gender norms that is often quite radical. The pageants' more friendly attitude toward female assertiveness has much to tell us about the flexibility and diversity of patriarchy, illustrating how patriarchal norms are not uniform across all social levels, but instead align with class identity, and how the patriarchal philosophy of one group can allow and even encourage certain characteristics in women that are vilified in other versions.[17]

While my discussion in this chapter focuses on particular pageants, I do not treat the different versions of these pageants as entirely separate entities. I am aware that my approach goes against the grain of current scholarship, which has emphasized the distinct nature of each of the four extant collections of biblical drama (Towneley, N-town, York, and Chester), as well as the scattered individual biblical pageants.[18] While this emphasis has rightly corrected a tendency to overlook differences between the various collections, it is also possible to become too balkanized in our approach to the biblical drama. It is important to recognize that the unruly Mrs. Noah exists not in one unique pageant but in several; the distaff-wielding mothers of the Innocents episode are not the eccentric creation of one community but are incorporated into four different pageants from a variety of regions in England. While we ought to appreciate the variations between different pageants and different groups of pageants, we should not lose sight of what their commonalities reveal about the interest they held not just for a small or eccentric audience but for large numbers of people, in a variety of different locales, over a long period of time.

Companionate Marriage and the Towneley *Noah*

One of the most celebrated characters of the English biblical drama is the unruly Mrs. Noah, famous for comically resisting her husband's command to board the ark. Three of the four complete Noah plays, as well as the fragmentary Newcastle pageant of Noah, feature an unruly uxor, a figure who does not exist in continental versions of the Noah story. Of all the English Noah pageants, the Towneley version stands out for its intense focus on the conflict between Mr. and Mrs. Noah and for its depiction of spousal violence.

In spite of its superficial resemblance to portrayals of nagging, shrewish wives in other comic poems, tales, and plays of the later Middle Ages, the Towneley *Noah* diverges considerably from obscene discourse in the matter of the unruly woman, introducing events and portraying the marital couple in ways that interrogate the discourse's tendency to villainize the unruly woman and to idealize violence as a constructive method of upholding male authority in the household. The Towneley Mrs. Noah is a contradictory figure, part obscene comedy harridan, part reliable partner whose labor and intelligence are essential to the functioning of the ark. In many respects, the pageants' revision of obscene comedy sexual politics evinces elements of the companionate view of marriage that historians identify as having developed in the late medieval and early modern period among the middle ranks of northern Europe. Unlike marital ideologies that value male dominance and female submission, companionate marriage envisions the union as a partnership among equals, made for the purposes of companionship, friendship, and mutual aid. In this model, patriarchal authority in the household is moderated and greater autonomy is granted to wives.[19]

That an assertive, clever woman might also be a productive member of her household is a notion foreign to the fabliau, which persistently associates such women with sexual misbehavior and social disruption. This same attitude is born out in many fifteenth-century English carols and comic tales. "In soro and car he led hys lyfe" goes one fifteenth-century carol, "That haue a shrow ontyll his wyfe."[20] Another carol specifies the torture a husband endures as he labors under his wife's greed:

> All þat I may swynk or swet,
> My wyfe it wyll bop drynk & ete;
> & I sey ovȝt she wyl me bete—
> carfull ys my hart þerfor!
>
> . . .
>
> If I say, "it shal be thus,"'
> She sey, "þou lyyst, charll, I-wovs!
> Wenest þou to ouercome me þus?"[21]

In misericords created in the fifteenth century, similarly, women are characterized as violent shrews who attack their husbands with distaffs, ladles, and flax mallets (see Figure 4). The fifteenth-century English comic tale, *The Tale of the Basin*, shows a similar distaste for feminine command. In the tale, a local "goodman" is being bankrupted by a lazy wife who commits adultery with a local priest. The beginning of the tale makes it clear that the reason for this troublesome state of affairs is that his assertive wife has too much authority in the household. The "goodman," the tale informs us, cannot even think of husbandry, but

> . . . did as she hym tolde . . .
> He þat hade bene a lorde
> Was noup at bedde ne at borde,
> Ne durst onys speke a worde
> Whan she bade be stille. (16–18, 32–35)[22]

At first, the Towneley play's Mrs. Noah appears to be an obscene comedy woman in the traditional mold. When Noah arrives home from a conversation with God, the uxor is full of complaints and vows to avenge herself on her husband with tricks and beatings: "What with gam and with gyle, / I shall smyte and smyle, / And qwite hym his mede" (310–12). Like the wives of the popular carols and the misericords, Mrs. Noah appears as a physically powerful woman, capable of taking on her husband in a physical fight. Her resistance to Noah's commands prompts two episodes of fisticuffs between the couple in which both parties suffer and neither wins. The baleful warning that Noah issues in the midst of the second violent episode bears a close resemblance to the husbandly complaints of fifteenth-century popular carols:

> Yee men that has wifys,
> Whyls thay ar yong,
> If ye luf youre lifys,
> Chastice thare tong,
> Me thynk my hert ryfys,
> Both levyr and long,
> To se sich stryfys
> Wedmen emong. (573–80)[23]

The Towneley *Noah* pageant is, however, more generous than most obscene comedy in allowing Mrs. Noah to present her side of the story. As Ruth Evans has pointed out, the Towneley *Noah* is remarkable for the interest it shows in female subjectivity, allowing the uxor to express her own perspective on marriage and to describe the difficulty of living under male authority.[24] Noah is an inadequate husband in her view because he ignores the family and fails to provide food. When he arrives home, she complains:

> Where has thou thus long be?
> To dede may we dryfe,
> Or lif, for the,
> For want. (279–82)

Other grievances concern Noah's fearfulness and his impotence: the uxor's remark that Noah has "lowsyd me of my bandys" (303; released me from the pain of childbirth) seems to imply a failure to perform sexually. Modern readers may dismiss the uxor's complaints, but, if Vern Bullough is correct in saying that the three basic tenets of masculinity in medieval Europe were "impregnating women, protecting dependents, and serving as a provider to one's family," then Mrs. Noah's grievances would likely have struck a chord with late medieval audiences.[25] Certainly her complaint about Noah's failure to acquire food would have resonated in fifteenth-century England, when food shortages still loomed as a very real possibility.[26]

Of course, Noah's biblical significance would have rendered the uxor's complaints about household failures somewhat comical. Nevertheless, the fact that these failings involve duties so central to the role of middle-rank men renders the uxor more sympathetic than a shrew like the wife of the fabliau *Sire hain et dame anieuse* (2.5) who frustrates her husband out of spite, serving him stewed vegetables when he wants peas and fresh-water fish when he wants salt, or like the violent women of the misericords, whose anger appears without justification.[27]

Nor does the play invest Noah's perspective with the kind of inviolability one might expect in a biblical patriarch. There is a disparity between what Noah reports about his wife and what appears on stage that undercuts the authority of his perspective. Before we meet the uxor herself, Noah characterizes her as a ferocious shrew:

> And I am agast
> That we get som fray
> Betwixt vs both,
> For she is full tethee,
> For litill oft angré;
> If any thyng wrang be,
> Soyne is she wroth. (267–73)

The events that follow reveal Noah's own short-temperedness and irascibility. Mrs. Noah offers up very little resistance to her husband before he bursts into obscenities and physical violence, calling her "ram-skyt" (ramshit) (313) and striking the first blow in their physical fight. Although fabliau-style husbands certainly fight back against their unruly wives, they are not typically cast as the instigators. Rather, it is the wife's bad behavior that provokes the husband's violence and that justifies its use. This is the case in *Sire hain et dame anieuse*, wherein the wife becomes so unruly the husband is forced to quell her rebellions once and for all by challenging her to a fight (quite literally) over the pants of the household (2.5.51).

Also notable in the characterization of Mrs. Noah is the total absence of the sexual misbehavior that fabliau and farce typically associated with the unruly woman. This excision is not only a feature of the Towneley *Noah* but of the biblical drama's unruly women generally. Although the "Troubles of Joseph" pageants address the stereotype of the sexually immoral wife, they do so only in a situation in which it is clearly erroneous. Other portraits of unruly wives, like the uxor of the Noah pageants, Gyll of the *Second Shepherd's Play*, or the mothers of the Innocents pageants, do not link female assertiveness with sexual misbehavior.[28]

The excision of adultery is significant for what it tells us about the drama's re-evaluation of female unruliness. Sexual misbehavior is the single element of the unruly woman's personality that is utterly indefensible, since it is not only a violation of gender norms but is also a sin and an act forbidden by medieval law.[29] Medieval society did not stigmatize any of the other qualities associated with the unruly woman—not her argumentativeness, her assertiveness, her petty violence, or even her lying—to the extent that it stigmatized adultery. By avoiding sexual misbehavior, pageants like the Towneley *Noah* create a space in which alternatives to the dominant gender norms can be explored more freely, since the unruly woman's other attributes were not so clearly or definitely proscribed.

The *Noah* pageant's most fascinating departure from obscene comedy lies in the way it moves past marital conflict to depict the couple as working partners on the ark. In this segment, the same unruly Mrs. Noah who caused Noah such trouble is now a reliable comrade. Although Mrs. Noah is rather more deferential to her husband after she boards the ark, it is also clear that the very qualities that made her so difficult to manage on land render her a useful partner at sea: namely, her independence, her work ethic, and her reliance on her own judgment. "Wife," Noah tells her, "tent the stere-tre, [tend the tiller] / And I shal asay / The depnes of the see" (625–28). "That shall I do ful wysely," she replies (629–30). If the uxor has mellowed somewhat in the ark phase of the pageant, so has Noah, who is kind and deferential to his wife, asking her advice on which bird ought to be released to seek dry land (683–87).

While the growth of companionate marriage through the late medieval and early modern periods is well known, its origins are more shadowy. Many historians have located it in the unique marriage patterns of northern Europe, in which couples married late, were approximately the same age, and inhabited a household populated only by the married couple and minor children (rather than the intergenerational households more common in the English aristocracy and in southern Europe).[30] In a recent article, Martha Howell asserts that companionate marriage emerges out of economic changes that saw the wealth of medieval families (particularly those of the middle ranks) shift from land to moveable goods. Moveable wealth, Howell asserts, means that the marital pair is "in charge of their own and their children's future to an extent unknown in previous generations, thrown together as 'partners in life'."[31] The emphasis on cooperation in companionate marriage grows out of the economic instability of early capitalism, which made partnership necessary to survival: "when property might disappear overnight or double in a few short years so that the material past could not predict the material future, a couple needed to combine energies to preserve what they had and secure what they did not."[32]

To a remarkable degree, the Towneley *Noah* pageant traces out the transformation that Howell describes. The Noahs begin rooted in the land and then are, quite literally, torn away from that land. As a unit containing all the family's possessions, the ark metaphorizes with great accuracy the moveable wealth that had become the basis for the prosperity of many middle-rank families in the later Middle Ages. More interesting still is the way the pageant traces out the concomitant change in gender politics, from a fabliau-style view of marriage as a power contest in the land segment of the pageant to the companionate marriage on the ark.

This is not to say that the Towneley *Noah* repudiates patriarchy. Indeed, it does quite the opposite. Noah is the undisputed director of affairs in the ark sequences, and the play gives him an analytic edge when it has him choose the dove to release while Mrs. Noah chooses the raven. It is, however, a moderated patriarchy, one not so extreme in its assertions of authority as obscene comedy would dictate: a husband's decisions are made in dialogue with his wife; the wife's judgment and abilities are respected, if still inferior.

While the Towneley *Noah* is exceptional among the Noah pageants for the intensity of its focus on the spouses, the other pageants reveal a similar fidelity to the companionate marriage philosophy of partnership and mutual aid. In the York *Noah*, the uxor critiques Noah's failure to inform her of the coming flood in ways that suggest a husband ought not to keep secrets from his wife. The Chester pageant delivers a more solidly authoritative portrait of Noah (who does not respond violently when his wife clouts him) but is just as invested as the Towneley play in the "unruly but useful" characterization of the uxor, featuring a Mrs. Noah who moves back and forth between the two roles, at one moment aiding in the building of the ark, then refusing to get on, helping to name the animals, then resisting Noah's commands.

Domestic Violence in the Towneley *Noah*

Feminist readers have expressed an understandable dismay at the beatings of the Noah pageants, particularly in the Towneley *Noah*, arguing that they trivialize and legitimize violence against women. Undoubtedly, in absolute terms, the Noah plays do not reflect the modern feminist understanding of domestic violence as a phenomenon that disproportionately victimizes women. Like all of the biblical drama, the Towneley *Noah* is not a pageant written by or for women. Nevertheless, relative to other iterations of obscene comedy, its depiction of violence and the changes it makes to the character of the husband are significant.

Traditionally, obscene comedy upholds husbands' moral authority as guardians of the social order and defenders of the status quo. It is the wife who disrupts and the husband who controls (or fails to control) her insurrection. These men may be stupid, greedy, or inept, but in fighting to maintain the hierarchy of marriage, they are typically the force of order. The linchpin of masculine control in obscene comedy is often violence. Like chivalric discourse, obscene comedy advocates violence as an effective method of securing social stability. Husbands who use violence to control unruly women are valorized as wise and effective, while those who do not are pilloried as fools who deserve their domination by women. In the fifteenth-century French farce *D'une Femme à qui son Voisin baille ung clistoire* [The woman whose neighbor gave her an enema], a wife commits adultery with her neighbor, who arrives at her house disguised as a doctor. The woman is soundly beaten by her husband when he discovers her plans.[33] Similarly, a number of fabliaux idealize violence as the only way to keep women in line. In *Berengier au lonc cul* (4.34), a rich peasant married to a penniless noblewoman pretends to ride out on knightly adventures. Hanging his armor on a tree and beating it with his own lance, the husband fakes martial combat, coming home with battered armor he claims was acquired in a fight. At first, his noble wife is intimidated, but, following him one day, she discovers her his secret. Freed from the threat of her husband's violence, the wife treats him with contempt and embraces her lover in his presence.

While the Towneley *Noah* may trivialize domestic violence by rendering it as a comical battle, it nevertheless does not idealize violence as an effective method of asserting the husband's authority. Violence in the Towneley *Noah* produces exhaustion and a stalemate from which the couple emerges only when one of them gives in and abandons the fight. In the same way that the *Book of Margery Kempe* characterizes controlling men as ludicrous fools, the Towneley *Noah* reverses the logic of obscene comedy, portraying the violent man as ineffective and out of control.

Uxor Redux: Mak and Gyll of the *Second Shepherd's Play*

The Towneley *Second Shepherd's Play* repeats the corrections that the Towneley *Noah* pageant makes to obscene comedy. In the pageant's opening scene, the Second Shepherd, like Noah, complains about the trials of living with a domineering wife:

> These men that ar wed
> Haue not all thare wyll;
> . . .
> God wayte thay ar led
> Full hard and full yll
> In bowere nor in bed
> Thay say noght thertyll
> This tyde. (105–6; 109–13)

In the sixty-line speech, he proceeds through a veritable anthology of obscene comedy misogamy: from expressing amazement at some men for marrying more than once; to warning young men that "Mekyll styll mowrnyng / Has wedyng home brought, / And grefys" (137–39); to complaining about his own shrewish wife: "I aue oone to my fere / As sharp as thystyll, / As rugh as a brere" (145–47).

As in the *Noah* play, the *Second Shepherd's Play* introduces questions regarding the misogynist man's judgment and reliability. Among all the familiar complaints, the pageant features one that we do not often see in obscene comedy. The bad temper of a wife in childbirth is first mentioned by the Second Shepherd (100–104) and is followed up by Mak when he enters a few hundred lines later. Along with his wife's drinking and laziness, Mak is particularly offended by the fact that every year she has a baby, an event for which he holds her wholly responsible:

> Bot s[h]o
> Etys as fast as she can,
> And ilk yere that commys to man
> She bryngys furth a lakan—
> And, som yeres, two (347–51)

While all the shepherds' complaints find ready analogues in songs, carols, sermons, and bawdy tales, the complaint about reproduction is rare. The reason for this is obvious when one considers the misogyny of obscene comedy: in seeking to castigate women as innately evil beings whose depredations can only be curbed by male dominance, obscene comedy must focus on feminine transgressions, rather than evils that arise from activities in which men also participate. The biological interdependency of reproduction necessarily mitigates against the obscene comedy configuration of blame, thus its absence from most misogynist iterations of the discourse. The complaints of the *Second Shepherds'* men about childbearing makes them into parodies of fabliau-style men, its foolishness casting doubt on the validity of their other, more traditional, complaints about female perfidy.

The pageant's interrogation of obscene comedy continues with its portrait of Gyll. Acerbic, disobedient, and disrespectful, Gyll is in many respects a classic unruly woman. Like the Towneley *Noah*, however, the *Second Shepherds' Play* diverges from obscene comedy by emphasizing Gyll's importance in the household. While the discourse characterizes women's crabbiness as innate, the *Second Shepherds' Play* links Gyll's refusal to answer the door and her exasperation with Mak to her work. Gyll is loath to open the door because she is busy spinning (430–33). In reply to Mak's accusations of laziness, Gyll emphasizes her labor and that of other women:

> Why, who wanders, who wakys?
> Who commys, who goes?
> Who brewys, who bakys?
> . . .
> Full wofull is the householde
> That wantys a woman (599–607)

The pageant also significantly alters the obscene comedy trope of the lying woman. While Gyll's fictions are certainly clever and outrageous enough to compete with those of the most crafty fabliau wife, the function of her trickery is very different. While the lies of the unruly woman are usually a detriment to her husband, Gyll's plot to hide the sheep in the cradle and pretend it is a new baby is aimed at supporting her husband by concealing his theft and securing additional food for her household. This is similar to the *Noah* pageant, in which the unruly Mrs. Noah is crucial to the successful operation of the ark.

By making Gyll the guiding intelligence of her household, the *Second Shepherds' Play* gives an unusual degree of latitude to female authority. The pageant's closest analogue, the mid-fifteenth-century French farce *Pathelin* (c. 1456), features a husband and wife team who steal a bolt of cloth from a draper, then craft a plan to hide the stolen cloth under the husband's pillow while he feigns illness. Although Pathelin's wife is featured criticizing her husband in the same way that Gyll criticizes Mak, it is the husband in this story who creates and directs the plan that the wife obediently follows.[34]

Gyll's lie is not successful. The trick is eventually discovered. Nevertheless, the pageant does not isolate Gyll's behavior as the cause of the couple's downfall, since she only lies to cover up Mak's theft of the sheep. Thus the couple's mutual crimes, rather than Gyll's own transgression, are punished at the pageant's conclusion.

Women's Work: The Social Context of Biblical Drama Shrews

Both the *Second Shepherds' Play* and the Noah pageants are attentive to the subject of women's labor. I have already noted Gyll's self-defense on the basis of her labor. That same interest in women's work is also evident in the Towneley *Noah* play, wherein the uxor refuses to board the ark in order to finish her spinning and wherein the useful labor she performs tending the tiller is essential to her value on the ark. Other versions of the *Noah* pageant also pay attention to the uxor's role as a laborer, featuring a Mrs. Noah who either works independently or aids in the building of the ark.[35]

Feminist readings of the pageants' attitude to women's work have often characterized them as negative and reactive. Citing Howell's research on the high labor status achieved by women in the towns in the century following the Black Death and the way this high status "must have threatened the patriarchal character of Europe's sex-gender system during the period they held it," Ruth Evans reads Noah's beating of his wife in the Towneley pageant as a response to that threat.[36] Katie Normington associates the Towneley beating with the decline in the status of women spinners and weavers in late fifteenth-century England. Further noting that the ark is a strictly hierarchical space, Normington asserts that the uxor's abandonment of her spinning and distaff when she boards the ark represents her submission to patriarchal authority.[37]

While Normington and Evans are right to identify a potential backlash against working women in these violent episodes, their approach to understanding women's labor in the pageants is too focused on specific incidents, historical events, and geographic locales. A more generalized approach is useful for two reasons. First, we must recognize that the pageants' textual history is so obscure as to make it very difficult to identify their gender politics with specific geographical locations or moments in English economic history. Second, a focus on particular episodes in which women are being controlled or put back in their place misses what these pageants have to tell us about the pervasive effect middle-rank people's dependence on women's labor had on their views of gender and marriage.

The textual history of most biblical drama, and in particular the Towneley collection, is so shadowy that it is very difficult to link them to particular moments in medieval English economic history. Analysis of the Towneley manuscript has recently dated it to the Marian period of 1553–58, decades after the writing and performance of the plays.[38] The exact date of the Towneley plays is, then, a matter of conjecture. This difficulty is emblematic of the problems that inhere in the dating of biblical drama generally, since it is highly likely that all the pageants were created at a date far earlier than their extant manuscripts.[39] Moreover, the repetitive and communal nature of the plays' creation, in which they were played over and over again, year after year (and possibly moderated or changed each time they were performed) also makes it impossible to locate their content in a specific historical moment.

Also difficult to maintain is any interpretation that grounds the pageants in larger urban environments. Again, the Towneley plays demonstrate a particularly vexed example of this problem. Although they were at one time equated with the cycles of Chester and York on the assumption that they were the documentary remnants of a similar urban cycle in Wakefield, Barbara Palmer has argued that the Towneley manuscript is "neither from Wakefield, nor a cycle" but is instead an artificial compilation of plays originating from a variety of areas, including Doncaster, Pontrefract, and Wakefield.[40] Thus the Towneley plays may well have originated from an environment considerably less urbanized than the plays of Chester and York. And yet, in many ways, their gender politics are similar to the ones found in those cycles.

Even if we cannot link the plays to a specific set of late medieval economic or social circumstances, we can be reasonably confident about their middle-rank affiliation. Earlier critics assumed that the plays must have been authored by clerics, but this view has been disputed in recent years. Noting the markedly higher levels of lay literacy in the later Middle Ages, as well as the fact that biblical drama did not grow up in towns with powerful ecclesiastical establishments,

Lawrence Clopper promotes the notion that the pageants were entirely lay productions.[41] The idea that, in the large towns, plays like those of York and Chester were controlled by merchant oligarchies, rather than the craftspeople who produced them, has also recently been disputed.[42] P. J. P Goldberg has argued for a slow evolution of the plays at York over the course of the late fourteenth and early fifteenth centuries. While the plays may have been decisively controlled by merchant elites in the later fifteenth century, Goldberg asserts, their creation lay with the artisanal guilds that originally produced them.[43] Other scholars have pointed out that the York pageants' role in upholding the privilege of urban elites is not necessarily antithetical to the expression of an artisanal viewpoint. Sarah Beckwith has argued that, even as the York plays serve as a ceremonial and administrative support to the ruling oligarchy of the city, many pageants articulate what she calls an "artisanal ideology" that undercuts the base of the merchant elite's power by putting an emphasis "on manufacture, or on making, rather than on the control of exchange mechanisms, through the manipulation of networks of supply and distribution."[44]

While little is known for certain about the Towneley plays, there is still much evidence that associates the collection generally, and particularly the plays of the "Wakefield Master," with the middle ranks.[45] Not only is much of the Towneley collection sourced from the York plays, but the textual associations with the town of Wakefield that are seen in both the *Noah* pageant and the *Second Shepherd's Play* (the Towneley manuscript lists the *Noah* pageant as *Processus Noe cum filiis Wakefield* and the *Second Shepherd's Play* refers to well-known landmarks in the Wakefield area) make it highly likely that they were produced by or in association with the residents of that town. While a number of scholars have noted that Wakefield would not, at this time, have featured the urbanized environment of Chester or York, it was nevertheless populated by members of the middle ranks. There is, moreover, in the *First and Second Shepherds' Plays* and in the Towneley *Magnus Heroditus*, a biting satire of landholders and the aristocratic discourse of chivalry that mitigates against these plays having been written by or for members of the landed classes.[46]

While Howell ascribes the development of companionate marriage to families' dependence on moveable wealth, the pageants suggest that the importance of women's labor to the survival of middle-rank families also informed their revised notions of appropriate gender behavior and marital power relations. It is notable that women's labor plays a prominent role in the biblical drama pageants that revise obscene comedy gender politics. Both Mrs. Noah and Gyll are

valuable because they are good workers. In discussing the importance of wom-
en's labor to the household-based industry of the late medieval town, David
Aers has remarked that we need to appreciate its potential "to destabilize the
received sex gender system and its ideology."[47] Examination of middle-rank
women's work across the board suggests that this view could apply to a much
broader swath of the medieval middle and lower ranks than just the members
of urban artisanal households.

While there are certainly variations in middle-rank women's labor across
time and geographic region in the later Middle Ages, there are also continuities.
No matter whether they were urban or rural and whether they existed in the late
fourteenth century or the early sixteenth, middle-rank communities depended
for their survival on women's work. Moreover, the work that middle-rank
women performed required precisely the kind of confidence and self-command
that the pageants value in their "unruly" wives. Among historians, there has
been considerable debate over whether the post-plague era represented a "golden
age" in which women, particularly urban women, experienced a higher degree of
freedom and independence than they did during previous or subsequent periods.[48] The historical conditions that interest me here are of a somewhat different
nature. Debates over a golden age for women are primarily concerned with the
extent to which women achieved a status *separate* from the family, in the sense
that they were permitted to trade or operate businesses independently. My own
focus in thinking about the biblical drama involves not women's independence
but rather their status within the family and the value accorded to their work as
members of the family unit.

In many respects, the conditions of middle-rank life would have favored
markedly different forms of behavior in women than those promoted by the
elites of medieval society. It is well known that the aristocracy and gentry of
medieval England, as well as urban merchant elites, followed a marriage pattern
wherein women married in their teens, often to men considerably older than
themselves.[49] This was not the case for members of the lower and middle ranks
of medieval English society, who followed the northwestern European marriage
pattern, whereby same-age couples married in their mid- to late twenties and set
up housekeeping separate from the familial home.[50] In the early marriage culture
of medieval elites, women's primary function was reproductive. Entering a
household staffed by servants and professional managers, the aristocratic wife
was not required to engage in managerial and productive tasks.[51] Indeed, the
household in the upper echelons of medieval society was "almost completely a
male preserve."[52] Although some wives in this social sector may have taken on

managerial tasks, particularly in their later years, family survival, economic and physical, did not require that they do so.[53] In these social arrangements, female submission, silence, and chastity were what best served the family's interests.

The conditions of middle-rank life in England cohered less easily with ideals that favored female passivity, submission, and silence. Whether they lived in large towns, market villages, or in the country, middle-rank women were, from the time of their marriage, required to manage a household independently, a job requiring assertiveness, independence, and self-command. In the "Ballad of a Tyrannical Husband" (1500), in which a husband unjustly blames his wife for failing to work, the wife provides a list of her tasks, which include caring for the children, keeping chickens, making meals, tending to the cow, brewing, making bread and butter, pounding flax, carding, and spinning.[54] Sue Niebrzydowski notes the difference between the feminine behaviors emphasized by the knight of La Tour Landry to gentlewomen, and those emphasized in the middle-rank *How the Goodwife Taught Her Daughter*, noting that, in the latter, there is much emphasis on the practical skills of housekeeping, while the former emphasizes the importance of noble birth, beauty, and good manners. As Niebrzydowski remarks, "such attributes are of secondary importance to a husband whose economic position required a wife who was no stranger to hard work."[55]

As well as managing the household, most middle-rank women also engaged in other forms of work whose success depended on intelligence and a reliance on one's own judgment. In York, the role of the wife in a craft workshop was so crucial that city ordinances allowed an artisan to take on an extra apprentice if he had no wife.[56] Among the middle-rank families of London, between 82 and 83 percent of men made their wives executors of their wills, a move that indicates a high level of trust in women's knowledge and honesty. Moreover, the merchants' confidence in their wives strongly suggests "a joint discussion of debts and deals" since the wife, as the executor of her husband's will, "had to know who owed money to the husband and to whom he owed money . . . had to know the business factors who were handling merchandise, what merchandise was abroad or in the country, who owed craftsmen payment, and what the craftsman might owe for raw materials."[57]

It is not only in the towns that we see women doing jobs requiring personality traits that elite gender ideology identified as inappropriate or unfeminine. Margaret Cappes was the wife of a small farmer, owning 10–20 acres of land. Margaret was reported for brewing each year for forty years in the mid-fifteenth century, suggesting that she independently operated an alehouse. The income from Margaret's work added considerably to the family's prosperity, allowing her husband to buy additional land and providing the generous dowries that enabled Margaret's three daughters to marry men of superior social station.[58] While details regarding Margaret Cappes's personality are not known, it is highly unlikely that deference, submission, and obedience would have contributed to her success in the business of selling ale.

Court records, too, suggest that middle-rank notions of appropriate gender behavior differed from those of medieval elites. Katherine French has revealed how all-female fundraising activities and the control accorded to middle-rank women over the physical features of the parish church through their role as church cleaners and caretakers caused friction with clergy members who felt that women's participation in these activities contradicted with ideals of feminine humility, obedience, and submission. The women's husbands and fathers, however, were less likely to object to this behavior. Charting differences in the rates of women being reported for speech crimes in the jurisdictions of Lincoln and Kent, French argues that laymen's understandings of speech crimes were far less gender-oriented than those exhibited by the clergy. In the Kent visitation, where the clergy dominated the proceedings, women were cited for speech crimes with greater frequency. In Lincoln, where lay churchwardens were more central to the process, speech crimes were more evenly divided between men and women, a phenomenon French ascribes to laymen's greater appreciation of the fact that women's "talking, leading, acting, and opining" benefited the parish and raised the family's status.[59]

One might ask how my argument regarding middle-rank men's favorable view of assertive women can be reconciled with the fact that these same men also display an increasing concern with women's social misbehavior.[60] Marjorie McIntosh's research into juries in England's market towns reveals a marked increase over the course of the fifteenth century in reports of "scolding." The overwhelming majority of those reported for scolding (an offense involving argumentative speech or the spreading of malicious gossip) were female. In fact, I do not think these two phenomena are contradictory or mutually exclusive. The increase in attempts to regulate women legally, indeed, may stand as the best evidence of their increasing status. In a culture where gender norms are stable, there is less need for legal regulation since the society itself regulates its members. It is only in a society of contradictory valences that the need for outside regulation, in the form of legal punishments, becomes necessary.

While the culture of the medieval middle ranks may have encouraged certain forms of female assertiveness, it nevertheless remained firmly patriarchal. Town ordinances continued to enforce female submission to male authority, excluding women from the "formal, direct exercise of public authority," and women continued to be subordinate to men, who controlled the crafts, guilds, and civic government.[61] Thus, even as the culture might have fostered female independence for economic reasons, its patriarchal nature was likely to encourage severe punishments of women who took the invitation to assertiveness into areas that put them in conflict with the culture's patriarchal norm. For this same reason, we can see the pageants at once disciplining female independence in certain forms (as in Noah's beating of the resistant spinning uxor) but also promoting it in others (as in the uxor's helpful work on the ark).

Women's Work, Cross-Dressing, and Gender Difference in the Biblical Drama

Reading the biblical drama in the context of middle-rank women's work also sheds light on another facet of the pageants' unruly women. The fact that women's roles in the drama were most likely played by adult men (rather than the adolescent actors of Shakespeare's time) has been used to support arguments for their misogyny.[62] Writing of her experience putting on modern performances of the *Noah* pageant, Meg Twycross writes that, when Mrs. Noah was played by a man, she "came over as an admitted caricature, an incarnation of Misrule"; when she was played by a woman, the uxor took on the status of a person and "her rebelliousness gains overtones and raises questions it was never meant to raise."[63] Twycross's analysis is grounded in the assumption that medieval and modern bodies are identical. Her observation that, in her own modern production, "even a smaller male Mrs. Noah becomes disproportionately large for a woman" is assumed to apply to medieval audiences and players as well.[64]

We should not, however, be so quick to assume that marked physical differences existed between men and women of the middling and lower orders of late medieval society. In a world without mechanization, a housewife's job required considerable physical strength, for the hauling of water and wood, as well as the washing of clothing, the beating of flax, and a variety of other household tasks. Both brewing and spinning—common occupations for middle- and lower-rank women—required considerable muscle. It is likely, then, that these women exhibited levels of muscularity unusual in middle-class women of the modern West. It has always been assumed that the uxor of the Chester *Noah* pageant is speaking about her physical abilities when she remarks, during the building of the ark, that "women bynne weak to underfoe / any great travell"

(67–68).[65] But since the alternate chore she suggests for these "weak" women is the hauling of timber (65), one wonders whether she is not referring to an intellectual or moral inferiority instead.[66]

We ought to remember, as we consider the transvestite medieval drama, that most of the female costumes were not made specifically for these adult men. Rather, they were borrowed. Thus, the men outfitted themselves *in the clothes of real women.*[67] The possibility that this exchange of clothes was predicated on small men borrowing the garments of large women only underlines my point regarding the physical equivalency between the sexes, for it shows that they were similar enough in size for some men—and perhaps many more men than we might imagine—to wear clothing made for a woman.

What may have been written on the bodies of the middle ranks, then, and what the transvestite theater may well have emphasized, is not sexual difference but sexual sameness. Writing of the early modern period, Mary Hartman makes a point that can also be applied to the later Middle Ages. Observing the early modern emphasis on sexual difference and the frequent lamentations in the literature of the period regarding women's insubordination, Hartman proposes that they are a reaction to the fact that men's and women's lives were becoming more and more similar and identifies that phenomenon with late marriage societies. Separate female and male roles and men's superiority, Hartman argues, were less discussed in early marriage societies because they were so obvious, being fully incorporated into the fabric of experience and in household structures.[68] In late marriage societies, where married couples were the same age and ran the household together, gender differences were less marked. Indeed, gender sameness is at the heart of the comedy that drives the Towneley *Noah* pageant when it features a couple equally matched in strength of body and will. The figuration of Mak and Gyll in the *Second Shepherd's Play* also emphasizes sexual sameness. Although the two have marital battles, they function as a pair throughout the play, sharing the same plot, the same crime, and the same punishment. This fact is even remarked upon at the play's conclusion by the second shepherd, who says of the couple, "Ye two are well feft / Sam in a stede" (894–95).

Marriage and Adultery in the "Troubles of Joseph" Pageants

The "Troubles of Joseph" pageants present another case study in how the biblical drama significantly alters the discourse of obscene comedy. All four of the largest extant biblical drama collections—Towneley, N-town, York, and Chester—as well as the Coventry *Shearman and Taylor's Play*, include a comical episode in which an elderly and impotent Joseph observes Mary's pregnancy and accuses her of sleeping with other men, while a calm Mary assures him that she has done nothing wrong. As many readers have noted, the episode is rooted in comical portrayals of cuckolded husbands and old men married to young women.[69]

The foolish, elderly Joseph is not unique to the biblical drama. As Louise Vasvari, Pamela Sheingorn, and others have demonstrated, the trope was a common one in medieval portrayals of Joseph.[70] While the belief in a sexless holy marriage was a necessary consequence of the Church's policy on Mary's perpetual virginity, the idea that a vigorous young man would participate in such an arrangement was sufficiently incredible to medieval audiences that the image of an elderly and impotent Joseph prevailed.[71] The idea was still troubling, however. Even if an impotent old man made the notion of chaste marriage credible, his impotence compromised his authority, since notions of marriage and masculinity situated sexual intercourse as a key element of male dominance in the marital relationship. As Vern Bullough has noted, "masculinity is equated with potency, and any sign of lack of virility is a threat to one's definition as a man."[72]

Like the Noah pageants, the "Troubles of Joseph" episodes do not dispute the paradigm of masculine authority in the household. And certainly in their portrayal of an elderly doddering Joseph, they evince the same discomfort with Joseph's celibate masculinity that we see in other medieval portrayals of the holy father. However, the pageants diverge from fabliau and farce in the way they approach the tropes of the cuckolded husband and of May-December marriages.

Medieval tales of cuckolded older husbands tend to run along a well-worn narrative track: the wife has a dalliance with a younger man, and the husband becomes suspicious; he confronts his wife, and she allays his suspicions with a comically unlikely story. In these tales, a man is never wrong to suspect his wife. In the fifteenth-century *Farce de Regnault qui se marie à Lavollée*, a group of advisors try to discourage Regnault from marrying, in one case singing, "Se tu prens jeune femme, / Cocu tu en seras; / Tu t'en repentiras" [If you take a young wife / You will be cuckolded / You will repent it] (76–78).[73] The most famous cuckolded old men in English literature are the husbands of Chaucer's *Miller's Tale* and *Merchant's Tale*. Although Chaucer often alters the fabliau, these two tales follow the Old French works in their attitude to a husband's suspicions: both Alisoun and May are doing exactly what their husbands suspect. In Chaucer's tales, and in many other versions of the *senex amans* story, the joke is on men who are too credulous. Like January of the *Merchant's Tale*, these men become laughingstocks for having faith in the probity of their adulterous wives. Many tales that do not feature May–December unions include similar plots of tricky wives. In *L'enfant qui fut remis au soleil* (5.48), which appears as both a fabliau and a sermon exemplum (and is cited in the N-Town "Trial of Joseph and Mary"), a wife tells her husband she conceived the child born during his long absence on a business trip through a snowflake (not believing her, the husband sells the child on his next trip, telling the wife that he "melted" in the sun).[74]

The "Troubles of Joseph" episodes take up the trope of the cuckolded old husband, but, because in this case the young wife under suspicion is Mary, the most virtuous woman in Christendom, the joke is turned on its head. Here, the husband is funny not because he is too credulous but because he is too suspicious. Instead of supporting the rigid and unvarying principle of women's perfidy, the "Troubles of Joseph" episodes do just the opposite, making a joke of misogynist suspicion and advocating a flexible intelligence that can discern between a good woman and a bad one.

Some might argue that Mary is so extraordinary that her story cannot be applied to gender relations in general. As Marina Warner has demonstrated, Mary's virtue is often an oppressive paradigm for women, setting a standard no woman can meet.[75] The case for Mary's exceptionalism in the "Troubles of Joseph" episodes would be persuasive if the episodes appeared as part of pageant collections that portray numerous incidents of female adultery. But this is not the case. Indeed, sexual misbehavior is notably absent from the pageants' depictions of unruly women. Given this context, the discernment reading is the more likely interpretation of the "Troubles of Joseph" episodes.

It is also worth noting that, even in his anger, Joseph steers clear of fabliau-style misogyny. Fabliau and farce frequently include misogynist condemnations of women's lust, mendacity, and weakness. While misogyny is not entirely absent from the "Troubles of Joseph" episodes (the Towneley Joseph says he does not blame Mary for having "[w]oman manners" [210]) it does not predominate. In all four of the "Troubles of Joseph" episodes, Joseph spends most of his time lamenting the foolishness of May-December marriages, rather than women's perfidy. The first phrases out of the Towneley Joseph's mouth when he learns of Mary's pregnancy are

> I irke full sore with my lyfe
> That euer I wed so yong a wyfe —
> That bargan may I ban

. . .

It is ill-cowpled of youth and elde (161–63, 170)

A similar lament is also the first thing we hear from the York Joseph, who asks, "For shame what shall I say, / that thus-gates now on mine old days / Have wedded a young wench to my wife, / And may not well trine [step properly] over two straws?" (10–13).[76] The Joseph of the N-Town pageant *Joseph's Doubt* issues a warning to all old men to "weddyth no wyf in no kynnys wyse / That is a yonge wench" (50–51), as does the Chester Joseph, who declares "God, lett never [an] ould man/ take to wife a yonge woman. . . . For accorde ther maye be none" (145–46, 149).

The plays' emphasis on the inappropriateness of May-December pairings locates the fault not in the women themselves but in the arrangement of the marriage, which is a male responsibility. Moreover, the plays characterize young women's adultery not as a mark of feminine wantonness but as a natural human response to an inappropriate match. Unlike many fabliaux and farces, the "Troubles of Joseph" episodes do not treat the female sex drive as a pathological impulse, destined to destroy society if not kept in tight bounds, but as a normal one that ought to be satisfied. As the Towneley Joseph says, "it is long of yowth-hede, / All swich wanton playes. / For yong women wyll nedys play them / With yong men, if old forsake them" (300–303). As is so often the case in the biblical drama, the approach of the "Troubles of Joseph" episodes is undeniably patriarchal (women are weak), but nevertheless displays a higher level of regard for women as human beings than we see in many other forms of obscene comedy.

Part II: Obscene Comedy and the Hidden Transcript in the Noah and Innocents Pageants

Comic episodes of the biblical drama not only revise dominant notions of gender and marriage, they are also a locus of middle-rank resistance to secular and ecclesiastical elites. The creators of the biblical drama deploy obscene comedy in the same way that we see it deployed in the writings of Langland and Chaucer and in the *Book of Margery Kempe*: as a discourse in which they can oppose the dominant ideology and criticize the power holders of their society with a severity that would have been impossible in more exalted discourses. By recognizing this function of obscene comedy, we can finally explain why the drama's creators were inspired to inject episodes of ludicrous comedy into

tragic biblical narratives like the Noah pageants and the Massacre of the Innocents plays. The plays' criticisms of established authority are not separate from
their revision of dominant notions of gender and marriage. As we shall see in
the ensuing discussion, the plays often present their revisions of sexual and
household politics as an important element of the same middle-rank identity
that asserts itself against the depredations of late medieval elites.

Resistance to Ecclesiastical Interpretations
of the Flood in the Noah Pageants

Although typological readings of the Noah pageants are now no longer in
vogue, most readers continue to assume that the pageants' producers and audiences would not have questioned the dominant theological interpretation of
the Noah story as a warning to sinners of God's righteous vengeance. According to this reading, Mrs. Noah's resistance to boarding the ark and her mourn-
ing for the drowned world represent spiritual errors that must be overcome
before the establishment of the new, post-Flood world. Assumptions regarding
the pageants' theological orthodoxy have also informed feminist interpretations that read the uxor as a misogynist caricature, since the plays cannot be
characterized as misogynist unless one assumes that the audience is being
invited to regard the uxor's resistance with contempt. In what follows, I wish to
interrogate these assumptions by pointing out how the Noah pageants resist
the dominant theological interpretation of the Flood as a story that is primarily illustrative of God's vengeance on humanity.

In medieval theology, sin and punishment for sin are regarded as the central themes of the Noah story. The Noah story was read in the Office for Sexa-
gesima week as an illustration of God's vengeance on sin. Mirk recites the Noah
story in his *Festial*, concluding, "Pus good men ze most vndyrstond how gret
vengeans God toke on pe world for wykednesse of synne."[77] Human death and
suffering are not, in this interpretation, to be pitied, but are regarded as the
righteous punishment of an offended God. Depictions of the Noah story in the
medieval visual arts often reflect the dominant theological interpretation, for-
bidding pity for the drowned by depicting them as corpses whose lifeless aspect
invites disgust rather than compassion. In the Bedford Hours (c. 1423), produced for the wedding of John, duke of Bedford, to Anne of Burgundy, an
illustration of the Noah story depicts dead bodies floating beside the ark, as well
as others that are partially beached, being eaten by carrion birds (see Figure 7).[78]

Cõment noel aps le deluge aruna a teric et nuft lors le britail et fift sacrifice et planta la vigne.

FIGURE 7. Animals disembark from the ark as dead bodies float nearby and are eaten by ravens. The Bedford Hours, c. 1410–1430. Add.MS.18850, fol. 016v.
© The British Library Board.

Such depictions are a constant in European art from the twelfth through the sixteenth century.[79]

With the arrival of the Black Death in the fourteenth century, the Noah story acquires a new prominence. Preachers and Church writers interpret the plague as God's intervention to draw humankind away from sin in ways analogous to the biblical Flood.[80] In a sermon of 1375, Thomas Brinson, bishop of Rochester, expresses contempt for the notion that "the pestilence and other misfortunes" can be attributed to astrological phenomena rather than to sin, asking advocates of astrology to "say what sort of planet reigned at the time of Noah, when God drowned the whole world except for eight souls, unless the planet of malice and sin. . . . Since the wretchedness of men was great on the earth, and all the thought of their heart was bent upon evil' [Gen. 6.5]. God himself, the best astrologer, said, 'The earth is filled with iniquity, therefore I will destroy them with the earth [Gen. 6.13]."[81]

Although the earliest manuscripts of the biblical drama are dated at least one hundred years after the Black Death, the theological interpretation of disease as divine punishment for sin is still relevant. This is not only because the first Noah plays may well have been created within decades of the Black Death but also because fatal epidemics were still well known to fifteenth-century audiences. As well as the plague, fifteenth-century England was beset with a variety of other highly contagious pathogens. In his study of epidemic disease in England over the fifty years between 1430 and 1480, Robert Gottfried finds that there were at least seven (and very likely ten) outbreaks of fatal epidemic disease on a national scale, a figure that leaves out the significant number of local epidemics occurring during the same period.[82] The most fatal and virulent epidemic of Gottfried's study occurred late in the fifteenth century, in 1479–80. The severity of this epidemic is attested by the author of the *Brut*, who notes that, in the years after Edward IV's invasion of France in 1475, "ther fylle a gret disse in Engelond callyd þe 'styche,' þat moche peeple deyde sodeynly þerof. And also anoper disse reyned aftyr þat, callyd þe 'fflyx' þat neuer was seen in Engelond before; & peple deyde hogely therof iij yer togedyr, in on place or oper."[83] As Gottfried notes, "few periods in history appear to have been subjected to as virulent, and, most important, as frequent outbreaks of infectious disease as was fifteenth century England."[84]

Throughout the fifteenth century, the Noah story continued to be cited in discussions that characterized epidemics as instances of God's vengeance on sinners.[85] In a Latin note appended to a fifteenth-century English translation of

John of Burgundy's famous medical treatise on the plague, an anonymous author intones,

> It should be known to all Christians that pestilence, and
> every other manifestation of God's vengeance, arises
> because of sin. It was for that reason that God first took
> vengeance in Heaven, when Lucifer fell; secondly in Para-
> dise, when Adam was driven out; thirdly throughout the
> whole world when all living things, except for those saved
> in Noah's ark, were destroyed in a cataclysm. . . . And there-
> fore it follows from these examples that pestilence arises
> from a multitude of sins.[86]

While it is true that the Noah pageants contain no explicit resistance to the orthodox interpretation of the Flood, this absence does not necessarily represent agreement. The work of James Scott is helpful in revealing how the Noah pageants' seeming complicity with the dominant view masks a deeper resistance to it. In Scott's reading of subordinates' response to coercive author-ity, lack of outright resistance in what he calls the "public transcript" of recorded history is not due to subordinates' complicity with the dominant ideology but to the "tactical prudence" of those who know that direct resis-tance will be met with severe punishment.[87] Subordinate dissent exists but is often invisible, occurring "offstage, beyond direct observation by the power-holders" in what Scott calls "the hidden transcript."[88]

Fear of reprisals does not mean that subordinate groups are disposed to keep their views entirely secret, since public articulations of resistance are empowering. When such articulations appear, however, they are often indirect and garbled in such a way as to make them "capable of two readings, one of which is innocuous." The innocuous meaning provides an "avenue of retreat" for the message's creators, should authorities accuse them of insubordination.[89] One of the best ways to express resistance safely is to clothe it in a ritual of "symbolic compliance" that seems, on the surface, to affirm the established order.[90]

Some episodes from fifteenth-century England suggest that the middle ranks did indeed use traditional rituals to express dissent and that they were well aware of how such rituals provided an avenue of retreat into innocuous meaning. Chris Humphrey notes the possibility of such an occurrence in "Gladman's rising" in Norwich in 1443. The incident involved one John Glad-man riding through the city on horseback, leading a procession of other burghers, at a time when members of the city were involved in a dispute with their ecclesiastical landlord over the local grain mills. Since the procession took place a full five weeks ahead of the proper day of the feast, Humphrey theorizes that it was a display of aggression intended to affect the outcome of negotiations over the mills. Because the procession was tied to a ritual display, however, such accusations were difficult to support. While a complaint made by the prior alleged that Gladman and his followers were inciting riot in the city, another account, found in the city records several years later, alleges that Gladman was simply engaging in a traditional Shrovetide procession, involving "makyng myrth, disportes and pleyes."[91] Thus the proximity of the Shrovetide holiday gave Gladman and his associates "a means of covering themselves" before those who would accuse them of rebellious intent.[92]

Evidence of a "hidden transcript" resisting the orthodox theology of the Noah story can be found in the three Noah pageants featuring an unruly Mrs. Noah. It is notable that the pageants diverge from medieval visual representations of the Flood by declining to represent the drowned. None of the pageants indicate either through stage directions or dialogue that they include such depictions. This absence cannot have been due to technical concerns. It would have been easy to represent the drowned in productions that already featured a ready stand-in for the ark in the form of the pageant wagon or scaffold. Nor can the cause be found in audience squeamishness, since the biblical drama is well known for its depictions of violence, both in the Passion sequence and in the Massacre of the Innocents plays.

Even more telling is the fact that the three unruly uxor pageants spend minimal time dwelling on the notion of the Flood as punishment for sin. This lack of emphasis stands in stark contrast to the N-town *Noah* pageant (the only one of the four complete extant Noah plays that does not feature an unruly uxor), which reflects the clerical interpretation of the narrative by dwelling extensively on sin. In the N-town play, a pious Mrs. Noah warns that "Synne offendyth God in his face / And agrevyth oure Lorde full ylle" (31–32), words whose sentiments are repeated several times over as each of the three Noah sons and each wife gives a separate speech in which he or she forswears sin and locates the cause of the Flood in sinful living. The difference in attitudes to sin between the N-town *Noah* and the three unruly uxor pageants is witnessed in a marked variance in word usage. The words "sin" or "sinful" appear thirty times in the N-Town Noah's 253 lines. They appear far less frequently in Chester (six times in 328 lines), York (eight times in 322 lines), and Towneley (eleven times in 559 lines).

Instead of sin and punishment, the obscene comedy Noah pageants focus on the human experience of catastrophe, emphasizing the family's struggle to survive. This is embodied not only in the pageants' interest in the Noah family's internal politics but also in the considerable stretches of text expended on the construction of the ark itself and on the practicalities of survival. Thus the obscene comedy Noah pageants are not simple instances of comic relief, meant to entertain illiterate audiences, but articulate a profoundly human-oriented approach to the Noah story.

The unruly uxor is the leading figure in this facet of the pageants. It is she who most often articulates the human (and humane) responses to the catastrophe. As Jane Tolmie has noted, Mrs. Noah "cares for the drowned world."[93] This element of her character is particularly evident in the Chester and York plays, where she frequently articulates a resistance to the brutalities of the Flood. In the Chester pageant, the uxor resists the idea that her "gossips" must die, saying "They shall not drowne, by sayncte John, / and I may save there life" (203–4), pausing to share a drink with them and threatening to leave Noah if he does not let them in. Similar expressions characterize the uxor of the York pageant. As well as refusing to board the ark, the York uxor demands that her "gossips" and relatives accompany the group and later grieves their deaths: "But Noah, where are now all our kin / And company we knew before?" (269–70).

In the York pageant, the uxor leads off a fascinating set of speeches by the Noah sons and daughters-in-law that focus on their desperation and grief over the coming destruction. In these speeches, the characters beg God for mercy and express puzzlement over the extremity of the punishment. "Yea, lord, as thou late vs be born / In this grete bale, some bote us bede" (169–70) begs one Noah son, while the other wonders about the Flood, "Fadir, what may this meruaylle mene? / Wherto made God medilerth and man?" (157–58). A Noah daughter-in-law, meanwhile, begs God to end the family's sorrow since they have understood his teachings (247–50).

In the Towneley pageant, as well, the uxor provides the human response to the flood, expressing fear when Noah tells her that the world shall be destroyed for sin ("I wote neuer whedir / I dase and I dedir / For ferd of that tayll" [453–55]) and anxiety about what it will be like to live in the ark ("Bot shall we here be pyned, / Noe, as have thou blis?" [480–81]). As in the York play, the Towneley uxor is the primary voice of grief for the drowned. When, after the Flood, Noah looks about and notes that all have been slain, Mrs. Noah expresses disbelief at their deaths, inquiring of Noah, "From thens agayn / May thei neuer wyn?" (792–93).

If the unruly uxor was featured in productions that emphasized sin and punishment, then interpreting her as an exemplar of sin or error would be justified. This is not, however, the case. That the pageants themselves contain subtle shifts of emphasis away from the themes of sin and punishment suggests that the uxor's words had a different purpose for their producers and original audiences. As I have illustrated in my discussion of *Piers Plowman* and the *Book of Margery Kempe*, one of the important functions of the unruly woman in English literary culture is as a figure through whom authors can articulate ideas that would otherwise be taboo, her comic ridiculousness functioning as a blind that allows her creator to air risky ideas in safety, since the unruly woman's words can always be dismissed as the utterances of an untutored shrew.

The importance of the unruly woman as a voice of explicit resistance in the Noah pageants is attested by the fact that the pageants' opposition to orthodox interpretations of the Flood is elsewhere manifested only passively, as an absence (an absence of the drowned, an absence of emphasis on sin). The pageants' authors can only bring themselves to voice explicit dissent in the person of the uxor. This is not to say that the pageants' creators were unaware that the uxor might be cast as an exemplar of spiritual error. Indeed, if Scott's theory regarding the necessity for an avenue of retreat is correct, the availability of this orthodox reading is crucial to enabling her resistance.

In this respect, the obscene Noah pageants represent a continuation of the "vernacular theology" that Nicholas Watson sees arising in the late fourteenth century.[94] While Watson believes that vernacular theology was extinguished in the anti-Lollard crackdown of the fifteenth century's first decades, the Noah plays suggest that it did not die.[95] In their resistance to punishment and their emphasis on humanity, the obscene comedy Noah pageants resemble the theology of Julian of Norwich, who also famously opposes the notion of a punitive God, presenting suffering as a means through which God draws humanity closer to himself.[96]

Class, Violence, and "the Hidden Transcript" in the Innocents Plays

The unruly woman's capacity for political expression is witnessed most remarkably in the "Massacre of the Innocents" pageants. The pageants dramatize the episode found in the Gospel of Matthew, wherein Herod, troubled by prophecies of Christ's birth, orders the murder of all male children under two years of age.[97] All six of the extant Innocents pageants embroider on their biblical source by depicting the slaughter of the children, a scene that Matthew (who only mentions Herod's edict) does not narrate. Four of the six pageants—the Chester, Towneley, Coventry, and Digby plays—inject the horrific episode with a ludicrous battle between the mothers and Herod's soldiers.[98] In the Chester, Coventry, and Towneley pageants, the soldiers and the mothers insult one another as the mothers fight back with distaffs and pot ladles; in the Digby *Killing of the Children*, a young aspiring knight named Watkyn is comically overcome by a group of distaff-wielding women and must be rescued by the other soldiers.

The unruly mothers are unique to English biblical drama, having no precedent in either the exegetical or liturgical traditions associated with the gospel story. In spite of their uniqueness, the pageants were, for many years, virtually ignored by scholars puzzled, and sometimes even offended, by their combination of murder and slapstick comedy (a "strange, humorous and vicious spectacle," in the words of one critic).[99] Recent years have seen a flowering of interest in the pageants among feminist scholars, As in the case of the Noah pageants, however, feminist readings of the Innocents plays have primarily regarded the unruly mothers as misogynist caricatures.[100] In two insightful studies, Theresa Coletti proposes that the pageants are more about gender than social difference, arguing that they counterpose a masculine preoccupation with status, lineage, and rank with the feminine sexual and maternal body.[101] Although Coletti credits the pageants with a powerful critique of patriarchy, proposing that the murderous soldiers call attention to "patriarchy's self-destructive capacities and its desire to purge the public realm of the maternal," she locates the positive feminine in the figures of St. Anne and the Holy Virgin, regarding the unruly Innocents mothers as misogynist figurations.[102]

While I agree that the pageants dramatize a conflict with public authority, and that gender is a crucial part of that conflict, I do not agree that they prioritize matters of gender over those of class or that their unruly mothers are simple instantiations of misogynist comedy. Two factors are crucial to our understanding of the Innocents pageants. First, we must recognize how the Innocents mothers—like the Noah pageants' unruly uxor and Gyll of the *Second Shepherd's Play*—diverge considerably from the unruly women typical of obscene comedy, even as they seem superficially to embody them. Second, we must understand how the plays' representations of gender and class are closely intertwined.

As I shall demonstrate, the Innocents plays make explicit the class-based differences in gender norms that I have described as being implicit in the Noah pageants and the *Second Shepherd's Play*. Understanding this aspect of the Innocents plays allows us to see how they issue a stringent critique of upper-class violence in the guise of ludicrous comedy. Indeed, one of the most stunning and yet least noted features of the plays is the fact that they exhibit a scene in which middle-rank people beat feudal authorities!

Although all of the obscene comedy Innocents pageants exhibit the phenomena I describe, I shall focus my analysis on the Digby *Killing of the Children*, the pageant that most clearly demonstrates the features I wish to highlight. The Digby *Killing of the Children* is one of four plays based on New Testament narrative that were put on to celebrate the feast Day of St. Anne in the late fifteenth or early sixteenth century in East Anglia. The play begins with Herod giving orders to his soldiers to kill the children. After Herod speaks, a young messenger, Watkyn, begs to be knighted. Herod agrees to do so if Watkyn can prove himself in the child-killing mission. Watkyn then comically professes to a terror of women bearing distaffs. When the knights arrive to kill the children, the women give battle, surrounding Watkyn and beating him with their distaffs until he is rescued by the other knights. The narrative is punctuated throughout with scenes of Mary's purification and of the holy family's flight to Egypt.

The Digby play identifies Herod and his knights closely with England's ruling class. Herod uses chivalric language when he refers to his soldiers as "knyghts" and vows to reward Watkyn with the title of "knyght aventururos" if he succeeds in the mission of killing the children (216).[103] When the knights embark on the infant-killing mission, they do so with the flourish and boasts typical of the chivalric language of warfare. We see similar patterns of identification in all the unruly mother Innocents pageants: the Chester play refers to the soldiers as "knights" (97) and gives them satiric titles like "Sir Lancher-deepe" (58); the Coventry play has Herod's minions speaking French and discussing their armor; in the Towneley *Magnus Heroditus* Herod speaks French and exhibits courtly manners, while his knights appear in full battle array.

It is undeniable that the Digby mothers reflect the misogynist stereotypes of obscene comedy: they are rude, crude, violent, and disorderly. We should, however, recognize that the mothers are identified not just by gender but also by class. In a work that has already highlighted class identity in its characterization of Herod and his "knights," the mothers are necessarily aligned with the urban middle ranks. This identity is affirmed by their status as residents of Bethlehem, their association with the carpenter Joseph and Mary his wife, and their use of distaffs and pot-ladles (both tools of middle-rank women's work).

Thus, the plays promote a kind of double vision of the conflict, wherein one can see it as a male-female battle typical of obscene comedy, or one can see it as a battle of the classes.

Modern readers, even those who identify the satire of chivalry implicit in the anachronistic characterization of Herod and his men, have seen the battle exclusively in terms of gender.[104] But would the plays' original audiences also have done so? To answer this question, we must consider the political culture of middle-rank people in fifteenth-century England. As any historian will admit, this is no easy task. The political beliefs and principles of the English middle and lower ranks are a classic example of Scott's "hidden transcript," since the systems of domination under which they lived gave them little opportunity for public or durable expressions of their politics. To say, however, that we cannot know much about the politics of fifteenth-century people is not to say we know nothing at all. The fifteenth century also includes a number of those rare instances of outbreak, in which the systems of domination break down sufficiently to make the hidden transcript publicly visible. A succession of popular uprisings throughout the fifteenth and early sixteenth centuries—in 1407, 1450, 1469, 1485, 1497, 1536, and 1549—as well as a series of significant local insurrections, attest to the ongoing discontent of middle- and lower-rank people, both urban and rural, with the ruling elites of their society.[105] Historians have increasingly come to see these outbreaks not as isolated incidents but as elements of "a deeper, active popular politics" among middle- and lower-rank people "that otherwise left few traces in the archives."[106] Thus, we can see the satire of Herod and his minions as part of what Simon Walker, using the terminology of James C. Scott, has called the "infra-politics" of late medieval England, a "broad area of discussion, complaint, and dissent that fell somewhere between wholehearted consent and open rebellion."[107]

The existence of a culture of resistance among the creators and audiences of the drama suggests that the class politics of the battle between the mothers and the soldiers was likely to have been much more visible to the pageants' original audiences than it has been to modern critics. A political, rather than gender-based, reading of the *Innocents* pageants allows us, for the first time, to justify their wide popularity. Mobilized and permitted by biblical narrative and the discourse of obscene comedy, the pageants allowed audiences to enjoy the intoxicating spectacle of middle-rank people beating feudal authorities. Scott's analyses are, once again, helpful in illuminating the pageants' appeal in this respect. For Scott, a crucial element in understanding the content of the hidden transcript lies in understanding the assault on human dignity inherent in systems of domination. In these systems, subordinates cannot fight back against insults and harm but must repress their anger for fear of severe reprisals from the dominant group. Citing the tradition of the duel, Scott points out that, in relationships of equal power, the victim of insult or harm can retain his or her human dignity by engaging in reciprocal action, meeting insult with aggression. All systems of domination produce a "routine harvest of insults and injury to human dignity." Subordinates, however, cannot take reciprocal action, since attempts to respond "in kind" are likely to be met with death, torture, or severe injury. Thus, the "hidden transcript" often acts out in fantasy the anger and reciprocal aggression denied by the presence of domination.[108]

A number of recorded episodes from the fifteenth century attest to the "routine harvest of insults and injury to human dignity" that Scott describes. Simon Payling's survey of judicial records in Nottinghamshire leaves him in little doubt that the ruling elites of English localities were frequently involved in acts of intimidation and extortion against members of the middle ranks. In 1414, for instance, Sir John Zouche was indicted for threatening a member of a coroner's jury and extorting forty shillings and a horse from him. In 1440, juries sitting before the justices of the peace accused Sir Hugh Willoughby of having several men falsely appealed of felony and extorting forty pounds from them.[109] These cases exhibit the "constant oppression and petty extortion" that Walker finds being practiced by royal and ducal officials in Lancashire in the names of their masters. A variety of other studies have charted the frequency with which the lesser gentry terrorized and blackmailed whole localities.[110] Most notable among these is the case of John Belsham, accused of fourteen separate crimes between 1422 and 1439, including three murders and six assaults. Belsham seems to have escaped punishment by attaching himself to the duke of Norfolk, and his only known instance of facing a jury was in 1441, when he was acquitted.[111] It is highly likely, moreover, that the extant records document only a small portion of the criminal behavior and violence of the late medieval English aristocracy and gentry. As Payling notes, "With the great men of the country able to exercise such a malign influence over the function of royal justice at the local level, it is unlikely that the recorded crimes of this sector of society represent anything approaching the total extent of their criminal activity."[112]

One might object, however, that, if this were really the meaning of the pageant as it was understood by its original audience, the very system of domination that I am describing would never have allowed it to be played. Here, once again, Scott's insights are illuminating. For Scott, the expression of resistance in the public transcript is not necessarily dependent on making sure members of the dominant group are not able to interpret the message, but on the extent to which that message is also open to an innocent or innocuous interpretation. Dominant groups in an oppressive society might recognize the possibility of dissent in a particular expression but will allow it, as long the opposition is not unambiguously articulated.[113] Expressions of folk or popular culture can thus articulate seditious notions without prompting a reaction from the powerful as long as the seditious expression also lends itself to an innocent construction.[114] In this respect, the plays' biblical content and their performance as part of a religious festival provide an alternate "innocent" reading, as does their seeming evocation of a conventional misogyny in the form of the unruly mothers.[115]

Child Murder and Misogynist Spectacle

Many readers have puzzled over the seemingly callous attitude to child murder evinced by the Innocents pageants. This view, however, is based on certain assumptions regarding the function of art that may well not have been shared by the plays' creators and original audience. Distaste at comedy in the midst of child murder is grounded in the belief that art ought to provide appropriate moral and emotional cues to its audience. Thus, a depiction of child murder ought to direct the audience to see that "this is sad" or "this is a horrific crime." This approach assumes a certain distance between the audience and the work of art they consume: onlookers feel pity because they witness an event that has happened to others and not to them. However, distance of this sort is discouraged by the anachronism of the Innocents pageants. By casting both the mothers and the soldiers in contemporary terms, the pageant invites its audience to read themselves into the drama. Given the violence and intimidation that was endemic to the coercive political system of late medieval England, the soldiers' assault on the mothers may well have had a much greater degree of immediacy for the pageant's original audiences than it does for modern ones.

In terms of audience response, the proximity of biblical narrative to historical reality is a double-edged sword. On the one hand, as an indictment of medieval elites, the anachronism of the child-killing scene is profoundly effective. An infant-killing mission cast in chivalric language highlights—in a way few other plots could—how aristocratic militarism had degenerated into horrific brutality against the very defenseless creatures it promised to protect.[116] As

Rosemary Woolf remarks of the Wakefield playwright, he was "aware of the romance ideals of chivalry and of the monstrous inappropriateness of killing babies as an activity for knights."[117] At the same time, a spectacle of the powerful inflicting suffering on the powerless threatens to affirm the completeness of that power in a way that demoralizes rather than uplifts. In his discussion of torture in Western penal systems up to the eighteenth century, Michel Foucault describes how public spectacles of extreme torture affirmed the power of the ruling order by making power visible, using the suffering body as "the anchoring point for a manifestation of power, an opportunity for affirming the dis-symmetry of forces" between the subject and the sovereign.[118] Similarly, in her study of the body in pain, Elaine Scarry notes the theatrical element of torture, which converts an inaccessible individual experience into a witness of power through a display of agency wherein the link between the pain and those inflicting it is self-consciously displayed, most often through the exhibition of the weapon: "having as its purpose the production of a fantastic illusion of power, torture is a grotesque piece of compensatory drama."[119]As spectacles, the Innocents pageants have the potential to affirm established power in the way that Foucault and Scarry describe, even as they condemn it on moral grounds, simply by virtue of the fact that Herod is not defeated or punished after the murders.[120]

In this respect, the obscene comedy episode between the soldiers and the mothers is crucial, for it destroys the pageant's ability to function as a spectacle of power. The disruptive force of the ludicrous battle is not rooted in the fact that the mothers fight back, since their self-defense is ultimately futile. Rather, the scene disrupts because it asserts an obscene comedy discourse of power that is the opposite of the one implicit in spectacles of torture. As I have noted throughout this study, obscene comedy's tendency to invert social hierarchies and to represent them as contingent and subject to change means that it always resists the established order on some level, even as it might seem to uphold it. This vision of power as contingent is precisely the opposite of the vision of power as total and incontestable that inheres in spectacles of torture.

By making the soldiers the stand-ins for the frustrated obscene comedy husband, afflicted with female shrewishness, the pageant characterizes military power as unstable and vulnerable. This is not an illusion, but rather gets at the basic instability already implicit in any display of violence by authorities. As Scarry points out, the infliction of torture is always sign of a regime's vulnerability: "It is precisely because the reality of that power is so highly contestable, the regime so unstable, that torture is being used."[121]

The fact that the Innocents pageants invite audiences to *laugh* at the soldiers, even as they commit the heinous crime of child murder, constitutes an attack on the soldiers' power. As the nineteenth-century Russian socialist Alexander Herzen has noted, the laughter of subordinates in the face of established powers disrupts and disperses their authority: "No one laughs in church, at court, on parade, before the head of their department, a police officer, or a German boss. House serfs have no right to smile in the presence of their masters. Only equals can laugh among themselves. If inferiors were permitted to laugh in front of their superiors and if they could not hold back their laughter, then you can forget about respect for rank."[122]

The Class of Gender in the Innocents Pageants: Joseph and Mary and the Unruly Woman

Although the plays' evocation of misogyny enables their critique of political authority, their gender politics, when examined closely, actually run against the misogynist discourse of obscene comedy. In their attitude to gender, the Innocents plays are quite similar to the Noah pageants and the Towneley *Second Shepherd's Play*. However, they go beyond the other pageants in identifying these revised gender norms specifically with the middle ranks.

Like so many of the biblical drama's unruly women, the fighting mothers of the Innocents pageants are characterized in terms that diverge from the obscene comedy tradition. In fabliau, farce, and popular lyrics, the unruly woman is always cast as an anti-social force, her disobedience, violence, and bad behavior threatening to destroy the social order. The Innocents pageants reverse this trajectory, making the unruly woman a force of moral rectitude, who resists the horrific act of child murder. Rather than being the destroyer of the social order, she is its fiercest guardian.

Insofar as they act in defense of middle-rank people in a contest with feudal authorities, the mothers of the Innocents pageants are also positioned as representatives of that class. By promoting the mothers' unruliness in this context, the pageants' creators announce a correlation between differing classes and differing gender norms, asserting a middle-rank vision of the usefully unruly woman against aristocratic norms of feminine obedience. For the creators of the

Innocents pageants, the unruly woman is not just a metaphor "for expressing the relations of all subordinates to their superiors" in the way Natalie Zemon Davis describes the unruly woman's role in early modern Europe.[123] Rather, she is a representative of middle-rank identity.

A number of details in the Digby *Killing of the Children* associate a gender politics of male dominance and female submission specifically with medieval elites, while identifying companionate-style male-female relationships with the middle ranks.[124] As well as equating Herod and his minions with unjust authority, the Digby *Killing of the Children* repeatedly associates them with a gender politics that equates masculinity with shows of force. When the young solider, Watkyn, expresses his fear of women bearing distaffs to Herod, the king's response makes it clear that he regards physical dominance over women as an integral part not just of knighthood but of masculine identity. "Nay, harlott!" Herod exclaims in outrage at Watkyn's confession, "Abyde stylle with my knightes, I warne the, /... / If thu quyte the like a *man* whille thu art ought!" (193, 196). This same notion is articulated when Watkyn expresses his fears to the other knights, one of whom responds with an ironic joke: "Watkyn, I loue the, for thu art euer a *man!*" while a second knight promises "thu shalt haue better wage, / If thu quyte the *manly* amonge the wyves."[125]

We can see a similar conflict between elite and middle-rank notions of acceptable gender behavior playing out in debates over certain aspects of the ritual culture of late medieval English towns. Hocktide rituals, which were popular in urban parishes in the fifteenth century, allowed women to raise money for the parish by chasing men down, binding them, and releasing them for a ransom. Ecclesiastical, aristocratic and, occasionally, civic authorities disapproved of these activities. In 1450, John Carpenter, bishop of Worcester, condemned the ritual, calling it a "noxious corruption"; in 1446, an activity called "hokking" was banned during Queen Margaret's visit to London. However, the persistence of Hocktide rituals attests to the fact that many townspeople did not find them offensive.[126]

The aristocratic promotion of total male dominance is opposed in the Digby *Killing of the Children* not only by the play's lionization of the unruly mothers but also by its representation of Joseph and Mary in the "Flight to Egypt" sequence, whose scenes are interspersed with the killing of the children narrative. The play's anachronism means that Joseph, as a carpenter, implicitly takes on a middle-rank identity. The gender politics of the Joseph-Mary marriage are markedly different from the theory of total masculine dominance pursued by Herod and his knights. In the Dibgy play's "Flight to Egypt" scenes, Mary is self-confident and assertive, often instructing her husband. "Gentyll spouse," she tells Joseph, "now do your diligens, /And brynge your asse, I pray you, a-non right" (259–60). Joseph, for his part, does not follow the theories of masculine domination forwarded by Herod and his knights but respectfully follows his wife's wishes. In the temple scene he avows, "ye shal me fynde plesant at every assaye; / to cherysshe you, wyf, gretly am I bounde" (531–32). Thus, the holy couple represents a vision of marriage that is quite similar to the companionate partnerships of the Noahs in the post-Flood sequence of the Towneley *Noah* pageant and of Mak and Gyll in the *Second Shepherd's Play*. Like these other couples, the Digby Mary and Joseph are figured as a team, working together against a common enemy.

This is not to suggest that the authors of the Digby play were feminists. In fact, there is nothing in the play to dispute the patriarchal framework visible in other obscene comedy pageants. Mary's higher-than-average level of precedence in the holy marriage is framed by the larger patriarchal authority of God, who ultimately directs the action. Moreover, it is no coincidence that the most vociferous promotion of the unruly woman comes in a place where actual husbands are not involved, since the mothers' husbands do not appear in any of the Massacre of the Innocents pageants.

The patriarchal sponsorship of female assertiveness and independence that we see in the biblical drama's obscene comedy pageants not only reveals a significant facet of middle-rank politics in the later Middle Ages, it also helps us to understand the vexed status of female sexuality in the modern West. Feminism is typically thought to exist in opposition to patriarchal social formations. The biblical drama shows us that, when other factors make a certain degree of feminine liberation profitable for men, a patriarchal culture can sponsor and promote forms of behavior that are typically identified as feminist while still retaining an outlook that is essentially patriarchal in its convictions regarding male superiority and its tendency to prioritize male perspectives and needs over those of women. While the biblical drama is capable of significantly revising women's roles, it remains in conformity with medieval norms when it comes to women's sexual and reproductive life because women's liberation in these areas did not serve men's interests. Indeed, one of the most unique features of biblical drama comedy lies in its commitment to severing the strong link made in the obscene comedy tradition between women's assertiveness and their sexual misbehavior. This medieval phenomenon sheds light on why economic liberation and the increased opportunities for work and education for women in the modern West have not been accompanied by a similarly extensive sexual liberation or alteration in family relations.[127] It helps explain, in other words, why western women can ascend to the highest echelons of government, business, and academia and yet still face sexual harassment and rape in large numbers as well as official restrictions on access to birth control and abortion

Conclusion

Lessons of the Medieval Obscene

The Digby *Killing of the Children* is a fitting last subject for this study, its remarkable expressions testifying to the interrogatory, innovative, and politically oriented culture of obscene comedy during the later Middle Ages. By connecting household and government, gender and political theory, the pageant reveals an acute understanding of how theories of the domestic and the familial inform those defining the relation of subordinates and superiors in other spheres. My aim in this study has been to demonstrate that the obscenity of this pageant—and of all the other works I have addressed—is not incidental to its insights, but constitutive of them.

Through its violation of social norms, obscenity creates a "no holds barred" space in which writers and actors not only shock with depictions of transgressive behavior, but use those transgressions to explore alternative ways of looking at the established order. Fusing the obscene with laughter, obscene comedy creates a sense of play and of suspension from the ordinary course of life that allows subordinates to expose the hypocrisies, injustices, and contradictions of the powerful and to examine their ideological justifications. This occurs not only because obscene play inherently invites experimentation but also because it performs a masking function, providing a safe space within a coercive political environment by allowing critiques to be dismissed (even as they are issued) as the ludicrous sayings of degraded characters. Exploiting the "hidden in plain sight" nature of medieval obscenity, wherein the public violation of taboos is permitted in certain marginalized spaces, fourteenth- and fifteenth-century English authors make public ideas and analyses that could not have been voiced in more authoritative and serious discourses.

Medieval Obscenity/Early Modern Censorship

Understanding the political valences of late medieval obscenity leads us to ask new questions not only of the period itself but of the one immediately following it. Well known as an era in which an increasingly centralized and potent royal government replaces the competing power structures of the Middle Ages, the sixteenth century also features the first attempts to censor the obscene. This new tendency is evident in sixteenth-century responses to Chaucer which, for the first time, begin to express concern over his "flat scrurrilitie" (to quote the Elizabethan courtier and writer John Harington).[1] Indeed, the process by which the sexual comes to be regarded as unsuitable for public display might even be said to begin in the late fifteenth century. The biblical drama, for all its interrogatory force, tends to veer away from sex in favor of exploring the more socially oriented forms of obscenity embodied in subordinates' resistance to superiors.[2] By the time Thomas Speight edits his edition of Chaucer's works in the late 1590s, lewdness is so much a part of Chaucer's reputation that Speight's friend Francis Beaumont feels obliged to defend it. Noting "the incivilitie *Chaucer* is charged withall," Beaumont excuses the great medieval writer on the basis that "His drift is to touch all sortes of men, and to discouer all vices of that Age."[3]

Other discussions of Chaucer in the sixteenth century indicate that early modern readers were well aware of the links between the poet's obscenity and his social critique. As well as having a reputation for lewdness, Chaucer was also known in the sixteenth century as a reformer and a satirist who rebuked the vices of his age.[4] In a commentary on Chaucer in his expanded edition of the *Book of Martyrs* (1570), John Foxe articulates a clear understanding of comedy's role in enabling a critique of established powers. Chaucer, Foxe writes, escaped the censorship of the bishops during Henry VIII's reign in spite of being a "right Wicleuvian" because his criticism of the Church was "done in myrth & covertly." Taking Chaucer's criticisms "but for jests and toyes," Foxe says, the bishops "yet permitted his bookes to be read" even as they condemned other works in the same vein.[5]

If the works and authors listed in the late sixteenth-century Bishop's Ban are any indication, Chaucer had a powerful influence on the obscene satire of the Elizabethan age. On June 1, 1599, the archbishop of Canterbury and the bishop of London ordered the Stationer's Company to round up, burn, and ban from future printing several literary texts.[6] While the ban was ostensibly aimed at "satyre," Lynda Boose has pointed out that the banned works are notable for their "sexualized, salacious tone."[7] The works were offensive not only for their social critique but because they harnessed the power of obscenity to express it. Thus the ban reflects what Linda Hunt and Joan de Jean have observed of censorship in later periods of European history: namely, that official concern over obscenity is prompted less by a concern over its exhibition than with its use in threatening or questioning the powerful.[8] As Boose observes, official concern over the works listed under the ban is prompted not only by their obscene satire but by the fact that they sought to disseminate it to a wider, nonelite audience through publication.[9]

Most fascinating in light of this study is the extent to which the authors named in the Bishops' Ban were careful readers of Chaucer's fabliaux. In *Virgidemiarum* (1597–98), a collection of "satyres," Joseph Hall cites the denizens of Chaucer's *Merchant's Tale* by name, comparing one of his own characters to "Chaucers frosty Janiuere."[10] Thomas Middleton, whose *Microcynicon: Six Snarling Satires* (1598) was also among the banned works, refers in a later text to Chaucer's style of "jest" and describes him as "that broad famous English poet."[11] In the prefatory material to his obscene work, *The Scourge of Villanie* (1598), John Marston cites Chaucer (along with Juvenal) as an influence.[12]

A similar objection to social invective fused with sexual explicitness appears to have prompted the censorship, in 1576, of George Gascoigne's *A Hundreth Sundrie Flowres*. Like the objects of the Bishops' Ban, Gascoigne's work sought a broader readership through publication and was censored for its "wanton speeches and lascivious phrases."[13] And, like many of the authors of the 1599 ban, Gascoigne is inspired by Chaucer, characterizing *A Hundreth Sundrie Flowres* as having been created after the model of "that worthy and famous Knight Sir Geffrey Chaucer," who, "after many pretie deuises spent in youth, for the obtayning a worthles victorie" spends his age "in discribing the right pathway to perfect felicitie."[14]

The censorship of sexual obscenity in the Elizabethan era raises new questions about the absence of explicit obscenity in the work of the premier authors of the period, Edmund Spenser and William Shakespeare. Of course, one can find the erotic, and even the bawdy, in the work of Spenser and Shakespeare, but their sexual representations are coy in comparison to the exposed genitalia and riotous, lower-class antics of Chaucer's fabliaux. The obscene may be present in Spenser and Shakespeare, but it is hidden, masked behind double entendre and linguistic play. This is worthy of remark. Why, in fact, did Spenser—so worshipful of Chaucer in other respects as the "well of Englishe undefyled"[15]— demure in the matter of the fabliau, the favorite genre of the *Canterbury Tales*?

Why did Shakespeare, a writer with a fondness for the bawdy and an attentive reader of Chaucer who often adopts the characters and plots of Chaucer's works in his own, never match the obscenity of the *Miller's* or *Reeve's Tales*? It is easy to naturalize these choices as simply differences in taste without inquiring how that altered sense of propriety actually came about. Given the censorship of sexually explicit, socially critical works in the late sixteenth century, we must ask to what extent the absence of the obscene in Spenser and Shakespeare is a matter of taste and to what extent it is an enforced absence resulting from the anti-establishment associations the obscene had acquired in English culture during the later Middle Ages.

The censorship we see being applied to sexual obscenity in the early modern period casts late medieval obscenity in a new light. It suggests that the growth and development of obscene comedy as a political discourse in the late medieval period represents a brief window of opportunity, when nonelite authors are able to experiment with using the obscene to examine and interrogate the established order before censorship, and the kind of centralized government that enables it, are able to obliterate or marginalize it. By the sixteenth century, authorities not only are able to recognize the danger of this new mode but have the means to ensure it does not reach a wide audience.

The political discourses uncovered by this study also pose questions regarding the suppression of the biblical drama in the sixteenth century. The traditional interpretation of the biblical drama's demise says that Protestant authorities suppressed it because of its Catholic doctrine.[16] This analysis is based on the assumption that the primary (indeed the only) subject matter of the drama is religious. As this study has revealed, however, the biblical drama also develops an articulate political critique of the ruling orders of English society. To what extent did this critique figure in the drama's suppression?

As Lawrence Clopper and others have pointed out, there are no clear parallels between the arrival of the Reformation in England and the suppression of the biblical drama. Although Henry VIII issues the Act of Supremacy establishing himself as head of the English Church in 1534, the playing of the northern cycles is only completely suppressed in the late sixteenth century.[17] Moreover there is much to indicate that the suppression of the drama and other carnival-style popular festivals is more closely related to official fears over political insurrection than with problematic religious meanings. Edward VI's Act of 1549, temporarily banning the performance of any play or interlude, was prompted by Kett's Rebellion, a popular revolt in Norfolk against land enclosure, which was itself sparked by the performance of a play.[18] Official moves leading to the demise of the northern cycles in the 1570s, meanwhile, follow closely on the heels of the Northern Rebellion of Catholic earls against Elizabeth's government in 1569.

In light of the politics of medieval obscenity, we must ask to what extent authorities' concerns about the "superstition" and extrabiblical content in the drama speak to theology and to what extent they tacitly recognize the drama's anti-establishment explorations. How did the Noah uxor and the unruly mothers of the Innocents pageants appear to the Elizabethan government in a century when middle- and lower-rank women were frequent participants in popular protests over enclosure and high food prices and when lower- and middle-rank men adopted the dress of the unruly woman to engage in protest?[19]

Medieval Obscenity/Modern Pornography

Medieval obscenity and modern pornography stand at two ends of a long historical development in the West, wherein explicit forms of sexual representation become more and more removed from mainstream discourse. Characterizing the privatization of sex as part of a broader trend toward separating the public and private realms from one another over a range of discourses and practices, Michael McKeon describes the gradual process whereby depictions of sex come to be regarded as apolitical forms of expression, intended exclusively for sexual stimulation.[20] The total depoliticization of sex is, however, a relatively recent occurrence. Until the eighteenth century, pornography still entertains a variety of rhetorical concerns, is still socially engaged, and is frequently comical.[21] It is only in the nineteenth century that representations of sex and sexuality begin to be separated from forms like satire, advice, and political commentary and become solely focused on sexual arousal.[22]

Yet the modern divide between sex and politics is an illusory one. If this study has shown anything, it is that violations of taboo are always, necessarily, engaged with the power relations of their society. Even as modern pornography claims to be about sex exclusively, it has remained relentlessly political. This, indeed, has been the core of the modern feminist objection to much heterosexual pornography. Responding to accusations of prudishness, the antiporn feminist Gail Dines insists that it is not the explicit sexual expression of modern Internet pornography to which she objects but the misogynist and racist politics it so frequently exhibits.[23]

Modern feminist analyses of pornography often reflect modernity's illusory divide, interpreting it as a primarily sexual form that relates only to issues of gender and sexuality, rather than exploring its connection to the larger political, economic, and social structure of Western society. Catharine MacKinnon, for instance, has famously drawn parallels between feminism and Marxism, but her analysis is based on the separation of the economic and the sexual. MacKinnon says that sex is to feminism as work is to Marxism, but does not consider how the two might be interdependent, for instance, how pornography might be used to uphold economic power relations by offering men disempowered by capitalism a compensatory source of power in the form of pornographic misogyny.[24] Even Linda Williams, who has done much to reveal the intellectual and cultural work of pornography, still mainly restricts its meaning to the realm of gender and sexuality.[25]

Feminists' failure to recognize obscenity's involvement in other concerns—an involvement that medieval obscenity renders visible—has created a false division between so called "pro" and "anti" porn feminists and has led both groups to lobby in favor of policies that ultimately undermine the feminist goal (common to both factions) of resisting the hatred of women. A failure to understand how deeply misogynist obscenity is imbricated in the power structures of the modern West has led to disastrous results in antiporn feminists' attempts to control pornographic misogyny through legal regulation.[26] Repeatedly, feminist campaigns to censor misogynist porn have instead led to censorship of gay and lesbian porn and other forms of insurgent, socially marginalized pornography.[27] Meanwhile, feminist advocates of free expression, who emphasize porn's capacity to undercut misogyny and oppressive gender norms, have overlooked the violations of human rights inherent in an exploitative pornography industry that extracts profits through the exhibition of racism and an increasingly violent misogyny.[28] This issue has acquired new urgency with the wide popularity of Internet porn, which, in combining the "three As" of accessibility, anonymity, and affordability, has become a $12 billion industry consisting of primarily male consumers.[29]

The study of medieval obscenity shows us that the core of the problems relating to pornography in the modern West lies not in sexual expression itself but in the public-private divide that still defines it. The Middle English iterations of obscene comedy that I have explored in this study may not meet the standards of modern feminist thought on gender and sexuality, yet they exceed the capacities of modern pornography in the simple fact that they *changed*. The penis in *Piers Plowman* is not like the penis in the fabliau or the penis that bedecks church architecture. Explicit representations of sex are configured very differently in the work of Chaucer and the fabliau or Latin elegiac comedy. The unruly woman of the biblical drama is not the unruly woman of the sermon exemplum.[30]

This is not something we can say about most of the heterosexual pornography produced over the last two hundred years, which is characterized by a formulaic repetitiousness.[31] The moment in the early nineteenth century when pornography is completely detached from other social and political concerns and becomes exclusively aimed at sexual stimulation is also the moment when it becomes frozen in time. In one of the very few instances in which the rate of modern cultural change is *slower* than that of the Middle Ages, heterosexual pornography from the nineteenth to the twenty-first centuries exhibits little alteration. Isolated, quite literally, in the bedroom, sexual representation has ceased to change with the culture around it, remaining disproportionately mired in hierarchical gender relations even as women have acquired unprecedented rights and liberties in Western society. The eroticization of female submission and male dominance that defines the popular gonzo porn site "Teens Love Huge Cocks" (wherein young women with "small" genitalia are penetrated by older men with "large" penises) is almost identical to that which defines *The Autobiography of a Flea*, published in 1887, wherein sixteen-year-old Bella is seduced by a well-endowed priest.[32]

Enacted in public and connected to the public dialogue, medieval representations of sex changed as their culture changed. While the Internet has made pornography much more widely available, it has, paradoxically, only deepened the public/private divide that isolates sexual representation in the modern West, making pornography consumption more private than it has ever been before.[33] The crisis that now confronts us with respect to modern pornography is that its Internet distribution has also, as Dines notes, given its misogynist and racist politics an unprecedented degree of dispersal and influence.[34]

The study of medieval obscenity suggests that the best way to deal with the malign politics of modern porn is not to censor it but to bring sex out of hiding and reconnect it to the culture's public life. Judith Butler has argued, using the theories of Foucault, that feminist attempts to censor violent and misogynist pornography will only end up "inadvertently but inevitably producing and authorizing . . . precisely the scenes of sexual violence and aggression they seek to censor."[35] Gesturing at the semiotic instability that has been the focus of this study, Butler proposes that this is because "limits are in a sense what fantasy loves most, what it incessantly thematizes and subordinates to its own aims."[36] While Butler's chosen term is "fantasy," she is actually addressing the nature of the obscene, which, as this study has illustrated, is always in dynamic conversation with the source of its prohibition. Thus, Butler argues, it is in deregulation and "in the production of a chaotic multiplicity of representations" that the authority and prevalence of a reductive and violent imagery can be defused.[37] Thus, the problem of modern misogynist porn is best regarded not only as a sexual issue but as an example of the more general difficulties relating to the free and democratic exchange of ideas in the modern media. In the same way that the economics of other forms of modern media result in the privileging of viewpoints that favor social power holders (as Noam Chomsky and others have pointed out), so the misogyny of modern Internet pornography serves the interests of its corporate financial backers.[38]

If the study of Middle English obscenity directs us to new ways of confronting modern pornography, it also illustrates the urgency of doing so. As my examination of the biblical drama has revealed, bourgeois patriarchy in the West was capable, from a very early stage in its development, of giving considerable latitude and freedom to women when doing so served its economic and political interests. The precondition of those freedoms, however, was the removal of female sexuality from the agenda of social change. The biblical drama might invite approval of Mrs. Noah's cleverness and it might honor female assertiveness, but it cannot and does not imagine new configurations of sexuality to go along with its changed standards of feminine conduct.

The separation of sexuality from other forms of female liberation still dogs the life of women in the modern West, particularly in the United States, where unprecedented levels of social, economic, and political autonomy for women exist alongside a still-misogynist and patriarchal sexual politics that attempts to control women's bodies and punish them for nonnormative sexual behavior.[39] In this respect, the *Book of Margery Kempe* is a revolutionary work not only in its fifteenth-century context but in the context of modern society as well. Inappropriate, rude, and shocking (in short, *obscene*), the *Book* contends that women's full entitlement in other areas of life cannot be achieved without confronting the cultural precepts that define their sexuality. In doing so, the *Book*'s medieval author grasps a truth that modern Western society has yet to confront.

NOTES

INTRODUCTION. OBSCENITY IN MEDIEVAL CULTURE AND LITERATURE

Epigraph: Chaucer, *Riverside Chaucer*. All subsequent citations of Chaucer's work are from this edition and will be cited by line number in parentheses in the text.

1. *Middle English Dictionary*, s.v. "Harlotrie."

2. Per Nykrog's argument that the French fabliau originated with "les riches seigneurs ou grands bourgeois" has been largely accepted within the field of fabliau studies, although it has been qualified somewhat by Jean Rychner, who notes that changes reflected in different editions of select fabliaux suggest they were being tailored to appeal to different audiences. The fact that such tales were part of upper-class entertainment repertoires is also attested by one of the major influences on the *Canterbury Tales*, Boccaccio's *Decameron*, which features upper-rank young men and women trading tales of similar obscenity. See Nykrog, *Les fabliaux*, 27; Rychner, *Contribution à l'étude des fabliaux*; Boccaccio, *Decameron*. For an account of the extant fabliaux in English or English-associated manuscripts, see Pearcy and Short, *Eighteen Anglo-Norman Fabliaux*, 1–5; Hines, *Fabliau in English*, 38–41.

3. Two recent studies of medieval scatological obscenity include Morrison, *Excrement in the Late Middle Ages*, and Allen, *On Farting*.

4. In attempting to define obscene comedy (which he calls "fabliau-like tales") in European literature, Dronke describes them as "amusing stories of deception and outwitting, especially of the sexual kind." Goodall believes that the fabliau's combination of sex and trickery is what distinguishes it from other stories, and Hines remarks on the "characteristic and pervasive atmosphere of sexuality and sensuality" in the fabliau. See Dronke, *Medieval Poet*, 146; Goodall, "History of the English Fabliau," 7; Hines, *Fabliau in English*, 35.

5. Nykrog, *Les fabliaux*, 53

6. Hines calls the taboo language of the fabliau "marked terms" that the culture labeled indecent or vulgar to varying degrees. Featuring such language in the title, he notes, seems to have influenced the popularity of certain fabliau. While more than half of the 120 fabliau recognized by the twentieth-century collection, the *Nouveau recueil complèt des fabliaux* (NRCF) exist in a single copy, several fabliaux with salacious titles exist in multiple manuscripts. These include, *Le chevalier qui fist parler les cons*, "The Knight Who Could Make Cunts Speak" (seven manuscript copies); *Cele qui se fist foutre sur la fosse de son mari*, "She Who Got Fucked on the Tomb of Her Husband" (six copies); and *Cele qui fu foutue et desfoutue*, "She Who Was Fucked and De-Fucked" (six copies). Fewer than twenty of the less racily titled fabliaux exist in four or more copies. See Hines, *Fabliau in English*, 19.

7. This is not to say that lexically oriented studies of medieval obscenity are not valuable and necessary, only that they are limited in terms of what they can say about obscene comedy as a cultural phenomenon in the Middle Ages. Some examples of studies that focus on the lexical character of

obscenity include Harris, "Inserting 'A grete tente'"; Muscatine, "Courtly Literature and Vulgar Language"; Wood, "The Wife of Bath and 'Speche Daungerous'"; Louise O. Vasvari, "Fowl Play in My Lady's Chamber"; Sheila Delany, "Anatomy of a Resisting Reader"; L. Benson, "The 'Queynte' Punnings of Chaucer's Critics."

8. For a review of the critical history of the genre, see Levy, *The Comic Text*, 1–29.

9. Scholarship on the visual arts has also produced some excellent analyses, including studies of manuscript marginalia, church carvings and misericords, and obscene badges. See Camille, *Image on the Edge*; Jermain and Weir, *Images of Lust*; Grössinger, *English Misericords*; and Koldeweij, "A Bare-Faced Roman de la Rose," "Lifting the Veil on Pilgrim Badges," and "The Wearing of Significant Badges."

10. Dronke, *Medieval Poet*, 146.

11. Busby, "*Dame Sirith*," 70.

12. Montaiglon and Raynaud, *Recueil général et complet des fabliaux*.

13. Bédier, *Les fabliaux*, 30,

14. Nykrog, *Les fabliaux*, 3–30.

15. See Pearcy and Short, *Eighteen Anglo-Norman*, 1–5. For a fuller history of debates over the fabliau, see Levy, *Comic Text*, 1–29.

16. Rychner, *Contribution à l'étude des fabliaux*, 45.

17. Cooke, "Middle English Comic Tales," 3152. For other discussions regarding the generic classification of English tales, see Goodall, "History of the English Fabliau"; Hines, *Fabliau in English*, 205–16.

18. Foucault, *Archaeology of Knowledge*, 41.

19. Ziolkowski, *Cambridge Songs*, 62–68.

20. For the Latin original, see Cohen, "*Comédie*" *latine*. For a translation, see *Babio*, in Fitzgerald and Sebastian, *Broadview Anthology of Medieval Drama*, 10–20.

21. Dronke, *Medieval Poet*, 156.

22. For a collection of extant fabliaux, see Noomen and van den Boogaard, 10 vols. *Nouveau Recueil Complet des Fabliaux*.

23. For English translations of Der Stricker, see Thomas, *Fables, Sermonettes, and Parables*. For English translations of *maeren*, see Classen, *Erotic Tales of Medieval Germany*. For English translations of the Italian *Il Novellino*, see Consoli, *One Hundred Ancient Tales*. No English translations of the Middle Dutch boerden exist, to my knowledge. For a translation into modern Dutch, see Lodder, *Van de man die graag dronk*. In addition several novelle and maeren as well as a number of later texts, are published as analogues for Chaucer's fabliaux in Benson and Andersson, *Literary Context of Chaucer's Fabliaux*.

24. Basevorn, "The Form of Preaching," 212.

25. These are accorded the following numbers in Tubach, *Index Exemplorum*: 6, 53, 60, 67, 183, 295, 320, 321, 328, 632, 661, 966, 969, 1127, 1159, 1626, 2158, 2267, 2268, 2401, 2408, 2895, 2706–8, 3176, 3182, 3299, 3557, 3686, 4319, 4353–54, 4451, 5243, 5246, 5271, 5275, 5277–78, 5279–80, 5284–85, 5289, 5291, 5294–95, 5311.

26. Vitry, *Sermones Vulgares*, 240.

27. Tubach, *Index Exemplorum*, 328. Another exempla (4451) features a husband who avenges himself against his wife after she explains the child of an adulterous union by claiming he was conceived with an icicle, a story that is also told in the fabliau *L'enfant qui fu remis au soleil* (5.48); the wife who gobbles the family meal and is punished in another exemplum (969) is very similar to the woman in the fabliau *Les perdris* (4.21). Other exempla with strong resemblances to fabliaux include 1127, the story of a wife who manages to escape her husband's wrath when her lover leaves his coat behind (very similar to *Le chevalier a la robe vermeille* (2.12); 2708, in which a husband sees his wife with her lover but is per-

suaded that herbs made him see double is similar to *Le prestre qui abevete* (8.98); in 3182, a foolish youth who learns his lesson after wanting to marry more than one woman is similar to the fabliau *Le vallet aus douze fames* (4.29); 5271, about a knight who dresses as a priest to hear his wife's confession resembles *Le chevalier qui fist sa fame confesse* (4.33). Another very popular exemplum, 661, repeats the plot of the English comic tale *Dame Sirith*. See Salisbury, *Trials and Joys of Marriage*, 29–43.

28. Bernard of Clairvaux, "Ad Clericos de Conversione," in *Sancti Bernardi Opera*, vol. 4, 59–116, 83; English translation: Evans, *Bernard of Clairvaux*, 13–14. Helen Cooper also notes that Eadmer gives an extended *similitude inter mulierem et voluntatem* in which the will is seen as poised between God and the devil as a woman is between her husband and the devil. See Cooper, "Gender and Personification," 33n3.

29. See MS. B.11.22., Trinity College, Cambridge; also cited in Camille, *Image on the Edge*, 56.

30. Camille, *Image on the Edge*, 48–50.

31. Ibid., 147–48.

32. Jermain and Weir, *Images of Lust*.

33. English translations of the *Decameron* are too well known and too numerous to list. English translations of the other works exist in the following editions: Ruiz, *The Book of Good Love*; Hurwood, *The Facetiae of Giovanni Francesco Poggio Bracciolini*; Leighton, *Merry Tales and Three Shrovetide Plays by Hans Sachs*; Aylett, *Translations of the Carnival Comedies by Hans Sachs*; Enders, *Farce of the Fart*. Several Schwänke as well as a number of *Fastnachtspiele* are translated in Benson and Andersson, *Literary Context of Chaucer's Fabliaux*.

34. For an index and description of misericords in medieval Europe, see Block, *Corpus of Medieval Misericords: France*; *Corpus of Medieval Misericords: Iberia*; *Corpus of Medieval Misericords: Belgium and Netherlands*. See also the "Elaine C. Block Database of Medieval Misericords," which includes 12,000 photographs of misericords from across Europe, "Index of Christian Art," http://ica.princeton .edu. For description and discussion of the badges, see Koldeweij, "A Bare-Faced Roman de la Rose"; Koldeweij, "Lifting the Veil on Pilgrim Badges"; Koldeweij, "The Wearing of Significant Badges."

35. Five other riddles play off a similar dynamic. For the Old English originals and modern English translations of the obscene Anglo-Saxon riddles, see Baum, *Anglo Saxon Riddles*, 57–60.

36. Wells et al., *Manual of the Writings in Middle English, 1050–1500*, 9: 3158 and 5: 1324. An additional tale, *A Peniworth of Witte*, exists in the Auchinleck manuscript (1330–40). Although the story of a merchant who learns the fickleness of his mistress and the value of his wife when he pretends to have lost all his wealth is told in a moralizing style that is not exactly comical, its close relation to the fabliau *Le bors pleine de sens* (2.8) by Jehan le Galois makes it worthy of mention. For a summary of the tale, see Cooke, "Middle English Comic Tales," 3159.

37. Melissa Furrow argues that the fabliau does not exist in English because English romances integrate elements of fabliau into their narratives in a way French romances do not. Keith Busby asserts that the lack of English fabliaux is due to the fact that English romances are not as interested as the French works in fine points of manners and psychological sensibilities. Because the fabliau's appeal lies primarily in its ability to overturn these notions, it had limited appeal to English-language audiences. See Furrow, "Middle English Fabliau"; Busby, "Conspicuous by Its Absence."

38. Bishop, "Influence of Plautus," 299.

39. Anstey, *Munimenta Academica*, 60. Translation mine.

40. These include four from MS London BL Harley 2253: *Le chevalier a la corbeille* (9.113); *Le chevalier qui fist parler les cons* (3.15); *Les trois dames qui troverent un vit* (8.96); and *La gageure* (10.114). There is also *Un chevalier, sa dame, et un clerk* (10.123), found in Cambridge Corpus Christi College MS 50; *Cele qui fu foutue et desfoutue* (4.30), found in MS Clermont-Ferrand Archives du Puy-de-Dome F2; and *Les quatre souhais de saint Martin* (4.31), found in Bodlein Library, Oxford, MS Digby 86. These are

listed in Hines, *Fabliau in English*, 39; Pearcy and Short, *Eighteen Anglo-Norman Fabliaux*; van den Boogaard, "Fabliau Anglo-Normand."

41. Hines, *Fabliau in English*, 38.

42. These are *D'un vilein e de sa femme*; *D'un autre vilein e de sa femme*; *D'un vilein e de sa femme cuntrarieuse*; *D'un riche humme e de sa fille*. See Pearcy and Short, *Eighteen Anglo-Norman Fabliaux*; Marie de France, *Fables of Marie de France*, numbers 44, 45, 94, 95.

43. Langland, *The Vision of Piers Plowman: A Critical Edition of the B-text*, Passus 10, line 45. See also Piers's advice to the knight to "Hold noght with none harlotes ne here noght hir tales" (6.52), or the Prologue's reference to "japeres and jangeleres" who remind the narrator of Paul's preaching that "Qui loquitur turpiloquium is Luciferes hyne," lines 35 and 39.

44. Mosher, *Exemplum*, 100–101 and 103.

45. Mirk, *Festial*, 192. Also cited in Mosher, 108.

46. "Sawles Warde," 86–109.

47. The *Alphabetum Narrationum*, the *Disciplina Clericalis*, and the exempla of Jacques de Vitry were circulating in England in the early fourteenth century because tales sourced from them appear in the *North English Homily Collection*. See Mosher, 79 and 96–97.

48. Jermain and Weir, *Images of Lust*, 23.

49. In a Chester Cathedral misericord, c. 1390, a woman grips a kneeling man by his tippet and beats him with a flax mallet.

50. For instance, in an early fourteenth-century Flemish book of hours held by Cambridge University, two young men shit into a bowl and carry it to a lady. See MS. B.11.22, *Image on the Edge*, 56. Examples of obscene English badges can be found in Spencer, *Pilgrim Souvenirs and Secular Badges*.

51. For discussions of the revisions of gender roles and marriage occurring in Europe at this time, see Burger, "In the Merchant's Bedchamber"; Carroll, *Painting and Politics in Northern Europe*, ch. 1; Lipton, *Affections of the Mind*; McSheffrey, *Marriage, Sex, and Civic Culture*.

52. Watson, "Censorship and Cultural Change."

53. Fowler, "Civil Death and the Maiden."

54. Davis, "Woman on Top," 127.

55. Hartman, *The Household and the Making of History*; Howell, "The Properties of Marriage."

56. Howell, "Properties of Marriage," 17–21.

57. Per Nykrog believes that explicit discussions of sexuality are not considered obscene in medieval culture because they did not offend, while Bruno Roy regards obscenity as a category that is "more aesthetic than moral in the Middle Ages." Charles Muscatine believes that the notion of obscenity is a courtly imposition on a culture that lacked such notions generally. See Nykrog, "Obscene or not Obscene," 331; Roy, "Getting to the Bottom of St. Caquette's Cult," 318; Muscatine "Courtly Literature and Vulgar Language."

58. Foucault *The History of Sexuality*; Lacquer, *Making Sex*.

59. Brundage, *Law, Sex, and Christian Society*.

60. Honigmann, "A Cultural Theory of Obscenity," 717.

61. La Barre, "Obscenity: An Anthropological Appraisal," 543.

62. Justice Potter Stewart, concurring in *Jacobellis v. Ohio*, 378 U.S. 184, 197 (1964).

63. For the last part of this definition, I am indebted to Henderson, *Maculate Muse*, 2.

64. *Miller v. California*, 413 U.S. 15 (1973).

65. Williams, *Obscenity and Film Censorship*, 124.

66. Camille, *Image on the Edge*, 13.

67. Fein, "Appendix: the Contents, Quires, and Independent Blocks of MS Harley 2253," 374–75.

68. Brundage, *Law, Sex, and Christian Society*, 246.

69. Karras, "*Leccherous Songys*," 243.

70. Ibid., 242.

71. Brundage, *Law, Sex, and Christian Society*, 6: "the legal regulation of marriage and divorce, together with the outlawing of bigamy and polygamy and the imposition of criminal sanctions on fornication, adultery, sodomy, fellatio, cunnilingus, and bestiality...are all based in large measure upon ideas and beliefs about sexual morality that became law in Christian Europe during the Middle Ages."

72. Melissa Furrow remarks that the very things romance is careful to exclude are the joy of the fabliau: bodily functions, obscene words, low-class people, lust, and greed. See Furrow, "Middle English Fabliau," 7. Simon Gaunt notes that, while there are some obscene troubadour lyrics, the use of overt obscenity in troubadour lyrics is rare. See Gaunt, "Obscene Hermeneutics in Troubadour Lyric," 90.

73. Baum, *Anglo Saxon Riddles*, 57–60.

74. Nykrog notes that every time the fabliau authors use the word "foutre" (fuck), they accompany the usage with a remark that insists very strongly on "le caractere grivois d'expression." See Nykrog, *Les fabliaux*, 211.

75. Translation from Eichmann and Du Val, *French Fabliau*, 2: 137.

76. de Lorris and de Meung, *Roman de la Rose*, lines 7220–28, trans. Dahlberg, *Romance of the Rose*, 133.

77. Ibid., lines 7429–32, trans. Dahlberg, *Romance of the Rose*, 135–36.

78. *Ménagier de Paris*, 129.

79. Translation: Bayard, *A Medieval Home Companion*, 93–94.

80. "Christine de Pisan, "Contre Le Romant de la Rose, 51.

81. Baird and Kane, *Querelle de la Rose*, 48–49.

82. Gerson, "Traité Contre le Roman de la Rose," 82.

83. Baird and Kane, *Querelle de la Rose*, 87.

84. Gerson, "Traité Contre le Roman de la Rose," 83.

85. Baird and Kane, *Querelle de la Rose*, 88.

86. Cited in Hunt, "Introduction," 13.

87. de Jean, *Reinvention of Obscenity*, 10–14.

88. Talvacchia, *Taking Positions*, 74.

89. Ibid., 9, and Wolk-Simon, "'Rapture to the Greedy Eyes',"54.

90. Findlen, "Humanism, Politics, and Pornography," 101.

91. Hunt, "Introduction," 10.

92. Findlen, "Humanism, Politics, and Pornography," 101. See also Talvacchia, *Taking Positions*, 74, who talks about the new index of forbidden books compiled by Clement VIII in 1596, which explicitly added the printing of licentious images to its prohibitions.

93. Hunt, "Pornography and the French Revolution," 307.

94. Caviness argues that artistic representations of the nude Eve are associated with shame and guilt in the Middle Ages but authorities did not respond to nude imagery with censorship because they counted on their ability to control viewers' responses. See Caviness, "Obscenity and Alterity," 160.

95. Karras, "*Leccherous Songys*," 243–44.

96. Clopper, "Middle English Drama," 742.

97. Loomis, "Some Evidence for Secular Theatres," 34.

98. Clopper, "Middle English Drama," 743.

99. Chambers, *Medieval Stage*, 91, and Clopper, "Middle English Drama," 744–45.

100. Clopper, "Miracula and *The Tretise of Miraclis Pleyinge*," 884.

101. Clopper, "Middle English Drama," 744.

102. Ibid., 744.

103. Marshall, "Theatre in the Middle Ages," 381.

104. Michael Camille notes that oral sex is rarely pictured in medieval art and never mentioned in the fabliau. Jermain and Weir find corbels in San Pedro de Cervantos in Spain that depict one man pulling apart the buttocks of another and two simians having anal sex, but they note such depictions are extremely rare. Also, it is significant that even these carvings do not depict human anal sex but must displace it onto animals. See Camille, *Image on the Edge*, 54; Jermain and Weir, *Images of Lust*, 101.

105. Minnis, *Fallible Authors*, 307.

106. Jermain and Weir, *Images of Lust*, 150.

107. Dunton-Downer, "Poetic Language and the Obscene," 34.

108. Morrison, *Excrement in the Late Middle Ages*, 33.

109. Thomas, "Alien Bodies," 228.

110. Camille, *Image on the Edge*, 143.

111. Although fabliau attitudes to gender are complex, the presence of a persistently misogynist ideology in the genre is well recognized. As Gaunt notes, "the fact remains that the fabliaux evoke and use a deeply misogynistic discourse, often to condemn . . . women's sexual desire." See Gaunt, *Gender and Genre*, 268. In terms of the genre's approach to rank, Per Nykrog notes that the fabliaux show a profound respect for the aristocracy and an equally profound disrespect for the peasantry, priests, and, much of the time, also the bourgeoisie. See Nykrog, *Les fabliaux*, 119.

112. The photographs of Robert Mapplethorpe use anal and genital imagery to challenge dominant views of heterosexuality and masculinity in modern American society. Eve Ensler's *Vagina Monologues* uses explicit discussions of female genitals to undercut patriarchal characterizations of women's sexuality. Mapplethorpe, *Mapplethorpe*; Ensler, *Vagina Monologues*.

113. MacKinnon, *Only Words*, argues that the protections afforded pornography under the First Amendment violate women's Fourteenth Amendment rights to equal protection, an abuse permitted and rendered invisible by a culture that relegates women to second-class status as human beings. Similarly, Dworkin, *Pornography: Men Possessing Women*, argues that pornography licenses violence against women in a way that dovetails with the oppression of women in Western society generally.

114. Carter notes that censorship of pornography in the modern West is more severe when it opposes the official order than when it affirms conventional heterosexual power relationships. See Carter, *The Sadeian Woman*, 96. Kipnis, *Bound and Gagged* (124) proposes that the magazine *Hustler* is the most reviled example of mass circulation pornography due to its oppositional political stance, rather than its explicit nudity.

115. Lessa, "Discursive Struggles Within Social Welfare," 284.

116. Lochrie, "Women's 'Pryvetees'," and Hansen, *Chaucer and the Fictions of Gender*, ch. 8.

117. Patterson, *Chaucer and the Subject of History*, 244–79.

118. Bakhtin, *Rabelais and His World*, 4.

119. Ibid., 10.

120. Eagleton, *Walter Benjamin*, 148; Eco, "The Frames of Comic 'Freedom'," 6.

121. Turner, *Libertines and Radicals*, 139. See also Stallybrass and White, *The Politics and Poetics of Transgression*, 19.

122. Stallybrass and White, *Politics and Poetics of Transgression*, 16.

123. Ibid.

124. Davis, "Woman on Top," 131.

125. Foucault, *The History of Sexuality*, 100–101.

126. Bakhtin, *Rabelais and His World*, 15.

127. Ibid., 10 and 34.

128. Turner, *From Ritual to Theatre*, 27.

129. Ibid., 53.

130. Ibid., 44.

131. Turner, "Frame, Flow, and Reflection," 101.

132. Sutton-Smith, "Games of Order and Disorder," cited in Turner, *From Ritual to Theatre*, 28.

COMEDY AND CRITIQUE: OBSCENITY AND LANGLAND'S REPROOF OF ESTABLISHED POWERS IN *PIERS PLOWMAN*

1. Langland, *Vision of Piers Plowman*, ed. A. V. S. Schmidt. All citations from the B version of *Piers Plowman* are taken from this edition and will hereafter be cited parenthetically in the text.

2. Nicolette Zeeman makes a similar point regarding *Piers Plowman*'s relation to the grail romances, noting that one cannot approach the subject as a source study because Langland's inventive and interactive modes of composition mean "we are unlikely to find in his poem the kinds of unchanged matter that would constitute, in a more explicitly referential author, plausible proof of source." Zeeman, "Tales of Piers and Perceval," 201.

3. "[A]nd to the werk we 3eden," says Lechery, describing intercourse with his mistress (C.VI.181). See Langland, *A New Annotated Edition of the C-text*, ed. Derek Pearsall. All citations of the C-text are taken from this edition and will hereafter be noted parenthetically in the text.

4. Edwin Craun (*Lies, Slander, and Obscenity*, ch. 5) discusses obscenity in *Piers Plowman*, but his focus is on viewing Langland's condemnations of minstrels and obscene speech in the context of the pastoral tradition, rather than Langland's own use of obscene comedy. The only other author who specifically addresses Langland's obscenity is Stephen A. Barney ("Langland's Mighty Line," 112, 115), who believes that passages like the description of the keen weapon and the impotence vignette are not obscene but evidence of Langland's unselfconscious attitude to sex and the body, an approach whose problems I have addressed in the introduction to this study.

5. For discussions of gender, see Baker and Morrison, "*The Luxury of Gender*"; Cooper, "Gender and Personification"; Davis, *Writing Masculinity*, ch. 1; Fowler, "Civil Death"; Lees, "Gender and Exchange"; Murphy, "Lady Holy Church and Meed the Maid"; Raskolnikov, "Promising the Female,"; Robertson, "Measurement and the 'Feminine' in *Piers Plowman*"; Tavormina, *Kindly Similitude*; Trigg, "The Traffic in Medieval Women." For discussions of secular genres in *Piers Plowman*, see: Bloomfield, *Fourteenth-Century Apocalypse*, introduction; Clifton, "The Romance Convention of the Disguised Duel"; Shepard, "Langland's Romances."

6. Bloomfield's survey of the different genres operational in *Piers Plowman*, for instance, notes that Langland manifests a sense of humor that is uncommon in the genre of allegorical dream vision but does not give the point extended consideration (*Fourteenth-Century Apocalypse*, 19). Others who briefly recognize Langland's use of comedy include Barney, *Penn Commentary*, 220; Galloway, *Penn Commentary*, 375; Harwood, "Dame Study," 7; Middleton, "Acts of Vagrancy," 289. One exception to the general tendency toward vagueness in descriptions of Langland's use of comedy and satire is Yunck, *Lineage of Lady Meed*.

7. The notion that Chaucer was familiar with *Piers Plowman* is becoming increasingly accepted. For arguments in favor of the connection, see Cooper, "Langland's and Chaucer's Prologues,"; Grady, "Chaucer Reading Langland"; Middleton, "Commentary on an Unacknowledged Text."

8. Bowers, *Chaucer and Langland*, 2–3.

9. Other condemnations of "harlotrye" in *Piers Plowman* include Reason's refusal to have ruth "Til lords and ladies loven alle truthe / Ad haten alle harlotrie, to heren it or to mouthen it" (B.4.114–15) and Piers' advice to the knight to "Hold noght with none harlots ne here noght hir tales, / And namely at the mete swiche men eschuwe / For it ben the develes disours, I do the to understonde" (B.6.52–4).

10. There is not much scholarship that explores Langland's views of secular politics, particularly his attitudes to the gentry and aristocracy. Scholarship that does explore Langland's politics tends to equate his traditionalism with a support of the ruling orders. Thus, David Aers explores Langland's attitudes to the poor in great detail but overlooks his critique of the aristocracy and gentry. Kathryn Kerby-Fulton, meanwhile, expresses the critical consensus when she reads the C-text revisions as an expression of Langland's "latent social conservatism." Furthermore, as Larry Scanlon notes, even New Historicist studies remain focused on ecclesiology. See Aers, *Community, Gender, and Individual Identity*, ch. 1; Kerby-Fulton, "Piers Plowman," 522; Scanlon, "King, Commons," 199.

11. Scanlon, "King, Commons," 199. The mid-century works in question are Donaldson, *C-Text and Its Poet*; Lewis, *Allegory of Love*; Robertson and Huppé, *Scriptural Tradition*.

12. Scanlon, "King, Commons," 207.

13. Ibid., 197–98.

14. Crane, "Writing Lesson of 1381," 211.

15. Dean, ed. *Mum and the Sothsegger*.

16. Barnie, *War in Medieval English Society*, 142–43.

17. Ibid., 143.

18. Scanlon, "King, Commons," 224.

19. Scott, *Arts of Resistance*, 148, 1–5.

20. Ibid., 157.

21. While one might rightly question whether Western democracies feature in practice the degree of free speech that they boast in theory, it is undeniable that the modern West allows a much greater latitude in public political commentary than existed in late medieval England.

22. Crowley, *The Vision of Pierce Plowman*, ii.

23. British Library, Add. MS 42130 (the "Luttrell Psalter") ff.170–73.

24. Ibid. ff. 60. For a further discussion and examples of obscene marginalia, see Camille, *Image on the Edge*.

25. Examples of fabliaux including oversexed, garrulous women include *Aloul* (3.14), *La borgoise d'Orliens* (3.19), *Le bouchier d'Abeville* (3.18), *Les braies au cordelier* (3.17), *Le chevalier a la robe vermeille* (2.12). Plots involving female sexual misbehavior are also legion in Latin elegiac comedy, including *Babio* (four of its five manuscripts are found in British libraries) *Milo, Lidia, Miles Gloriosus*. For the Latin originals of the elegiac comedies, see Cohen,*"Comédie" latine*. For English translations, see Crawford, "Secular Latin Comedies." Adulterous women are also the subject of many sermon exempla. See Tubach, *Index Exemplorum*, 966 (about a priest locked inside a cabinetmaker's chest after an adulterous liaison with the man's wife); 1127 (about a woman's plot to cover her adultery); 2895 (about a king and knight who leave home after their wives are unfaithful, only to learn that even a girl locked in a cupboard by her husband manages to commit adultery); 4319 (about a wife and mother-in-law who hide her adultery by holding up a sheet to conceal her lover when the husband returns unexpectedly).

26. "Dame Sirith" in Salisbury, *Trials and Joys*, 29–43.

27. Galloway notes that, in English law from the thirteenth century on, members of the royal family holding inheritance from the king-in-chief would need the king's license to marry. Galloway, *Penn Commentary*, 267.

28. Yunck and others have identified Meed with the arrival of the money economy, which could perhaps more easily be characterized as a force outside traditional medieval society. See Yunck, *Lineage of Lady Meed*; Aers, "Class, Gender"; Pearsall, ed., introduction to *Annotated Edition of the C-Text*, 11. However, I agree with John Burrow, who argues that the economy of bribery as Langland portrays it is nothing new but is actually typical of a traditional mixed economy. Burrow, "Lady Meed," 117.

29. The husband of *Sire hain* (2.5.76–79) is similarly laughable and degraded, responding in kind to his wife's scolding. "Dieus! fet Hains, com tu me tiens cort! / A paines os je dire mot! / Grant honte ai quant mon voisin m'ot / Que tu me maines si viument!" (Says Master Ham, "God help me, you're / so touchy, I can't say a word! / I'd hate to think our neighbor heard / you treat me so contemptibly!") See Dubin, 78–91.

30. My citation here is from Text A of the "Textes Diplomatiques" in NRCF, 208.

31. One might say that, as the king's ward, Meed approximates the position of a daughter. As I elaborate in greater detail in my discussion of Chaucer's *Reeve's Tale* in Chapter 2, father-daughter relationships are not the primary territory of obscene comedy. Daughters do appear occasionally, as in *La damoiselle qui ne pooit öir parler de foutre* (4.26), but they are not common in a discourse that is primarily focused on husband-wife relations. Moreover, even when daughters do appear in the fabliau, they are not characterized as individuals who thwart and undermine their fathers in the way that an obscene comedy wife thwarts her husband.

32. The tale exists in two fourteenth-century manuscripts. See Crawford, "Secular Latin Comedies," 65. Boccaccio knew of the tale and narrated it in *Decameron* 7.9.

33. Lidia" in Cohen, ed., "*Comédie*" *latine*, 229, lines 81–32, trans. *Lidia*, in Elliott, *Seven Medieval Latin Comedies*, xlvi, lines 81–83.

34. Lyons, "*Avoir* and *Savoir*." Cited in Gaunt, *Gender and Genre*, 235.

35. Trigg, "Traffic in Medieval Women," 25.

36. Fowler, "Civil Death," 779. Fowler makes her point in the service of her notion that Meed represents agency without intent, an argument with which I am not wholly in agreement, given Meed's plentiful display of intent during her self-defense.

37. A similar speech also exists in an eleventh-century poem that includes a speech by Queen Pecunia describing, among other things, her corruption of virgins. Cited in Yunck, *Lineage of Lady Meed*, 78.

38. Galloway, *Penn Commentary*, 315. The relevant passage in the *Nichomachean Ethics* is 4.1, on "Liberality." See Bartlett and Collins, *Nichomachean Ethics*, 67–72.

39. Galloway, *Penn Commentary*, 372, notes that that the reciprocal granting of gifts and favors is a common practice in Langland's time, as was the practice of using arbitration to settle complains about property outside official courtrooms and legal procedures.

40. Trigg, "Traffic in Medieval Women," 25.

41. Galloway, *Penn Commentary*, 370.

42. Robertson, "Measurement,"188.

43. Baker and Morrison argue that Langland lacks Chaucer's interest in gender and warn against burdening his text "with more claims for gender than it can reasonably support" ("*The Luxury of Gender*," 43, 65).

44. Cooper, "Gender and Personification," 44. This observation is also made in Robertson, "Measurement," 168.

45. Middleton, "Narration," 95, 100.

46. Baldwin, *Guidebook*, 140; Boitani, *English Medieval Narrative*, 93; Simpson, *Introduction to the B-Text*, 108–10; Steiner, *Reading* Piers Plowman, 98, 124–25.

47. For a description of the procedures of university debate, see Novikoff, *Medieval Culture of Disputation*, ch. 5.

48. Middleton, "Narration," 98.

49. Simpson, *Introduction to the B-Text*, 91; Steiner, *Reading* Piers Plowman, 97.

50. Middleton, "Narration," 92–94.

51. Cooper, "Gender and Personification," 32, and Raskolnikov, "Promising the Female," 81.

52. Obscene comedy narratives featuring shrewish wives that predate Langland include fabliaux like *Les quatre souhais saint Martin* (4.31), *La coille noire* (5.46), *Sire hain et dame anieuse* (2.5), and *La dame escoillee* (8.83). Marie de France's *Fables* also feature two tales of quarrelsome and contrary women; see 94 and 95. A number of exempla also feature shrewish wives. See Tubach, *Index Exemplorum*, 3557 (about a wife who nags her husband until he buys her a gown), 4353 (about a man who pits another shrew against his quarrelsome wife), 4354 (about a man who tames a shrew by killing his dog, cat, and horse before her eyes when they fail to obey him), 5284 (about a wife who persists in calling her husband evil, even when she is drowning), 5285 (about a wife so contrary that, when she falls into a river, her husband is convinced she will float upstream).

53. Trans. Dubin, "Four Wishes," lines 32–34; 38–41.

54. See, for instance, Tavormina, *Kindly Similitude*, 162; Robertson, "Measurement," 187.

55. Zeeman, *Discourse of Desire*, 109–56; Simpson, *Introduction to the B-Text*, ch. 3; Steiner, *Reading* Piers Plowman, ch. 4.

56. *Latin Vulgate*, trans. Douay Rheims Bible. All subsequent citations are taken from these sources and will be cited parenthetically in the text.

57. Zeeman, *Discourse of Desire*, 120.

58. For a study of the word and its uses in English political culture, see Watts, "Public or Plebs."

59. Scanlon, "King, Commons," 212, 204.

60. Johnson, *Reading Piers Plowman and the Pilgrim's Progress*, 99–101.

61. Similarly, the wife of *La coille noir* (5.46), elicits a certain audience sympathy when she complains of the dirt collected on the testicles of her peasant husband, and the audience of *Sir hain et dame anieuse* (2.5) is invited to laugh along with the wife's outrageous resistance to her husband's authority, a resistance that extends to quite literally fighting him for the pants of the household.

62. Simpson, *Introduction to the B-Text*, 95; Zeeman, *Discourse of Desire*, 70–74.

63. See Bernard of Clairvaux, "Ad Clericos de Conversione," 83; English translation Evans, *Bernard of Clairvaux*, 13–14.

64. *Sawles Warde*, in *Medieval English Prose for Women*, 87.

65. Johnson, *Reading* Piers Plowman *and the* Pilgrim's Progress, 99.

66. Jacobus de Voragine, "Sancto Gregorio."

67. For example, Adams, "Piers' Pardon"; Aers, *Salvation and Sin*; Pearsall, "The Idea of Universal Salvation"; Watson, "Visions of Inclusion."

68. Aers, *Salvation and Sin*, for instance, focuses on Langland's engagement with Augustinian versus semi-Pelagian notions of redemption.

69. The phrase appears in Deut. 32:35 and Rom. 12:19.

70. Watson, "Visions of Inclusion," 158.

71. In the Latin Vulgate, Paul speaks in the third person of "a man" who is taken to heaven. The verb in the Vulgate is thus the third-person "audivit," rather than the first-person "audivi" that Langland cites. See 2 Corinthians 12:4.

72. Zeeman, *Discourse of Desire*, 23; Simpson, *Introduction to the B-Text*, 128.

73. Bradwardine, *De Causa Dei*. For a discussion of these debates, see Baldwin, *Guidebook*, 140–41, and Simpson, *Introduction to the B-Text*, 116–17. Anxieties regarding the justice of the fate of "virtuous" pagans like Aristotle, Plato, and Virgil—who must be in hell, according to the Church's doctrine of salvation through baptism and reception of the sacraments—is witnessed in ongoing debates about their fate from the first through the fourteenth centuries. For a further discussion of these debates, see Vitto, *The Virtuous Pagan*, introduction and chap. 1.

74. Somerset, *Clerical Discourse*, 39. For the identification of Scripture with the Bible or biblical teaching and Ymaginatif with the power to think through images, see Simpson, *Introduction to the B-Text*, 107, 91. Zeeman, *Discourse of Desire*, argues for a more capacious definition of these terms, positing that Scripture may refer to many texts of revelation, both biblical and nonbiblical (146) and that Ymaginatif personifies the via imaginativa, one of the partly rational inner senses of the soul, associated with dreams and images (246). However, her reading is still focused on the meanings produced by allegory in the vision.

75. For an excellent discussion of Ymaginatif's contradictions and his dubious claim as an authoritative voice on grace, see Somerset, *Clerical Discourse*, 39–49.

76. Bergson, *Laughter*, 8–9.

77. Pearsall, "Universal Salvation," 264.

78. The use of force in overcoming the unruly woman is a common trope of obscene comedy. In *La dame escoille* (8.83), a son-in-law literally "castrates" his shrewish mother-in-law by cutting open her buttock and "pulling out" her testicles (really the testicles of a bull he has commandeered for the purpose). Sometimes even force cannot work, as gruesomely narrated in Marie's fable of the quarrelsome wife who continues to argue with her husband, even after he cuts out her tongue. See Marie de France, *Fables*, 94.

79. Aers (*Chaucer, Langland*, 61) writes of the conclusion of Passus XX that "as we follow Conscience out of holy church we are participating in an exit from the visible church and a flight from its traditional claims to be the sole mediator of the means of grace."

80. Tavormina, *Kindly Similitude*, 209.

81. Ibid., 210.

82. Calabrese, "Being a Man in *Piers Plowman*," 166–68 and 170.

83. Paxson, "Queering *Piers Plowman*," 22.

84. Translation mine.

85. These values are emphasized persistently over the course of the poem. One of the more explicit declarations occurs in Passus V, when Piers describes the seven sisters that serve truth as abstinence, humility, charity, chastity, patience, peace, and largess (B.5.618–23).

86. Tavormina, *Kindly Similitude*, 93.

87. Raskolnikov, "Promising the Female," 102.

88. Robertson, "Measurement," 187.

89. "Reuthe" in Middle English is used primarily to denote "pity." It also has a secondary meaning signifying remorse or regret, which might suggest that Will's wife is simply annoyed at his sufferings. I would argue that it is perfectly consistent with Langland's approach to this marriage that both meanings apply. See *Middle English Dictionary*, s.v. "reuthe."

90. Nor can we regard Will's memories of their sexual relations as an example of sinful sexual behavior, given Langland's fulsome approval of licit married sexuality in Wit's speech and elsewhere. See Tavormina, *Kindly Similitude*, 99 and 178, for a discussion of Langland's positive attitude to licit marital sexuality.

91. Davis (*Writing Masculinity*, 35) remarks that Langland's citations reveal his often unspoken interest in marriage to be an enduring preoccupation. See also Cooper, "Gender and Personification," 44, and Tavormina, *Kindly Similitude*, x.

92. Tavormina, *Kindly Similitude*, 219.

93. Fowler, "Civil Death," 760.

94. Ibid., 767.

95. Bullough, "On Being Male," 43.

CHAPTER 2. CHAUCER'S POETICS OF THE OBSCENE: CLASSICAL
NARRATIVE AND FABLIAU POLITICS IN FRAGMENT ONE
OF THE CANTERBURY TALES AND THE LEGEND OF GOOD WOMEN

1. See note 47 below.

2. Exceptions to the general distaste for the *Reeve's Tale* include Crocker, "Affective Politics";
Frank, "*Reeve's Tale* and the Comedy of Limitation"; Olsen, "*Reeve's Tale* as Fabliau."

3. Kolve, *Chaucer and the Imagery of Narrative*, 255; Charles Muscatine describes the *Reeve's Tale*
as exhibiting "a particularly bilious view of life." *Chaucer and the French Tradition*, 204.

4. Patterson, *Chaucer and the Subject of History*, 276. These views continue to be echoed in very
recent scholarship, like that of Allman, who concludes that "The *Reeve's Prologue* and *Tale* ... stand as
one of the *Canterbury Tales*' most sustained examinations of failed sociality and unsatisfied desire at
both dramatic and narrative levels." Allman, "Sociolinguistics, Literature, and the *Reeve's Tale*," 403.

5. Lorde, "Master's Tools," 110.

6. Patterson, *Chaucer and the Subject of History*, 169.

7. For other feminist analyses on the similarities between the *Knight's Tale* and the *Miller's Tale*,
see Karma Lochrie, "Women's 'Pryvetees'"; Elaine Hansen, *Chaucer and the Fictions of Gender*, 208–44.

8. For a discussion of the medieval family and its moderation of the *patria potestas* doctrine on
the basis of Pauline injunctions to regard the family as a moral unit, see Herlihy, "Family and Religious
Ideologies in Medieval Europe," 159.

9. Wallace notes how Chaucer's own fears about becoming a victim of tyrannical violence are
reflected in his interest in the rhetorical powers of wives to allay that violence. Wallace, *Chaucerian
Polity*, 214.

10. Hansen, *Chaucer and the Fictions of Gender*, 240–42.

11. Beidler, "The Reeve's Tale," 23.

12 The Flemish tale, *Een bispel van .ij. clerken*, is a fourteenth-century derivative of the French
Gombert. The two German versions are *The Students' Adventure* [*Das Studentenabenteuer*] and *Way-
wardwight and Lustymite* [*Irregang und Girregar*]. For a discussion and list of the analogues, see Beidler,
"The *Reeve's Tale*"; Benson and Andersson, *Literary Context of Chaucer's Fabliaux*, 79–87.

13. Dewar, "Introduction," *Statius' Thebaid IX*, xxxvii–xlv. For an account of Statius' popularity
in medieval schools, see Orme, *English Schools*, 102.

14. Dominik, *The Mythic Voice of Statius*, xiv.

15. Latin: Statius, *Thebaid* in *Statius: with an English Translation by J. H. Mozley*, Book 1, Lines
150–56; translation: *Thebaid*, trans. A. D. Melville.

16. Ibid., Book 1, Lines 125–30.

17. Karras, *From Boys to Men*, 21. See also Kaeuper, *War, Justice, and Public Order*, 192.

18. For further discussion of the Chaucer's and Boccaccio's treatment of the *Thebaid*, see Anderson, *Before the Knight's Tale*; Hanning, "Noble Designs and Chaos"; Wetherbee, "Romance and Epic";
Patterson, *Chaucer and Subject of History*, ch. 3.

19. Anderson, *Before the Knight's Tale*, 50.

20. Wetherbee, "Romance and Epic," 306.

21. Ibid, 305; Patterson, *Chaucer and the Subject of History*, 168.

22. This includes not only Ariadne, whom Theseus was seen to have seduced and abandoned, but also his youthful rape of Perigune, daughter of Siris and Helen and his role as a helper in Pirithous' plan to rape Persephone. For a discussion of Theseus' checkered past, see Hagedorne, *Abandoned Women*, 75–90; Mills, *Athenian Empire*, 6–25.

23. Wetherbee, 312–13, and Hagedorn, 78.

24. Krueger, *Women Readers*, 40.

25. The *Thebaid* is exceptional among classical epics for its willingness to present a female perspective on war, in Hypsipyle's narrative in Book 5 and the account of the Argive women in Book 12. For further discussion of the *Thebaid*'s perspective on women and its influence on Chaucer, see Sanok, "Criseyde, Cassandre, and the *Thebaid*."

26. Hagedorn, *Abandoned Women*, 101.

27. The notion that the *Miller's Tale* presents an unqualified opposition to the *Knight's Tale* has a long critical history. Huppé, for instance, asserts that the *Miller's Tale* contrasts the *Knight's Tale* by showing up its world of courtly pretense with a story of realistic and believable characters, see Huppé, *A Reading of the Canterbury Tales*, 49–90. Even more politicized readings of the first fragment continue to credit the *Miller's Tale* with a strong opposition to the Knight. Paul Strohm, for instance, argues that the *Miller's Tale* rebuts the *Knight's Tale* with "a celebration of the mercantile or commercial attitude of calculation in one's own interest." Strohm, *Social Chaucer*, 133–41. Similarly, Lee Patterson argues that the *Miller's Tale*'s peasant resistance of courtly convention enables Chaucer to liberate himself from the circumscriptions of aristocratic ideology that defined the first half of his career. Patterson, *Chaucer and the Subject of History*, 40.

28. Glenn Burger notes how the *Miller's Tale* depicts non-normative masculine behavior and in doing so, loosens the class and gender hierarchies of the *Knight's Tale*. However, Burger also concludes that the tale "ends with a vision of chastened masculinity and restored social control that . . . reproduces the moralitas of the *Knight's Tale*." Burger, *Chaucer's Queer Nation*, 37, 23.

29. Nykrog, *Fabliaux*.

30. Rychner investigated Nykrog's claims with a study of the fabliau manuscript tradition. His study emphasized the adaptability of the fabliau to a wide variety of social contexts and argued that the works, particularly in later incarnations, could not be strictly identified with any one class. Rychner, *Contribution à l'étude des fabliaux*.

31. In a debate that is typical of the scholarly difficulty in classifying the fabliau as a genre, early scholarship identified only eight Anglo-Norman fabliaux. However, Pearcy and Short argue that this number is based on overly narrow classifications and, classifying a number of Marie de France's fables as fabliaux, they have argued that there are 18 fabliaux in Anglo-Norman. Pearcy and Short, *Eighteen Anglo-Norman Fabliaux*, 1–5.

32. van den Boogaard, "Le Fabliau Anglo-Normand," 66–77, argues for the aristocratic provenance of the fabliau in England based not only on the language of the texts but also in the preponderance of aristocratic characters in the Anglo-Norman fabliaux. For a discussion of the now defunct theory regarding an oral tradition of English fabliaux, see the Introduction to this study, n36.

33. Indeed, the fabliau interest in romance is, for Nykrog, conclusive evidence of its aristocratic character, since only an audience closely familiar with romance would have understood the fabliau's subtle and detailed references. Nyrog, *Fabliaux*, 74–86.

34. Foucault, "History of Systems of Thought," 199.

35. Burns, *Bodytalk*, 28; Gaunt, *Gender and Genre*, 268.

36. Translation: Benson and Andersson, *Literary Context of Chaucer's Fabliaux*, 95.

37. Lochrie, "Women's 'Pryvetees,'" 303; Hansen, *Chaucer and the Fictions of Gender*, 209.

38. Gaunt, *Gender and Genre*, 239.

39. Foucault, *History of Sexuality*, 100–101.

40. The B-version of *Le meunier et les deus clers* (7.80) is the only one in which the clerks are aware of the miller's theft of their grain before having intercourse with the wife and daughter (indeed, *Le meunier* is the only version of the tale even to include the motif of the thieving miller). However, here the knowledge functions only as an additional justification for the clerks' sex with the wife and daughter, rather than its prime motivator, as it is in the *Reeve's Tale*. The clerk in *Le meunier*, B, has already stolen the ring from the andiron in his plot to seduce the daughter when he notices the stolen grain that the miller has hidden.

41. Tolkien, "Chaucer as Philologist," asserts that the clerks' northern accents would have made them sound oafish to a metropolitan audience.

42. Bourdieu, *Masculine Domination*, 52.   •

43. Corinne Saunders describes the *Knight's Tale*'s repeated evocations of rape and abduction, from the fact that Theseus' wife, Hypolita has been won in battle, to the distribution of Emelyne as a prize against her will. Saunders, *Rape and Ravishment*, 287–90.

44. Most fabliaux do not depict the kind of gruesome violence against women that is called up by Absolon's use of the hot kolter on Alison. Only one fabliau, *La dame escoillee* (8.83), engages in this kind of violence.

45. Kolve, *Imagery of Narrative*, 251, describes the rapes as acts which "loosen the women's bridles." Woods, "Logic of Deprivation," 155–6, describes Malyne as obtaining a "long deferred emotional well being" from her sex with the clerk. Recent studies that have discussed the impact of rape on the scene include: Kohanski, "In Search of Malyne"; Barnett, "Chaucer's Deflection of Rape"; Breuer, "Being Intolerant." Others acknowledge the importance of the scene in the *Reeve's Tale* and identify it as rape, but do not provide an extended analysis of it or of Malyne. See Cannon, "Chaucer and Rape," 83–84; Saunders, *Rape and Ravishment*, 298–300.

46. Cannon, "Chaucer and Rape," 84, writes that the episodes involving Malyne and her mother are *not* rapes according to the 'cherles termes' of the fabliau.

47. *Cele qui fu foutue et desfoutue* (4.30). The Anglo-Norman fabliau *La gageure* (10.114) also revolves around a trick. In this case, a serving girl has promised a squire her body if he will kiss her anus. When she offers him her backside for the kiss, however, he has intercourse with her instead. The two are later married. Similarly, in the Old French fabliau *La damoisele qui songoit* (4.25) a young man assails a maiden while she is asleep (as Aleyn does to Malyne in the *Reeve's Tale*). In *La damoisele*, rape is a non-traumatic occurrence that quickly becomes a comic game of one-upmanship. The young woman has a pleasant sexual dream as the young man has intercourse with her four times. When she awakens, she excoriates him for taking her virginity but also demands more of the same, a task the exhausted rapist finds difficult to repeat.

48. Brundage, "Rape and Seduction," 143.

49. Woods, "Rape and Pedagogical Rhetoric."

50. Statius, *Achilleid*, 360–1.

51. Ovid, *Ars Amatoria*, Book 1, lines 697–700.

52. Saunders, *Rape and Ravishment*, 187.

53. For a discussion of rape in the pastourelle, see Gravdal, *Ravishing Maidens*, 166. The rape of Hersent in the *Roman de Renart* is another example, but this takes place only in the distancing medium of the beast fable.

54. Wolfthal, *Images of Rape*, 181.

55. Brundage, "Rape and Marriage," 67.

56. Quoted in Brundage, *Law, Sex, and Christian Society*, 396.

57. Wolfthal, *Images of Rape*, 36.

58. Crane notes that Theseus's capitulation to the women expands and dignifies his masculinity. Crane, *Gender and Romance*, 16–26. Similarly, Ingham notes that the excessively emotional weeping of the tale's female characters is essential to the Knight's construction of Theseus as a wise and moderate ruler. Ingham, "Homosociality and Creative Masculinity," 33–35.

59. Crocker, "Affective Politics," 232.

60. In the *Morte Arthur*: "I sall *auntre* me anes hys egle to touche," (360); and in John Lydgate, *Troy Book*, "He . . . was . . . On with þe first for to *auntre* his lyf" (2.230). Cited in *Middle English Dictionary*, Part B1, 529.

61. Ovid, *Ars Amatoria*, Book 1, lines 691–93.

62. Woods, "Rape and Pedagogical Rhetoric," 60.

63. See note 25 above.

64. Malyne's obscurity has also been noted by Kohanski, "In Search of Malyne."

65. This is according to my own survey of the extant fabliaux listed in the NRCF.

66. All three fabliau analogues feature a jealous father who locks his daughter in a corn bin every night to ensure her virginity. This, however, is not linked to any social ambitions on the father's part.

67. The Ariadne also refers to yet another betraying daughter when Chaucer the narrator remarks on Scylla at the legend's outset.

68. Gratian. *Decretum*, Causa. 30, quaestio 9.2, canon 1.

69. Brundage *Law, Sex, and Christian Society*, 238, 243, 275, 437–8, 500. See also Walker, "Punishing Convicted Ravishers"; Walker, "Common Law Juries," 706; Helmholz, *Marriage Litigation*, 90; Noonan, Jr, "Marriage in the Middle Ages."

70. According to Butler, force in marriage accounts for 11 per cent of fourteenth century, and 13 per cent of fifteenth century cases of marriage litigation heard by the Archbishop of York's consistory court. Butler, "'I Will Never Consent to be Wedded," 251. In the fifteenth century, when the teenaged Margery Paston secretly wed the bailiff, her parents put her under house arrest on one of the family estates for two years and forbade her to communicate with her husband. However, the bishop of Norwich ordered that she be reunited with her husband after determining that her marriage was valid. Haskell, "The Paston Women."

71. Helmholz, *Marriage Litigation*, 90–94.

72. Walker, "Punishing Convicted Ravishers," 237. Also see Post, "Ravishment of Women," 153, and Post, "Sir Thomas West," 24.

73. Bellamy, *Criminal Trial*, 167; and Post, "Ravishment of Women," 158. The earlier Westminster I (1275) also aided families by classifying both sexual assault and abduction according to the same term, thereby allowing families to prosecute abduction, which had formerly not been classified as an offense. See Bellamy, *Criminal Trial*, 167.

74. *Statutes of the Realm*, 2:27. Also cited in Kelly, "Statutes of Rapes," 371.

75. Bellamy, *Criminal Trial*, 167; and Post, "Sir Thomas West," 27–30.

76. "Disparagen," means "to degrade (sb.) socially (i.e., for marrying below rank or without proper ceremony)." *Middle English Dictionary Online*, s.v. "disparagen." Chaucer uses the term again in the *Wife of Bath's Tale*, when the young knight laments upon his marriage to the poor old hag, "Allas, that any of my nacioun / Sholde euere so foule disparaged be!" (1069).

77. Patterson, *Chaucer and the Subject of History*, 240. Lowes believes that the Ariadne in the *Legend* must have been written before the *Knight's Tale*, but that is only because he cannot imagine Chaucer authoring the obscene content of Ariadne before his beautifully poetic treatment of Emelye in

the *Knight's Tale*. Patterson dismisses this view, noting only that the *Legend*'s Ariadne must have been written some time after *Troilus and Criseyde* was finished and circulating in court circles. The only additional evidence for dating is the omission, in the second version of the *Legend*'s Prologue, to Queen Anne and her palace at Sheen, an indication that Chaucer was still working on this portion of the *Legend* after the Queen's death in 1394. See Lowes, "Prologue to the *Legend of Good Women*," 808; Patterson, *Chaucer and the Subject of History*, 236 n. 17.

78. For a full list of parallels between the Ariadne, the *Teseida*, and the *Knight's Tale*, see Percival, *Chaucer's Legendary Good Women*, 185–88; Patterson, *Chaucer and the Subject of History*, 238–240; Lowes, "Prologue to the *Legend of Good Women*," 804–10.

79. Boccaccio, *Teseida*, Book 3, Stanza 11

80. Percival, *Chaucer's Legendary Good Women*, 186.

81. Ibid, 186.

82. Ibid, 188; see also Patterson, *Chaucer and the Subject of History*, 238–39.

83. Patterson, *Chaucer and the Subject of History*, 240, also notes that this biting attitude toward aristocratic pretentions is most explicit in the *Legend of Ariadne*.

84. Percival, *Chaucer's Legendary Good Women*, 178, 181.

85. Patterson, *Chaucer and the Subject of History*, 241.

86. Delany, "Logic of Obscenity," 196.

87. Ibid, 196–97.

88. Percival, *Chaucer's Legendary Good Women*, 183.

89. Ibid, 183.

90. Mills, *Michel Foucault*, 74.

91. The notion of a particular character speaking in a culturally predetermined script that fails to express that character's true wishes and feelings is discussed by Crane, *Gender and Romance*, in the context of Dorigen's speech in the *Franklin's Tale*. Crane argues that Dorigen's desire to refuse Aurelius "is at odds with courtly discourses that do not admit a language of refusal" (65).

CHAPTER 3. THE HENPECKED SUBJECT: MISOGYNY, POETRY, AND MASCULINE COMMUNITY IN THE WRITING OF JOHN LYDGATE

1. "Ballade on an Ale Seller" is a case in point. While it appears to call up an obscene comedy woman, it is actually a work of serious misogyny focused on a favorite Lydgatean theme, women's fickleness. "Prohemy of a Mariage Betwixt an Olde Man and a Yonge Wife" is a livelier piece, but its authorship has, quite rightly, been disputed. MacCracken, "The Lydgate Canon," xlviii, believes the rhymes are against authorship by Lydgate. For the poems, see Lydgate, *Minor Poems*, Part II, 429–32 and 27–46. Unless otherwise noted, all citations from Lydgate's drama and short poems are taken from Halliwell, ed., *Minor Poems of Dan John Lydgate*, and will be cited hereafter by line numbers in parentheses in the text.

2. Renoir, "On the Date," 32; Pearsall, *John Lydgate*, 188; Schirmer, *Culture of the XVth Century*, 106.

3. Recent analyses include Epstein, "Lydgate's Mummings"; Nolan, *Making of Public Culture*, 120–83; Sponsler, *Queen's Dumbshows*, 173–80.

4. The single exception to this rule is *Bycorne and Chychevache*, which appears to have been a commissioned piece made "at the request of a werthy citeseyn [worthy citizen] of London." See Lydgate, *Mummings and Entertainments*.

5. Even in his own time, Lydgate was recognized as a woman hater. The author of "A Reproof to Lydgate," which scolds the poet for his negative attitude toward women, seems assured of his audience's

convictions regarding Lydgate's misogyny. See Hammond, *English Verse*, 200–201. Similarly, the London copyist John Shirley wryly annotates Lydgate's *A Lover's New Year Gift* as an "Amerous balade by Lydgate þat haþe loste his thanke of wymmen." See Lydgate, *The Minor Poems*, Part II, 424.

6. For a discussion of the important role played by misogyny in the establishment of clerical superiority, see Elliott, *Spiritual Marriage*, 132–52.

7. For discussions of the role of the family-state analogy in early modern society, see Schochet, *Patriarchalism in Political Thought*; Hill, *Society and Puritanism*; Amussen, *An Ordered Society*; Shaffer, "Missing Wives."

8. For a discussion of the role and importance of the "state as body" metaphor in medieval society, see Coleman, *History of Political Thought*, 23, 42; Franklin, "Sovereignty and the Mixed Constitution," 326; Burke, "Tacitism, Scepticism, and Reason of State," 480; Malcolm, "Hobbes and Spinoza," 539–42; and Kantorowicz, *The King's Two Bodies*.

9. Scanlon, "King, Commons," 197–98.

10. Although there is no incontrovertible evidence for the date of the *Mumming at Hertford*, itineraries and contemporary account books indicate that Henry VI was most likely at Hertford for Christmas of 1427. For evidence supporting a 1427 date, see Green, "Three Fifteenth-Century Notes," 15–16; Pearsall, *Bio-Bibliography*, 28; and Nolan, *Making of Public Culture*, 156–57.

11. See note 3 above.

12. Nolan, *Public Culture*, 24, sees the mumming as announcing Lydgate's rejection of Chaucerian comedy; Epstein, "Resistance to Drama," 339 and 345, sees it as resisting drama and its association with lower-order grievances against elites; Sponsler, *Queen's Dumbshows*, 180, reads it as a warning to Catherine of Valois not to overstep her bounds.

13. Nolan, *Public Culture*, 167, explicitly rejects the notion that the performance is about gender, regarding its central concern to be genre. Epstein, "Resistance to Drama," does not mention gender. Sponsler, *Queen's Dumbshows*, is interested in the role of gender in Hertford, but only insofar as it pertains to Catherine of Valois.

14. Nolan, *Public Culture*, 154–56.

15. Langland, too, describes fabliau-like tales using the term "harlotrye." Dame Study remarks on the goods that "harlotes...And japeris and jogelours and jangleris of gestes" win from the rich, who eagerly consume their "vile harlotrye" while ignoring those who speak of Christine doctrine (B.X.30–31, 45). Other examples of Langlandian usage of the term include include Reason's refusal to have ruth "Til lords and ladies loven alle truthe / And haten alle harlotrie, to heren it or to mouthen it" (B.4.114–15) and Piers's advice to the knight to "Hold noght with none harlots ne here noght hir tales, / And namely at the mete swiche men eschuwe / For it ben the develes disours, I do the to understonde" (B.6.52–54).

16. See, for instance, Symkyn of the *Reeve's Tale* or January of the *Merchant's Tale*. Even the cuckolded John of the *Miller's Tale* begins from a dictatorial position, holding his young wife Allison "narwe in cage" (3224).

17. Examples of vigorous masculine self-defense in the fabliau include the husband of *Sire hain et dame anieuse* (2.5) who defeats his domineering wife after challenging her to a battle over the trousers of the household and the husband of *Le fevre de creil* (5.42) who catches his adulterous wife and beats her.

18. Furrow, *Ten Fifteenth-Century Comic Poems*, 53–64.

19. Estimates have dated this piece to the latter half of the fifteenth century, but this does not completely rule out an influence of this farce or something like it on Lydgate since, as I shall be discussing in more detail below, the farces are notoriously difficult to date.

20. *Farce des Drois de la Porte Bodès*, in Cohen, ed., *Recueil de farces*, 159–64. English translation appears in Enders, *Farce of the Fart*, 86–106.

21. In the entire *Mumming at Hertford*, there is only one phrase that might possibly construe adultery, when the presenter remarks in telling of Beatrice's abuse of Robin with a distaff that "With suche a metyerde she haþe shape him an hoode" (54). The phrase to "shape an hoode" can connote cuckoldry but can also simply mean to deceive. See *Middle English Dictionary*, s.v. "shapen (v.)." Given that the rest of the Beatrice-Robin narrative makes no mention of other men but is entirely concerned with Beatrice's slovenliness and drunkenness, the invocation of adultery here is vague at best.

22. Chaucer's *Miller's Tale, Reeve's Tale, Shipman's Tale*, and *Merchant's Tale* all feature female adultery.

23. See my discussion of the *Troy Book* and the *Fall of Princes* below.

24. Nolan, *Making of Public Culture*, 156.

25. As I discuss below, the *Mumming at Hertford* is suffused with legal language. Chaucer makes brief use of the trope when he has the Wife of Bath remark of her first three husbands, "I governed hem so wel, after my lawe, / That ech of hem ful blisful was" (219–20).

26. One fabliau, *La coille noire* (5.46), does feature a wife pleading in court for relief from a bad marriage. However, both the tale's content and conclusion illustrate the foolishness of such an appeal. In the end, the husband shames his wife into recognizing that submitting the matter to a court was wrong.

27. One of Chaucer's fabliau-esque narratives, the *Summoner's Tale*, does move out of the domestic space and into the court of the local lord. However, this tale does not concern household politics but rather the probity of friars.

28. Muir, "Farces, *Sotties*," 329. The earliest farce-like work, *Le garcon et l'aveugle*, dates from about 1280, and the term "farce" is used to designate a dramatic work as early as 1398, when a Parisian document forbids the playing of "jeux de personnages par maniere des farces." See Muir, "Farces, *Sotties*," 330.

29. Ibid., 330.

30. Pearsall, *Bio-Bibliography*, 26–27.

31. De Julleville, *Histoire du théâtre*, 2: 190. Also cited in Enders, *Farce of the Fart*, 12.

32. Pearsall, *John Lydgate*, 179–80.

33. Furrow, *Comic Poems*, 64. These attitudes are also rife in the fabliau. The husband of the fabliau *Berengier au lonc cul* (4.34), for instance, is a peasant who pretends to engage in knightly battles. When his noble wife discovers that he is a coward, she takes over the house, sleeping openly with her lover and treating him with contempt, leading the narrator to opine at the tale's conclusion that "A mol pastor chie los laine" (When the shepherd is weak, the wolf shits wool).

34. During the baseline period 1370–1399, in McIntosh's study, only 14 percent of the lesser courts under observation reported any types of wrongdoing, but, by the 1460s–70s, the figure had risen to 40 percent. In the 1520s–1530s, the proportion of courts addressing misbehavior climbed to 54 percent, before reaching a peak of 59 percent in the 1580s–1590s. See McIntosh, *Controlling Misbehavior*, 10.

35. Ibid., 73, reports that 71 to 86 percent of the courts that mentioned scolding during this period named women only.

36. McIntosh, "Finding a Language for Misconduct," 90–91.

37. Utley, *The Crooked Rib*, 64.

38. Watts, "The Pressure of the Public," 172. Similarly, Barron has marveled at "the quite sophisticated political awareness displayed by tailors and skinners and other artisans, about the way in which their urban community should be governed." See Barron, "Political Culture of Medieval London," 130.

39. Watts, "Pressure of the Public," 171.

40. Rollison, *Commonwealth of the People*, 257.

41. Gibson, *Theatre of Devotion*, 119.

42. Gottfried, *Bury St. Edmunds*, 6.

43. Watts describes how language reflects the ways lower-ranking men and women gradually get edged out of the political community, in spite of their improving legal status and prosperity: while the 1381 rebels' claim to be part of the "commune" was a claim to governance, as the fifteenth century progresses, "to be 'common' is less and less to be part of the public and more and more to be part of the plebs." See Watts, "Pressure of the Public," 179. The same point is also made in Hilton, *Bond Men Made Free*, 176–77, and Strohm, *Hochon's Arrow*, 34–45.

44. McSheffrey, "Jurors, Respectable Masculinity," 272.

45. Coleman, *History of Political Thought*, 39, writes that in medieval English society the words *libertas* or *franchise* mean "a power to act in affairs of the community and to exert influence on one's fellows, free from the interference of sovereign government. It is a privilege granted by some higher authority that acknowledges a capacity to engage in independent action, to exercise power and authority. In England, franchises developed to signify jurisdictional powers either of a rural aristocracy or of urban corporations." For a description of franchises and their role in urban communities, see Hilton, *English and French Towns*, 127.

46. Bickley, *Little Red Book of Bristol*, 2: 155. Similarly, John Shillingford describes the seizure of a city in the following way: "The sayde Cyte . . . was seysed yn to the Kyngis handys . . . the sayde libertees and franchises . . . shuld be expired and extynt." See Moore, *Letters and Papers of John Shillingford*, 126.

47. This is very much in line with an already extant Lancastrian tendency, witnessed in the persecution of Lollardy and other forms of heresy. Strohm, *England's Empty Throne*, 182.

48. Similarly, Sponsler notes that Lydgate's *Mumming for Mercers and Goldsmiths* resolves the problem of "alien" merchants in London by "turning unwelcome competitors into beneficent gift-givers and supporters of the mayor's authority." Sponsler, "Alien Nation," 229.

49. Ibid., 235.

50. *Bycorne and Chychevache* describes the presenter as a figure dressed "in poet-wyse." See Lydgate, "Bycorne and Chychevache," in Hammond, ed., *English Verse*, 115.

51. Lawton, "Dullness," 793.

52. Crawford, "King's Burden?" 37.

53. Levin, "Catherine of Valois," 95.

54. Green, "Three Fifteenth-Century Notes," 16.

55. See Sponsler, *Queen's Dumbshows*, 173–80.

56. Pearsall, *Bio-Bibliography*, 28.

57. Muir, "Farces, *Sotties*," 330.

58. Earenfight, *Queenship*, 95–115.

59. Ibid., 11. Among other things, queens could use the fees generated from formal requests for intercession to fund poor relief and other charitable acts, thereby enlarging their economic power.

60. Jean de Froissart, *Oeuvres*, 215. Translated by Strohm, in *Hochon's Arrow*, 100.

61. Cited in Strohm, *Hochon's Arrow*, 106.

62. Strohm, *Empty Throne*, 257n37.

63. Jacob, *Fifteenth Century*, 226; Strickland, *Lives of the Queens*, 3:148. Also cited in Sponsler, *Queen's Dumbshows*, 256n44.

64. See notes 7 and 8 above.

65. John of Salisbury, *Policratus*. Other works that use the image of the body politic include Marie de France, "Fable of a Man," 25; Christine de Pisan, *Book of the Body Politic*; Guillaume de Deguileville, *Le Pèlerinage de l'âme*.

66. Scanlon, *Narrative, Authority and Power*, 335.

67. Guido delle Colonne, *Historia Destructionis Troiae*, 17.

68. Ibid., 68.

69. Calling the ironic passages in *Troy Book* and *Fall of Princes* "among Lydgate's happier achievements," Pearsall remarks that the poet "found in the conventionalized patterns of the anti-feminist dialogue the opportunity for a degree of complexity and irony and 'suspension' in his account of human behavior which he could rarely manage elsewhere." See Pearsall, *John Lydgate*, 237–38.

70. Meyer-Lee, *Poets and Power*, 61–62.

71. Chance, "Christine de Pizan," 246.

72. The debate was well known and admired enough that, when the manuscript that Christine had given to Isabeau was purchased by John, Duke of Bedford, when he was regent in France during Henry VI's minority, he brought it back to England for his wife, Jacqueeta of Luxembourg. See Summit, *Lost Property*, 69.

73. Ibid., 68 and 70.

74. Meyer-Lee, *Poets and Power*, 63.

75. Ibid., 64.

76. Elliott, *Spiritual Marriage*, 132–94.

77. Meyer-Lee, *Poets and Power*, 65–66.

78. While Lydgate may mention Guido at other junctures, these citations are limited to a simple reference to Guido as source, rather than an active critique or analysis.

79. Summit, *Lost Property*, 68.

80. Rich, "When We Dead Awaken," discusses the strong aversion to anger in women in Western culture and its effects on nineteenth- and twentieth-century women writers.

81. Christine de Pisan, *Epistre au dieu d'amours*, 10–14, and *Livre de la Cité des Dames*.

82. Lydgate, *Fall of Princes*. All citations from the *Fall of Princes* are taken from this text and are cited, parenthetically, by line numbers, in the text.

83. The most outstanding example of this is Christine's eulogy for Joan of Arc in her last known work. See Christine, *Ditié de Jeanne d'Arc*.

84. Valente, "Joan of Navarre," 288–89.

85. Levin, "Catherine of Valois," 95.

86. Patterson, "Making Identities," 89.

87. The Middle English romance *Sir Orfeo* emphasizes Orpheus's great love for Eurydice when it depicts him falling into grief and living like a wild man after her disappearance and risking his life to save her.

88. Scanlon, *Narrative, Authority, and Power*, 339.

89. Ibid., 337.

90. David Lawton describes Lydgate as "always emphatic for peace," a stance that has also been noted by others. See Lawton, "Dullness," 779; Baswell, *Troy Book*, 222; C. David Benson, "Civic Lydgate," 147; Patterson, "Making Identities," 74; Straker, "Deference and Difference," 20.

91. Stone, *Family, Sex, and Marriage*, 153 and 7.

CHAPTER 4. "RYTH WIKKED": CHRISTIAN ETHICS AND THE UNRULY HOLY WOMAN IN THE *BOOK OF MARGERY KEMPE*

1. Over more than ten years of teaching the *Book of Margery Kempe* to graduate and undergraduate classes, I have found that students invariably find portions of the *Book* amusing. Lochrie, *Translations of the Flesh*, 137, notes a similar experience.

2. Kempe, *The Book of Margery Kempe*. All citations are taken from this edition and are hereafter cited parenthetically in the text by page number.

3. Allen, "Letter."

4. Riddy, "Text and Self," 444; Thornton, *English Pastoral*, 2; Goodman, *Margery Kempe and Her World*, 69. Staley, *Dissenting Fictions*, 164, also remarks on the *Book's* comic elements.

5. Goodman, *Margery Kempe and Her World*, 69; Thornton, *English Pastoral*, 2.

6. The works addressing Margery's relation to late medieval religious culture are numerous. A few examples include Ashley, "Historicizing Margery"; Barr, *Willing to Know God*; Beckwith, "Very Material Mysticism"; Beckwith, "Problems of Authority"; Gibson, *Theatre of Devotion*; Salih, *Versions of Virginity*.

7. Lochrie, *Translations of the Flesh*, ch. 4.

8. Ibid., 9.

9. See, for instance, Delany, "Sexual Economics"; Ellis, "Merchant's Wife's Tale"; Wilson, "Margery and Alison: Women on Top."

10. Margery may well have witnessed the York Corpus Christi cycle in 1413. The performance of a play in Lynn is recorded on Corpus Christi Day, 1385. In addition, there exists a note of "a play" before a great lady of the neighborhood in 1409–10 that suggests that the town did, at least occasionally, host dramas. See Allen and Meech, "Notes," 333.

11. Based on my own observation; see my discussion of St. Margaret's Church in the section, "Revision of Obscene Comedy Tropes of Female Sexuality."

12. McDonald, "A York Primer," 196.

13. Strohm, "Chaucer's Fifteenth-Century Audience," 23.

14. Benson, *Public Piers Plowman*, 115, notes that both *Piers Plowman* and the *Book of Margery Kempe* contain a marginal character on a passionate quest for religious salvation in an England where Christian devotion must compete with more worldly concerns.

15. Mitchell observes in a recent bibliographic study that "the facticity of the book is still implicitly or explicitly assumed" by the vast majority of critics. Mitchell, *Scholarship, Community, and Criticism*, 86.

16. For the lack of documents corroborating the *Book's* events, see "Appendix III. Extracts from Documents," in Meech, ed., *The Book of Margery Kempe*, ed. Meech, 358–75. Staley provides a list of events in the *Book* that could plausibly have shown up on official records and notes the total absence of evidence of any of the events the *Book* reports. Thus, for instance, the trial at Leicester is described as a public one, yet neither the *Records of the Burough of Leicester* nor *The Register of Bishop Philip Repingdon* mention any such event. Similarly, the account in the final pages of the *Book* of Margery's peregrination through London, preaching, which must have occurred in the summer of 1434, finds no corroboration in the *Register of Henry Chichele*, then archbishop of Canterbury, in spite of the fact that his register is extraordinarily rich in the details of daily life and that Chichele himself had a strong interest in maintaining Church orthodoxy, which would have led him to inquire into the activities of a woman who seemed to be engaging in public preaching. See Staley, *Dissenting Fictions*, 173, and Rees Jones, "Margery Kempe and the Bishops," 379.

17. Rees Jones, "Margery Kempe and the Bishops," 379n9.

18. Lawton, "Voice, Authority, and Blasphemy," 100–101.

19. Voaden, *God's Words*, 112–13.

20. Evans, "The *Book of Margery Kempe*."

21. For a discussion of the possibility that the author is a literate female, see Staley, Introduction, x–xi, and Staley, *Dissenting Fictions*, 78. For the theory that the *Book* is entirely fictional, see Rees Jones, "Margery Kempe and the Bishops." For the theory that the narrative of an original Margery was shaped by her scribe, see Hirsh, "Author and Scribe"; Watson, "The Making of the *Book of Margery Kempe*."

22. As Staley points out, one section of the manuscript already gives evidence of scribal contribution. The story of Margery preparing a hot cawdel for the virgin is bracketed and crossed out. Moreover, the marginal annotations in the manuscript—made by residents of the Carthusian monastery of Mountgrace—show a strong desire on the part of the manuscript's readers to organize the text "by casting its narratives in terms familiar to the monastic reader." Thus, when Margery is clothed in white, a hand in the margin writes "nota de vestura," and Margery's story of the priest, the bear, and the pear tree is labeled "narracion" to set it apart as a story separate from the *Book*'s main text. See Staley, *Dissenting Fictions*, 7, and Staley, "*The Book of Margery Kempe*: Introduction," 4–5.

23. Kerby-Fulton and Justice, "Langlandian Reading Circles," 70.

24. Ibid., 71.

25. See, for instance, Hirsh, "Author and Scribe," and Watson, "The Making of the *Book of Margery Kempe*."

26. French, "To Free Them from Binding."

27. Allen, "Prefatory Note," lxiv, describes Margery in these terms.

28. Ashley, "Historicizing Margery," 371, sees the *Book* as a text "with rhetorical strategies aimed at making Margery a saint." Salih, *Versions of Virginity*, 174, "does not believe that it does stretch credulity to suggest that the *Book* is aware of the possibility of canonization." Similarly, Barr, *Willing to Know God*, 212, says that "the primary goal of Kempe's text is the establishment of Margery's authenticity as a visionary in response to the many critics that she encounters."

29. Voaden, *God's Words*, 112.

30. De Vitry, *Vita Maria Oigniacensi*, 53.

31. For the association between brewing and female unruliness, see Bennett, "Misogyny, Popular Culture," 181.

32. De Vitry, *Vita Maria Oigniacensi*, ch. 11.

33. Voaden, *God's Words*, 128.

34. Voaden remarks that "at least three people are writing this book, and none of them is particularly good at it." Ibid., 113.

35. Matthew 19: 30, *Vulgate*. The statement is repeated in Matthew 20: 16, Mark 10: 31, and Luke 13: 30.

36. Shklar, "'Cobham's Daughter'," 282–84.

37. McIntosh, *Controlling Misbehavior*, 58.

38. Ibid., 10, 58, 157; Ingram, "'Scolding Women'," 53.

39. Shklar, "'Cobham's Daughter'," 288.

40. Tubach, *Index Exemplorum*, 4354.

41. Ibid., 5294 and 5291.

42. Translation mine.

43. All of the following assume that the trials are factually based: Aers, *Community, Gender*, ch. 2; Arnold, "Margery's Trials,"; Watson, "Making of the *Book of Margery Kempe*." Shklar acknowledges the possibility that Margery Kempe's trials could be "a fictive enterprise," but her otherwise very insightful analysis still assumes an equivalency between the rhetorical goals of Margery the character and those of the author. See Shklar, "'Cobham's Daughter'."

44. While the narrator elsewhere mentions other historically identifiable individuals, like the Carmelites Alan of Lynn and William Sowthfeld, and Margery's confessor, Robert Spryngold, these individuals are not high-ranking clerics in the manner of Lincoln, Worcester, York, and Arundel.

45. The eight accusations are the monks' threat that "you shall be burnt as a Lollard" in Chapter 13; the threat by the woman in the pilche outside Arundel's court that Margery ought to be "at Smith-

field" in Chapter 16; the mayor of Leicester's accusation of Lollardy in Chapter 46; the people who call Margery "a lollard and a heretic" in Chapter 52; the accusation by the Duke of Bedford's men that Margery is "the greatest Loller in the country" and the men who call her a Lollard in Hessle (both in Chapter 53); the accusation by the Duke of Bedford's men and the friar that she is "Cobham's daughter" in Chapter 54; and her arrest "as a Lollard" at the Humber in Chapter 55.

46. The single accusation of Lollardy that lies outside the trials or Arundel-Lincoln segment is the exception that proves the rule. The reference is found in Chapter 13, the next chapter but one before the meeting with the bishop of Lincoln. This is the episode at Canterbury, featuring the elderly monk who wishes Margery shut in a house of stone. After their argument, the monks accuse Margery of Lollardy and threaten her with burning (42). Interestingly, this chapter shares with the other two segments a mention of a high-ranking authority: the old monk, we are told, was once treasurer to the queen (41). The fact that two seemingly unrelated and rare elements in the *Book* (the reference to Lollardy and to high-ranking secular authority) occur together in this chapter, as they do in the Arundel-Lincoln and trials segments, strongly suggests a pointed rhetorical purpose in the juxtaposition of these two references and also raises the possibility that Chapter 13 may be, like the other two segments, an insertion.

47. Evans points out four more additional uses of the first person in the narrative voice, but these are not necessarily remarks in the voice of the character, Margery, and could, conceivably, be attributed to the voice of a narrator. The use of the first-person voice in the bishop episode is the only instance that I know of in the *Book* wherein the voice must be that of a character in the narrative (although not necessarily Margery herself) because it comments on action within the narrative itself. Evans, *"Book of Margery Kempe,"* 8.

48. Cole has also asked why there is so much Lollardy in the *Book*. Like many readers, however, Cole sees the *Book* as a product of its protagonist whose primary rhetorical goal is to establish her religious authority. Thus, Cole argues that Lollardy is being primarily invoked not as the basis of a critique but as what he calls "an affective form," that is, a discourse of shame that allows Kempe to clarify her own affective piety. Cole, *Literature and Heresy*, ch. 7.

49. Shklar, "'Cobham's Daughter,'" 278.

50. For a discussion about the convergence of heresy and treason in the second quarter of the fifteenth century, see Aston, "Lollardy and Sedition"; Forrest, *Detection of Heresy*, 150, 191, and 222; McNiven, *Heresy and Politics*, 224–25.

51. For a discussion of the chilling effect of the English Church's anti-heresy campaign on vernacular writing about religion, see Watson, "Censorship and Cultural Change."

52. *Examination of Master William Thorpe*, 114. For another discussion of the contrast between Arundel's personality in these two sources, see Staley, *Dissenting Fictions*, 147–49.

53. For the symbolic relation between white and virginity in the Middle Ages, see Erler, "White Clothes."

54. For a discussion of white's other associations, see Salih, *Versions of Virginity*, 217–24. For a discussion of white's association with radical forms of continental piety, see Wilson, "Communities of Dissent."

55. McNiven, *Heresy and Politics*, 86–87.

56. Leff, *Heresy in the Later Middle Ages*, 596; McNiven, *Heresy and Politics*, 87.

57. Aston, "Lollardy and Sedition," 32, 34.

58. Forrest, *Detection of Heresy*, 45.

59. Cited in ibid., 16.

60. Ibid., 213.

61. Ibid., 156.

62. McNiven, *Heresy and Politics*, 113, writes that, in spite of Arundel's interest in rooting out heresy, "the events of Henry IV's reign give very little support to the thesis that the Archbishop saw the regular burning of heretics as a vital element in his campaign." On the Continent, as well, Church officials were also aware of the importance of compassion in the Christian tradition, even if their actions were not always in accordance with it. For a discussion of this, see Leff, *Heresy in the Later Middle Ages*, 599.

63. Thomson, *Later Lollards*, 140.

64. *Dame Sirith*, 29–52.

65. Other tales of clever old women include *La vielle truande* (4.37) and *Auberee* (1.4). In *Auberee*, the old woman outwits a rigid, moralistic husband so thoroughly that, in spite of his discovery of his young wife's adultery, he ends the tale in complete faith as to her innocence and purity.

66. Chaucer's obscene comedy frequently accentuates this conflict: thus, the possessive John of the *Miller's Tale* is bested by Nicholas and Alison; Symkyn of the *Reeve's Tale* is defeated by his two guests; January of the *Merchant's Tale* is fooled by May; and the merchant of the *Shipman's Tale* is tricked by his wife.

67. Gaunt, *Gender and Genre*, 237.

68. Aston, "Lollardy and Sedition," 12; Shklar, "'Cobham's Daughter'," 284. For an extended discussion of the links between Lollardy and feminine preaching, see Lochrie, *Translations of the Flesh*, 107–13.

69. Margery's description of the woman's loud voice is a slight exaggeration of the original, which reads, "extollens vocem quaedam mulier de turba dixit illi" [a certain woman from the crowd, lifting up her voice] (Lk. 11: 27). Also somewhat altered is Christ's response, which corrects the woman slightly by saying "quinimmo beati, qui audiunt verbum Dei et custodiunt illud" (*rather* blessed are they who hear the word of God and keep it); my italics.

70. Lochrie, *Translations of the Flesh*, 111–12.

71. Obscene comedy may also have left its mark on hagiography. Winstead has noted how, by the fifteenth century, the fragile virgin martyrs of high medieval legend had become aggressive to the point of unruliness. Winstead, *Virgin Martyrs*, 64–111.

72. Tout, "Bowet, Henry (d. 1423)"; McNiven, *Heresy and Politics*, 70.

73. Staley refers to the Beverly episode as "a scene of female triumph as potentially riotous as any presented by the Miller or the Wife of Bath or the Merchant, all of whom stress the fundamental chicanery and intractability of the weaker sex." Staley, *Dissenting Fictions*, 105.

74. Scott, *Arts of Resistance*, 157.

75. Aston, *Lollards and Reformers*, 29; Leff, *Heresy in the Later Middle Ages*, 603–4.

76. *Middle English Dictionary*, s.v. "Charité."

77. McNamer, *Affective Meditation*, 212n43.

78. Staley, *Dissenting Fictions*, 161.

79. In the fabliau *La borgoise d'Orliens* (3.19), for instance, an adulterous wife defeats her husband by marshaling the household servants to her cause.

80. McNamer, *Affective Meditation*, 151–52.

81. This is also Moore's conclusion in his famous study of heresy: "heretics and Jews owed their persecution in the first place not to the hatred of the people, but to the decisions of princes and prelates. In neither case have we found grounds to justify a description of the persecutor merely as the agents of society at large." Moore, *Persecuting Society*, 123.

82. Three examples of the numerous fabliau that feature the trope of the tricky, adulterous wife and the do-right husband are *Les braies au cordelier* (3.17), in which a wife uses a clever stratagem to hide her dalliance with a local Franciscan; *Le cuvier* (5.44), in which a wife hides her lover from her husband under a washing tub; and *Le prestre crucefié* (4.27).

83. Based on my own observations.

84. *L'enfant qui fu remis au soleil* (5.48). This trope is also central to *Le fevre du Creil* (5.42), in which a blacksmith's wife attempts to hide her lust for her husband's apprentice by pretending to be affronted at a description of the apprentice's large genitals.

85. Ziolkowski, "Obscenities of Old Women," 81.

86. These are the plots of the English *Dame Sirith*, the fabliau *Auberee* (1.4), and the Latin elegiac comedy *Pamphilus de Amore*.

87. Bennett cites a Chester ordinance of 1540–41 that banned women between the ages of fourteen and forty from keeping an alehouse on the grounds that they incited "wantonny and braules frays and other inconvenyents," causing "grete slaunders and dishonest report of this citie." Bennett, "Misogyny, Popular Culture," 181.

88. Dorothea's greatest temptation, according to Marienwerder, is despair. He never figures her being tempted by sexual feeling. Marienwerder, *Life of Dorothea of Montau*, 93.

89. Karras, "Leccherous Songys," 234–40.

90. The passage is frequently excerpted in anthologies. See Greenblatt et al., *Norton Anthology of English Literature*, 385–86; Damrosch et al., *Longman Anthology of English Literature*, 536–37.

91. For a definition of companionate marriage, see Howell, "Properties of Marriage," 18; Stone, *Family, Sex, and Marriage*, 8.

92. Lipton, *Affections of the Mind*, 130–32.

93. Lipton also remarks that Margery's marriage with Christ combines the companionate ideals of her earthly marriage (143).

94. Indeed, this statement was seen as so outrageous by one the *Book*'s medieval annotators that he felt obliged to correct it. The original text of Christ's promise reads "for I schal sodeynly sle thine husbonde." A late fifteenth-century hand has written in the margins "the flesshely lust in" with a black cross daubed with red after it corresponding to a similar cross after "sle" so that Christ is slaying the fleshly lust in John rather than John himself, as the text originally states. For a description of the marginalia and its location, see Meech, "Notes," 21n2.

95. In a similar way, Carroll sees the *Arnolfini Portrait* using its depiction of marriage as a union governed by contract and consent to underscore the sociable and cooperative character of other economic and political relations, including the merchant's relation to his clients and notions of consensual government. Carroll, *Painting and Politics*, 3–27.

CHAPTER 5. WOMEN'S WORK, COMPANIONATE MARRIAGE, AND MASS DEATH IN THE BIBLICAL DRAMA

1. Determining the dates of the biblical drama is notoriously difficult. While the manuscript of the York plays dates from the second last quarter of the fifteenth century, the first mention of drama in the civic registers of York dates from 1376, at which point pageant wagons were already in use. The manuscript of the Towneley plays, once thought to date from the mid- to late fifteenth century, has most recently been dated to the mid-sixteenth century, although the date of the plays' creation was

likely much earlier. While all five manuscripts of the Chester plays date from the late fifteenth and six-teenth centuries, the earliest known reference to the cycle is in 1422. See Wells et al., eds., *A Manual of the Writings in Middle English*, 5: 1317–37; Palmer, "'Recycling the Wakefield Cycle'"; Johnston and Rogerson, eds., *Records of Early English Drama: York*, 3.

2. *Bibliotheca Towneleiana*, 45.

3. A search of the Modern Language Association International Bibliography reveals about forty entries each for the Noah plays and the Towneley *Second Shepherd's Play*, compared to seventeen entries for the crucifixion plays and fifteen entries for the Towneley *Mactacio Abel*, itself a pageant the involves a fair amount of comedy, although not of the sexual kind.

4. In an influential 1940 article, John Watt calls most biblical drama "pretty sorry stuff" because its "odd items of bickering among characters, monologue acts, and occasional slapstick stuff" result in "a lack of unity and economy in the plays." Watt, "Dramatic Unity," 271.

5. For typological readings of the uxor, see Kolve, *Play Called Corpus Christi*, 150, and Woolf, *English Mystery Plays*, 136. For a critique of typological readings, see Helterman, *Symbolic Action*, 51–52.

6. James, "Ritual, Drama, and the Social Body," 27; Flannigan, "Liminality, Carnival, and Social Structure," 58; Phythian-Adams, "Ceremony and the Citizen," 69.

7. Evans, "Body Politics."

8. This represents a welcome change from the situation that Coletti described in 1990 when she wrote that "feminist criticism of medieval drama is largely unrealized." Coletti, "A Feminist Approach," 79.

9. An important exception is Evans's analysis of the Wakefield *Noah* pageant, wherein she argues that the uxor gestures toward a gendered subjectivity and difference unacknowledged in most farcical comedy. Evans, "Feminist Re-Enactments."

10. Coletti, "A Feminist Approach," 82. Similarly, Coletti asserts that the Digby *Killing of the Innocents* interrogates misogyny only when it juxtaposes a virtuous Saint Anne against the stereotypi-cally unruly mothers. Coletti, "Geneology, Sexuality," 46.

11. Fitzgerald, "Manning the Ark," 352, and Fitzgerald, *Drama of Masculinity*, 6.

12. Tolmie, "Mrs. Noah and Didactic Abuses," 31.

13. For examples of this approach, see Axton, *European Drama*, 186; Hill-Vasquez, *Sacred Play-ers*, 146.

14. Dentith, *Bakhtinian Thought*, 75.

15. Humphrey, *Politics of Carnival*, 60.

16. The list of studies on companionate marriage is too long to recite here. Notable entries include Howell, "Properties of Marriage"; Stone, *Family, Sex, and Marriage*; Fleming, *Family and Household*; Shorter, *Making of Modern Family*; Watt, *Making of Modern Marriage*.

17. The anachronism of using a term like "class" to describe medieval social relations has long been a subject of debate. My own view is that, while it is true that certain denotations of class (for instance, those that are based on a notion of proletariat-capitalist relations) are an inappropriate para-digm by which to interpret medieval social relations, a more generalized use of the term to denote an awareness of social difference based on differing levels of economic power and different modes of labor is a useful term of description. It is in the latter sense that I use it in this chapter.

18. For instance, Palmer has rightly noted that the Towneley pageant appears to be a collection of plays, perhaps compiled after the fact and perhaps never performed together and, thus, is markedly dif-ferent from the York and Chester cycles, which were clearly played together. See Palmer, "Recycling the Wakefield Cycle," and Palmer, "'Wakefield Cycle' Revisited."

19. For a definition of companionate marriage, see Howell, "Properties of Marriage," 18; Stone, *Family, Sex, and Marriage*, 8.

20. Greene, ed., *Early English Carols*, no. 404, 240.

21. Ibid.

22. *The Tale of the Basin*, 54. This work can be found in Furrow, *Ten Fifteenth-Century Comic Poems*,

23. All citations are from Stevens and Cawley, eds., *The Towneley Plays*, and will be cited by line number parenthetically in the text.

24. According to Evans, the speech invites the audience to confront "a radical idea of the subject, as a figure who breaks away from embodying social or communal forces, and who becomes the source of a difference in view." Evans, "Feminist Re-Enactments," 151.

25. Bullough, "On Being Male," 34.

26. For a discussion of grain shortages in London and other English towns in the fifteenth century, see Keene, "Crisis Management in London's Food Supply"; Lee, "Grain Shortages."

27. For a discussion of the husband-wife battles of the English misericords, see Grössinger, *English Misericords*.

28. Coletti, "A Feminist Approach," 82, has also observed the drama's excision of adultery.

29. In her discussion of jurors in English market towns, McIntosh notes that one of the problems the jurors faced was that behaviors, like scolding, which they believed threatened the peace of their communities, were not forbidden by law. McIntosh, "Finding a Language for Misconduct," 91.

30. The theory of a distinctive marriage and household system in northwestern Europe is first put forward in Hajnal, "European Marriage Patterns." For works relating that pattern to companionate marriage, see Macfarlane, *Marriage and Love*; Hanawalt, *Ties That Bound*.

31. Howell, "Properties of Marriage," 49.

32. Ibid., 60.

33. Cohen, *Recueil de farces françaises*, 28, 219–36; translated by Enders as *Playing Doctor, or, Taking the Plunge*, in *Farce of the Fart*, 199–218.

34. Tissier, *Recueil des farces*, 14–40.

35. In the Chester play, uxor and the Noah daughters-in-law help with the building of the ark. In the York *Noah*, the uxor says she has "tolis to trusse." See Lumiansky and Mills, eds., *Chester Mystery Cycle*, vol. 1, Play III, lines 65–76; *York Plays*, Play IX, line 110.

36. Evans, "Feminist Re-Enactments," 154.

37. Normington, *Gender and Medieval Drama*, 131.

38. Palmer, "'Recycling the Wakefield Cycle'," 88.

39. See note 1 above.

40. Palmer, "'Recycling the Wakefield Cycle'," 88. Palmer's theories are debatable. Goldberg, for instance, has disputed her dismissal of Wakefield as a possible locale for a dramatic cycle, noting that there is evidence for a Corpus Christi play at Wakefield and strong evidence to connect a number of the pageants to Wakefield. Goldberg, "From Tableaux to Text," 253n36. Nevertheless, the mere fact that such debates exist shows the difficulties involved in readings that depend on locating the pageants at a specific historical moment or in a specific locale.

41. Clopper, "Civic Religious Drama and Ceremony."

42. For the view that the York pageants were controlled by civic oligarchies, see Dobson, "Craft Guilds and City"; Swanson, "The Illusion of Economic Structure."

43. Goldberg, "From Tableaux to Text." Christie also argues convincingly for craft association influence on the plays, noting "that while the York cycle as a whole was authorized by the civic government, the

individual pageants were largely funded and produced by the associations. The crafts collected pageant silver from their members . . . they built and repaired pageant wagons; they begged, borrowed, and bought costumes, props, and materials for special effects; they paid for rehearsals, refreshments, and performances. Without their participation, there would have been no Play." Christie, "Bridging the Jurisdictional Divide," 54.

44. Beckwith, *Signifying God*, 53.

45. The fact that the Towneley manuscript resided with a gentry family does not mitigate against a middle-rank association in the time of its creation, for the family's association with the plays dates only from the postmedieval period.

46. Nisse has argued that the Wakefield author exhibits a self-conscious ruralism, taking the York plays as his primary exemplar and writing his contributions "in polemical contrast to the urban form of the Corpus Christi cycle" (*Defining Acts*, 78). While the Wakefield author may have differentiated him or herself from the urban world of York, it does not necessarily follow that the two groups, rural and urban, always had opposed interests or were completely alien to each other in every respect.

47. Aers, "Rewriting the Middle Ages," 235.

48. Barron and Goldberg have theorized that labor shortages induced by the plague of the mid-fourteenth century, combined with the rise of the home-based industrial system, created conditions in which women were able to obtain unprecedented levels of autonomy and status. Judith Bennett has opposed this view, asserting that a "patriarchal equilibrium" ensured that any gains women achieved in one area were balanced out by deficits in others. McIntosh has sketched out a middle ground by tracking fluctuations in women's participation in the market economy. See Goldberg, *Women, Work and Life Cycle*; Barron, "'The Golden Age' of Women in Medieval London"; Bennett, *History Matters*; McIntosh, *Working Women in English Society*.

49. Harris, *English Aristocratic Women*, 56–57.

50. Hajnal, "European Marriage Patterns"; Goldberg, *Women, Work and Life Cycle*, 225–32; McSheffrey, *Marriage, Sex, and Civic Culture*, 17.

51. High-ranking noblewomen might live in households composed of upward of 50 people. See Ward, *English Noblewomen*, 51.

52. Ibid., 53.

53. Ward notes numerous instances in which women did take on managerial roles. My point here is not to deny that women of the aristocracy and gentry did so, but that their participation was not necessary to familial survival in the way it was for the women of middle- and lower-rank families.

54. "Ballad of a Tyrannical Husband," 85–89.

55. Niebrzydowski, *Bonoure and Buxum*, 182.

56. Swanson, *Medieval British Towns*, 51.

57. Hanawalt, *Wealth of Wives*, 120.

58. McIntosh, *Working Women*, 148.

59. French, *Good Women of the Parish*, 219.

60. See my discussion in Chapter 3, in the section "The Mumming at Hertford and the Legal Regulation of the Shrew."

61. Howell, "Citizenship and Gender," 37.

62. Since there are two records of male cast members playing female roles for several years running, it seems unlikely that the female parts in the biblical drama were given to prepubescent boys, as they were in the Renaissance. See Twycross, "'Transvestism'," 144, and Normington, *Gender and Medieval Drama*, 64–65.

63. Twycross, "'Transvestism'," 162.

64. Ibid., 164. Jane Tolmie, "Mrs. Noah and Didactic Abuses," 17–19, also regards a transvestite Mrs. Noah as emphasizing the misogynist elements of the play.

65. See, for instance, Normington, *Gender and Medieval Drama*, 127.

66. All citations from the Chester plays are taken from Lumiansky and Mills, eds., *Chester Mystery Cycle*, and are cited parenthetically, by line number, in the text.

67. Records from Coventry note a payment "to Maisturres grymesby for lendyng off her geir ffor pylatts wyfe" (to Mistress Grimesby for lending of her gear for Pilate's wife). Cited in Twycross, "'Transvestism',"125.

68. Hartman, *Household and the Making of History*, 51.

69. Baird and Baird, "Hegge *Joseph's Return.*"

70. For discussions of Joseph's inferior and ridiculous status in later medieval religious culture, see Huizinga, *Autumn of the Middle Ages*, 193–96; Sheingorn, "Joseph the Carpenter's Failure at Familial Discipline'"; and Vasvari, "Joseph on the Margin."

71. According to Elliott, *Spiritual Marriage*, 141, clerical opposition to celibate marriage was, in part, fueled by beliefs regarding the importance of intercourse in maintaining male dominance.

72. Bullough, "On Being Male," 43.

73. *Farce de Regnault qui se marie à Lavollée*, in Cohen, *Recueil de farces françaises*, VII, 51–56. Translation mine.

74. In the farce *Resjouy d'Amours*, a husband suspects his wife of adultery and sets the house on fire to "smoke out" the lover. However, the quick-thinking wife stuffs her lover in a sack and asks her husband to carry it out, claiming it contains all their worldly goods. The husband, failing to see a lover escaping the flames, regrets his suspicions and asks his wife for forgiveness. The husband of the *Farce de Patinier*, in Cohen, tries to expose his cheating wife by arranging a trick with his neighbor. Unfortunately, the neighbor, who is, in fact, the wife's lover, takes advantage of the situation, and the husband is cuckolded again. See Cohen, *Recueil de farces françaises*, 135–43, 273–82.

75. Warner, *Alone of All Her Sex.*

76. All citations of the York plays are taken from Beadle, ed., *York Plays*, and will be cited parenthetically, by line number, in the text.

77. Wenzel, *Latin Sermon Collections*, 60; Mirk, *Mirk's Festial*, 72.

78. British Library Add. MS 18850, f.016v.

79. In Chartres Cathedral (artstor), the early thirteenth-century Noah window includes a panel depicting the ark, surrounded by several other panels depicting the drowned floating in the floodwaters, as well as a vulture tearing at the flesh of a corpse. A few more of the many examples of medieval depictions of the drowned as inanimate dead bodies include the Ramsey Psalter (c. 1310), MS M.0302, fol.01v, and a Norman Book of Hours (c. 1440) Bodleian Libary MS Auct. D inf. 2. 11, fol. 059v.

80. Horrox, *Black Death*, 242. See also, Byrne, *Encyclopedia of Pestilence*, 64; Boeckl, *Images of Plague and Pestilence*, 42 and 190. The notion of plague as a punishment for sin is something Langland repeats several times in *Piers Plowman*. In Passus XII, Ymaginatif advises Will to amend himself abjuring that "thow hast ben warned ofte / With poustees of pestilences, with poverte and with angres — / And with thise bitter baleises God beteth his deere children" (10–12).

81. *Sermons of Thomas Brinton*, no. 70. Also cited in Horrox, *Black Death*, 145. See also *Chronicon Abbatiae de Parco Ludae*, 38–39; Simon de Covino, "De Judicio Solis in Conviviis Saturni," 206–8; "Cortusii Patavini Duo," cols. 926–27. Also cited in Horrox, *Black Death*, 67, 165, and 35.

82. Gottfried, *Epidemic Disease*, 50. For a table charting all of the known epidemics, both local and national, occurring in the fifteenth century, see 48.

83. Brie, *The Brut*, 604.

84. Gottfried, *Epidemic Disease*, 225.

85. Thomas Forestier's *Tractus Contra Pestilentium, Thenasmonium, et Dissinterium*, printed in 1490, advocates divine wrath as a cause of pestilence, as does an anonymous treatise written in English during the same period. Both are cited in Gottfried, *Epidemic Disease*, 68–69.

86. British Library, Sloane MS 965, fos. 143–45. Cited and translated in Horrox, *Black Death*, 193.

87. Scott, *Arts of Resistance*, 15.

88. Ibid., 1–5.

89. Ibid., 157.

90. Ibid., 166.

91. Humphrey, *Politics of Carnival*, 63–77.

92. Ibid., 76.

93. Tolmie, "Mrs. Noah and Didactic Abuses," 11.

94. Watson, "Visions of Inclusion."

95. Watson, "Censorship and Cultural Change," 823–25.

96. This is embodied in Julian's famous dictum that "Sin is behovabil." See Julian of Norwich, *Shewings*, 72.

97. Matt. 2:16e.

98. Neither the York nor the N-Town Innocents pageants include obscene comedy, choosing instead to emphasize the mothers' pathos.

99. Coldeway, "Non-Cycle Plays," 194.

100. Coletti, "'Ther be but women'"; Coletti, "Geneology, Sexuality, and Sacred Power," 46. Similarly, Tolmie believes that the Innocents plays connect the unruly mothers to Eve and original sin, asserting that the pageants link the mothers' ineffectual resistance to their inferior status as females. Tolmie, "Spinning Women." An exception to this is Ryan, who sees the women as heroic figures and analyzes the women's speech in the context of legal constructs of slander: "Womanly Weaponry."

101. Coletti, "'Ther be but women'," and Colletti, "Geneology, Sexuality, and Sacred Power."

102. Coletti, "Geneology, Sexuality, and Sacred Power," 43. Sponsler, *Drama and Resistance*, 145, also sees the conflict of the plays as primarily one about gender.

103. Baker et al., eds., *Candlemes Day*. All citations are taken from this edition and will be cited parenthetically, by line number, in the text.

104. See, for instance, Woolf, *English Mystery Plays*, 205; Weimann, *Shakespeare and the Popular Tradition*, 65–72.

105. For discussions of the series of popular revolts in the fifteenth century and their links with a broader culture of discontent with medieval authorities, see Bennet, "Henry VII and the Northern Rising"; Fletcher and MacCulloch, *Tudor Rebellions*; Fryde, *Peasants and Landlords*; Rollison, *Commonwealth of the People*, ch. 5; Watts, "Pressure of the Public"; and Wood, *1549 Rebellions*.

106. Wood, *1549 Rebllions*, 4; Rollison, *Commonwealth of the People*, 240.

107. Walker, "Rumour, Sedition and Popular Protest," 33.

108. Scott, *Arts of Resistance*, 37–38.

109. Payling, *Political Society*, 188–89.

110. Harriss, *Shaping the Nation*, 201–2; Carpenter, *Locality and Polity*, 432–33; Wright, *Derbyshire Gentry*, 134–37; Maddern, *Violence and Social Order*, 154–66; Powell, *Kingship, Law, and Society*, 123–24, 217–21, 238–39.

111. Maddern, *Violence and Social Order*, 154–62.

112. Payling, *Political Society*, 189. Similarly, Harriss, *Shaping the Nation*, 201, notes that "No realistic measurement can be made of gentry violence either overall or at different times and places. . . .

many individual acts of violence must have gone unrecorded both from reluctance of juries of yeoman to indict their superiors and from victims too frightened to petition for redress."

113. Scott, *Arts of Resistance*, 57.

114. Ibid., 158.

115. Scott (159) notes that popular religious rituals that ostensibly celebrate the tenets of the dominant faith are particularly useful as vehicles for seditious meaning since their religiosity would seem to support the established order. He cites a Filipino use of the tradition of a passion play to convey a dissent from elite culture. Herod's different religious identity also works as a distancing mechanism. All of the plays are careful to emphasize his non-Christian identity by having him or his minions swear by "Mahoun." See Chester (55), Towneley (184), Digby (127), and Coventry (516). All citations of the Coventry *Shearmen and Tailor's Play* are taken from Happé, ed., *English Mystery Plays*, and are cited parenthetically in the text by line number.

116. Patterson, *Chaucer and the Subject of History*, 171.

117. Woolf, *English Mystery Plays*, 205.

118. Foucault, *Discipline and Punish*, 55.

119. Scarry, *Body in Pain*, 28.

120. The discomfort of biblical drama creators with this aspect of the biblical story is illustrated by the Chester pageant, which adds the extrabiblical detail of having Herod die at the pageant's conclusion, after learning that his own son was killed by the soldiers (397–433).

121. Scarry, *Body in Pain*, 27.

122. Herzen, "A Letter Criticizing *The Bell* [1858]," 69.

123. Davis, "Woman on Top," 127.

124. Burger notes a similar association between the middle ranks and interrogations of gender norms in his discussion of Chaucer's Wife of Bath. The Wife's female masculinity exhibits a fourteenth-century attempt to think about dominant masculinity differently. Because her desire to profit and make the most of her position aligns with the ambitions of middle-rank men, this attempt at reconsidering gender is also one that reconsiders social hierarchies. Burger, *Chaucer's Queer Nation*, 79–100.

125. Italics throughout this paragraph are mine.

126. French, "To Free Them from Binding."

127. The conflict between women's professional successes and ideals of feminine behavior in the family has most recently been examined by French feminist philosopher Élisabeth Badinter, who notes a backlash against working mothers in the emergence of parenting philosophies that advocate extensive parental investment in and contact with children. See Badinter, *The Conflict*.

CONCLUSION. LESSONS OF THE MEDIEVAL OBSCENE

1. Cited in Spurgeon, *Five Hundred Years*, Part 1, 134. Chaucer is also condemned on similar grounds by Thomas Drant in 1567 (100).

2. Camille also notes the beginnings of a dislike for explicit sex in the later fifteenth century among manuscript illuminators. While thirteenth- and fourteenth-century illuminators depict body parts and sexuality freely, fifteenth-century illuminators are less likely to do so. Even so, other forms of art, like the medieval badges, retain their interest in explicit representation through the fifteenth century. See Camille, "Obscenity Under Erasure."

3. Spurgeon, *Five Hundred Years*, 146.

4. Ibid., xix.

5. Foxe, *Ecclesiasticall History*, 2: 965.

6. Auchter, *Dictionary of Literary and Dramatic Censorship*, 163–64; Boose, "Elizabethan Pornography," 185.

7. Boose, "Elizabethan Pornography," 187.

8. Hunt, "Pornography and the French Revolution," 307 and de Jean, *Reinvention of Obscenity*, 10–14. "See also "Media Control and the Regulation of the Obscene" in the Introduction to this study.

9. A similar work, Thomas Nashe's *The Choice of Valentines*, was not singled out for censorship because it appeared in manuscript and was thus restricted to an elite readership. See Boose, "Elizabethan Pornography," 187–90.

10. Spurgeon, *Five Hundred Years*, 158.

11. Ibid., 179 and 197; for Middleton's other references to Chaucer, see 187.

12. Ibid., 158.

13. Gascoigne, *Complete Works*, 2. Also cited in McCoy, "Wages of Courtly Success," 30.

14. Spurgeon, *Five Hundred Years*, part 4, 38.

15. Spenser, *Faerie Queene*, IV.ii.32.8–9.

16. For the traditional view that the drama's suppression was due to its Catholic content, see Gardiner, *Mysteries' End*.

17. Clopper, "Persistence of 'Medieval Drama'," 287–89.

18. Gardiner, *Mysteries' End*, 60; Dillon, *Language and Stage*, 86.

19. For a discussion of male protesters' use of the unruly woman during the early modern period, see Davis, "Woman on Top," 148–49. Wood, *1549 Rebellions*, 117, describes how elites during Kett's Rebellion were particularly disturbed by the women rioters, who were said to have been "clamorous, loude," giving out "outcries shout[s], hallow[s]." Wood, *1549 Rebellions*, 13, also describes women's leadership in the food riots of Norwich in 1532.

20. McKeon, *Secret History*, 269–319.

21. Ibid., 312. For a description of the growing tendency to censor obscenity, see Hunt, "Pornography and the French Revolution"; Talvacchia, *Taking Positions*, 4–19. For descriptions of the humorous and satirical content of obscenity in early modern England, see Moulton, *Before Pornography*, 6. Similarly, in a study of seventeenth-century pornography, Sarah Toulalan notes that the genre is remarkable for often including comic narratives, as well philosophical musings. See Toulalan, *Imagining Sex*, 34.

22. Hunt, introduction to *Invention of Pornography*, 23; McKeon, *Secret History*, 300.

23. Dines, *Pornland*, x.

24. MacKinnon, "Feminism, Marxism, Method, and the State." Some fascinating recent work by the sociologist Jennifer A. Johnson examines the interdependence of porn and capitalism, theorizing that misogynist porn offers men disempowered by capitalism a compensatory trade-off in the form of a fantasy of power. See Johnson, "To Catch a Curious Clicker."

25. Williams's analysis identifies pornography's obsession with finding out the "truth" of women's difference, embodied in its focus on filming women's genitalia, a bid that fails because it cannot represent women's sexual pleasure visually. See Williams, *Hard Core*, 113–14.

26. The leading voice in these efforts is that of Catharine MacKinnon, who has campaigned to use U.S. civil law and the equal protection guarantee of the Fourteenth Amendment to attack pornography. See MacKinnon, *Only Words*.

27. For instance, the Canadian Supreme Court decision *R. v. Butler* (1992) was hailed by feminists because it allowed for the legal censorship of pornography when the material in question could be found to violate women's rights to equality under the Canadian Charter of Rights and Freedoms. Six weeks after the decision, however, Toronto police brought charges against the Glad Day Bookshop, a

gay and lesbian bookstore, for selling a lesbian erotic fiction magazine. A host of other charges followed in which the new law was used to censor nonconventional representations of sexuality. See Cossman and Bell, introduction to *Bad Attitude/s on Trial*, 4–8.

28. For pro-porn feminism, see Strossen, *Defending Pornography*; Willis, "Lust Horizons"; Bright, *Sexual State of the Union*; Cossman and Bell, *Bad Attitude/s*.

29. Chris Morris, "Porn Industry Feeling Upbeat About 2014," *NBC News*, June 3, 2014; Johnson, "To Catch a Curious Clicker," 147.

30. Although Middle English writers are the subject of this study, change is not exclusive to them. The fabliau and the Latin elegiac comedy are themselves alterations of previous iterations of obscene comedy. The twelfth-century Latin elegiac comedies are different from the classical works that inspired them; the fabliaux are different from the Latin elegiac comedies.

31. This is a feature of pornography that a number of modern commentators have observed. See, for instance, Drucilla Cornell, who refers to the "frozen violence and rigid gender identities" of modern porn; perhaps surprisingly, Vladimir Nabokov, who observes porn's mediocrity, commercialism, and strict rules of narration; and Isabelle Barker, who notes that "most pornography fashions fantasy through the rigidity of scripted performance" and rehearses "again and again" a story that is "steeped in sexual hierarchies." See Cornell, introduction to *Feminism and Pornography*, 11; Nabokov, cited in Dworkin, "Against the Male Flood," 25; and Barker, "Editing Pornography," 650.

32. "Teens Love Huge Cocks," http://www.realitykings.com/teens-love-huge-cocks/home.htm; Avery, *Autobiography of a Flea*.

33. Whereas the era of pornographic films required audiences to travel to a theater and watch with others and whereas DVD porn required a trip to the video store, the Internet is steamed right into the home computer with no required human contact at any point.

34. Dines, *Pornland*, 80.

35. Butler, "Force of Fantasy," 493.

36. Ibid.

37. Ibid., 504.

38. See Chomsky and Herman, *Manufacturing Consent*.

39. Consider, for instance, the attacks on access to birth control and abortion that have recently occurred in the United States.

BIBLIOGRAPHY

MANUSCRIPT SOURCES

Bibliothèque National de France
  MS Fr.25526
British Library
  Add. MS 42130 (the "Luttrell Psalter")
  Sloane MS 965
  Add. MS 18850
Morgan Library
  MS M.0754
  MS 302 (the "Ramsey Psalter")
Oxford Bodleian Library
  MS Acut. D. Inf. 2. 11
Trinity College, Cambridge
  MS. B.11.22.

PUBLISHED PRIMARY SOURCES

Anstey, Henry, ed. *Munimenta Academica or, Documents Illustrative of Academical Life and Studies at Oxford, Part 1, Libri Cancellarii et Procuratorum.* London: Longmans, Green, Reader, and Dyer, 1868.

Aristotle's Nichomachean Ethics. Trans. Robert C. Bartlett and Susan D. Collins. Chicago: University of Chicago Press, 2011.

Avery, Edward. *The Autobiography of a Flea.* London, 1887.

A/Y Memorandum Book, 1419. In *Records of Early English Drama: York,* ed. Alexandra F. Johnston and Margaret Rogerson. Toronto: University of Toronto Press, 1979.

Baird, Joseph L., and John R. Kane, ed. and trans. *La Querelle de la Rose: Letters and Documents.* Chapel Hill: North Carolina Studies in Romance Languages and Literatures, 1978.

"Ballad of a Tyrannical Husband." In Salisbury, *The Trials and Joys of Marriage,* 85–89.

Baker, Donald C. et al., eds. *Candlemes Day and the Kyllyng of þe Children of Israelle.* In *The Late Medieval Religious Plays of Bodleian MSS. Digby 133 and E Museo 160.* Oxford: EETS, 1982.

Baum, Paul F., ed. and trans. *Anglo Saxon Riddles of the Exeter Book.* Durham, N.C.: Duke University Press, 1963.

Bayard, Tania, trans. *A Medieval Home Companion: Housekeeping in the Fourteenth Century.* New York: HarperCollins, 1991.

Beadle, Richard, ed. *The York Plays*. London: E. Arnold, 1982.

Benson, Larry D., and Theodore M. Andersson, eds. and trans. *The Literary Context of Chaucer's Fabliaux: Texts and Translations*. Indianapolis: Bobbs-Merrill, 1971.

Bernard of Clairvaux. "Ad Clericos de Conversione." In *Sancti Bernardi Opera*, vol. 4, 59–116.

———. *Sancti Bernardi Opera*. Ed. J. Leclerq, C. H. Talbot, and H. M. Rochais. Rome: Editiones Cistercienses, 1957–77.

Bernard of Clairvaux: Selected Works. Trans. and ed. G. R. Evans. New York: Paulist, 1987.

Biblia Sacra: Iuxta Vulgatam versionem. 2 vols. Ed. Robert Weber. Stuttgart: Württembergische Bibelanstalt, 1969.

Bibliotheca Towneleiana: A Catalogue of the Curious and Extensive Library of the Late John Towneley, Esq. London, 1814.

Bickley, F. B., ed. *The Little Red Book of Bristol*. 2 vols. Bristol, 1900.

Block Elaine C. *Corpus of Medieval Misericords: Belgium and the Netherlands*. Turnhout: Brepols, 2010.

———. *Corpus of Medieval Misericords. France*. Turnhout: Brepols, 2003.

———. *Corpus of Medieval Misericords. Iberia: Portugal-Spain*. Turnhout: Brepols, 2004.

Boccaccio, Giovanni. *Decameron*. Ed. Jonathan Usher. Trans. Guido Waldman. Oxford: Oxford University Press, 1993.

———. *Teseida: Della nozze d'Emilia*. Ed. Aurelio Rancaglia. Bari: Gius, Laterza, et Figle, 1941.

Bradwardine, Thomas. *De causa Dei contra Pelagium et de virtute causarum ad suos Mertonenses, libri tres*. Ed. Henry Saville. London: 1618. Rpr. Frankfurt: Minerva, 1964.

———. "On the Cause of God Against Pelagius." In *Forerunners of the Reformation: The Shape of Late Medieval Thought*, ed. Heiko A. Oberman, trans. Paul L. Nyhus, 151–64. Cambridge: James Clark, 1966.

Brie, Friedrich W. D., ed. *The Brut, or the Chronicles of England*. Vol. 2. London: EETS, 1908.

Brinton, Thomas. *The Sermons of Thomas Brinton*. Ed. Sister Mary Aquinas Devlin. 3rd ser. 85–86. London: Camden Society, 1954.

Chaucer, Geoffrey. *The Riverside Chaucer*. Ed. Larry Benson et al. New York: Houghton Mifflin, 1987.

Christine de Pisan. *The Book of the Body Politic*. Trans. K. L. Forhan. Cambridge: Cambridge University Press, 1994.

———. *Ditié de Jeanne d'Arc*. Ed. Angus J. Kennedy and Kenneth Varty. Oxford: Society for the Study of Medieval Languages and Literature, 1977.

———. *Epistre au dieu d'amours*. In *Poems of Cupid, God of Love*, ed., Thelma S. Fenster and Mary C. Erler, 33–73. Leiden: Brill, 1990.

———. "L'Épistre Cristine au Prevost de Lisle, envoyé par la dicte contre *Le Romnant de la Rose*." In Hicks, *Le Débat*, 49–57.

———. "*Le Livre de la Cité des Dames of Christine de Pisan*: A Critical Edition." Ed. Maureen Cheney Curnow. Ph.D. dissertation, Vanderbilt University, 1975.

Chronicon Abbatiae de Parco Ludae: The Chronicle of Louth Park Abbey. Horncastle, 1891.

Classen, Albrecht, trans. *Erotic Tales of Medieval Germany*. Tempe: Arizona Center for Medieval and Renaissance Studies, 2007.

Cohen, Gustave, ed. *La "Comédie" latine en France au XIIe siècle*. Paris: Belles-Lettres, 1931.

———, ed. *Recueil de farces françaises inédites du XVe siècle*. Cambridge, Mass.: Medieval Academy of America, 1949.

Consoli, Joseph P., ed and trans. *The Novellino or One Hundred Ancient Tales*. New York: Garland, 1997.

Corpus of the Misericords at Chester Cathedral. http://www.misericords.co.uk/chester_des.html.

"Cortusii Patavini Duo, sive Gulielmi at Abrigeti Cortusiorum, Historia de Novitatibus Paduae et Lombardiae ab anno MCCLVI usque ad MCCCLXIV." In *Rerum Italicarum Scriptores* XII, ed. L. A. Muratori. Milan, 1728. Cols 926–27.

"Coventry Shearmen and Tailor's Play." In *English Mystery Plays*, ed. Peter Happé. London: Penguin, 1975.

Crawford, James Martin, trans. "The Secular Latin Comedies of Twelfth Century France." Ph.D. dissertation, Indiana University, 1977.

Crowley, Robert, ed. *The Vision of Pierce Plowman, newlye imprynted after the authours olde copy*. London: Owen Rogers, 1561. Early English Books Online.

Damrosch, David et al., eds. *The Longman Anthology of English Literature*. 4th ed. Vol. 1A. New York: Longman, 2009.

Der Stricker. *Fables, Sermonettes, and Parables by Der Stricker*. Trans. J. W. Thomas. 2 vols. Lewiston, N.Y.: Edwin Mellen, 1999.

Dubin, Nathaniel E., trans. *The Fabliaux*. New York: Liveright, 2013.

Eichmann, Raymond, and John Du Val, eds. and trans. *The French Fabliau: B.N. MS. 837*. New York: Garland, 1984.

Elliott, Alison Goddard, ed. and trans. *Seven Medieval Comedies*. New York: Garland, 1984.

Enders, Jody, ed. and trans. *The Farce of the Fart and Other Ribaldries: Twelve Medieval French Plays in Modern English*. Philadelphia: University of Pennsylvania Press, 2011.

Ensler, Eve. *The Vagina Monologues*. New York: Villard, 1998.

The Examination of Master William Thorpe. In *Fifteenth Century Prose and Verse*, ed. William Pollard, 90–174. Westminster: Archibald Constable, 1903.

Foxe, John. *Ecclesiasticall history contaynyng the Actes and Monumentes of thynges passed in euery Kynges tyme in this Realme*. London: John Day, 1570. Vol. 2, 965. Early English Books Online.

Furrow, Melissa ed. *Ten Fifteenth-Century Comic Poems*. New York: Garland, 1985.

Gascoigne, George. *The Complete Works*. Vol. 1. Ed. John W. Cunliffe. Cambridge: Cambridge University Press, 1910.

Gerson, Jean. "Traité contre le Roman de la Rose." In Hicks, *Le Débat*, 59–87.

Gratian. *Decretum*. Ed. Emil Friedberg. Leipzig, 1879.

Greenblatt, Stephen et al., eds. *The Norton Anthology of English Literature*. 8th ed. Vol. 1. New York: Norton, 2006.

Greene, Richard Leighton, ed. *The Early English Carols*. Oxford: Clarendon, 1935.

Guido delle Colonne. *Historia Destructionis Troiae*. Trans. Mary Elizabeth Meek. Bloomington: Indiana University Press, 1974.

Guillaume de Deguileville. *Le Pèlerinage de l'âme*. Ed. J. J. Stürzinger. London: Roxburghe Club, 1895.

Guillaume de Lorris et Jean de Meung. *Le Roman de la Rose*. Ed. Pierre Marteau. Paris, 1878.

———. *The Romance of the Rose*. Trans. and ed. Charles Dahlberg. Princeton, N.J.: Princeton University Press, 1971.

Halliwell, J. O., ed. *A Selection from the Minor Poems of Dan John Lydgate*. London: Percy Society, 1840.

Hammond, Eleanor, ed. *English Verse Between Chaucer and Surrey*. Durham, N.C.: Duke University Press, 1927.

Henri d'Andeli. *Les Dits d'Henri d'Andeli*. Ed. Alain Corbellari. Paris: Champion, 2003.

Hicks, Erik, ed. *Le Débat sur* Le Roman de la Rose. Paris: Champion, 1977.

Horrox, Rosemary, trans. and ed. *The Black Death*. Manchester: Manchester University Press, 1994.

Jacobus de Voragine. "Sancto Gregorio." In *Legenda Aurea vulgo historia lombardica dicta*, ed. Theodore Grässe, 188–202. Lipsiae: Impensis Librariae Arnoldianae, 1850.

Jacques de Vitry. *The Exempla or Illustrative Stories from the Sermones Vulgares of Jacques de Vitry*. Ed. Thomas Frederick Crane. London: D. Nutt, 1890.

———. *Vita Maria Oigniacensi in Naurcensis Belgii diocecesi*. Ed. Danile Papebroeck. Paris: 1867.

Jean de Froissart. *Oeuvres*. Ed. Kervyn de Lettenhove. Brussels: Devaux, 1868, 1869, 1872.

John of Salisbury. *Policratus*. Ed. and trans. C. J. Nederman. Cambridge: Cambridge University Press, 1990.

Johnston, Alexandra F., and Margaret Rogerson, eds. *Records of Early English Drama: York*. Toronto: University of Toronto Press, 1979.

Julian of Norwich. *The Shewings of Julian of Norwich*. Ed. Georgina Ronan Crampton. Kalamazoo, Mich.: Medieval Institute Publications, 1994.

Kempe, Margery. *The Book of Margery Kempe*. Ed. Lynn Staley. Rochester, N.Y.: Medieval Institute Publications, 1996.

Langland, William. *Piers Plowman: A New Annotated Edition of the C-text*. Ed. Derek Pearsall. Exeter: University of Exeter Press, 2008.

———. *The Vision of Piers Plowman: A Critical Edition of the B-text based on Trinity College Cambrige MS B.15.17*. Ed. A. V. S. Schmidt. London: Everyman, 1978.

Lodder, Fred, ed. *Van de man die graag dronk en andere Middelnederlandse komische verhalen*. Trans. Karel Eykman. Amsterdam: Prometheus, 2002.

Lumiansky, R. M., and David Mills, eds. *The Chester Mystery Cycle*. 2 vols. London: EETS, 1974.

Lydgate, John. *The Fall of Princes*. 4 vols. Ed. Henry Bergen. EETS e.s. 121, 122, 123, 124. Oxford: Oxford University Press, 1924–27, 1967; Chadwyk-Healey, 1992.

———. *The Minor Poems of John Lydgate*. 2 vols. Ed. Henry Noble MacCracken. EETS o.s. 192. Oxford: Oxford University Press, 1934, 1961.

———. *Mummings and Entertainments*. Ed. Claire Sponsler. Kalamazoo, Mich.: Medieval Institute Publications.

Mapplethorpe, Robert. *Mapplethorpe*. Kempen: Te Neues, 1992.

Marie de France. *The Fables of Marie de France*. Trans. Mary Lou Martin. Birmingham, Ala.: Summa, 1984.

———. *Marie de France: Fables*. Ed. A. Ewert and Ronald C. Johnston. Oxford: Blackwell, 1942.

Marienwerder, Johannes. *The Life of Dorothea of Montau: A Fourteenth-Century Recluse*. Trans. Ute Stargardt. Lewiston, N.Y.: Edwin Mellen Press, 1997.

———. *Vita Dorotheae Montoviensis Johannis Marienwerder*. Ed. Hans Westphal with Anneliese Triller. Cologne/Graz: Böhlau, 1964.

McSheffrey, Shannon, ed. and trans. *Love and Marriage in Late Medieval London*. Kalamazoo, Mich.: Medieval Institute Publications, 1995.

Ménagier de Paris. *Le Ménagier de Paris*. Ed. Georgine E. Brereton and Janet M. Ferrier. Oxford: Clarendon 1981.

Middle English Dictionary. Ed. Hans Kurath et al. Ann Arbor: University of Michigan Press, 1957.

Millet, Bella, and Jocelyn Wogan-Browne, eds. and trans. *Medieval English Prose for Women: From the Katherine Group and Ancrene Wisse*. Oxford: Clarendon, 1990

Mirk, John. *John Mirk's Festial, Edited from British Library MS Cotton Caludius A*. Ed. Susan Powell. Oxford: Oxford University Press, 2011.

Montaiglon, Anatole de, and Gaston Raynaud, eds., *Recueil général et complet des fabliaux des XIIIe et XIVe siècles*. Paris: Librairie des Bibliophiles, 1872–90.

Moore, Stuart A., ed., *Letters and Papers of John Shillingford, Mayor of Exeter 1447–50*. Westminster: Printed for the Camden Society, 1871.

Mum and the Sothsegger. In *Richard the Redeless and Mum and the Sothsegger*, ed. James M. Dean. Kalamazoo, Mich.: Medieval Institute Publications, 2000.

Noomen, Willem, and Nico van den Boogaard, eds. *Nouveau recueil complèt des fabliaux*. 10 vols. Assen: Van Gorcum, 1983–98.

Ovid. *Ars Amatoria*. In *The Art of Love and Other Poems, with an English translation by J. H. Mozley*. Loeb Classical Library. New York: Putnam, 1929.

Pamphilus de Amore. In Elliott, *Seven Medieval Latin Comedies*.

Robert of Basevorn. "The Form of Preaching." Trans. Leopold Krul. In *Three Medieval Rhetorical Arts*, ed. James J. Murphy, 109–216. Berkeley: University of California Press, 1971.

———. *Forma Praedicandi*. In *Artes Praedicandi: Contribution à l'histoire de la rhétorique au moyen âge*, ed. Th.-M. Charland. Institut d'Études Médiévales d'Ottawa 7, 233–323. Paris: Vrin, 1936.

Ruiz, Juan. *The Book of Good Love*. Trans. Elizabeth Drayson Macdonald. London: Everyman, 1999.

———. *El Libro de Buen Amor*. Alicante: Biblioteca Virtual de Miguel de Cervantes, 2000.

Sachs, Hans. *Merry Tales and Three Shrovetide Plays by Hans Sachs, now first done into English verse by William Leighton*. London: D. Nutt, 1910. Rpr. Westport, Conn.: Hyperion, 1978.

———. *Translations of the Carnival Comedies by Hans Sachs (1494–1576)*. Trans. Robert Aylett. Lewiston, N.Y.: Edwin Mellen, 1994.

Salisbury, Eve, ed. *The Trials and Joys of Marriage*. Kalamazoo, Mich.: Medieval Institute, 2002.

Sawles Warde. In Millet and Wogan-Browne, *Medieval English Prose for Women*, 86–109.

Simon de Covino. "De Judicio Solis in Conviviis Saturni." In *Bibliotheque de l'école des Chartes* 2, ed. E. Venables, 206–8. 1840–41.

Spenser, Edmund. *The Faerie Queene*. Ed. A. C. Hamilton. New York: Longman, 1977.

Spurgeon, Carolyn, ed. *Five Hundred Years of Chaucer Criticism and Allusion (1357–1900)*. 3 vols. Cambridge: Cambridge University Press, 1925.

Statius, Publius Papinius. *Achilleid*. Vol. 3 of *Statius*. Ed. and trans. D. R. Shackleton Bailey. Cambridge, Mass: Harvard University Press, 2003.

———. *Statius: With an English Translation by J. H. Mozley*. 2 vols. London: W. Heinemann, 1928.

———. *Statius' Thebaid IX*. Ed. and trans. Michael Dewar. Oxford Classical Monographs. Oxford: Clarendon, 1991.

———. *Thebaid*. Trans. A. D. Melville. Oxford: Clarendon, 1992.

The Statutes of the Realm. 12 vols. London: Dawsons of Pall Mall, 1810–28.

Stevens, Martin, and A. C. Cawley, eds. *The Towneley Plays*. Oxford: EETS, 1994.

Symes, Carol, trans. *Babio*. In *The Broadview Anthology of Medieval Drama*. Ed. Christina M. Fitzgerald and John T. Sebastian, 10–20. Toronto: Broadview, 2013.

Tissier, André, ed. *Recueil des farces, 1450–1550*. Genève: Droz, 1986.

Tubach, Frederic C. *Index Exemplorum: A Handbook of Medieval Religious Tales*. Helsinki: Suomalainen Tiedeakatemia, 1969.

Wells, John Edwin, et al., eds. *A Manual of the Writings in Middle English*. 5 vols. Hamden, Conn.: Shoestring Press, 1975.

Ziolkowski, Jan, ed. and trans. *The Cambridge Songs (Carmina Cantabrigiensia)*. New York: Garland, 1994.

SECONDARY SOURCES

Adams, Robert. "Piers' Pardon and Langland's Semi-Pelagianism." *Traditio* 39 (1983): 367–418.

Aers, David. *Chaucer, Langland and the Creative Imagination*. London: Routledge, 1980.

———. *Community, Gender, and Individual Identity: English Writing, 1360–1430*. London: Routledge, 1988.

———. "Class, Gender, Medieval Criticism, and *Piers Plowman*." In *Class and Gender in Early English Literature*, ed. Britton J. Harwood and Gillian R. Overing, 59–75. Bloomington: Indiana University Press, 1994.

———. "Rewriting the Middle Ages: Some Suggestions." *Journal of Medieval and Renaissance Studies* 18, 2 (1988): 221–40.

———. *Salvation and Sin: Augustine, Langland, and Fourteenth-Century Theology.* Notre Dame, Ind.: University of Notre Dame Press, 2009.

Allen, Hope Emily. Letter to the Editor. *Times*, December 27, 1934, 15.

———. Prefatory Note to *The Book of Margery Kempe*, ed. Sanford Brown Meech, liii–lxviii. London: Early English Text Society, 1940. (EETS)

Allen, Hope Emily, and Sanford Brown Meech. Notes to *The Book of Margery Kempe*, ed. Sanford Brown Meech, 255–350. London: EETS, 1940.

Allen, Valerie. *On Farting: Language and Laughter in the Middle Ages.* New York: Palgrave, 2007.

Allman, W. W. "Sociolinguistics, Literature, and the *Reeve's Tale*." *English Studies: A Journal of English Language and Literature* 85, 5 (2004): 385–404.

Amussen, Susan Dwyer. *An Ordered Society: Gender and Class in Early Modern England.* New York: Columbia University Press, 1988.

Anderson, David. *Before the Knight's Tale: Imitation of Classical Epic in Boccaccio's* Teseida. Philadelphia: University of Pennsylvania Press, 1988.

Arnold, John H. "Margery's Trials: Heresy, Lollardy and Dissent." In *A Companion to the Book of Margery Kempe*, ed. John H. Arnold and Katherine Lewis, 75–93. Cambridge: Brewer, 2004.

Ashley, Kathleen. "Historicizing Margery: The *Book of Margery Kempe* as Social Text." *Journal of Medieval and Early Modern Studies* 28 (1998): 371–88.

Aston, Margaret. *Lollards and Reformers: Images and Literacy in Late Medieval Religion.* London: Hambledon, 1984.

———. "Lollardy and Sedition, 1381–1431." *Past and Present* 17, 1 (1960): 1–44.

Auchter, Dorothy. *Dictionary of Literary and Dramatic Censorship in Tudor and Stuart England.* Westwood, Conn.: Greenwood, 2001.

Axton, Richard. *European Drama of the Early Middle Ages.* Pittsburgh: University of Pittsburgh Press, 1975.

Badinter, Élisabeth. *The Conflict: How Modern Motherhood Undermines the Status of Women.* Trans. Adriana Hunter. New York: Metropolitan Books, 2012.

Baird, Joseph, and Lorrayne Y. Baird. "Fabliau Form and the Hegge *Joseph's Return*." *Chaucer Review* 8, 2 (1973): 159–66.

Baker, Joan, and Susan Signe Morrison. "The Luxury of Gender: *Piers Plowman* B.9 and the *Merchant's Tale*." In Hewett-Smith, *William Langland's* Piers Plowman, 41–67.

Barker, Isabelle. "Editing Pornography." In Cornell, *Feminism and Pornography*, 643–52.

Bakhtin, Mikhail. *Rabelais and His World*, Trans. Helene Iswolsky. Cambridge, Mass.: MIT Press, 1968.

Baldwin, Anna. *A Guidebook to* Piers Plowman. New York: Palgrave Macmillan, 2007.

Bardsley, Sandy. *Venomous Tongues: Speech and Gender in Late Medieval England.* Philadelphia: University of Pennsylvania Press, 2006.

Barnett, Pamela. "'And shortly for to sayn they were aton': Chaucer's Deflection of Rape in the *Reeve's* and *Franklin's Tales*." *Women's Studies: An Interdisciplinary Journal* 22 (1993): 145–62.

Barney, Stephen A. "Langland's Mighty Line." In Hewett-Smith, *William Langland's* Piers Plowman, 103–18.

———. *The Penn Commentary on* Piers Plowman. Vol. 5, *C Passūs 20–22; B Passūs 18–20*. Philadelphia: University of Pennsylvania Press, 2006.

Barnie, John. *War in Medieval English Society: Social Values in the Hundred Years War, 1337–99*. Ithaca, N.Y.: Cornell University Press, 1974.

Barr, Jessica. *Willing to Know God: Dreamers and Visionaries in the Later Middle Ages*. Columbus: Ohio State University Press, 2010.

Barron, Caroline M. "'The Golden Age' of Women in Medieval London." In *Medieval Women in Southern England*, 35–85. Reading Medieval Studies 15. Reading: University of Reading, Graduate Centre for Medieval Studies, 1989.

———. "The Political Culture of Medieval London." In *The Fifteenth Century IV: Political Culture in Late Medieval Britain*, ed. Linda Clark and Christine Carpenter, 111–33. London: Boydell, 2004.

Baswell, Christopher. "*Troy Book*: How Lydgate Translates Chaucer into Latin." In *Translation Theory and Practice in the Middle Ages*, ed. Jeanette Beer. 215–37. Kalamazoo, Mich.: Medieval Institute, 1997.

Beckwith, Sarah. "Problems of Authority in Late Medieval English Mysticism: Language, Agency, and Authority in the *Book of Margery Kempe*." *Exemplaria* 4, 1 (1992): 172–99.

———. *Signifying God: Social Relation and Symbolic Act in the York Corpus Christi Plays*. Chicago: University of Chicago Press, 2001.

———. "A Very Material Mysticism: The Medieval Mysticism of Margery Kempe." In *Medieval Literature: Criticism, Ideology and History*, ed. David Aers, 34–57. New York: St. Martin's, 1986.

Bédier, Joseph. *Les fabliaux: Études de littérature populaire et d'histoire littéraire du moyen âge*. Paris: Champion, 1893.

Beidler, Peter. "The *Reeve's Tale*." In *Sources and Analogues of the* Canterbury Tales, ed. Robert M. Correale and Mary Hamel, vol. 1, 23–74. Suffolk: Brewer, 2002.

Bellamy, John G. *The Criminal Trial in Later Medieval England: Felony Before the Courts from Edward I to the Sixteenth Century*. Toronto: University of Toronto Press, 1998.

Bennett, Judith. *History Matters: Patriarchy and the Challenge of Feminism*. Manchester: Manchester University Press, 2006.

———. "Misogyny, Popular Culture and Women's Work." *History Workshop: A Journal of Socialist and Feminist Historians* 31, 1 (1991): 166–88.

Bennett, Michael J. "Henry VII and the Northern Rising of 1489." *English Historical Review* 105 (1990): 34–59.

Benson, C. David. "Civic Lydgate: The Poet and London." In *John Lydgate: Poetry, Culture, and Lancastrian England*, ed. Larry Scanlon and James Simpson, 147–68. Notre Dame, Ind.: University of Notre Dame Press, 2006.

———. *Public Piers Plowman: Modern Scholarship and Late Medieval English Culture*. University Park: Pennsylvania State University Press, 2005.

Benson, Larry. "The 'Queynte' Punnings of Chaucer's Critics." In *Studies in the Age of Chaucer, Proceedings* 2, ed. Paul Strohm and Thomas Heffernan, 23–47. Knoxville, Tenn.: New Chaucer Society, 1985.

Bergson, Henri. *Laughter: An Essay on the Meaning of the Comic*. Trans. Cloudesley Brereton and Fred Rothwell. London: Macmillan, 1911.

Bishop, Kathleen. "The Influence of Plautus and Latin Elegaic Comedy on the Fabliaux of Chaucer." *Chaucer Review* 35, 3 (2001): 294–317.

Bloch, R. Howard. *The Scandal of the Fabliau*. Chicago: University of Chicago Press, 1986.

Bloomfield, Morton W. *Piers Plowman as a Fourteenth-Century Apocalypse*. New Brunswick, N.J.: Rutgers University Press, 1961.

Boeckl, Christine M., ed. *Images of Plague and Pestilence: Iconography and Iconology*. Kirksville, Mo.: Truman State University Press, 2000.

Boitani, Piero. *English Medieval Narrative in the Thirteenth and Fourteenth Centuries*. Trans. Joan Krakover Hall. Cambridge: Cambridge University Press, 1982.

Boose, Lynda E. "The 1599 Bishop's Ban, Elizabethan Pornography, and the Sexualization of the Jacobean Stage." In *Enclosure Acts: Sexuality, Property, and Culture in Early Modern England*, ed. Richard Burt and John Michael Archer, 185–200. Ithaca, N.Y.: Cornell University Press, 1994.

Bourdieu, Pierre. *Masculine Domination*. Trans. Richard Nice. Stanford, Calif.: Stanford University Press, 2001.

Bowers, John. *Chaucer and Langland: The Antagonistic Tradition*. Notre Dame, Ind.: University of Notre Dame Press, 2007.

Breuer, Heidi. "Being Intolerant: Rape Is Not Seduction (in the *Reeve's Tale* or Anywhere Else)." In *The Canterbury Tales Revisited: 21st Century Interpretations*, ed. Kathleen Bishop, 1–15. Newcastle: Cambridge Scholars Publishing, 2008.

Bright, Susie. *Susie Bright's Sexual State of the Union*. New York: Simon and Schuster, 1997.

Brown, Andrew. *Church and Society in England: 1000–1500*. New York: Palgrave Macmillan, 2003.

Brundage, James. *Law, Sex and Christian Society in Medieval Europe*. Chicago: University of Chicago Press, 1987.

———. "Rape and Marriage in Medieval Canon Law." *Revue de Droit Canonique* 28 (1978): 62–75.

———. "Rape and Seduction in the Medieval Canon Law." In *Sexual Practices and the Medieval Church*, ed. Vern Bullough, 141–48. Buffalo, N.Y.: Prometheus, 1982.

Bullough, Vern. "On Being Male in the Middle Ages." In *Medieval Masculinities: Regarding Men in the Middle Ages*, ed. Clare A. Lees, 31–46. Minneapolis: University of Minnesota Press, 1994.

Burger, Glenn. *Chaucer's Queer Nation*. Minneapolis: University of Minnesota Press, 2003.

———. "In the Merchant's Bedchamber." In *Thresholds of Medieval Visual Culture: Liminal Spaces*, ed. Elina Gertsman and Jill Stevenson, 239–59. Woodbridge: Boydell, 2012.

Burke, Peter. "Tacitism, Scepticism, and Reason of State," In Burns, *Cambridge History of Political Thought*, 479–98.

Burns, E. Jane. *Bodytalk: When Women Speak in Old French Literature*. Philadelphia: University of Pennsylvania Press, 1993.

Burns, J. H., ed. *The Cambridge History of Political Thought: 1450–1700*. Cambridge: Cambridge University Press, 1991.

Burrow, J. A. "Lady Meed and the Power of Money." *Medium Aevum* 74 (2005): 113–18.

Busby, Keith. "Conspicuous by Its Absence: The English Fabliau." *Dutch Quarterly Review of Anglo-American Letters* 12 (1981): 30–41.

———. "*Dame Sirith* and *De Clerico et Puella*." In *Companion to Early Middle English Literature*, ed. N. H. G. E. Veldhoen and H. Aertsen, 69–81. Amsterdam: VU University Press, 1995.

Butler, Judith. "The Force of Fantasy: Feminism, Mapplethorpe, and Discursive Excess." In Cornell, *Feminism and Pornography*, 487–508.

Butler, Sara. "'I Will Never Consent to be Wedded with You!': Coerced Marriage in the Courts of Medieval England." *Canadian Journal of History* 39 (2004): 247–70.

Byrne, Joseph Patrick, ed. *The Encyclopedia of Pestilence, Pandemics, and Plagues*. Westport, Conn.: Greenwood, 2008.

Calabrese, Michael. "Being a Man in *Piers Plowman* and *Troilus and Criseyde*." In *Men and Masculinities in Chaucer's* Troilus and Criseyde, ed. Tison Pugh and Marcia Smith Marzec, 161–82. Cambridge: Brewer, 2008.

Camille, Michael. *Image on the Edge: The Margins of Medieval Art*. London: Reaktion, 1992.

———. "Obscenity Under Erasure: Censorship in Medieval Illuminated Manuscripts." In Ziolkowski, *Obscenity*, 139–54.

Cannon, Christopher. "Chaucer and Rape: Uncertainty's Certainties." *Studies in the Age of Chaucer* 22 (2000): 67–92.

Carpenter, Christine. *Locality and Polity: A Study of Warwickshire Landed Society, 1401–1499*. Cambridge: Cambridge University Press, 1992.

Carroll, Margaret D. *Painting and Politics in Northern Europe: Van Eyck, Bruegel, Rubens, and Their Contemporaries*. University Park: Pennsylvania State University Press, 2008.

Carter, Angela. *The Sadeian Woman*. London: Virago, 2006.

Caviness, Madeline H. "Obscenity and Alterity: Images That Shock and Offend Us/Them, Now/Then?" In Ziolkowski, *Obscenity*, 155–75.

Chambers, E. K. *The Medieval Stage*. Oxford: Clarendon, 1903.

Chance, Jane. "Christine de Pizan as Literary Mother: Women's Authority and Subjectivity in *The Floure and the Leafe* and *The Assembly of Ladies*." In *The City of Scholars: New Approaches to Christine de Pizan*, ed. Margarete Zimmerman and Dina DeRentiis, 245–59. Berlin: Walter de Gruyter, 1994.

Chomsky, Noam, and Edward S. Herman. *Manufacturing Consent: The Political Economy of the Mass Media*. New York: Pantheon, 1988.

Christie, Sheila K. "Bridging the Jurisdictional Divide: The Masons and the York Corpus Christi Play." In *The York Mystery Plays: Performance in the City*, ed. Margaret Rogerson, 53–74. Woodbridge: York Medieval Press, 2011.

Clifton, Nicole. "The Romance Convention of the Disguised Duel and the Climax of *Piers Plowman*." *Yearbook of Langland Studies* 7 (1993): 123–28.

Clopper, Lawrence. "Lay and Clerical Impact on Civic Religious Drama and Ceremony." *Contexts for Early English Drama*, ed. Marianne G. Briscoe and John C. Coldewey, 103–37. Indianapolis: Indiana University Press, 1989.

———. "Middle English Drama: From Ungodly Ludi to Sacred Play." In *The Cambridge History of Medieval English Literature*, ed. David Wallace, 739–66. Cambridge: Cambridge University Press, 1999.

———. "Miracula and *The Tretise of Miraclis Pleyinge*." *Speculum* 65 (1990): 878–905.

———. "The Persistence of 'Medieval Drama' in the Tudor and Elizabethan Periods." In *Drama, Play, and Game: English Festive Culture in the Medieval and Early Modern Period*, 268–93. Chicago: University of Chicago Press, 2001.

Coldewey, John. "The Non-Cycle Plays and the East Anglian Tradition." In *The Cambridge Companion to Medieval English Theatre*, ed. Richard Beadle, 189–210. Cambridge: Cambridge University Press, 1994.

Cole, Andrew. *Literature and Heresy in the Age of Chaucer*. Cambridge: Cambridge University Press, 2008.

Coleman, Janet. *A History of Political Thought: From the Middle Ages to the Renaissance*. Oxford: Oxford University Press, 2000.

Coletti, Theresa. "A Feminist Approach to the Corpus Christi Cycles." In *Approaches to Teaching Medieval Drama*, ed. Richard K. Emmerson, 78–89. New York: Modern Language Association, 1990.

———. "Geneology, Sexuality, and Sacred Power: The Saint Anne Dedication of the Digby *Candlemas Day and the Killing of the Children of Israel*." *Journal of Medieval and Early Modern Studies* 29, 1 (1999): 25–59.

———. "'Ther be but women': Gender Conflict and Gender Identity in the Middle English Innocents Plays." *Medievalia* 18 (1995): 245–61

Cooke, Thomas. "Tales." in *A Manual of Writings in Middle English, 1050–1500*, vol. 9, 3138–3328. Hamden, Conn: Archon, 1992.

Cooper, Helen. "Gender and Personification in *Piers Plowman*." *Yearbook of Langland Studies* 5 (1991): 31–48.

———. "Langland's and Chaucer's Prologues." *Yearbook of Langland Studies* 1 (1987): 71–81.

Cornell, Drucilla, ed. *Feminism and Pornography*. Oxford: Oxford University Press, 2000.

———. "Introduction." In Cornell, *Feminism and Pornography*, 1–16.

Cossman, Brenda, and Shannon Bell. Introduction. In *Bad Attitude/s on Trial: Pornography, Feminism, and the Butler Decision*, ed. Brenda Cossman et al., 3–47. Toronto: University of Toronto Press, 1997.

Crane, Susan. *Gender and Romance in Chaucer's Canterbury Tales*. Princeton, N.J.: Princeton University Press, 1994.

———. "The Writing Lesson of 1381." In *Chaucer's England: Literature in Historical Context*, ed. Barbara Hanawalt, 201–21. Minneapolis: University of Minnesota Press, 1992.

Craun, Edwin. *Lies, Slander, and Obscenity in Medieval English Literature: Pastoral Rhetoric and the Deviant Speaker*. Cambridge: Cambridge University Press, 1997.

Crawford, Anne. "The King's Burden? The Consequences of Royal Marriage in Fifteenth-Century England." In *Patronage, the Crown and the Provinces in Later Medieval England*, ed. Ralph A. Griffiths, 33–56. Gloucester: Sutton Humanities Press, 1981.

Crocker, Holly. "Affective Politics in Chaucer's *Reeve's Tale*: 'Cherl' Masculinity After 1381." *Studies in the Age of Chaucer* 29 (2007): 225–58.

Davis, Isabel. *Writing Masculinity in the Later Middle Ages*. Cambridge: Cambridge University Press, 2007.

Davis, Natalie. "Women on Top." In *Society and Culture in Early Modern France: Eight Essays*, 124–51. Stanford, Calif.: Stanford University Press, 1975.

De Jean, Joan. *The Reinvention of Obscenity: Sex, Lies, and Tabloids in Early Modern France*. Chicago: University of Chicago Press, 2002.

De Julleville, Petit. *Histoire du théâtre en France: Les Mystères*. Paris: Hachette, 1880.

Delany, Sheila. "Anatomy of a Resisting Reader: Some Implications of Resistance to Sexual Word Play in Medieval Literature." *Exemplaria* 4 (1992): 7–34.

———. "The Logic of Obscenity in Chaucer's *Legend of Good Women*." *Florilegium* 7 (1985): 189–205.

———. "Sexual Economics, Chaucer's Wife of Bath, and the *Book of Margery Kempe*." *Minnesota Review* 5 (1975): 105–15.

Dentith, Simon. *Bakhtinian Thought: An Introductory Reader*. London: Routledge, 1995.

Dewar, Michael. "Introduction." *Statius' Thebaid IX*, ed. with English translation and commentary by Michael Dewar, xv–xlviii. Oxford Classical Monographs. Oxford: Clarendon, 1991.

Dillon, Jeanette. *Language and Stage in Medieval and Renaissance England*. Cambridge: Cambridge University Press, 1998.

Dines, Gail. *Pornland: How Porn Has Hijacked Our Sexuality*. Boston: Beacon, 2010.

Dobson, R. B. "Craft Guilds and City: The Historical Origins of the York Mystery Plays Reassessed." In *The Stage as Mirror: Civic Theatre in Late Medieval Europe*, ed. Alan E. Knight, 91–106. Cambridge: Brewer, 1997.

Dodds, Ben, and Christian D. Liddy, eds. *Commercial Activity, Markets, and Entrepreneurs in the Middle Ages: Essays in Honour of Richard Britnell*. Woodbridge: Boydell and Brewer, 2011.

Dominik, William J. *The Mythic Voice of Statius: Power and Politics in the Thebaid*. Leiden: Brill, 1994.

Donaldson, E. Talbot. *"Piers Plowman": The C-Text and Its Poet*. New Haven, Conn.: Yale University Press, 1949.

Dronke, Peter. *The Medieval Poet and His World*. Rome: Edizioni di Sotria e Letteratura, 1984.

Dunton-Downer, Leslie. "Poetic Language and the Obscene." In Ziolkowski, *Obscenity*, 19–38.

Dworkin, Andrea. "Against the Male Flood: Censorship, Pornography, and Equality." In Cornell, *Feminism and Pornography*, 19–38.

——. *Pornography: Men Possessing Women*. New York: Plume, 1991.

Eagleton, Terry. *Walter Benjamin, Or, Towards a Revolutionary Criticism*. London: Verso, 1981.

Earenfight, Theresa. *Queenship in Medieval Europe*. New York: Palgrave, 2013.

Eco, Umberto. "The Frames of Comic 'Freedom'." In *Carnival!* ed. Thomas A. Sebeok, 1–9. Berlin: Mouton 1984.

Elliott, Dyan. *Spiritual Marriage: Sexual Abstinence in Medieval Wedlock*. Princeton, N. J.: Princeton University Press, 1993.

Ellis, Deborah. "The Merchant's Wife's Tale: Language, Sex and Commerce in Margery Kempe and in Chaucer." *Exemplaria* 2 (1990): 595–626.

Epstein, Robert. "Lydgate's Mummings and the Aristocratic Resistance to Drama." *Comparative Drama* 36 (2002): 337–58.

Erler, Mary C. "Margery Kempe's White Clothes." *Medium Aevum* 62, 1 (1993): 78–83.

Evans, Ruth. "Body Politics: Engendering the Medieval Cycle Drama." In *Feminist Readings in Middle English Literature: The Wife of Bath and All Her Sect*, ed. Ruth Evans and Lesley Johnson, 112–39. New York: Routledge, 1994.

——. "*The Book of Margery Kempe*." In *A Companion to Medieval English Literature and Culture c. 1350–c. 1500*, ed. Peter Brown. London: Blackwell, 2007.

——. "Feminist Re-Enactments: Gender and the Towneley Uxor Noe." In *A Wyf Ther Was: Essays in Honour of Paule Mertens-Fonck*, ed. Juliette Dor, 141–54. Liège: University of Liège, 1992.

Fein, Susanna. "Appendix: The Contents, Quires, and Independent Blocks of MS Harley 2253." In *Studies in the Harley Manuscript: The Scribes, Contents, and Social Contexts of British Library MS 2253*. Kalamazoo, Mich.: Medieval Institute Publications, 2000.

Findlen, Paula. "Humanism, Politics, and Pornography in Renaissance Italy." In Hunt, *Invention of Pornography*, 49–108.

Fitzgerald, Christina. *The Drama of Masculinity and Medieval English Guild Culture*. New York: Palgrave, 2007.

——. "Manning the Ark in York and Chester." *Exemplaria* 15, 2 (2003): 351–84.

Flanigan, C. Clifford. "Liminality, Carnival, and Social Structure: The Case of Late Medieval Biblical Drama." In *Victor Turner and the Construction of Cultural Criticism: Between Literature and Anthropology*, ed. Kathleen Ashley, 42–63. Bloomington: Indiana University Press, 1990.

Fleming, Peter. *Family and Household in Medieval England*. Basingstoke: Palgrave, 2001.

Fletcher, Anthony, and Diarmaid MacCulloch. *Tudor Rebellions*. 5th ed. New York: Routledge, 2008.

Forrest, Ian. *The Detection of Heresy in Late Medieval England*. New York: Oxford University Press, 2005.

Foucault, Michel. *The Archaeology of Knowledge*. Trans. A. M. Sheridan Smith. 1972. New York: Routledge Classics, 2002.

——. *Discipline and Punish: The Birth of the Prison*. Trans. Alan Sheridan. 2nd ed. New York: Vintage, 1995.

——. *The History of Sexuality*. Vol. 1. Trans. Robert Hurley. London: Penguin, 1998.

——. "History of Systems of Thought." In *Language, Countermemory, Practice: Selected Essays and Interviews by Michel Foucault*, ed. Donald F. Bouchard, trans. Donald F. Bouchard and Sherry Simon, 199–204. Ithaca, N.Y.: Cornell University Press, 1977.

Fowler, Elizabeth. "Civil Death and the Maiden: Agency and the Conditions of Contract in *Piers Plowman*." *Speculum* 70 (1995): 760–92.

Frank, Robert Worth, Jr. "The *Reeve's Tale* and the Comedy of Limitation." In *Directions in Literary Criticism: Contemporary Approaches to Literature*, ed. Stanley Weintraub and Phillip Young, 53–69. University Park: Pennsylvania University Press, 1973.

Franklin, Julian H. "Sovereignty and the Mixed Constitution: Bodin and His Critics." In Burns, *Cambridge History of Political Thought*, 298–328.

French, Katherine. *The Good Women of the Parish: Gender and Religion After the Black Death*. Philadelphia: University of Pennsylvania Press, 2008.

———. "To Free Them from Binding: Women in the Late Medieval English Parish." *Journal of Interdisciplinary History* 27 (1997): 387–412.

Friedman, John Block. *Orpheus in the Middle Ages*. Cambridge, Mass.: Harvard University Press, 1970.

Fryde, E. B. *Peasants and Landlords in Later Medieval England*. New York: St. Martin's, 1996.

Furrow, Melissa. "Middle English Fabliau and Modern Myth." *ELH* 56, 1 (1989): 1–18.

Galloway, Andrew. *The Penn Commentary on* Piers Plowman, *Volume 1*. Philadelphia: University of Pennsylvania Press, 2006.

Gardiner, Harold C. *Mysteries' End: An Investigation of the Last Days of the Medieval Religious Stage*. New Haven, Conn.: Yale University Press, 1946. Rpt. New York: Archon, 1967.

Gaunt, Simon. *Gender and Genre in Medieval French Literature*. Cambridge: Cambridge University Press, 1995.

———. "Obscene Hermeneutics in Troubadour Lyric." In *Medieval Obscenities*, ed. Nicola McDonald, 85–104. York: York Medieval Press, 2006.

Gibson, Gail McMurray. *Theatre of Devotion: East Anglian Drama and Society in the Late Middle Ages*. Chicago: University of Chicago Press, 1989.

Goldberg, P. J. P. "From Tableaux to Text: The York Corpus Christi Play ca. 1378–1428." *Viator: Medieval and Renaissance Studies* 43 (2012): 247–76.

———. *Women, Work and Life Cycle in a Medieval Economy: Women in York and Yorkshire*. Oxford: Oxford University Press, 1992.

Goodall, Peter. "An Outline History of the English Fabliau After Chaucer." *Journal of Australian Universities Language and Literature Association* 57 (1982): 5–23.

Goodman, Anthony. *Margery Kempe and Her World*. Edinburgh: Longman, 2002.

Gottfried, Robert S. *Bury St. Edmunds and the Urban Crisis: 1290–1539*. Princeton, N.J.: Princeton University Press, 1982.

———. *Epidemic Disease in Fifteenth-Century England: The Medical Response and the Demographic Consequences*. New Brunswick, N.J.: Rutgers University Press, 1978.

Grady, Frank. "Chaucer Reading Langland: *The House of Fame*." *Studies in the Age of Chaucer* 18 (1996): 3–23.

Gravdal, Kathryn. *Ravishing Maidens: Writing Rape in Medieval French Literature and Law*. Philadelphia: University of Pennsylvania Press, 1991.

Green, Richard Firth. "Three Fifteenth-Century Notes." *English Language Notes* 14 (1976): 14–17

Grössinger, Christina. *The World Upside-Down: English Misericords*. London: Harvey Miller, 1997.

Hagedorne, Suzanne. *Abandoned Women: Rewriting the Classics in Dante, Boccaccio and Chaucer*. Ann Arbor: University of Michigan Press, 2004.

Hajnal, John. "European Marriage Patterns in Perspective." In *Population in History: Essays in Historical Demography*, ed. D. V. Glass and D. E. C. Eversley, 101–43. London: Edward Arnold, 1965.

Hanawalt, Barbara. *The Ties That Bound: Peasant Families in Medieval England*. Oxford: Oxford University Press, 1986.

———. *The Wealth of Wives: Women, Law, and Economy in Late Medieval London*. Oxford: Oxford University Press, 2007.

Hanning, R. W. "'The Struggle Between Noble Designs and Chaos': The Literary Tradition of Chaucer's Knight's Tale." *Literary Review* 23 (1980): 519–41.

Hansen, Elaine Tuttle. *Chaucer and the Fictions of Gender.* Berkeley: University of California Press, 1992.

Harris, Barbara J. *English Aristocratic Women, 1450–1550: Marriage and Family, Property and Careers.* Oxford: Oxford University Press, 2002.

Harris, Carissa M. "Inserting 'A grete tente, a thrifty, and a long': Sexual Obscenity and Scribal Innovation in Fifteenth-Century Manuscripts of *The Canterbury Tales*." *Essays in Medieval Studies* 27 (2011): 45–60.

Harriss, Gerald. *Shaping the Nation: England, 1360–1461.* Oxford: Clarendon, 2005.

Hartman, Mary S. *The Household and the Making of History: A Subversive View of the Western Past.* Cambridge: Cambridge University Press, 2004.

Harwood, Britton J. "Dame Study and the Place of Orality in *Piers Plowman*." *ELH* 57, 1 (1990): 1–17.

Haskell, Ann S. "The Paston Women on Marriage in Fifteenth-Century England." *Viator* 4 (1973): 459–71.

Helmholz, Richard. *Marriage Litigation in Medieval England.* Cambridge: Cambridge University Press, 1974.

Helterman, Jeffrey. *Symbolic Action in the Plays of the Wakefield Master.* Athens: University of Georgia Press, 1981.

Henderson, Jeffrey. *The Maculate Muse.* New Haven, Conn.: Yale University Press, 1975.

Herlihy, David. "The Family and Religious Ideologies in Medieval Europe." In *Women, Family, and Society in Medieval Europe: Historical Essays, 1978–1991*, 154–73. Providence, R.I.: Berghahn Books, 1995.

Herzen, Alexander. "A Letter Criticizing *The Bell* [1858]." In *A Herzen Reader*, ed. and trans. Kathleen Parthé, 68–69. Chicago: Northwestern University Press, 2012.

Hewett-Smith, Kathleen M., ed. *William Langland's* Piers Plowman: *A Book of Essays.* New York: Routledge, 2001.

Hill, Christopher. *Society and Puritanism in Pre-Revolutionary England.* New York: Schocken, 1964.

Hill-Vasquez, Heather. *Sacred Players: The Politics of Response in the Middle English Drama.* Washington, D.C.: Catholic University of America Press, 2007.

Hilton, Rodney. *Bond Men Made Free: Medieval Peasant Movements and the Uprising of 1381.* New York: Viking, 1973.

———. *English and French Towns in Feudal Society.* Cambridge: Cambridge University Press, 1992.

Hines, John. *The Fabliau in English.* New York: Longman, 1993.

Hirsh, John C. "Author and Scribe in *The Book of Margery Kempe*." *Medium Aevum* 44 (1975): 145–50.

Honigmann, John Joseph. "A Cultural Theory of Obscenity." *Journal of Criminal Psychopathology* 5 (1944): 715–33.

Howell, Martha. "Citizenship and Gender: Women's Political Status in Northern Medieval Cities." In *Women and Power in the Middle Ages*, ed. Mary Erler and Maryanne Kowaleski, 37–60. Athens: University of Georgia Press, 1987.

———. "The Properties of Marriage in Late Medieval Europe: Commercial Wealth and the Creation of Modern Marriage." In *Love, Marriage, and Family Ties in the Later Middle Ages*, ed. Isabel Davis, Miriam Müller, and Sarah Rees Jones, 17–61. Turnhout: Brepols, 2001.

Huizinga, Johan. *The Autumn of the Middle Ages.* Trans. Rodney J. Payton and Ulrich Mammitzsch. Chicago: University of Chicago Press, 1996.

Humphrey, Chris. *The Politics of Carnival: Festive Misrule in Medieval England.* Manchester: Manchester University Press, 2001.

Hunt, Lynn. "Introduction." In Hunt, *Invention of Pornography*, 9–45.

———. "Pornography and the French Revolution." In Hunt, *Invention of Pornography*, 301–39.

———. ed. *The Invention of Pornography: Obscenity and the Origins of Modernity 1500–1800*. New York: Zone Books, 1993.

Huppé, Bernard. *A Reading of the Canterbury Tales*. Albany: State University of New York Press, 1964.

Hurwood, Bernhardt J. *The Facetiae of Giovanni Francesco Poggio Bracciolini: A New Translation by Bernhardt J. Hurwood*. New York: Award Books, 1968.

Ingham, Patricia. "Homosociality and Creative Masculinity in the *Knight's Tale*." In *Masculinities in Chaucer: Approaches to Maleness in the* Canterbury Tales, ed. Peter Beidler, 23–35. Cambridge: Brewer, 1998.

Ingram, Martin. "'Scolding women cucked or washed': A Crisis in Gender Relations in Early Modern England?" In *Women, Crime, and the Courts in Early Modern England*, ed. Jennifer Kermode and Garthine Walker, 48–80. Chapel Hill: University of North Carolina Press, 1994.

Jacob, Ernest Fraser. *The Fifteenth Century: 1399–1485*. Oxford: Oxford University Press, 1969.

James, Mervyn. "Ritual, Drama, and the Social Body in the Late Medieval English Town." *Past and Present 98* (1983): 3–29.

Jensen, Robert. *Getting Off: Pornography and the End of Masculinity*. Cambridge, Mass.: South End Press, 2007.

Jermain, James, and Anthony Weir. *Images of Lust: Sexual Carvings in Medieval Churches*. London: Batsford, 1986.

Johnson, Barbara. *Reading* Piers Plowman *and the* Pilgrim's Progress: *Reception and the Protestant Reader*. Carbondale: Southern Illinois University Press, 1992.

Johnson, Jennifer A. "To Catch A Curious Clicker: A Social Network Analysis of the Online Pornography Industry." In *Everyday Pornography*, ed. Karen Boyle, 147–62. New York: Routledge, 2010.

Justice, Steven. "The Genres of Piers Plowman." *Viator* 19 (1988): 291–306.

Kaeuper, Richard. *War, Justice, and Public Order: England and France in the Later Middle Ages*. Oxford: Clarendon, 1988.

Kantorowicz, Ernst H. *The King's Two Bodies: A Study in Mediaeval Political Theology*. Princeton, N. J.: Princeton University Press, 1957.

Karras, Ruth Mazo. *From Boys to Men: Formations of Masculinity in Late Medieval Europe*. Philadelphia: University of Pennsylvania Press, 2003.

———. "*Lecherous Songys*: Medieval Sexuality in Word and Deed." In Ziolkowski, *Obscenity*, 233–45.

Keene, Derek. "Crisis Management in London's Food Supply." In Dodds and Liddy, *Markets, and Entrepreneurs*, 45–62.

Kelly, Henry Ansgar. "Statutes of Rapes and Alleged Ravishers of Wives." *Viator* 28 (1997): 361–419.

Kerby-Fulton, Kathryn. "Piers Plowman." In *The Cambridge History of Medieval English Literature*, ed. David Wallace, 513–38. Cambridge: Cambridge University Press, 1999.

Kerby-Fulton, Kathryn, and Steven Justice. "Langlandian Reading Circles and the Civil Service in London and Dublin, 1380–1427." *New Medieval Literatures* 1 (1997): 59–83.

Kimmel, Michael S. *Guyland: The Perilous World Where Boys Become Men*. New York: Harper Collins, 2008.

Kipnis, Laura. *Bound and Gagged: Pornography and the Politics of Fantasy in America*. New York: Grove Press, 1996.

Kohanski, Tamarah. "In Search of Malyne." *Chaucer Review* 27 (1995): 228–38.

Koldeweij, A. M. "A Bare-Faced Roman de la Rose (Paris, B.N. ms. Fr25526) and Some Late Medieval Mass-Produced Badges of a Sexual Nature." In *Flanders in a European Perspective: Manuscript Illumination in Flanders and Abroad,* ed. M. Smeyers and B. Cardon, 499–516. Leuven: Peeters, 1994.

———. "Lifting the Veil on Pilgrim Badges." In *Pilgrimage Explored*, ed. J. Stopford, 161–88. York Studies in Medieval Theology. York: York Medieval Press, 1999.

———. "The Wearing of Significant Badges, Religious and Secular: The Social Meaning of a Behavioral Pattern." In *Showing Status: Representation of Social Positions in the Late Middle Ages*, ed. Willem Blockmans and A. Janse, 307–28. Turnhout: Brepols, 1999.

Kolve, V. A. *Chaucer and the Imagery of Narrative: The First Five Canterbury Tales*. Stanford, Calif.: Stanford University Press, 1984.

———. *The Play Called Corpus Christi*. Stanford, Calif.: Stanford University Press, 1966.

Krueger, Roberta. *Women Readers and the Ideology of Gender in Old French Verse Romance*. Cambridge: Cambridge University Press, 1993.

La Barre, Weston. "Obscenity: An Anthropological Appraisal." *Law and Contemporary Problems* 20 (1955): 533–43.

Lacquer, Thomas. *Making Sex: Body and Gender from the Greeks to Freud*. Cambridge, Mass.: Harvard University Press, 1990.

Lawton, David. "Dullness and the Fifteenth Century." *English Literary History* 54 (1987): 761–99.

———. "Voice, Authority, and Blasphemy in *The Book of Margery Kempe*." In *Margery Kempe: A Book of Essays*, ed. S. J. McEntire, 93–115. New York: Garland, 1992.

Lee, John S. "Grain Shortages in Late Medieval Towns." In Dodds and Liddy, *Markets, and Entrepreneurs*, 63–80.

Lees, Clare. "Gender and Exchange in *Piers Plowman*." In *Class and Gender in Early English Literature*, ed. Britton J. Harwood and Gillian Overing, 112–30. Bloomington: Indiana University Press, 1994.

Leff, Gordon. *Heresy in the Later Middle Ages: The Relation of Heterodoxy to Dissent c. 1250–c.1450*. Manchester: Manchester University Press, 1967.

Lessa, Iara. "Discursive Struggles Within Social Welfare: Restaging Teen Motherhood." *British Journal of Social Work* 36 (2006): 283–98.

Levin, Carole. "Catherine of Valois." In *Historical Dictionary of Late Medieval England, 1272–1485*, ed. Ronald H. Fritze, William Baxter Robison, and Ann E. Faulkner, 94–95. Westport, Conn.: Greenwood Press, 2002.

Levy, Brian. *The Comic Text: Patterns and Images in the Old French Fabliaux*. Amsterdam: Rodopi, 2000.

Lewis, C. S. *The Allegory of Love: A Study in Medieval Tradition*. London: Oxford University Press, 1936.

Lipton, Emma. *Affections of the Mind: The Politics of Sacramental Marriage in Late Medieval English Literature*. Notre Dame, Ind.: Notre Dame University Press, 2007.

Lochrie, Karma. *Margery Kempe and Translations of the Flesh*. Philadelphia: University of Pennsylvania Press, 1991.

———. "Women's 'Pryvetees' and Fabliau Politics in the Miller's Tale." *Exemplaria* 6 (1994): 287–304.

Loomis, Roger. "Some Evidence for Secular Theatres in the Twelfth and Thirteenth Centuries." *Theatre Annual* 3 (1945): 33–43.

Lorde, Audre. "The Master's Tools Will Never Dismantle the Master's House." In *Sister Outsider*, 110–13. New York: Crossing Press, 1984.

Lowes, J. L. "The Prologue to the *Legend of Good Women* Considered in Its Chronological Relations." *PMLA* 20 (1905): 789–864.

Lyons, Gabrielle. "*Avoir* and *Savoir*: A Strategic Approach to the Old French Fabliaux." Ph.D. dissertation, Cambridge University, 1992.

MacCracken, Henry Noble. "The Lydgate Canon." In *The Minor Poems of John Lydgate*, Part II, ed. Henry Noble MacCracken. EETS, e.s. 107. Oxford: Oxford University Press, 1911, 1962.

Macfarlane, Alan. *Marriage and Love in England*. New York: Blackwell, 1986.

MacKinnon, Catharine. "Feminism, Marxism, Method, and the State: An Agenda for Theory." *Signs* 7 (1982): 515–44.

———. *Only Words*. Cambridge, Mass.: Harvard University Press, 1993.

Maddern, Philippa C. *Violence and Social Order: East Anglia, 1422–42*. Oxford: Clarendon, 1992.

Malcolm, Noel. "Hobbes and Spinoza," In Burns, *Cambridge History of Political Thought*, 530–60.

Marshall, Mary. "Theatre in the Middle Ages: Evidence from Dictionaries and Glosses." *Symposium* 4, 2 (1950): 366–89.

McCoy, Richard. "Gascoigne's 'Poemata castrata': The Wages of Courtly Success." *Criticism* 27 (1985): 29–55.

McDonald, Nicola. "A York Primer and Its Alphabet: Reading Medieval Women in a Lay Household." In *The Oxford Handbook of Medieval Literature in English*, ed. Elaine Treharne and Greg Walker, 181–99. Oxford: Oxford University Press, 2010.

McIntosh, Marjorie. *Controlling Misbehavior in England, 1370–1600*. Cambridge: Cambridge University Press, 1998.

———. "Finding a Language for Misconduct: Jurors in Fifteenth-Century Local Courts." In *Bodies and Disciplines: Intersections of Literature and History in Fifteenth-Century England*, ed. Barbara Hanawalt and David Wallace, 87–122. Minneapolis: University of Minnesota Press, 1996.

———. *Working Women in English Society: 1300–1620*. Cambridge: Cambridge University Press, 2005.

McKeon, Michael. *The Secret History of Domesticity: Public, Private, and the Division of Knowledge*. Baltimore: Johns Hopkins University Press, 2005.

McNamer, Sarah. *Affective Meditation and the Invention of Medieval Compassion*. Philadelphia: University of Pennsylvania Press, 2009.

McNiven, Peter. *Heresy and Politics in the Reign of Henry IV: The Burning of John Badby*. Woodbridge: Boydell and Brewer, 1987.

McSheffrey, Shannon. "Jurors, Respectable Masculinity, and Christian Morality: A Comment on Marjorie McIntosh's *Controlling Misbehavior*." *Journal of British Studies* 37 (1998): 269–78.

———. *Marriage, Sex, and Civic Culture in Late Medieval London*. Philadelphia: University of Pennsylvania Press, 2006

Meech, Sanford B. "Notes." In *The Book of Margery Kempe: The Text from the Unique Ms. Owned by Colonel W. Butler-Bowdon*, vol. 1, ed. Sanford Brown Meech and Hope Emily Allen. London: EETS, 1940.

Meyer-Lee, Robert. *Poets and Power from Chaucer to Wyatt*. Cambridge: Cambridge University Press, 2007.

Middleton, Anne. "Acts of Vagrancy: The C Version 'Autobiography' and the Statute of 1388." In *Written Work: Langland, Labor, and Authorship*, ed. Steven Justice and Kathryn Kerby-Fulton, 208–317. Philadelphia: University of Pennsylvania Press, 1997.

———. "Commentary on an Unacknowledged Text: Chaucer's Debt to Langland." *Yearbook of Langland Studies* 24 (2010): 113–37.

———. "Narration and the Invention of Experience: Episodic Form in *Piers Plowman*." In *The Wisdom of Poetry: Essays in Early English Literature in Honor of Morton W. Bloomfield*, ed. Larry D. Benson and Siegfried Wenzel, 91–122. Kalamazoo, Mich.: Medieval Institute, 1982.

Mills, Sara. *Michel Foucault*. Routledge Critical Thinkers Series. New York: Routledge, 2003.

Mills, Sophie. *Theseus, Tragedy, and the Athenian Empire*. Oxford: Clarendon, 1997.

Minnis, Alastair. *Fallible Authors: Chaucer's Pardoner and Wife of Bath*. Philadelphia: University of Pennsylvania Press, 2008.

Mitchell, Marea. *The Book of Margery Kempe: Scholarship, Community, and Criticism*. New York: Peter Lang, 2005

Moore, R. I. *The Formation of a Persecuting Society: Power and Deviance in Western Europe 950–1250*. Oxford: Blackwell, 1987.

Morrison, Susan Signe. *Excrement in the Late Middle Ages: Sacred Filth and Chaucer's Fecopoetics*. New York: Palgrave, 2008.

Mosher, J. A. *The Exemplum in the Early Religious and Didactic Literature of England*. New York: Columbia University Press, 1911.

Moulton, Ian Frederick. *Before Pornography: Erotic Writings in Early Modern England*. Oxford: Oxford University Press, 2000.

Muir, Lynette R. "Farces, *Sotties*, and Moralities." In *The Medieval European Stage: 500–1550*, ed. William Tydeman, 279–345. Cambridge: Cambridge University Press, 2001.

Murphy, Colette. "Lady Holy Church and Meed the Maid: Re-Envisioning Female Personifications in *Piers Plowman*." In *Feminist Readings in Middle English Literature: The Wife of Bath and All Her Sect*, ed. Ruth Evans and Lesley Johnson, 104–64. London: Routledge: 1994.

Muscatine, Charles. *Chaucer and the French Tradition*. Berkeley: University of California Press, 1957.

———. "Courtly Literature and Vulgar Language." In *Court and Poet: Selected Proceedings of the Third Congress of the International Courtly Literature Society*, ed. Glyn S. Burgess, 1–19. Liverpool: Francis Cairns, 1981.

Niebrzydowski, Sue. *Bonoure and Buxum: A Study of Wives in Late Medieval English Literature*. Bern: Peter Lang, 2006.

Nisse, Ruth. *Defining Acts: Drama and the Politics of Interpretation in Late Medieval England*. Notre Dame, Ind.: University of Notre Dame Press, 2005.

Nolan, Maura. *John Lydgate and the Making of Public Culture*. Cambridge: Cambridge University Press, 2005.

Noonan, John T. "Marriage in the Middle Ages, 1: The Power to Chose." *Viator* 4 (1973): 419–34.

Normington, Katie. *Gender and Medieval Drama*. Cambridge: Brewer, 2004.

Novikoff, Alex J. *The Medieval Culture of Disputation*. Philadelphia: University of Pennsylvania Press, 2013.

Nykrog, Per. *Les fabliaux*. Copenhagen: Ejnar Munksgaard, 1957.

———. "Obscene or not Obscene: On Lady Reason, Jean de Meun and the Fisherman from Pont-seur Seine." In Ziolkowski, *Obscenity*, 319–31.

Olsen, Glending. "The *Reeve's Tale* as Fabliau." *Modern Language Quarterly* 35 (1974): 219–30.

Orme, Nicholas. *English Schools in the Middle Ages*. New York: Methuen, 1973.

Palmer, Barbara. "'Recycling the Wakefield Cycle': The Records." *Research Opportunities in Renaissance Drama* 41 (2002): 88–130.

———. "'Towneley Plays' or 'Wakefield Cycle' Revisted." *Comparative Drama* 21 (1988): 318–48.

Patterson, Lee. *Chaucer and the Subject of History*. Madison: University of Wisconsin Press, 1991.

———. "Making Identities: Henry V and John Lydgate in Fifteenth-Century England." In *New Historical Literary Study: Essays on Reproducing Texts, Representing History*, ed. Jeffrey N. Cox and Larry J. Reynolds, 69–107. Princeton, N.J.: Princeton University Press, 1993.

Paxson, James J. "Queering *Piers Plowman*: The Copula(tion)s of Figures in Medieval Allegory." *Rhetoric Society Quarterly* 29 (1999): 21–29.

Payling, Simon. *Political Society in Lancastrian England: The Greater Gentry of Nottinghamshire*. Oxford: Clarendon, 1991.

Pearcy, Roy J., and Ian Short, "Introduction." In *Eighteen Anglo-Norman Fabliaux*. London: Anglo-Norman Text Society, 2000.

Pearsall, Derek. "The Idea of Universal Salvation in *Piers Plowman* B and C." *Journal of Medieval and Early Modern Studies* 39 (2009): 257–81.

———. *John Lydgate*. London: Routledge and Kegan Paul, 1970.

———. *John Lydgate (1371–1449): A Bio-Bibliography*. English Literary Studies Monograph Series 71. Victoria, B.C.: University of Victoria Press, 1997.

Percival, Florence. *Chaucer's Legendary Good Women*. Cambridge: Cambridge University Press, 1998.

Pettit, Thomas. "'Here Comes I, Jack Straw': English Folk Drama and Social Revolt." *Folklore* 95, 1 (1984): 3–20.

Phythian-Adams, Charles. "Ceremony and the Citizen: The Communal Year at Coventry, 1450–1550." In *Crisis and Order in English Towns, 1500–1700: Essays in Urban History*, ed. Peter Clark and Paul Slack, 57–85. Toronto: University of Toronto Press, 1972.

Post, J. B. "Ravishment of Women and the Statutes of Westminister." In *Legal Records and the Historian*, ed. J. H. Baker, 150–64. London: Royal Historical Society, 1978.

———. "Sir Thomas West and the Statute of Rapes, 1382." *Bulletin of the Institute of Historical Research* 53 (1980): 24–30.

Powell, Edward. *Kingship, Law, and Society: Criminal Justice in the Reign of Henry V*. Oxford: Clarendon, 1989.

Raskolnikov, Masha. "Promising the Female, Delivering the Male: Transformations of Gender in *Piers Plowman*." *Yearbook of Langland Studies* 19, 1 (2006): 81–105.

Rees Jones, Sarah. "'A Peler of Holy Church': Margery Kempe and the Bishops." In *Medieval Women: Texts and Contexts in Late Medieval Britain: Essays for Felicity Riddy*, ed. Jocelyn Wogan-Brown et al., 377–91. Turnhout: Brepols, 2000.

Renoir, Alain. "On the Date of John Lydgate's 'Mumming at Hertford'." *Archive für das Studium der Neurenen Sprachen un Literaturen* 198 (1961): 32–33.

Rich, Adrienne. "When We Dead Awaken: Writing as Re-Vision." *College English* 34 (1972): 18–30.

Riddy, Felicity. "Text and Self in the *Book of Margery Kempe*." In *Voices in Dialogue: Reading Women in the Middle Ages*, ed. Linda Olson and Kathryn Kerby-Fulton, 435–53. Notre Dame, Ind.: University of Notre Dame Press, 2005.

Robertson, D. W., and Bernard F. Huppé. *Piers Plowman and Scriptural Tradition*. Princeton, N.J.: Princeton University Press, 1951.

Robertson, Elizabeth. "Measurement and the 'Feminine' in *Piers Plowman*: A Response to Recent Studies of Langland and Gender." In Hewett-Smith, *William Langland's* Piers Plowman, 167–92.

Rollison, David. *A Commonwealth of the People: Popular Politics and England's Long Social Revolution, 1066–1649*. Cambridge: Cambridge University Press, 2010.

Roy, Bruno. "Getting to the Bottom of St. Caquette's Cult." In Ziolkowski, *Obscenity*, 308–18.

Ryan, Denise. "Womanly Weaponry: Language and Power in the Chester *Slaughter of the Innocents*." *Studies in Philology* 98 (2001): 76–92.

Rychner, Jean. *Contribution à l'étude des fabliaux: Variantes, remaniements, dégradations*. 2 vols. Geneva: Droz, 1960.

Salih, Sarah. *Versions of Virginity in Late Medieval England*. Cambridge: Brewer, 2001.

Sanok, Catherine. "Criseyde, Cassandre, and the *Thebaid*: Women and the Theban Subtext of Chaucer's *Troilus and Criseyde*." *Studies in the Age of Chaucer* 20 (1998): 41–71.

Saunders, Corinne. *Rape and Ravishment in the Literature of Medieval England*. Cambridge: D.S. Brewer, 2001.

Scanlon, Larry. "King, Commons, and Kind Wit: Langland's National Vision and the Rising of 1381." In *Imagining a Medieval English Nation*, ed. Kathy Lavezzo, 191–233. Minneapolis: University of Minnesota Press, 2004.

———. *Narrative, Authority and Power: The Medieval Exemplum and the Chaucerian Tradition*. Cambridge: Cambridge University Press, 1994.

Scarry, Elaine. *The Body in Pain: The Making and Unmaking of the World*. Oxford: Oxford University Press, 1985.

Schirmer, Walter F. *John Lydgate: A Study in the Culture of the XVth Century*. Trans. Ann E. Keep. London: Methuen, 1961.

Schochet, G. J. *Patriarchalism in Political Thought: The Authoritarian Family and Political Speculation and Attitudes Especially in Seventeenth-Century England*. New York: Basic Books, 1975.

Scott, James C. *Domination and the Arts of Resistance: Hidden Transcripts*. New Haven, Conn.: Yale University Press, 1990.

Shaffer, Gina Victoria. "The Missing Wives of Leviathan." *Seventeenth Century* 29 (2004): 53–68.

Sheingorn, Pamela. "Joseph the Carpenter's Failure at Familial Discipline." In *Insights and Interpretations: Studies in Celebration of the Eighty-Fifth Anniversary of the Index of Christian Art*, ed. Colum Hourihane, 156–67. Princeton, N.J.: Princeton University Press, 2002.

Shepard, Stephen H. A. "Langland's Romances," In Hewett-Smith, *William Langland's* Piers Plowman, 69–81.

Shklar, Ruth Nisse. "'Cobham's Daughter': Margery Kempe and the Power of Heterodox Thinking." *Modern Language Quarterly* 56 (1995): 277–304.

Shorter, Edward. *The Making of the Modern Family*. New York: Basic Books, 1975.

Simpson, James. *Piers Plowman: An Introduction to the B-Text*. London: Longman, 1990.

Soble, Alan. *Pornography: Marxism, Feminism, and the Future of Sexuality*. New Haven, Conn.: Yale University Press, 1986.

Somerset, Fiona. *Clerical Discourse and Lay Audience in Late Medieval England*. Cambridge: Cambridge University Press, 1998.

Spencer, Brian. *Pilgrim Souvenirs and Secular Badges*. Medieval Finds from Excavations in London 7. London: Stationery Office, 1998.

Sponsler, Claire. "Alien Nation: London's Aliens and Lydgate's Mummings for the Mercers and Goldsmiths." In *The Post-Colonial Middle Ages*, ed. Jeffrey Jerome Cohen, 229–42. New York: Palgrave Macmillan, 2001.

———. *Drama and Resistance: Bodies, Goods, and Theatricality in Late Medieval England*. Minneapolis: University of Minnesota Press, 1997.

———. *The Queen's Dumbshows: John Lydgate and the Making of Early Theater*. Philadelphia: University of Pennsylvania Press, 2014.

Staley, Lynn. *Margery Kempe's Dissenting Fictions*. Philadelphia: University of Pennsylvania Press, 1994.

———. "Introduction." In *The Book of Margery Kempe*, ed. and trans. Lynn Staley, vii–xix. New York: Norton, 2001.

———. "*The Book of Margery Kempe*: Introduction." In *The Book of Margery Kempe*, ed. Lynn Staley, 1–16. Kalamazoo, Mich.: Medieval Institute Publications, 1996.

Stallybrass, Peter, and Allon White. *The Politics and Poetics of Transgression*. Ithaca, N.Y.: Cornell University Press, 1986.

Steiner, Emily. *Reading* Piers Plowman. Cambridge: Cambridge University Press, 2013.

Stone, Lawrence. *The Family, Sex, and Marriage in England, 1500–1800*. New York: Harper & Row, 1977.

Straker, Scott-Morgan. "Deference and Difference: Lydgate, Chaucer, and the *Siege of Thebes*." *Review of English Studies* 52 (2001): 1–21.

Strickland, Agnes. *Lives of the Queens of England*. Vol. 3. Philadelphia: Lea & Blanchard, 1841.

Strohm, Paul. "Chaucer's Fifteenth-Century Audience and the Narrowing of the 'Chaucer Tradition'." *Studies in the Age of Chaucer* 4 (1982): 3–32.

———. *England's Empty Throne: Usurpation and the Language of Legitimation, 1399–1422*. New Haven, Conn.: Yale University Press, 1998.

———. *Hochon's Arrow: The Social Imagination of Fourteenth-Century Texts*. Princeton, N.J.: Princeton University Press, 1992.

———. *Social Chaucer*. Cambridge, Mass: Harvard University Press, 1989.

Strossen, Nadine. *Defending Pornography: Free Speech, Sex, and the Fight for Women's Rights*. New York: NYU Press, 2000.

Summit, Jennifer. *Lost Property: The Woman Writer and English Literary History, 1380–1589*. Chicago: University of Chicago Press, 2000.

Sutton-Smith, Brian. "Games of Order and Disorder." Paper presented at the Annual Meeting of the American Anthropological Society, Toronto, December 1972.

Swanson, Heather. "The Illusion of Economic Structure: Craft Guilds in Late Medieval English Towns." *Past and Present* 121 (1988): 29–48.

———. *Medieval British Towns*. London: Macmillan, 1999.

Talvacchia, Bette. *Taking Positions: On the Erotic in Renaissance Culture*. Princeton, N.J.: Princeton University Press, 1999.

Tavormina, Teresa. *Kindly Similitude: Marriage and Family in* Piers Plowman. Cambridge: Brewer, 1995.

Thomas, Alfred. "Alien Bodies: Exclusion, Obscenity, and Social Control in *The Ointment Seller*." In Ziolkowski, *Obscenity*, 214–30.

Thomson, John A. F. *The Later Lollards, 1414–1520*. London: Oxford University Press, 1967.

Thornton, Martin. *Margery Kempe: An Example in the English Pastoral Tradition*. London: SPCK, 1960.

Tolkien, J. R. R. "Chaucer as Philologist: *The Reeve's Tale*." *Transactions of the Philological Society* (1934): 1–70.

Tolmie, Jane. "Mrs. Noah and Didactic Abuses." *Early Theatre* 5 (2002): 11–35.

———. "Spinning Women and Manly Soldiers: Grief and Game in the English Massacre Plays." In *Laments for the Lost in Medieval Literature*, ed. Jane Tolmie and M. J. Toswell, 283–98. Turnhout: Brepols, 2010.

Toulalan, Sarah. *Imagining Sex: Pornography and Bodies in Seventeenth-Century England*. Oxford: Oxford University Press, 2007.

Tout, T. F. "Bowet, Henry (d. 1423)." In *Oxford Dictionary of National Biography*. Oxford: Oxford University Press, 2004.

Trigg, Stephanie. "The Traffic in Medieval Women: Alice Perrers, Feminist Criticism and *Piers Plowman*." *Yearbook of Langland Studies* 12 (1998): 5–29.

Turner, James Grantham. *Libertines and Radicals in Early Modern London*. Cambridge: Cambridge University Press, 2002.

Turner, Victor. "Frame, Flow, and Reflection: Ritual Drama as Public Liminality." *Japanese Journal of Religious Studies* 6, 4 (1979): 465–99.

———. *From Ritual to Theatre: The Human Seriousness of Play*. New York: Performing Arts Journal, 1982.

———. *Process, Performance, and Pilgrimage: A Study of Comparative Symbology*. New Delhi: Concept Publishing, 1979.

Twycross, Meg. "'Transvestism' in the Mystery Plays." *Medieval English Theatre* 5, 2 (1983): 123–80.

Utley, Francis. *The Crooked Rib: An Analytical Index to the Argument About Women in English and Scots Literature to the End of the Year 1568*. Columbus: Ohio State University Press, 1944.

Valente, Clare. "Joan of Navarre." In *Historical Dictionary of Late Medieval England, 1272–1485*, ed. Ronald H. Fritze, William Baxter Robison, and Ann E. Faulkner, 288–89. Westport, Conn.: Greenwood, 2002.

van den Boogaard, Nico. "Le Fabliau Anglo-Normand." In *Third International Beast Epic, Fable and Fabliau Colloquium, Proceedings*, ed. Jan Goossens and Timothy Sodmann, 66–77. Vienna: Böhlau, 1981.

Vasvari, Louise O. "Fowl Play in My Lady's Chamber: Textual Harassment of a Middle English Pornithological Riddle and Visual Pun." In Ziolkowsky, *Obscenity*, 108–38.

———. "Joseph on the Margin: The Merod Tryptic and Medieval Spectacle." *Medievalia* 18 (1995): 163–89.

Vitto, Cindy L. *The Virtuous Pagan in Middle English Literature*. Philadelphia: American Philosophical Society, 1989.

Voaden, Rosalyn. *God's Words, Women's Voices: The Discernment of Spirits in the Writing of Late-Medieval Women Visionaries*. Woodbridge: York Medieval Press, 1999.

Vulgate Bible: Douay-Rheims Translation. Ed. Edgar Swift. Cambridge, Mass.: Harvard University Press, 2010.

Walker, Simon. "Rumour, Sedition and Popular Protest in the Reign of Henry IV." *Past and Present* 166 (2000): 31–65.

Walker, Sue Sheridan. "Common Law Juries and Feudal Marriage Customs in Medieval England: The Pleas of Ravishment." *University of Illinois Law Review* 3 (1984): 705–18.

———. "Punishing Convicted Ravishers: Statutory Strictures and Actual Practice in Thirteenth- and Fourteenth-Century England." *Journal of Medieval History* 13 (1987): 237–50

Wallace, David. *Chaucerian Polity: Absolutist Lineages and Associational Forms in England and Italy*. Stanford, Calif.: Stanford University Press, 1997.

Ward, Jennifer C. *English Noblewomen in the Later Middle Ages*. London: Longman, 1992.

Warner, Marina. *Alone of All Her Sex: The Myth and Cult of the Virgin Mary*. London: Vintage, 1976.

Watson, Nicholas. "Censorship and Cultural Change in Late Medieval England: Vernacular Theology, the Oxford Translation Debate, and Arundel's Constitutions of 1409." *Speculum* 70 (1995): 822–64.

———. "The Making of the *Book of Margery Kempe*." In *Voices in Dialogue: Reading Women in the Middle Ages*, ed. Linda Olsen and Kathryn Kerby-Fulton, 395–434. Notre Dame, Ind.: University of Notre Dame Press, 2005.

———. "Visions of Inclusion: Universal Salvation and Vernacular Theology in Pre-Reformation England." *Journal of Medieval and Early Modern Studies* 27 (1997): 145–87.

Watt, John. "The Dramatic Unity of the *Secunda Pastorum*." In *Essays and Studies in Honor of Carleton Brown*, ed. Percy Waldron Long, 158–66. New York: New York University Press, 1940.

Watt, Richard. *The Making of Modern Marriage: Matrimonial Control and the Rise of Sentiment in Neuchâtel, 1550–1800*. Ithaca, N.Y.: Cornell University Press, 1992.

Watts, John. "The Pressure of the Public on Later Medieval Politics." In *The Fifteenth Century IV: Political Culture in Late Medieval Britain*, ed. Linda Clark and Christine Carpenter, 159–80. Woodbridge: Boydell, 2004.

———. "Public or Plebs: The Changing Meaning of 'the Commons,' 1381–1549." In *Power and Identity in the Middle Ages: Essays in Memory of Rees Davis*, 242–60. Oxford: Oxford University Press, 2007.

Weimann, Robert. *Shakespeare and the Popular Tradition in the Theatre*, ed. Robert Shwartz, 65–72. Baltimore: Johns Hopkins University Press, 1978.

Wenzel, Siegfried. *Latin Sermon Collections from Later Medieval England*. Cambridge: Cambridge University Press, 2005.

Wetherbee, Winthrop. "Romance and Epic in Chaucer's Knight's Tale." *Exemplaria* 2 (1990): 303–28.

Williams, Bernard, ed. *Obscenity and Film Censorship: An Abridgement of the Williams Report*. Cambridge: Cambridge University Press, 1982.

Williams, Linda. *Hard Core: Power, Pleasure, and the "Frenzy of the Visible."* Berkeley: University of California Press, 1989.

Willis, Ellen. "Lust Horizons: The 'Voice' and the Women's Movement." *Village Voice*, October 18, 2005.

Wilson, Janet. "Communities of Dissent: The Secular and Ecclesiastical Communities of Margery Kempe's *Book*." In *Medieval Women in Their Communities*, ed. Diane Watt, 155–85. Cardiff: University of Wales Press, 1997.

———. "Margery and Alison: Women on Top." In *Margery Kempe: A Book of Essays*, ed. Sandra J. McEntire, 223–37. New York: Garland, 1992.

Winstead, Karen. *Virgin Martyrs: Legends of Sainthood in Late Medieval England*. Ithaca, N.Y.: Cornell University Press, 1997.

Wolfthal, Diane. *Images of Rape: The "Heroic" Tradition and Its Alternatives*. Cambridge: Cambridge University Press, 1999.

Wolk-Simon, Linda. "'Rapture to the Greedy Eyes': Profane Love in the Renaissance." In *Art and Love in Renaissance Italy*, ed. Andrea Bayer, 43–58. New York: Metropolitan Museum of Art, 2008.

Wood, Andy. *The 1549 Rebellions and the Making of Early Modern England*. Cambridge: Cambridge University Press, 2007.

Wood, Chauncey. "The Wife of Bath and 'Speche Daungerous'." In *Chaucer and Language*, ed. Robert Myles and David Williams, 33–43. Quebec City: McGill-Queen's University Press, 2001.

Woods, Marjorie Curry. "Rape and the Pedagogical Rhetoric of Sexual Violence." In *Criticism and Dissent in the Middle Ages*, ed. Rita Copeland, 56–86. Cambridge: Cambridge University Press, 1996.

Woods, William F. "The Logic of Deprivation in the *Reeve's Tale*." *Chaucer Review* 30, 2 (1995): 150–63.

Woolf, Rosemary. *The English Mystery Plays*. London: Routledge and Kegan Paul, 1972.

Wright, Susan M. *Derbyshire Gentry in the Fifteenth Century*. Chesterfield: Derbyshire Record Society, 1983.

Yunck, John. *The Lineage of Lady Meed: The Development of Mediaeval Venality Satire*. Notre Dame, Ind.: University of Notre Dame Press, 1963.

Zeeman, Nicolette. Piers Plowman *and the Medieval Discourse of Desire*. Cambridge: Cambridge University Press, 2006.

———. "Tales of Piers and Perceval: *Piers Plowman* and the Grail Romances." *Yearbook of Langland Studies* 22 (2008): 199–236.

Ziolkowski, Jan. "The Obscenities of Old Women: Vetularity and Vernacularity." In Ziolkowski, *Obscenity*, 73–89.

———, ed. *Obscenity: Social Control and Artistic Creation in the European Middle Ages*. Leiden: Brill, 1998.

INDEX

abortion, 228

Act of Supremacy (Henry VIII), 232

adultery, 2, 5, 13, 45–47, 72, 87, 93, 113, 120, 129, 141, 150, 156, 167, 177–78, 188–89, 193, 196, 198, 208, 210–11; woman taken in (John 8: 1–11), 181. *See also* sexual misbehavior

Aers, David, 204

affective piety, 176

alewives, 125, 178–79, 205–6

allegory, 11, 36, 40, 44–45, 48–49, 51–54, 60–63, 67, 138–39

Allen, Hope Emily, 149

Anne of Bohemia, 130

anti-feminist satire, 124

Aretino, Pietro, 22–23

Ariadne, 79–80, 84, 101–2, 105. *See also* Chaucer; *Legend of Good Women*

aristocracy, 17, 23, 27, 31–32, 39, 45, 56, 60, 65, 79, 85, 87, 90, 98, 101, 103, 104, 108–9, 116, 124, 126, 129, 132, 135, 143, 145, 196, 204, 220, 222–23, 225–26; aristocratic wards, 45; ideology of, 31, 74, 79, 81, 89, 105–6, 108–10, 203; women of, 105, 107, 131, 135, 137, 139, 143–44, 204, 225. *See also* elites; gentry

Aristotle, 6; *Ethics*, 50

Arnolfini Portrait, 261n95

artisans, 183, 203–5. *See also* guilds

Arundel, Thomas (archbishop of Canterbury) 160–62, 164, 171, 175, 260n62

aube, 76, 110

Augustine of Hippo, St., 180

Autobiography of a Flea, 235

Badby, John, 162, 171

badges (obscene), 9, 11–12

Badinter, Élisabeth, 267n127

Bakhtin, Mikhail, 28–29

"Ballad of a Tyrannical Husband," 205

Basochiens, 9, 121

Beaumont, Francis, 230

Beckwith, Sarah, 203

Bedford Hours, 212–13

Bennett, Judith, 178

Bergson, Henri, 68–69

Bernard of Clairvaux, 6, 17, 24, 63

bestiality, 25

Bible, 67, 142: Book of Job, 57; Gospel According to Luke, 169–70; Gospel According to Matthew, 158, 218–19; Isaiah, 63; picture bibles, 95; Psalm 10, 58–59; Psalm 72, 57–58

biblical drama, 8, 13, 29, 32, 44, 150, 152, 155, 184, 187, 188–228, 230, 232, 235–36; dating of, 202, 261n1; and middle ranks, 203, 263n43; transvestism in, 208. *See also* Coventry *Shearman and Taylor's Play*; "Massacre of the Innocents" plays; Noah plays, N-Town plays; *Second Shepherd's Play*; Towneley plays; "Troubles of Joseph" plays; York plays

Bishop's Ban of 1599, 230

Black Death, 13, 14, 124, 201; as evidence of God's vengeance, 214–15

BnF MS FR.25526, 8, 41

Boccaccio, Giovanni, 140–41; *Decameron*, 8, 81; *Teseida*, 82–84, 105–6

Boethius, Anicius Manlius Severinus, *The Consolation of Philosophy*, 62, 68

Book of Margery Kempe, 13, 32, 51, 149–87, 191, 198, 211, 218; scribes of 153–54, 159, 236

Boose, Lynda, 230–31

Bourdieu, Pierre, 92

Bowers, John, 37

Bowet, Henry, archbishop of York, 149, 157, 161–62, 168–73, 175–76, 178.

Bracciolini, Poggio, 8

ACKNOWLEDGMENTS

As a student of literature I am keenly aware that no work is produced in isolation but is a product of the community from which it springs. The same can be said of literary scholarship. It is my pleasure to acknowledge the community that helped produce this book. Larry Scanlon started me on the first steps of this journey many years ago when, in discussing research topics he said, "Why not do the fabliau?" His careful attention in the early stages of this project and advice at later stages has been indispensable to me. Thanks also go to my colleagues who read this work in its earliest form: Susan Crane, Chris Chism, and Rita Copeland. Their encouragement then, and in the ensuing years, has been most valuable.

The ideas in this book, particularly with respect to the Old French fabliaux, were honed by R. Howard Bloch and the wonderful company of scholars who participated in his NEH seminar on the fabliaux at Yale University in 2003: Dorothy Schrader, Judith Tschann, Jean Jost, Kat Tracy, Nathaniel Dubin, Mary Leech, Peter Beidler and Ellen Friedrich. For their perceptive comments on chapters in various forms, I am indebted to Ruth Evans, Susan Nakely, Masha Raskolnikov, Elizabeth Scala, Nicole Smith, Fiona Somerset, Tara Williams, and especially Holly Crocker. This project would not have been the same without the support and encouragement of colleagues who conversed with me and/or hosted me on various panels over the years, including Gina Aloni, Jennifer Brown, Susanna Fein, Geraldine Heng, Emma Lipton, Liz McAvoy, Tison Pugh and David Raybin. I am grateful to Carissa Harris for her gracious encouragement at a crucial juncture. Thanks also to Glenn Burger and Eve Salisbury, who read the manuscript for the University of Pennsylvania Press, and whose insights clarified my thoughts and sharpened my writing, as well as to the editorial guidance of Jerry Singerman and Ruth Mazo Karras.

East Carolina University has been my scholarly home for many years and has provided the foundational community for this project. Members of the British Literature Ink Writing Group (BLING) kept me on track through the sleep-deprived years of babies and small children. I am forever grateful to Gregg Hecimovich, Anne Mallory, Brian Glover, and Sean Morris for the warmth and brilliance that provided a welcome respite from sippy cups and diaper changes. Thanks also go to my other ECU colleagues, Margaret Bauer and Amanda Klein, who set the bar high for scholarly achievement, as well as Anna Froula, Marame Gueye, Su-ching Huang, Andrea Kitta, Joyce Middleton, Ken Parille, Mikko Tuhkanen, McKay Sundwall, and the early modernists who have kept a lonely medievalist company in the "pre-1800" lands: David Wilson-Okamura, Marianne Montgomery, Jeffrey Johnson, and Tom Herron. My fellow ECU medievalists in other fields provided excellent context. Thanks to Anne-Hélène Miller for discussing the fabliau with me and to Purification Martinez for drawing my attention to Juan Ruiz. I am particularly indebted to Charles Fantazzi, for his expertise in Latin. The staff at the ECU Interlibrary loan department have been my faithful helpers these many years, particularly the late Lynda Werdal, who once cheered me by remarking, "You order very interesting books." My students at ECU have inspired me with their intelligent and humorous responses to medieval literature and their enthusiastic reception of feminist literary criticism.

Many parents will attest that intellectual work is impossible if one is worrying about one's children. I am grateful to the women who gave me precious peace of mind throughout this project by caring for my children with kindness, competence, and patience. Particular thanks go to Kim Burge, Meghan Boyce, and Allison Deese. My in-laws, Kaur and Bimla Sidhu, and my stepmother, Mary Nolan, provided encouragement, childcare, hospitality and superlative meals on many occasions. My sister, Jusna Nolan, has been my constant cheerleader and companion. Her faithfulness and loyalty stand out as an ideal of how to be a friend and a sister. My parents have provided a model to me of lives lived with ethical commitment. The dedication says it all.

For the inspiration and decades of faithful friendship they have provided, I am grateful to my own favorite unruly women: Kaelynne Koval, Ann Shin, Victoria Stoett, Maya Socolovsky, and especially Misao Boyd and Asiya Khalid Rolston, my two honorary sisters. My greatest thanks go to my husband, Rajinder Sidhu, whose wisdom, humor, and compassion inspire me daily, and to my three children, Ciaran, Naveen, and Sitara, who grew from birth to elementary school during the writing of this book and whose enduring fondness for fart jokes and lower body humor have meant that, even when I was not at my desk, I was never far from the obscene.

Parts of this book have previously appeared in "'To Late for to Crie": Female Desire, Fabliau Politics, and Classical Legend in Chaucer's Reeve's Tale," *Exemplaria: A Journal of Theory in Medieval and Renaissance Studies* 21 (2009): 3–23; and "Henpecked Husbands, Unruly Wives, and Royal Authority in Lydgate's *Mumming at Hertford*," *Chaucer Review* 42 (2008): 431–60. Permission to use these materials is gratefully acknowledged.